Organizing Workers in the Shadow of Slavery

Organizing Workers in the Shadow of Slavery

GLOBAL INEQUALITY, RACIAL BOUNDARIES, AND THE RISE OF UNIONS IN AMERICAN AND BRITISH CAPITALISM, 1870–1929

Rudi Batzell

The University of Chicago Press CHICAGO AND LONDON

The University of Chicago Press, Chicago 60637
The University of Chicago Press, Ltd., London
© 2025 by The University of Chicago
Published 2025
Printed in the United States of America

34 33 32 31 30 29 28 27 26 25   1 2 3 4 5

ISBN-13: 978-0-226-83876-2 (cloth)
ISBN-13: 978-0-226-83878-6 (paper)
ISBN-13: 978-0-226-83877-9 (e-book)
DOI: https://doi.org/10.7208/chicago/9780226838779.001.0001

Library of Congress Cataloging-in-Publication Data

Names: Batzell, Rudi, author.
Title: Organizing workers in the shadow of slavery : global
    inequality, racial boundaries, and the rise of unions in
    American and British capitalism, 1870–1929 / Rudi Batzell.
Description: Chicago : The University of Chicago Press, 2025. |
    Includes bibliographical references and index.
Identifiers: LCCN 2024036118 | ISBN 9780226838762 (cloth)
    | ISBN 9780226838786 (paperback) | ISBN 9780226838779
    (e-book)
Subjects: LCSH: Labor unions—United States—History. |
    Labor unions—England—History. | Discrimination in
    employment—United States. | African Americans—
    Employment.
Classification: LCC HD6508.B38 2025 | DDC 331.880973—dc23/
    eng/20241009
LC record available at https://lccn.loc.gov/2024036118

Contents

Introduction

In April and May of 1912, workers along Baltimore's waterfront launched an unprecedented inclusive mass organizing effort that led to what Maryland officials called "one of the largest strikes [in] Baltimore" history.[1] This remarkable effort followed many failed attempts at inclusive unionism in the United States. The strike's failure encapsulates one of the central arguments of this book: that the shadow of slavery, most visible in the structures of regionally and racially divided labor markets, confined the US labor movement within narrow, exclusive boundaries during its formative years from the 1870s to the 1920s. It was not, as most scholars have argued, exceptionally intense state or employer hostility that defeated inclusive unionism in the US.[2] Rather, the structural legacies of slavery gave employers a crucial weapon: strikebreakers. This book provides a sustained comparison of labor organizing and racial boundary-making in the US and Britain. Whereas the US labor movement remained weak and narrow, British workers succeeded in organizing broad, inclusive unions during the late nineteenth century. The 1912 strike in Baltimore brings this comparison into focus, since it represented an attempt to transplant inclusive British unionism to the US waterfront.

The 1912 strike was led by a recently formed union, the National Transport Workers Federation (NTWF). Experienced British union leaders came to the US, organized the NTWF, and attempted to amalgamate the various waterfront unions into an inclusive industrial coalition, building directly on their successful experience in Liverpool during the 1911 General Strike. Initially, this organizing effort seemed promising. Employers were "amazed on learning that the longshoremen, heretofore unorganized, had been affiliated almost overnight with" a new, ambitious union.[3] From its spontaneous start on April 9, 1912, the Baltimore waterfront strike remained tense but calm for two weeks until conflicts between strikers and strikebreakers led to widespread rioting and violence.

Employers turned immediately to strikebreakers. Around one thousand black strikebreakers were employed at the Light Street wharves moving Chesapeake Bay freight, with at least five hundred hired in a single day.[4] These were local African American workers who strategically used the strike to move into occupations that had previously been closed to them. Strict occupational racial boundaries in the US meant that strikes were among the only available opportunities for black workers to gain access to lucrative jobs. While some black workers joined the NTWF, many others rebuffed union organizers as they recalled organized US labor's well-established record of keeping black workers out of desirable jobs. Within a week of the strike's start, employers were making more secure arrangements for housing some two hundred strikebreakers imported from outside the city.[5] Payday for the strikebreakers created a racialized spectacle that hardened racial boundaries. Predominantly white strikers looked on menacingly as predominantly black strikebreakers collected their pay: "A great throng of strikers gathered to see the negroes and some whites get their money.... Feeling was running high among the longshoremen as they saw the colored men counting the greenbacks, and threats were heard in many directions."[6]

Despite early signs of trouble, during the initial weeks the NTWF managed to sustain of a degree of solidarity between black and white workers and win broad sympathy from the public and local government. Key government authorities in Baltimore were supportive of the strike and partially frustrated the efforts of owners and managers to deploy strikebreakers. City councillor William J. Lang, representing the Twenty-Fourth Ward on the waterfront, "protested strongly against the use of the [city police] patrol to carry away strikebreakers" from pickets, since these imported workers were "taking the bread out of the mouths of the people of several precincts in the Twenty-fourth ward."[7] The police captain defended his actions, stating that the "situation looked dangerous" and "a serious riot with fatal results would have occurred, had I permitted the negros to walk [unprotected] through the crowded streets."[8] But after this complaint, the police shifted from protecting strikebreakers to making strikebreaking more challenging for employers. Most notably, a "foremen of the strikebreakers" was arrested and "fined $25 and costs ... for carrying a concealed weapon."[9] The city council appointed a committee, led by the mayor and sympathetic to the strikers, to meet with the union to see if arbitration could be arranged.[10] Charles Fox, chief of the State Bureau of Statistics and Information, convened hearings on the strike on May 4; to the intense annoyance of the employers, he compelled company officials to give testimony.[11] The conclusion of this "official investigation of the strike situation" was reported as a victory for the strikers. The State Bureau report endorsed both an increase of wages and the recognition of the union.[12] Thus far, it might seem that the NTWF was on course for victory in 1912.

As the strike entered its third week, however, racial hostility between strikers and strikebreakers escalated. When the workday ended on April 27, strikebreakers faced "women, armed with sticks and crying 'Scab!' and 'Go back from where you came!' . . . as they left the docks."[13] Later that evening, police took over 100 black strikebreakers into custody to protect them from a growing crowd: "About 5,000 men, women, and children crowded the streets in the immediate neighborhood of the big piers crying and yelling at the negroes as they were rushed by in the automobile under police guard."[14] The next night, as the police stepped back from protecting strikebreakers under political pressure, the strike turned bloody. "A crowd of about 25 negro strikebreakers, working on the North German Lloyd steamship Rhein," came into conflict with "a crowd of white strikers." After an "argument between the negroes and the white men . . . one of the negroes was knocked down" and another black strikebreaker "fired a pistol five times into the crowd of strikers," leading to one white worker being seriously wounded.[15] As the injured white striker struggled for his life in the hospital, violence escalated the next day. Strikers assaulted the ship used to house and feed the strikebreakers: "500 union longshoremen broke through the lines of police and railroad detectives at Locust Point . . . and made a savage attack on 125 strikebreakers who were being fed on the steamer Maggie."[16] The next day, "about 500 striking longshoremen attacked the Northern Central Railway pier" to stop strikebreakers from unloading a ship.[17] Sporadic, smaller-scale violence by white workers against black strikebreakers, and African Americans in Baltimore more generally, continued over the coming weeks.[18] May 6 brought more large-scale rioting after strikers learned of the death of the injured white worker.[19] Although black Baltimoreans were subjected to widespread terror, the violence did not stop Baltimore employers from using strikebreakers, whatever the collateral costs. At the end of the strike, the Sun marveled at the many "thousands of dollars . . . spent to bring strikebreakers to Baltimore."[20] The Baltimore longshoremen were defeated, and the NTWF's experiment with inclusive unionism collapsed only a few months later.

Baltimore in 1912 speaks to far broader patterns of geographic inequality, migration, and the overlapping construction of craft, racial, and nativist boundaries by organized workers in the late nineteenth and early twentieth centuries. This book offers a comparative history of four cities situated within the uneven regional geographies of the British and American empires.[21] The archival research and arguments that follow are grounded in the local urban experiences of workers in the steel centers of Pittsburgh and Sheffield and the transportation hubs of Baltimore and Liverpool. These were all leading provincial cities of comparable size and importance and with similar yet distinctive economic foundations. Baltimore offers insight into a city long shaped by the history of slavery, while Liverpool was the provincial city most connected to the British maritime empire. In contrast, while Sheffield steelmakers were leading armaments manufacturers for the imperial war machine, the city remained comparatively isolated from flows of labor across the British Empire. Similarly, in contrast to Baltimore's long history of slavery, Pittsburgh reveals how white workers responded to the arrival of African Americans into the industrial North from the 1890s through to the Great Migration. While Pittsburgh and Baltimore ultimately followed quite similar trajectories in labor organizing and racial boundary-making, Liverpool and Sheffield offer a striking contrast.

To understand the diverging trajectories of urban labor movements, it is necessary to place these cities in the context of their local "near-peripheries": Ireland within the UK and the South within the US. Both of these near-peripheries were comparatively poor, mainly agricultural regions that provided migrant low-wage labor, strikebreakers, and competition to their respective urban-industrial cores. The US South and Ireland in this era could both be understood as part of the "Global South": regions marked by colonial domination, land expropriation, and coerced and enslaved labor. But these local near-peripheries had contrasting trajectories during the later nineteenth and twentieth centuries. Mass movements in Ireland secured land reform and national independence; in the US land reform was defeated and an anti-democratic, authoritarian, and white-supremacist Jim Crow regime consolidated power. The broadest scale of comparison operates at the level of settler-colonial empires. While workers in the US moved to the high-wage Western frontier secured through militarized dispossession, British workers moved overseas, in particular to the high-wage settler-colonial dominions of Canada, Australia, and South Africa.[22] This comparative perspective—urban, regional, and imperial—not only illuminates the causes of diverging trajectories of labor organizing and racial boundary-making in the US and the UK, but also offers new clarity on the enduring power of racism as rooted in the uneven economic geography of global capitalism.

Global Inequality, Migration, and the Rise of Unions

Our current moment is one of severe and seemingly intractable inequalities. These inequalities are registered in unequal wealth between the rich and poor, by the durable chasm between workers' wages in the Global North and South, and by racial inequalities in earnings and wealth alongside poverty and mass incarceration. Some have called this a "New Gilded Age" and a "New Jim Crow." The unequal geographical consequences of a warming planet have been described as "climate apartheid."[23] Corporate investments and technocratic interventions have failed to meaningfully address these challenges. Surely the effort to challenge these inequalities must come from below, from mass social movements organized by the vast majority of humanity left comparatively poor and powerless. Yet when workers organize, they rarely do so inclusively. The universal proletariat envisioned by Marx and hoped for by socialists has not appeared. This book asks two related questions. First: why were some workers able to mobilize relatively inclusively, as in Britain, while in the United States, the labor movement remained narrow and unrepresentative of the broader working class? In pointing to racial boundaries as the central answer to this question, we are challenged to confront a second, even larger question: what is the relationship between racism and capitalism?[24] To address these questions, this book offers a locally grounded comparative history of union formation and racial boundary-making by workers in the American and British empires during the late nineteenth and early twentieth centuries.

Three dimensions of inequality—class, race, and economic geography—were, and remain, inextricably intertwined in the history of capitalism. Their intersections explain the ability of British workers to organize broad, inclusive unions at the beginning of the twentieth century, whereas in the US the labor movement remained narrowly confined within craft, racial, and nativist boundaries during its formative years. In these years modern bureaucratic labor unions emerged and took permanent form, while white supremacy flourished globally in Jim Crow America, White Australia, and South Africa. Setting the pattern for the populist xenophobia sweeping the Global North today, in the early twentieth century mass movements of anti-immigrant nativism barricaded high-wage labor markets against migrants from low-wage peripheries.[25] The following chapters will explore how, as working-class movements organized to challenge the power of capital, they also reconstructed and entrenched capitalism's geographic and racial boundaries. As Fordist mass-production capitalism reshaped the working class's social worlds in their homes, neighborhoods, and leisure after 1890, the same social transformations that produced a more cohesive, integrated working class in Britain produced enduring patterns of segregation and structural inequality in the United States.

This era from the 1870s to the 1920s was not only the formative period for the rise of organized labor, but also marked the origins of modern racism. The parallel was no coincidence. Prior to the mid-nineteenth century, slavery had kept enslaved laborers immobilized under their masters' command. High transport costs meant that merchants and financiers played a leading role in directing long-distance migration for all but the most affluent. But with the spread of emancipation across the Atlantic and the decline in transportation costs due to both steam shipping and railroads after the 1870s, workers from low-wage, colonized, or formerly slave-based regions across the Global South came into direct contact, and potential competition, with workers in high-wage industrialized and urban cores across the Global North.[26] Up to the mid-nineteenth century, racial boundary-making had been a primarily top-down project driven by elites: militarist entrepreneurs, plantation owners and overseers, colonial administrators, and land-hungry colonial settlers who aimed to conquer, dispossess, and rule the indigenous and enslaved masses on the peripheries of global capitalism.[27]

After 1870, racism was increasingly driven from the bottom up, by organized workers in new labor unions and mass political parties in the Global North. This created a new, pervasive regime of racial inequality in global labor markets, occupations, and housing that has largely endured to the present. Racism and capitalism emerged together, but the late nineteenth century marked a crucial disjuncture from "top-down" to "bottom-up" racial boundary-making. This intensification of racial boundaries was perceptible to many at the turn of the century. Jean Finot, an early and influential critic of racialized thinking, was struck by the novelty, intensity, and global scope of racism in the early twentieth century. In 1911 Finot noted how "the conception of races, once so innocent, has cast as it were a veil of tragedy over the surface of the earth," with the world's population "divided into unequal fractions" with "superior peoples, peoples chosen to govern" and "others, inferior, slaves of the first, enduring the suspicion and contempt which come to them from all sides."[28] This global division into "rulers" who prospered and governed and "inferiors" who labored and suffered marked the global shadow of slavery, an integrated structure of geographical, class, and racial inequality that persisted long after emancipation and continues to mark our present.

For most readers, these hierarchies of race and class will be instantly

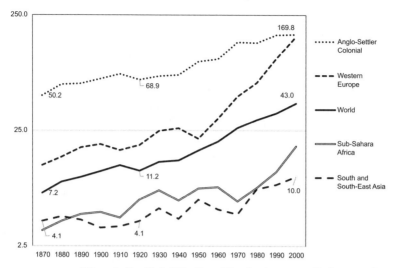

FIGURE I.1 Wages in the Global North and South, 1870–2000. Real wages of building laborers given in the number of subsistence baskets purchasable with a daily wage. *Source*: OECD, "Regional Averages of Real Wages of Building Labourers, 1820s–2000s: Number of Subsistence Baskets That a Daily Wage Buys, Decadal Averages" (Paris: Organisation for Economic Co-operation and Development, 2014).

recognizable given their daily visibility across much of the English-speaking world. Historians and social scientists have long exchanged polemics about the relative importance of and relationship between class, often seen as more "real" and structural, and race, often treated as secondary and "ideological."[29] But to unpack their connections it is necessary to foreground a third, less immediately obvious dimension of capitalist inequality: economic geography. As seen in figure I.1, capitalism's uneven economic geography is revealed most decisively in the chasm between high-wage cores and low-wage peripheries. This divide has endured as a defining feature of capitalist inequality. Yet this structure is both less visible to everyday observers and largely underdeveloped in scholarship on labor and race. Economic geography disappears when scholarship remains statically situated in local and national containers.

The rise of capitalism in the seventeenth and eighteenth centuries marked a geographical rupture in global economic history. Never before had the world been so intensely connected yet so profoundly unequal. This newly integrated world was stitched together, as Onur Ince has observed, by "the constitutive role of extra-economic coercion": "Colonial land grabs, plantation slavery, and the forced deindustrialization of imperial dependencies configure as crucial moments in the global formation of capitalism."[30] Drawing on earlier divisions between rulers and ruled, conquerors and conquered, distinctively modern racial ideologies developed to explain and map this integrated, unequal world.[31] If capitalists and imperial officials had initially charted the racialized geography of the Global North and South, core and periphery, after the 1870s it was organized labor that mobilized to defend and extend racialized boundaries. The material conditions of capitalism's global rise produced racism, a novel system of organizing space, social difference, power, and boundaries. Modern racism reorganized and consolidated premodern forms of prejudice and group hostility. Initially elaborated by mobile elites, with the rise of global mass migration racial boundary-making became a populist project driven by workers. Racism and capitalism arose together, but the social basis of racial boundary-making changed with emancipation, the explosion in global migration, and the rise of organized labor during the late nineteenth century.

By centering the struggles of organized workers to control socially and geographically bounded labor markets, this approach breaks with the culturalism of most studies of racism and class formation. Instead it foregrounds an economic, or materialist, interpretation of racial boundary-making rooted in the local and geographical hierarchies of labor markets. Figure I.1 illustrates the entrenched divide between the material conditions of life and labor in the Global North and South. Although Japan, and later China, have moved East Asia into the middle-income range in the twentieth century, the most striking feature of the long-term history of global wages is the intractable inequality between North and South, core and periphery. In the 1870s laborers in the Global South earned a tenth of the real wages earned by those in the Global North; at the start of the twenty-first century, the gap has actually grown, with Global South wages today only a sixteenth of those in the Global North.

While wage inequality is the simplest marker of cores and peripheries, politics also have profound importance. Across the history of capitalism, cores in the Global North have been distinguished by more powerful, autonomous states in which popular movements have successfully secured democratic rights and protections.[32] In contrast, peripheries in the Global South have been characterized by relatively weak, destabilized, subordinated or colonial regimes in which popular movements and democratic processes have been largely crushed. While directly foregrounding the impact of slavery in the United States, the "Shadow" invoked by the title aims illustrate this broader, global division of economic and political power in the history of capitalism.

This approach ultimately turns "American Exceptionalism" on its head. If spatially static, Eurocentric "nation-state" comparisons are abandoned in favor of a more appropriate, geographically flexible approach, the US experience of racial boundary-making appears not unusual, but exemplary of broader, imperial processes of geographic inequality, migration, and racialized class formation.[33] While the labor movement in the US was far narrower than in Britain itself, when the US as a continental empire is compared to the broader British maritime empire, the US no longer appears exceptional. Instead the US, in combining a leading industrial core and a large slave-labor periphery within its domestic political space, appears as a spatially and chronologically compressed configuration of capitalism's global inequalities. The US experience of racially bounded, narrow labor organizing had close parallels in the British maritime sector, in the racist nativism of White Australia, and in South Africa's color bar. The US compressed these dispersed imperial economic geographies within a single continental empire and nation-state.

As unsettling as it may be, the argument here is that racism is not aberrant or dysfunctional within the structures of global capitalism. Interpretations that foreground the contingent political construction of racism often miss or discount the deeper structural, material underpinnings that drive and sustain racial boundary-making.[34] Racism, as morally objectional and unjust as it may be, is not a misperception of workers' "real interests" in specific, immediate contexts. It is rather a rational and inevitable product of locally bounded class-formation and labor movements within capitalism's combined and uneven development.[35] Following the work of Eduard Bonilla-Silva and Moon-Kie Jung, this study finds that racism is not a deviation from some "normal" inclusive solidarity, but a structurally constitutive and functional dimension of globally unequal capitalist political economies.[36]

Capitalism and Racism

Capitalism, and racial capitalism in particular, has received renewed attention from scholars over the past decade. The extensive literature on slavery and capitalism has offered crucial insights, but research has mostly focused on the top of the social formation: finance, insurance, capitalists, and trading networks. Slavery is understood as commodity and capital, but rarely as labor. In the aftermath of the 2008 crisis, it is not surprising that debt and finance have loomed so large in the study of capitalism. While the power dynamic between creditors and debtors is undeniably important, capitalism's most novel, distinctive structural features are capital's command of commodified labor, both enslaved and wage laborers, and the global domination of metropolitan cores over the populations, politics, land, and resources of global peripheries. Histories of capitalism, and in particular, studies of racial capitalism, cannot afford to lose sight of workers and labor markets.[37] Especially in the US, history and economic history have for decades traveled on diverging paths. In giving central importance to labor markets, and to the findings of economic historians, I hope to demonstrate the value of sustained engagement with the robust and impressive array of empirical research done by economic historians.[38]

In this book, racism is examined through historically and geographically located "boundary-making" processes rather than notions of culture and identity.[39] Racism, treated in primarily psychological and cultural terms of "othering" by scholars in the dominant whiteness studies tradition, is here interpreted as a social process rooted in geographically located material structures, and in the power differentials that arise from access to or exclusion from property, income, and political rights.[40] While in tension at points, materialist and culturalist approaches to racism are in other ways compatible. They answer different kinds of historical questions. A materialist approach helps us understand when, where, and why racial boundary-making occurs. A culturalist approach, on the other hand, can speak to the personal, social, and cultural experiences of navigating, surviving, and fighting for justice within a racialized social formation. In building this materialist perspective on racial boundary-making, the book draws on insights from several classic studies in the black radical tradition.

W. E. B. Du Bois's *Black Reconstruction* remains an indispensable starting point. Although whiteness scholars have made much of a passing comment on the "psychological wage" of whiteness, the core of Du Bois's argument centers on the origins and development of a racially and regionally divided working class: "The proletariat is usually envisioned as united, but their real interests were represented in America by four sets of people: the freed Negro, the Southern poor white, and the Northern skilled and common laborer."[41] Du Bois recognized that the objective interests of workers in the US were cross-cut by racial and regional inequalities, as well as by the craft divide between low- and high-wage workers. In explaining the origins of this divided working class, I also follow Du Bois. In *Black Reconstruction*, Du Bois repeatedly returns to the failure of land redistribution during Reconstruction as the pivotal moment in the creation of a structurally divided working class.[42] These working-class divisions were not psychological delusions, but had an immediate, material basis on which racial boundaries were built and defended. Thus the US labor movement of "Northern skilled" white workers represented a narrow fraction of the larger working class, a narrow movement that Du Bois aptly labels "craft and race" unions.[43]

Sterling D. Spero and Abram Lincoln Harris, two contemporaries of Du Bois, though somewhat less well known, provide a second interpretative foundation in *The Black Worker*. Writing in 1930, Spero and Harris trace the trajectory of the US labor movement up to the 1920s and emphasize the connections between a racially and regionally divided labor market, migration, and strikebreaking. Although labor historians have widely acknowledged racialized strikebreaking in individual cases, few since Spero and Harris have given it systematic interpretive consideration.[44] Using the conception of a "reserve army of labor," Spero and Harris argue that the regionally and racially divided labor markets of the US produced the narrow craft and racial boundaries of the American labor movement.[45] They show how "rural workers, the numerically most important part of the Negro labor supply, became an industrial reserve" that could be used by employers for cheap, rapid strikebreaking.[46] Upending assumptions of a structurally uniform working class, Du Bois, Spero, and Harris provide a framework with which to analyze labor organizing and race, not just in the United States, but globally: access to land, regional wage differentials between cores and peripheries motivating labor migration, local wage differentials between craftsmen and common laborers, and given these labor market structures, the opportunities and costs of strikebreaking for employers and inclusive unionism for workers.

Race, in Stuart Hall's crucial formulation, is the "modality in which class is 'lived,' the medium through which class relations are experienced."[47] This fertile but sometimes elusive suggestion must be grounded in economic geography. As Hall notes, "racial structures cannot be understood adequately outside the framework of quite specific sets of economic relations," and he identifies these concrete relations as "conquest, colonization, and mercantilist domination" and more generally "relations between developed metropolitan and 'underdeveloped' satellite economic regions of the world economy."[48] Processes of class formation are always geographically contained within local social contexts. Because class formation must be rooted in local ties and concrete, directly experienced solidarities, it is also always necessarily bounded by the reach of these local ties. Working class formation is always implicitly, and often explicitly, racialized by its particular position in capitalism's uneven economic geography. While rooted in the tradition of class-formation studies pioneered by E. P. Thompson, the book aims to move this tradition forward by centering attention on economic geography and the necessarily constitutive role of racial boundary-making in processes of working-class formation.[49]

As Charles Postel writes in his recent history of struggles for equality, "too often, fraternity and solidarity rested on division and exclusion."[50] Yet these boundaries were hardly a unique or contingent "American dilemma."

Whether this always implicit racialization is realized and articulated in hard, defined racial boundary-making depends on the local contingencies of history. Certain countries, such as Britain in the early twentieth century, where race appeared less significant, were in fact temporarily situated within flows of capital and labor that allowed racial boundaries to fade into the implicit background. Shifts in the global economy, in particular growing waves of labor migration to high-wage cores in Europe since World War II, have made explicit the always implicit racial content of working-class formation across Britain and the rest of Europe. From a global perspective over the *longue durée*, patterns of working-class formation that are not explicitly racialized seem to be the far more unusual, contingent, and temporary experience.

Outline and Limits

The book is divided into three parts, moving forward chronologically and offering a descending perspective, moving from a largely structural analysis from 30,000 feet in the opening chapters to a finely grained social history of daily life in the final chapters. Part I sets the stage in the 1870s and 1880s at the most macro level of analysis, establishing broad structural conditions in terms of land reform, labor markets, migration, and strikebreaking. Part II is focused on the pivot of the 1890s, and moves to an intermediate, "meso" level of analysis, attempting to understand how unions navigated this crucial decade when inclusive union organizing survived in the UK, while in the US labor organizing retreated behind narrow craft, racial, and nativist boundaries. Finally, part III moves forward to the first two decades of the twentieth century, and roots the analysis of labor and racial boundary-making in the "micro" social history of everyday life, leisure, homes, and neighborhoods. During these decades, new working-class experiences, aspirations, and forms of collective action produced a newly integrated working class in the UK and a profoundly fractured and segregated working class in the US.

Part I compares structural conditions in terms of land reform in the US South and Ireland, the precarious initial rise of inclusive unionism, and the force of strikebreakers recruited from rural near-peripheries. Chapter 1 examines the US South and Ireland as comparable rural near-peripheries that supplied low-wage labor and strikebreakers to the industrial cores of the US and the UK in the nineteenth century. However, the success of land reform in Ireland, and its trajectory of wage convergence with the rest of the UK, meant that by the turn of the century, Irish low-wage rural migrants no longer threatened inclusive efforts to organize workers in Britain. In contrast, the failure of land reform during Reconstruction created a massive reserve army of labor—politically, socially, and economically oppressed African Americans—in the US South. Chapter 2 examines the parallel—and quite similar—eruptions of broad inclusive organizing in the US and the UK: the Knights of Labor and the New Unions. The initial rise and fall of these labor movements look remarkably similar. Where their paths diverged was in their ability to survive the 1890s. Chapter 3 shows that with access to a regionally and racially divided labor market, US employers could easily and cheaply recruit strikebreakers to defeat attempts to organize beyond narrow craft boundaries. As a result, inclusive unionism collapsed in the US but survived in the UK. The rural struggles for land in the Irish Land War and the Reconstruction South thus laid the foundations of the diverging patterns of working-class organizing in the urban metropoles during the 1890s.

Part II shifts to an intermediate level of institutions and strategy. Labor leaders responded to different structural conditions with different organizing strategies. In the US, faced with strikebreaking, low-wage labor migration, and sharp divisions between high-wage craft workers and low-wage common laborers, organized workers turned decisively in the 1890s to drawing craft, racial, and nativist boundaries around their movements. Chapter 4 examines why craft boundaries prevented collaboration in the US, but craft unions in the UK remained more flexible. The next two chapters focus on the US. Chapter 5 traces how racial boundaries hardened and organized white workers embraced white supremacy during the 1890s. In parallel, chapter 6 follows a similar trajectory for nativism against European immigrants during this same decade. American labor leaders who witnessed mass immigration and extensive and effective racialized strikebreaking in the 1890s concluded that only a narrow, restriction-oriented labor movement of native-born, white, locally established craft workers could survive. Offering a comparison to the preceding two chapters, chapter 7 examines the broader British settler-colonial maritime empire. Similar but distinct patterns of racial boundary-making coalesced at the turn of the century. In the British maritime sector, and across the broader empire in Australia and South Africa, organized workers turned to racial boundary-making and nativist exclusion to control labor markets and protect privileged access to preferable jobs. However, within Britain, these imperial experiences resonated unevenly. In Liverpool, as a maritime port, racial boundary-making was both materially relevant for local workers and recognized in the broader empire. In contrast, racialized imperial class formation was far less clearly recognized in Sheffield.

Finally, part III concludes with workers themselves, their daily experiences, and how the rise of durable, bureaucratic unions marked a reorientation of demands and collective action. Parallel cultural and social experiences produced a new kind of "Fordist" working class in the early twentieth century. In the UK, this remade Fordist working class was more cohesive and integrated; in the US, even more divided and segregated. Chapter 8 traces the growth of working-class industrial suburbs and the leisure and consumption practices these new, improved homes offered. Chapter 9 examines how organized sports provided the setting for the cultivation of a new kind of Fordist working-class masculinity based on bureaucratic routines, repertoires, and dispositions. Building from these experiences of new homes, consumption, commercial leisure, and sports, chapter 10 shows how both the tactics and the demands of working-class collective action changed. Crowds and direct street politics declined, channeled into more formal bureaucratic collective bargaining, and workers moved away from demands for autonomy toward more materialistic demands (more money for less time) in a new kind of redistributive politics. In the US, this new politics was forged in a racialized context of divided neighborhoods, social worlds, and sports. With the rise of statist, redistributive welfare politics, racial boundaries also took new shapes in the twentieth century. Who was an eligible, deserving citizen, and who was an ineligible outsider to be excluded from expanding state benefits, marked as alien and unworthy? As the state distributed a new kind of social citizenship, who was a citizen became a more pressing question, and racial boundaries around citizenship hardened.

This book aims to offer new clarity on fundamental questions that have long animated historical and social science research: why was the US working-class movement so narrow? What is the relationship between class, race, and capitalism? Through extensive archival research, and by building interpretive connections between often isolated fields and historiographies, I hope to have provided novel and compelling answers to these questions. Yet in developing these arguments, the limits of this perspective must also be acknowledged. While the mechanisms of global inequality, migration, and class formation described here are a central, indeed I would contend a primary, driver of racial boundary-making, this is far from an exhaustive account. Antisemitism, for example, is a topic of enormous importance in modern political and economic history. However, the historical logics motivating antisemitism appear to be related but also distinct, rooted more in the rise of mass nationalistic politics than in labor organizing in the late nineteenth century. This book does not attempt to even scratch the surface of this important field of research.[51] Similarly, the question of caste, and India's unquestionably central place in the British Empire, cannot be considered. Again, distinctive processes and regimes of racial boundary-formation appear to be at work there. And indeed, in much of Latin America, the complex interaction of sizable settler-colonial, indigenous, and formerly enslaved populations creates distinctive patterns in labor markets, land regimes, and racial boundary-making. The analysis of racism and class formation offered here does not claim to be universal or all-encompassing, only broadly applicable across multiple contexts. Additionally, while gender and working-class masculinity are considered, women workers, both in the paid workforce and in the unpaid labor of social reproduction, appear only at the margins here.[52] A parallel project, which has been completed in conjunction with this research, puts gender domination and household work and power at the center of the making of modern capitalist inequality, and is forthcoming.[53]

Last, a qualification and clarification on the materialist underpinnings of this argument. Ultimately, there is a fundamental, reflexive interdependence between the material world of things and resources and the cultural world of symbols and meaning.[54] I have placed my finger on the materialist side of the interpretative scale since economic geography and labor markets are so essential, yet also so widely overlooked or minimized in the existing scholarship. At the same time, some "economistic" Marxists have disparaged struggles against racism on the symbolic, representational, or cultural front. The argument developed here does not share this rejection. Racial domination should be challenged on all fronts. Still, the history traced here suggests that combating racial domination at its roots requires changing not what people believe, but what they earn and own. Materially substantial reparations and redistribution, at a national and global level, must be part of any strategy toward racial justice. At a local level, this suggests attention to racial discrimination in labor markets, hiring, and housing.[55] At a global level, as long as an enormous chasm separates the wages of workers in the Global North and Global South, the wells of racial boundary-making will be continuously replenished.

While the outlook offered here may seem gloomy, Ireland's escape from colonial and racialized subordination in the nineteenth century offers a ray of hope. What would it take to make the Global South Ireland? Open borders allowed Irish emigrants to set sail for favorable labor markets, and successful, extensive land reform transformed the balance of social power in the countryside and mitigated the unequal geographical structure of labor markets within the UK. In contrast, the failure of land reform in

Reconstruction continues to reverberate in the United States. The struggle of African Americans for reparations for slavery is justifiably accounted for by the long-delayed "forty acres and a mule" that were widely, and plausibly, expected after emancipation. As long as a yawning wealth gap divides white and black working-class households, and as long as similar white and black job-seekers experience dramatically different responses from employers in the labor market, white supremacy will have secure material foundations.[56] Racial domination deserves to be confronted on all fronts. But efforts to build a more just world—to finally lift the shadow of slavery—will fall short if we fail to consider class, labor markets, and capitalism's uneven economic geography as ongoing drivers of racial boundary-making and brutal racial domination.

PART I

Rural Peripheries, Labor Uprisings, and the Migrant Strikebreaker

The Negro unerringly and insistently led the way. The main question to which the Negroes returned again and again was the problem of owning land. . . . Again and again, crudely but logically, the Negroes expressed their right to the land and the deep importance of this right. . . . For 250 years the Negroes had worked on this land, and by every analogy in history, when they were emancipated the land ought to have belonged in large part to the workers.

W. E. B. DU BOIS, *Black Reconstruction in America*,
"The Price of Disaster," 367

In *Black Reconstruction*, W. E. B Du Bois connected the history of the North and the South, of white and black workers, to explain the origins of a divided working class from the failure of land reform during Reconstruction: "Northern labor leaders and the mass of the North were slow in realizing that the center of the South's labor problem was the land."[1] Land reform failed in the United States, and this failure marks the founding moment of a fractured US working class. Had Reconstruction provided "each one of the million Negro families a forty-acre freehold," Du Bois imagines, the US could have had "a basis for real democracy," a united and powerful working class that "might easily have transformed the modern world."[2] For Du Bois, this possibility of a powerful, inclusive, globally transformative US working class foundered on the failure of land reform during Reconstruction.

Why has the labor movement in the US been comparatively narrow, confined primarily to relatively well-paid white workers? The late nineteenth century rise of unions within industrial cities must be understood within the context of surrounding rural near-peripheries. In contrast to European states, the United States had a domestic, internal near-periphery marked by the shadow of slavery. In the US South, the cheap labor of disenfranchised and violently subordinated African Americans formed a vast Jim Crow reserve army, available to be recruited by capitalists, especially for the purposes of defeating unions through strikebreaking. The distinctive narrow shape of the US labor movement arose from racial boundaries workers built at the intersection of class and economic geography. Until the shocks of the boll weevil and World War I, northward migration was contained by strict racial boundaries in Northern labor markets and a lack of literacy and information among black Southerners.[3] But even if the total number of migrants was small, the strategic availability of this reserve army in a regionally and racially divided labor market gave US capitalists a crucial weapon against labor unions. As Ray Stannard Baker observed in 1908, the African American migrant laborer from the South was "overflowing his boundaries in all directions, expanding more rapidly, perhaps, than any other element in the urban population" of Northern cities.[4] The origins of the *labor movement* must be understood within the context of an unprecedented *movement of labor* across capitalism's uneven economic geography in the late nineteenth and early twentieth centuries. This uneven economic geography grew from slavery, emancipation, and the failure of land redistribution during Reconstruction.

The rise of organized labor in the late nineteenth century marked a change in the spatial scale on which workers mobilized collectively. Up to the 1870s, workers organized locally, and largely informally, within particular neighborhoods, trades, and cities. As workers began to build more durable, centralized unions that attempted to mobilize across broader geographies, the significance of uneven capitalist development became ever more apparent. Following calls for greater attention to the connections between agricultural and industrial workers, part I begins with a comparison of rural near-peripheries that surrounded the four cities of Pittsburgh, Baltimore, Sheffield, and Liverpool: the US South and Ireland.[5] In an era of global mass migration conditions in the countryside, especially in immediately accessible near-peripheries, shaped labor markets and union organizing in the urban core.

During the late 1880s, workers in both the United States and the United Kingdom succeeded for the first time in organizing inclusively, bringing masses of workers into impressively broad labor unions. However, these parallel labor uprisings produced dramatically different results: while in the US the Knights of Labor were crushed out of existence over the 1890s, in the UK the New Unions survived, and ultimately created the foundation for a far broader, more inclusive labor movement. The contrasting fate of the Knights and the new British unions arose largely from their experience of strikebreaking—the practice of employers recruiting re-

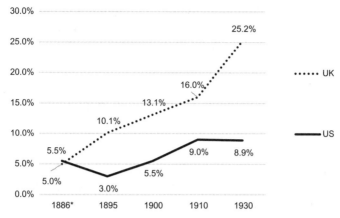

FIGURE P1.1 Union membership as a percentage of the workforce in the US and the UK. The year 1920 has been excluded since the spike in union membership obscured the growing gap between the US and UK. In 1920, UK membership reached 48.2 percent and the US reached 16.7 percent of the workforce. *Sources:* George Sayers Bain, *Profiles of Union Growth: A Comparative Statistical Portrait of Eight Countries* (Oxford: Blackwell, 1980), 170, table 10.1. Figures for the US in 1886 are necessarily estimates, but at the height of the Knights of Labor in 1886, union density in the US likely matched or slightly exceeded that UK; see Larry G. Gerber, "Shifting Perspectives on American Exceptionalism: Recent Literature on American Labor Relations and Labor Politics," *Journal of American Studies* 31, no. 2 (1997): 257n10.

placement workers who allowed capitalists to resume production and ignore the demands of strikers. As figure P1.1 shows, in the mid-1880s, when the Knights of Labor reached the height of their power, the rate of union membership in the US was similar to, and likely even exceeded, the rate of membership in the UK. The 1890s marked an initial moment of clear divergence. The US labor movement, battered by massive and effective strikebreaking, most visibly by African American workers recruited from the Jim Crow South, retreated into the narrow, racialized boundaries of craft unionism where workers were more protected from strikebreaking. In contrast, while employers also aimed to crush the New Unions in the UK during the 1890s, the transformation of the Irish countryside as a result of successful land reform meant that cheap and abundant strikebreakers were no longer easily accessible, and UK employers, despite militant and impressively organized attempts, found it expensive and difficult to break strikes.

Scholars have generally argued that exceptional levels of state and employer hostility explain the narrow boundaries of the US labor movement.[6] Yet during the crucial 1890s, when the survival of inclusive unionism hung in the balance, employers in both countries launched powerful counterattacks on labor, and British and American authorities proved more than willing to use police and military force to protect strikebreaking. If anything, the British counterattack on labor was more organized and militant. But British employers also found strikebreaking expensive and difficult compared to their American counterparts. From the early twentieth century, the relationship between the state, employers, and labor clearly diverged in the two countries. In the early twentieth century the British state began to shift toward a more neutral position as organized labor gained greater influence, and after 1910, British authorities generally refused to use police and military power to protect strikebreakers in the interests of employers. During the upsurge in labor organizing and militancy after World War I, the state played a drastically different role in the US and the UK. Yet, if the 1890s were the critical years during which the boundaries of the labor movement consolidated, this divergence in state posture toward employers and labor was not the cause but the result of the growth of mass, inclusive unionism in the UK.

The broad, inclusive union movement of the United Kingdom and the narrow, craft union movement of the United States diverged because similar labor uprisings that aimed to organize inclusively attempted to survive in two very different labor market contexts. In the US, the failure of land reform, disenfranchisement, and the rise of Jim Crow created a vulnerable, desperate reserve army of labor that could be quickly and cheaply recruited for strikebreaking. In the UK, while poor Irish farmers had been used extensively as strikebreakers in the early and mid-nineteenth century, the success of land reform, access to voting rights, and disappearing wage differentials between Britain and Ireland meant that by the 1890s the UK no longer had a near-periphery that could quickly and cheaply provide large numbers of strikebreakers.

Near-Peripheries

LAND AND THE RESERVE ARMY OF LABOR

When James Daly of the Irish Land League was released from a Sligo jail in 1878, his speech offered a rallying cry that could have as easily come from an African American Radical Republican in the US South at the same time: "Truly is the dawn of freedom appearing—truly the emancipation of the tenant farmers of Ireland. The south is awakening, slowly but surely."[1] In the 1870s both recently emancipated African Americans in the US South and Irish farmers under British colonial control were a largely landless, mostly desperately poor people. The mid-nineteenth century witnessed a global upsurge of rural uprisings that attempted, in part, to secure access to land for impoverished rural producers: the Taiping Rebellion in China, the Great Brigandage in Italy, the Land War in Ireland, and Radical Reconstruction in the US South.[2] Most were defeated, but the exceptional case of Ireland shows that these rural struggles could transform the terms on which labor from low-wage peripheries was swept into metropolitan labor markets. Impoverished rural producers in both Ireland and the US South understood their future, full emancipation in terms of gaining access to land. Although rarely connected, these two parallel struggles in rural peripheries would prove crucial in shaping how urban workers organized in both the United States and the United Kingdom.

George Campbell, a Liberal MP from Scotland and supporter of land reform in Ireland, toured the US in 1878. For him the parallel between the struggle of African Americans for land and the plight of Irish tenants was clear. According to this Scotsman, the black farmer in the South would be provided with "facilities for making himself . . . a small landowner," just as Liberal promoters of land reform in the UK had "sought to do for the Irish farmer."[3] Campbell imagined a similar process of land reform would unfold in both countries. However, he misread the situation, and the promise and expectation of land reform in the US South was quickly betrayed. In contrast, and quite exceptionally in a global context, Irish rural producers won a series of significant victories as part of an escalating revolutionary movement toward independence. By the 1920s, Irish nationalists had founded the Republic and broken from the colonial subjugation imposed by the United Kingdom. In contrast, African Americans' aspirations for forty acres and a mule after emancipation were defeated. Rather than a mass, democratic movement that culminated in the independence of the Irish Republic, in the US South white-supremacist Redeemers consolidated an economically, politically, and socially oppressive regime that tightly controlled access to land and imposed draconian restrictions on labor. Reconstruction marked the founding moment of the US working class, and the Irish Land War played a similar role for the British working class. The rural settlements reached in the late nineteenth century established the possibilities and constraints for subsequent efforts at inclusive working-class organization in urban cores.[4]

Toward Jim Crow: The Betrayal of Land Reform in the US South

During the Civil War, enslaved African Americans destroyed the conditions of their own bondage by refusing to work, demanding compensation, and fleeing to fight for the Union Army. Alongside their newly won freedom, most former slaves anticipated securing access to land. As W. E. B. Du Bois wrote in *Black Reconstruction*, most fundamentally after emancipation "black folk wanted two things": "first, land which they could own and work" that would "make them independent"; and second, "they wanted to know. . . . They were consumed with curiosity at the meaning of the world . . . with desire for schools."[5] For African Americans at the end of the Civil War, the "only real question . . . was not whether the lands belonging to the former slaveholders would be divided and distributed, but when and how."[6] The question of land redistribution moved through three distinct stages: first, military interventions in wartime; second, a struggle over the scope of the Freedmen's Bureau, the federal agency most directly charged with administering Reconstruction; and last, a revival of land redistribution during Radical Reconstruction (1868–1877), from party conventions, to state constitutions, and in the exceptional case of South Carolina, to successful land reform legislation during the 1870s. Not only did most formerly enslaved African Americans fail to secure the land they had so widely expected, but from the early 1870s, rising Ku Klux Klan terrorists assassinated black politicians, community leaders, and white Republican allies, closing the brief but profoundly consequential period of real democracy in the US South. White-supremacist "Redemption" was a gradual and uneven process across the US South. By the 1880s, a consolidating Jim Crow racial order not only systematically disenfranchised African Americans and many poor whites, it also profoundly curtailed the legal rights and protections of landless rural producers. School funding was withdrawn, illiteracy remained widespread, and poor, rural African Americans remained immobilized within the constraints of an oppressive Jim Crow economy.

The question of control over Southern land erupted during the war. Under the Second Confiscation Act of 1862, in theory all Confederates faced the forfeiture of their property. However, this could only be achieved through court proceedings, and at Lincoln's insistence, forfeited land was to be returned to heirs after the death of the traitorous landholder. In practice, although it raised broader political uncertainty about the legitimacy of Confederate claims to property, the Confiscation Act had little impact on actual landholding. Ultimately, far more land came under federal control due to nonpayment of taxes.[7] As the war ground to a close in January 1865 Sherman, in collaboration with Secretary of War Edwin Stanton, issued Special Field Order 15, setting aside the South Carolina Sea Islands and a coastal district thirty miles inland for settlement by formerly enslaved families on forty-acre plots. Although aligned with freedpeople's aspirations, this was a military measure designed not to transform the Southern social order but to relieve Sherman's army of its large following of impoverished African Americans seeking shelter and support.[8] By granting freedpeople plots of land, Sherman hoped to alleviate pressure on his army. Despite its pragmatic origins, the order produced transformative results. By June of 1865, some forty thousand former slaves had been settled on four hundred thousand acres of "Sherman Land." From this experiment in wartime land redistribution came the ubiquitous expectation that freedom would be supported on a foundation of "forty acres and a mule." As the war concluded, formerly enslaved African Americans were "convinced that the federal government had committed itself to land redistribution."[9]

The next stage in the struggle over land in the US South came with the passage of the Freedmen's Bureau bill in March 1865. The full title of this agency was the Bureau of Refugees, Freedmen and Abandoned Lands.[10] As the last part indicates, the Bureau was authorized "to divide abandoned and confiscated land into forty-acre plots, for rental to freedmen and loyal refugees and eventual sale."[11] The federal government controlled 850,000 acres in 1865, sufficient for more than 20,000 homesteads in forty-acre plots, enough "to make a start toward creating a black yeomanry."[12] Lincoln's assassination and Johnson's ascension to the presidency in April 1865 immediately called into question the goals and scope of the Bureau.

In June 1864, Johnson's vision of Reconstruction had appeared to include far-reaching possibilities, including land redistribution: "I say if their immense plantations were divided up and parceled out . . . it would give more good citizens to the Commonwealth, increase the wages of our mechanics, enrich the markets of our city, [and] enliven the arteries of trade."[13] However, a year later, Johnson had abandoned his agrarian radicalism and had become vehemently opposed to such transformative measures. Anticipating Johnson's hostility to the Bureau's mission, in July of 1865 the Director ordered its agents to establish forty-acre tracts for freedpeople as rapidly as possible. However, Johnson's pardons for nearly all Southern rebels soon created a legal battle over federally controlled land. Johnson ultimately forced the Freedmen's Bureau to restore nearly all land to pardoned Confederates.[14] Through his pardons and executive orders, Johnson foreclosed federal land reform. As Eric Foner has written, Johnson "had in effect abrogated the Confiscation Act and unilaterally amended the law creating the Bureau."[15] Johnson also worked to undo wartime land redistribution. Of the forty thousand plots distributed under Sherman, only two thousand remained in the hands of freedpeople after Johnson collaborated with the governor of South Carolina to block the validation of Sherman's land titles.[16] As Francis L. Cardozo explained during the South Carolina Constitutional Convention, the freedpeople had "held out hope of confiscation. General Sherman did confiscate; gave the lands to the freedmen; and if it were not for President Johnson they would have them now."[17]

Reconstruction was both a moment of revolutionary possibility and a profound defeat. It forces a consideration of what might have been. As Roger Ransom has written, in comparison to Johnson, Lincoln "would have been slower to pardon, more land would have remained under the Freedmen's Bureau's control," and it seems plausible that there might have been "some path to land ownership through purchase and distribution" for a significant proportion of the formerly enslaved.[18] Lincoln's assassination and Johnson's rise to the presidency ensured that the Freedmen's Bureau would never redistribute the "Abandoned Lands" of Confederate traitors. In September of 1865, the same month that Johnson foreclosed all possibility of land reform by the Bureau, Thaddeus Stevens and a small number of Radical Republicans in Congress proposed an even more revolutionary intervention: the confiscation by seizure of four hundred million acres from the wealthiest tenth of Southerners. With this vast expropriation, forty acres would be guaranteed for every formerly enslaved household, and in an effort to build broader support, the majority of the land would be auctioned off in small plots to fund pensions for all Union veterans.[19] Stevens argued that land reform was necessary to avoid a "war of races," since with secure access to land African Americans would "not be compelled to work for [former masters] upon unfair terms."[20] While an important reminder of the ambition and insight of a few Radical Republicans, Stevens's proposals never came close to being seriously considered in Congress.

While Johnson effectively killed land redistribution at the federal level, at the state level the Reconstruction Act of 1867 reopened the question of land reform. The act overturned Johnson's permissive approach to former Confederates and put Radical Republicans in Congress in control of Reconstruction. Most importantly, the act required universal male suffrage (that is, including all black men) in the elections for constitutional conventions in formerly Confederate states. As Republicans prepared to rewrite state constitutions and govern, party conventions across the South divided between predominantly black "confiscation radicals" and white moderates committed to policies appealing to landowners and Northern investors.[21] The possibilities of Radical Reconstruction after 1868 "rekindled the persistent dream of landownership" among African Americans in the South.[22] Poor white farmers from upcountry districts were also supportive of land redistribution, more to punish the planter elite and diminish their influence than to elevate the formerly enslaved.[23]

Yet only in South Carolina, with its powerful majority of black voters and legislators, was there meaningful land redistribution during Radical Reconstruction. During the 1868 Constitutional Convention in South Carolina, Francis Cardozo argued that "one of the greatest bulwarks of slavery was the infernal plantation system, one man owning his thousand, another his twenty, another his fifty thousand acres of land. . . . Let the lands of the South be similarly divided" to the small farms of the North, and the South could enjoy real freedom and prosperity.[24] The South Carolina Land Commission, authorized by the state constitution of 1868, was initially plagued by corruption and inefficiency, but after Cardozo reorganized and rationalized the Commission as Secretary of State, it began an impressive intervention in South Carolina's rural social order. Roughly fourteen thousand black families, around a seventh of the state's black households, along with a handful of whites, received a total of 112,404 acres of land through the Commission.[25] One study of Richland County, South Carolina, where thirty-nine African American households received title to 1,399 acres of land, found that over a century later, ten of those families "continue[d] to own largely intact parcels of land."[26] Families that received land often produced community leaders, including "ministers, politicians, and educators," for the local black community.[27] The Land Commission "experiment worked to an impressive and significant degree" in places where it helped portions of the black community "rise up out of the bonds of landlessness."[28] On the whole, we as yet know all too little about the long-term experiences of the thousands of African Americans in South Carolina who benefited from land redistribution during Reconstruction.

George Campbell, the Scottish Liberal MP who toured the US South in 1878, viewed the South Carolina Land Commission as a model and parallel for unfolding efforts at land reform in the UK: "In South Carolina . . . they have done more for themselves than in most states," since during Reconstruction "the State Government established a commission [to] settle freedmen upon [lands] on fair terms of payment, on exactly the plan recommended by the last Parliamentary Commission on Irish land."[29] Campbell visited some of the black farmers on redistributed land, and "was greatly interested in the independent and self-supporting rural communities which I there found."[30] As Reconstruction ended and as the Land War gained momentum, observers such as Campbell, although very few later scholars, recognized the clear parallels between these two agrarian near-peripheries.

In contrast to these successes in South Carolina, little meaningful land reform occurred elsewhere. Despite the state of Mississippi gaining control of some six million acres for failure to pay taxes, around 95 percent of this land found its way back to its original owners through collusion and intimidation at auctions.[31] An effort to promote ownership by African Americans on vacant federal land through the Southern Homestead Act, enacted by Republicans in 1866, produced negligible results since the land available was marginal and lacked access to necessary infrastructure.[32] Benjamin S. Turner, a black congressman from Alabama, proposed a national land commission bill in the 1870s, but his bill never came up for a vote, and the national Republican Party showed no interest in national land redistribution efforts.[33]

The remarkable achievement of Reconstruction was a commitment to inclusive political democracy and equality before the law, at least for men. Yet African American political influence during Radical Reconstruction in the South was brief. With the spread of Ku Klux Klan terror across the Southern countryside, African Americans in the South lost the ability to influence the political process, and white supremacy was restored in Southern politics. Rebecca Scott writes that the "denial of access to land consigned most former slaves and their descendants to the role of wage-paid farm laborers, and political defeat blocked the compensating possibility of organizing as workers."[34] In 1887, when some six thousand sugarcane field laborers went on strike with the Knights of Labor, the state militia and bands of white vigilantes massacred and terrorized the workers, leaving at least thirty African American men dead.[35] Political disenfranchisement not only made laborers vulnerable, but the few black landowners also struggled in an increasingly hostile legal and political environment. Black rural producers continued to fight for "land reform, education, and the elimination of the poll tax" through organizations like the Cooperative Workers Alliance and Colored Farmers Alliance in the 1880s and 1890s, but mass arrests, white militias, and violence foreclosed sustained political opposition.[36] Agrarian protest was fundamentally fractured in the 1890s between the white and black farmers' alliances, and when a Cotton Pickers' League attempted to "improve the lot of landless black tenants" through a mass strike in 1891, the movement was violently repressed.[37] By 1900 African Americans in the fertile cotton regions of the South owned a smaller share of the land than they did at the end of Reconstruction.[38] As we will see below, disenfranchisement of African Americans in the 1870s stands in sharp contrast to the enfranchisement of poor, rural Irish men in the 1880s, thus providing a key pivot point toward extending land reform in Ireland and foreclosing any renewed possibilities in the South.

The demand of the freedpeople for land had all too often been met with "surprise and ridicule," Du Bois noted in *Black Reconstruction*.[39] While nearly all efforts at land reform failed in the mid-nineteenth century, a comparison with Ireland makes it clear that transformative land reform was possible under the right political conditions. The longer sweep of US military history is also suggestive. While the US Army and War Department's Freedmen's Bureau was cut short in any effort to remake the Southern agrarian order in the 1870s, after World War II, US military authorities imposed far-reaching land reform in occupied Japan and Korea.[40] Du Bois also emphasizes a comparative, global context in *Black Reconstruction*: the "Italian and Russian serf" were "given definite rights in the land" in the nineteenth century, and workers in Europe used their electoral power "to redistribute wealth and income," but "only the American Negro slave was emancipated without such rights and in the end this spelled for him the continuation of his slavery."[41]

In the United States vagrancy laws, anti-enticement measures, convict leasing, and lien laws all empowered landowners and creditors and weakened the position of rural producers.[42] As figure 1.1 shows, African American farming households faced a desperate and deteriorating position at the turn of the twentieth century. The number of landowners stagnated and began to decline, while impoverished croppers came to predominate over somewhat more independent and prosperous tenants. This marked a grim economic retreat for rural African Americans as Jim Crow white suprem-

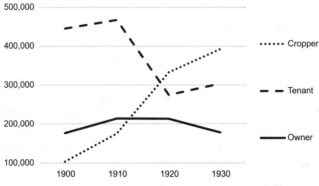

FIGURE 1.1 Black farming households in the US, 1900–30. *Source*: Lee J. Alston
and Kyle D. Kauffman, "Up, Down, and Off the Agricultural Ladder: New Evidence
and Implications of Agricultural Mobility for Blacks in the Postbellum South,"
Agricultural History 72, no. 2 (1998): 273, table.

acy consolidated across the US South. As Ransom and Sutch argue in their
economic history of emancipation, whites used violence to keep African
Americans from "gaining an education, practicing a trade, or purchasing
land," and thus "systematically prevented blacks from following the three
routes most commonly traveled by other Americans in their quest for self-
advancement."[43] By contrast Ireland, Britain's near-periphery and source
of low-wage industrial labor in the nineteenth century, charted a strikingly
different trajectory.

Toward Independence: The Long Land War in Ireland

As Klan terror destroyed the last remnants of Radical Republican power
in the late 1870s, the Irish Land War was beginning across the Atlantic.
The Land War of 1879–82 erupted from the accumulated pressures of three
decades of social transformation and class conflict in Ireland. After the
famine of the 1840s, Irish agriculture shifted from crop farming to pastur-
ing animals, and to facilitate this transformation, some seventy thousand
evictions took place between 1846 and 1853. New capitalist investors, such
as one Glasgow shipbuilder who purchased nearly thirty thousand acres in
Ireland, increasingly viewed their new estates as commodities on an active
land market, with little regard for the customary rights of their tenants.[44]
The Land War would reverse this trajectory toward concentrated private
landholding, and put Ireland on a very different course than the US South.
After the Land War, landlords lost the right to evict tenants. Rents were
no longer set by the market, but by judicial commissions that favored the

interests of tenant rural producers. In the 1880s, as African Americans were being systematically disenfranchised in the US South, poor, rural Irish men won the right to vote. Finally, in the first decade of the twentieth century, politically empowered and legally protected Irish tenants transformed themselves into small landholders through government-financed land redistribution schemes. The period from 1875 to World War I witnessed a gradual but far-reaching revolution in Irish land tenure, with the share of farm owner-operators rising from only 3 percent to over 60 percent by 1916.[45]

Fueled by decades of economic transformation and growing social conflict, the first tentative steps toward land reform came in 1870. Gladstone's Liberal Government aimed to resolve growing tensions in the Irish countryside by giving customary protections for tenants ("Ulster Custom") the force of law. The Irish Land Act of 1870 required compensation from landlords for any improvements made to the land or premises by tenants, compensation for the disruption of eviction in cases other than nonpayment of rent, as well as access to government loans at 5 percent interest if a landlord was willing to sell to tenants. While the 1870 Act failed to bring agrarian peace or produce significant transfers of land, it offered a symbolic measure of protection to Irish tenants, raised expectations, and set the stage for the Irish Land War of 1879–82.[46]

In April of 1879, as the date for the annual collection of rents approached, a mass meeting in County Mayo organized by James Daly and Michael Davitt attracted thousands and marked the formation of the Irish Land League. This meeting launched what came to be known as the Land War. Although the social roots of this struggle came from the impoverished western districts that had suffered through successive crop failures, the leadership of the Land League tilted toward more prosperous tenant farmers and urban shopkeepers. This more affluent leadership tried to avoid issues like confiscation and land redistribution and distanced themselves from widespread social violence.[47] The years of the Land War saw widespread "agrarian outrages" in which landlords (and often compliant, collaborating tenants) were murdered, mobbed, and terrorized for setting rents at market rates and evicting tenants.[48] Several differences with the US South are notable. African Americans very rarely resorted to social violence in advancing their political aims, likely for reasons of both principle and prudence. Even more importantly, unlike African Americans in the US South, among whom there was only a minuscule middle class, the impoverished Irish benefited from the early leadership and political connections of more prosperous farmers and wealthier urban leaders within the context of a cross-class nationalist mobilization.[49]

During the Land War, the Land League demanded the three "Fs": Fair Rent, Fixity of Tenure, and Free Sale. After two years of organized political protest by the Land League as well as extensive agrarian violence in the poorest districts, in 1881 the newly re-elected Liberal Government passed a Land Act. The 1881 Act essentially granted the Land League's demands: tenants gained a secure right to their land without fear of eviction, and rents would be fixed at "fair" rates by a judicial tribunal, a intervention that severely curtailed private property rights and "dramatically reduced landlords' control over their estates."[50] Under the Act, tenants could request judicial revision of their rents every fifteen years. In the first round of revisions in 1881–82 rents were reduced by an average of 21 percent, and in the second round in 1896–97, rents were reduced by a further 18 percent.[51] These protections applied to existing, permanent tenancies, but landlords increasingly escaped rent-control regulations by letting land on eleven-month contracts that did not fall under the regulations of the 1881 Land Act. Nevertheless, over much of rural Ireland, the Land War and the ensuing 1881 Land Act effectively ended private property for many landlords.

Even if middle-class leadership pushed the Land League away from more radical demands, it helped to create a political context in which poorer Irish farmers could later make more transformative demands for land redistribution. In the years that followed the Land War, the cross-class alliance of the Land League broke down as tensions increased between prosperous large tenants at the top and small tenants and landless laborers at the bottom. Paralleling the agrarian populism that swept the US South and West in the same years, two figures in the Irish countryside met with increasing popular hostility: the "large grazier," who operated more than two hundred acres of pasturage, and the "shopkeeper grazier," who used debt to keep small farmers under control.[52] With the franchise reform of 1884, even poor men in the Irish countryside gained the right to vote. Strikingly, during these same years, African Americans and many poor whites in the South were losing the franchise, first through Klan terrorism in the 1870s and 1880s, and from the 1890s, through Jim Crow constitutional and legal restrictions.[53]

Facing continuing social violence and electoral pressure from the Irish poor, the 1891 Land Act created a new administrative agency in Ireland, the Congested Districts Board, which aimed to make small, poverty-stricken farms large enough to be viably operated. Impressively, the Board managed to enlarge the holdings of some sixteen thousand small tenants.[54] Large landholders, unsurprisingly, usually refused to sell their land to the Board for redistribution. Landlord resistance and the Board's official sanction of land redistribution encouraged even moderate nationalist leaders to take up the issue. This led to the formation of the United Irish League in 1898, the "first major Irish nationalist organization to adopt land redistribution as its most fundamental and defining policy."[55] While not as spectacular in terms of agrarian violence, the growing mass movement of the United Irish League once again produced a legislative response from the UK government. The 1903 (Wyndham) and 1909 (Birrell) Land Acts overcame landlord resistance to redistribution, first by the carrot of financial incentives to sell, and then with the stick of allowing for compulsory purchase by the Land Commission.[56] By 1913, 250,000 tenants had secured holdings of land covering some eight million acres through these Acts, and when combined with the work of the Congested Districts Board and the Land and Estate Commissioners, around 285,000 Irish tenants were transformed into landowners in these years, covering a terrain of 9.3 million acres, or around half the agricultural land in Ireland.[57] By the end of the 1920s, an escalating sequence of mass mobilization, nationalist political agitation, concessionary legislation, and revolutionary upheaval had transformed social relations in the Irish countryside. Landlords and tenants, the dominant figures of the Irish countryside up to the late nineteenth century, had disappeared, replaced by small owner-occupiers who farmed sufficient land to guarantee what was understood at the time as a decent standard of living.

The example of the Land League and the struggle for land reform in Ireland resonated strongly in the United States, even if the parallels to the struggles of African Americans in the South were only occasionally recognized. Terence Powderly, the most important labor leader of the 1880s, was also Vice President of the American Land League, and Henry George told his mass following that the struggle "between Irish landlords and Irish tenants" highlighted the "great social problem of modern civilization."[58] Thomas T. Fortune, perhaps the first black socialist, published *Black & White: Land, Labor, and Politics in the South* in 1884. Fortune hailed the "most desperate struggle" in Ireland, where "monopoly in land" had become "so explosive that it can only be appropriately described as 'dynamitic,'" and he bitterly condemned the failure of land redistribution during Reconstruction.[59] Decades later, the Socialist Party in Texas renamed their Renters' Union the Land League of America under the leadership of Tom Hickey, a "firebrand socialist stump speaker originally from Ireland," and drawing inspiration from the struggle for land in the Mexican Revolution.[60] In the 1920s, the Irish struggle continued to resonate. Harry Haywood, the black Communist who helped develop the US Communist Party's interpretation of African Americans as an oppressed nation with a rightful claim to the soil of the black belt region of the South, spent time at the Lenin School in the Soviet Union where he met a group of Irish revolutionaries. He recalled that his friendship with these Irish radicals led him to embrace the national self-determination thesis: "As a result of my association with the Irish, I became deeply interested in the Irish question, seeing in it a number of parallels to U.S. Blacks."[61]

Near-Peripheries and Urban Labor Markets: Migrants and the Threat of Low Wages

The late nineteenth century was an age of unprecedented mass migration. As the *Sheffield Independent* noted, "men whose sole capital is the labour of their one pair of hands naturally prefer to take that labour to the market where the best terms are available." According to the *Independent*, "Irish labourers [did] not leave their native fields and become bricklayers labourers" in English cities "because they have ceased to love or care for the claims of their own island, but because they know that [in Britain] they can sell their labour for considerably more."[62] Uneven economic geography underpinned the mass migrations of labor in the late nineteenth century. Most moves occurred between rural districts and adjacent, growing urban centers. These short journeys sometimes set in motion longer, transoceanic movements across the Atlantic, Pacific, or South China Sea. As Adam McKeown shows, there were three major destination regions of mass long-distance migration in the years from 1846–1940, with some fifty-five million Europeans moving to the Americas, forty-eight million Chinese and Indians moving to Southeast Asia and across the Pacific Rim, and forty-six million Koreans, Russians, and others moving to Japan, Manchuria, and Siberia.[63] The uneven terrain of capitalism's economic geography encouraged these unprecedented flows from the global countryside to industrial cores. As McKeown argues, in the late nineteenth century, the "rise of a global economy centered on European, North American, and Japanese industrialization was the context for the increased long-distance migration of settlers and workers."[64] Many of these migrants hoped that industrial wage labor would be temporary, pursued only for enough time to accumulate funds to reestablish themselves in their rural homes. As an investigator found among rural African American migrants in Northern cities at the turn of the century: "I have yet to find one who wanted to go back" to the South, "unless he had accumulated enough to buy land."[65] Although geographically dispersed, access to land, migration, and the formation of urban-industrial working classes were closely bound together.

Globally, various near-peripheries provided labor to adjacent industrializing cores. Korea sent workers to the Japanese Empire; Southern

Italy provided migrants for the Italian industrial north and France; African homelands in South Africa supplied the mining industry; the Polish regions of Imperial Germany and the Habsburg Empire served German industry. All of these near-peripheries featured repressive political institutions that crushed resistance and denied rural producers control over land.[66] We can draw global connections between the violently repressive social environments of these agrarian peripheries. Just as African Americans fled lynching, many Jews from eastern Europe fled pogroms. At the turn of the century, for example, the organized workers of the Donbass-Dnepr heavy industrial region of Imperial Russia not only mobilized militant mass strikes but also turned with ferocious brutality against Jews.[67]

Hunger for land was widespread, but the US experience of defeat was far more typical than the surprising success of Irish rural producers. Most often, aspirations for land were crushed. In 1854 Hong Xiuquan's Taiping peasant rebellion in China promulgated the "Land System of the Heavenly Dynasty," which proposed to abolish private ownership and allocate all individuals—men, women, and children—a plot of land. Although this decree was reprinted in 1860, suggesting that "the rebels continued to accord land redistribution a place in their ideology," the "pressures of war and the demand for revenue prevented them from carrying out such a vast undertaking."[68] Had the Taiping revolt transformed the Chinese countryside in the 1850s, giving rural producers land, and thus more autonomy, bargaining power, and increased wages, Chinese labor migration would likely have been substantially lower in the late nineteenth century, provoking less vehement racial boundary-making by organized workers across the Global North. Similarly, Enrico Dal Lago's comparison of what Du Bois called the "General Strike" of enslaved African Americans during the Civil War and the Great Brigandage of the Southern Italian peasants in the 1860s suggests that the shared history of rural class struggle shaped the mass migrations of rural Italians and African Americans in the late nineteenth century.[69]

Agrarian struggles over land shaped how, when, and on what terms rural people migrated to urban cores. Defeated in their efforts to win control of land and trapped in a cycle of debt, landless Italian and Chinese tenants and African American sharecroppers entered the emerging global labor market from a position of profound vulnerability. With little security and few options remaining as a "fall-back position" in the countryside, they entered the urban labor market obliged to take the lowest-paid work at the bottom of the production hierarchy. In contrast, by the 1890s the desperation of the midcentury Irish peasantry had passed. Emigration to Britain decreased substantially, and those who chose to migrate could do so more selectively when particularly favorable opportunities became available. While rural producers across the world demanded political rights and land redistribution in the late nineteenth century, the success of the Long Land War in Ireland was highly unusual.[70] The only comparable cases of extensive land reform occurred in Russia after the 1905 and 1917 Revolutions and after 1915 during the Mexican Revolution.[71]

Regional wage differentials between rural near-peripheries and urban, industrial cores motivated the movement of migrant workers seeking higher wages. In the mid-nineteenth century, regional wage differentials between Ireland and Britain were substantial, and British workers feared the threat of low-wage Irish competition. As an 1868 editorial in *The Times* noted, the "principal fault" of the "Celtic invaders" was their tendency to "lessen the rates of wages" in British cities. An official of the miners' union recalled that British workers had been "driven to America by the wage competition" of Irish "strangers."[72] Yet, despite these high wage differentials in the mid-nineteenth century, by the twentieth century, British-Irish wage differentials had declined significantly. The ratio between British and Irish unskilled urban wages declined from 1.71 in the 1850s to 1.16 by 1910, close to parity, erasing a stark geographical divide in just over half a century.[73] In addition to land reform, the Irish were able to migrate before immigration restrictions spread in the early twentieth century. Largely open global borders allowed Irish emigrants to move freely to desirable labor markets, and previously low Irish wages converged with the broader North Atlantic. While migration certainly played a leading role, land reform also raised agricultural wages in Ireland. This massive decline in the wage differential reduced the incentives for migrants from rural Ireland to seek work in Britain. Irish beneficiaries of land reform withdrew household labor from the wage labor market, thereby decreasing the supply of labor and raising agricultural wages.[74] Migration from Ireland to Britain plummeted in the late nineteenth century.[75] Tenants' transformation into landowners, converging wages, and reduced migration meant that by the 1890s migrant Irish laborers no longer posed a threat to British workers, either as low-wage competition or as strikebreakers.

The story was far different within the United States. Economic historians have stressed the "remarkably uneven" integration of US labor markets between 1870 and 1914. As Gavin Wright has argued, the "South has been distinctive in many ways besides its wage rates: in its farming methods, in its racial segregation, in its entrepreneurship, in its political economy," but all these, he notes, have "their roots in the separateness of the Southern labor market."[76] While Northern, Midwestern, and eventually Western labor markets converged through a sustained process of integration, this "coincided with the persistent failure of integration between northern and southern labor markets."[77] Rosenbloom shows that in urban labor markets, earnings in the South Atlantic region were 16 percent below Northern wages in 1879; by 1914 the Southern wage gap deficit had increased to 26 percent below Northern wages. The initially labor-scarce south-central states had higher wages in the 1870s, but by the early twentieth century there was "a convergence of wage levels within the two southern regions" at a depressed Southern regional rate well below the rest of the United States.[78] While Irish wages converged with British wages, during the same years in the US substantial regional wage differentials increased, providing a strong and increasing incentive for migrants to move from the low-wage South to the industrial cities of the North. As Ray Stannard Baker observed in 1908, Northerners who glanced "Southward" could "almost see the army of Negroes gathering from out the cities, villages and farms, bringing nothing with them but a buoyant hope in a distant freedom, but tramping always Northward."[79]

The importance of land reform for the US labor movement was not entirely lost on observers after the Civil War.[80] While the vast majority of labor papers lined up behind the Democratic Party during Reconstruction, the lonely voice of the Boston *Daily Evening Voice* proclaimed the importance of Radical Reconstruction, African American voting rights, and land redistribution for the future of the labor movement.[81] It was not only moral justice, but economic self-interest. Land redistribution would reduce the pool of insecure agricultural workers, raise Southern wages, and reduce the incentive to migrate North, flooding urban labor markets.[82] This was a prescient vision, anticipating the findings of development economists more recently that land reform had the potential to produce a high-wage, high-consumption economy.[83] However, Northern workers did not respond to this vision, subscriptions to the *Daily Evening Voice* plummeted, and the paper folded in 1867. While momentarily visible, a Northern labor and Southern land-reform alliance never gained meaningful traction.

In the 1880s and 1890s United States, Northern white workers and manufacturing capitalists had a clear sense of the challenge posed by entrenched regional and racial wage differentials. A US immigration inspector recalled that in 1886 Henry W. Blair, described as the best advocate of the "cause of labor in the Senate," had warned that "the time was soon coming when Northern workmen would have to contend with the cheap negro of the South." Senator Blair promoted his proposal for federal control of education, and the provision of expanded education in the South, in terms of the self-interest of white Northern workers in a regionally and racially divided labor market: "The negro must be educated or he will be a constant menace to Northern workmen."[84] In 1889 the *Pittsburgh Dispatch* reported on a survey of "9,000 negro employees" and the relative wages paid to these black workers in the Southern iron and steel industry, noting that manufacturers were "practically unanimous in the opinion that for common labor in the Southern States, the negro is more efficient and useful than the white."[85] Later the same year, the paper again noted the "enormous wages" earned in Pittsburgh compared to "those which negro labor begets in the South."[86] A review of iron and steel production in 1890 highlighted the competitive difficulties faced by Northern manufacturers. The South enjoyed "great advantages in the manufacture of pig iron" due to the "cheapness of labor in the Southern states."[87] A month later, the *Pittsburgh Dispatch* noted that the owners of "Southern iron mills" based their claims to "future pre-eminence in the markets of the world" on the basis of being able to pay "unskilled negro labor in the mills . . . 50 cents per day."[88] Suggesting the close attention paid to questions of relative regional wages in early 1890s Pittsburgh, a letter to the editor pointed out that these figures were exaggerated, since "common labor in the South [was] uniformly paid $1 per day."[89] In March 1891, an interview with a "well-known pig-iron broker" in Pittsburgh on the increase in cheap Southern competition suggested that the root cause was that "labor is very cheap there."[90] The broker expected, with rather naïve faith in the laws of supply and demand, that "in the next few years Southern labor will successfully demand the same wages as are paid in the North."[91] This expectation proved misguided, as North-South wage differentials remained entrenched.

The persistence of high regional wage differentials in the United States forced Northerners to ponder the causes and consequences of long-term economic divergence. In 1891 another iron broker who had "spent nearly the whole of last winter in the South" criticized the tendency in Pittsburgh for manufacturers to "bury their heads in the sand and imagine that they are the only people in the country who can make iron." The broker reported that "labor in the South costs 25 or 30 per cent less than at the North," and in several states, the use of "convict labor in their coal and their ore mines" allowed for drastically reduced labor costs.[92] Asked if Southern wages would rise, this broker was less optimistic. He pointed to the "refusal of white men to take black men into their unions," but he speculated that in "time that may change."[93] In 1904, in an article reflecting on the "white movement southward" with capital establishing new industries seeking lower wages, and the "negro movement to the North" seeking higher wages, the *Pittsburgh Daily Post* noted that "by the operation of irresistible laws, there will be great negro populations in many Northern states" and this impending migration "vastly concerns the working people and the wage-earners of the North."[94]

Entrenched wage differentials provided an opportunity for employers and labor recruiters. Immediately after the Civil War, the emerging labor press raised concerns that a massive emigration company had been organized to transfer two to three hundred thousand black workers from the South to Northern manufacturing cities in order to keep down wages and break strikes.[95] While these fears proved exaggerated, by the 1880s employers in major cities interested in strikebreaking could turn to "a well developed network of employment agencies capable of supplying large numbers of unskilled workers," many of them recruited over substantial distances.[96] Just as Irish immigration to Britain was dwindling to a trickle in the late nineteenth century as wages on the two islands converged, African American migration from the South more than doubled, jumping from 88,000 black migrants moving North in the 1880s to 185,000 in the 1890s.[97] This number of permanent migrants likely underestimates the total movement, since many if not most Southern migrants returned South.

Already from the late 1880s, Northern employers explicitly sought a supply of low-wage black workers from the South. An 1889 classified from Pittsburgh sought "100 colored laborers—Wages $1.50 per day."[98] In 1890 a "leading contractor" in Pittsburgh reportedly found "Italian labor . . . so unsatisfactory that it will be discarded and colored labor tried in its place."[99] A few days later, the *Pittsburgh Dispatch* reported on the arrival of "150 colored laborers . . . from the South over the Baltimore and Ohio road."[100] As part of this racialized reassignment of the most objectionable work from Italians to black workers, the "son of the senior partner of the firm was in "Virginia . . . and will bring the colored men back with him."[101] While many firms such as this Pittsburgh building contractor might dispatch a trusted official to recruit labor in the South, some entrepreneurs organized labor recruiting businesses to take advantage of the large regional wage differentials by moving workers from the South into Northern labor markets. As a 1905 report observed, "stories of an outside world where wages are relatively large . . . continually reach his ears," and the Southern black migrant "cares not that the skilled trades are closed to him." He would answer the call "that some great corporation is seeking large numbers of men" distributed in "all the cities and many smaller villages" where "employment agencies" operated to send black workers north.[102]

One such labor recruiter became prominent in Pittsburgh. In September 1890 the *Pittsburgh Dispatch* provided a detailed profile of the work of F. Z. S. Peregrino, a labor recruiter whose house on Wylie Avenue was

FIGURE 1.2 Francis Peregrino, labor recruiter in Pittsburgh and South Africa.
Source: Heather MacAlister, *Ancestors Research South Africa*, https://www
.ancestors.co.za/francis-peregrino.

"painted in bold letters... that it is his business to furnish colored laborers of all sort direct from the South."[103] Peregrino (figure 1.2) was the son of an Afro-Brazilian born in Accra in the Gold Coast colony of the British Empire. He lived in England for most of his youth, where he married a white woman from the United States; they arrived in Pittsburgh in 1887.[104] At the Fourth Avenue office, the *Dispatch* reporter found "Mrs. Peregrino... very busy with numerous ladies and gentlemen who were anxious to secure help direct from the Sunny South."[105] The paper reported that Mr. Peregrino was on his "semi-monthly trip" to the South, and he was expected to return with "22 women and several men;" according to his wife, business was "very brisk" and was "rapidly on the increase." "We have no difficulty in getting all the people we want," Mrs. Peregrino explained, since "the wages paid in the South are so small that it is almost impossible to live.... Laborers there receive 75 cents per day.... They consider the $1.50 a day they can get in Pittsburg a princely salary." Mrs. Peregrino was also eager to dispel some potential misconceptions about their business. Southern imported labor received the "same compensation here that natives do." In addition, "Mr. Peregrino has made it a point never to take orders for men to take the places of strikers."[106] This strong disavowal suggests that already in the early 1890s Southern labor recruiters supplying black workers to Northern labor markets were strongly associated with strikebreaking. In August 1891, a classified for Peregrino's business offered "Cooks, Chambermaids, butlers, farm hands and every kind of colored help from the South"; a few months later, Peregrino was advertising his services "to manufacturers, mine owners, contractors and others: Every class of colored labor imported direct from the South."[107] Revealing striking global parallels between urban cores and rural near-peripheries, after his time in Pittsburgh, Peregrino moved to South Africa, where he spent much of his time "pursuing his role as a labour-broker and a conduit for Africans living in the interior" to employment in the white-controlled mines.[108]

Labor recruiters often experienced hostile reactions from both Northerners and Southerners. In the North, as we will see in chapter 5, white workers typically reacted with intense hostility and violence when black workers attempted to enter new segments of the workforce. Southern migrants also experienced hostility from more prosperous long-term black residents in Northern cities. The minuscule but relatively prosperous existing community of African Americans in Pittsburgh was deeply concerned about the increasing influx of poor black migrant workers from the South.[109] In 1891 African American ministers in Pittsburgh condemned the "evil-disposed white people" and the "immigrant agents" who "persuaded Southern colored laborers" to come to Pittsburgh.[110] The ministers noted the "crowding of many colored workmen into a single mill has thrown men out of employment."[111] Thus a double boundary hindered even more extensive movement of black workers from the low-wage South to the high-wage North. Rural black tenants were "locked in" to the South by limited literacy, confined social ties, and unreliable information; they were also "locked out" of Northern labor markets by the hostility of white workers as well as some Northern African Americans who might have been expected to be their allies and supporters.

Southern resistance to labor recruitment was even more intense. The *Pittsburgh Dispatch* noted that whenever labor recruiters attempted "to remove any portion of the negroes of the South," white Southern employers rose "in arms against it," indicating "the determination" of Southern whites "to retain the cheap labor of the region."[112] In 1891, the *Pittsburgh Dispatch* reported on the experiences of Charles Jones, a labor recruiter who went to North Carolina "to secure 500 negro laborers," but was forced to flee from mob violence. As Jones reported: "I came near being mobbed three times. . . . A committee waited on me five minutes after I got off the train and gave me 30 minutes to leave town. I had to leave the place on foot and walk ten miles to the next station."[113] Jones warned that labor recruiters were "going to get lynched if they don't mind."[114] Southern resistance to labor recruiters was not limited to vigilante intimidation and violence. To protect the interests of planters, Southern states passed laws that required prohibitively expensive licenses for labor recruiters and imposed large fines for labor enticement to deter recruitment of employed workers. Suresh Naidu shows that anti-enticement laws were an important "example of labor legislation, pervasive in the postbellum South, that benefited white employers at the expense of black workers," and finds that a 10 percent increase in the enticement fines corresponded to a 12 percent decrease in the probability of sharecroppers moving, with a negative impact on wages and returns to experience for wage-earners as well.[115] Thus sharecroppers were "most affected by anti-enticement laws," with "substantial spillover effects into the agricultural wage labor market."[116] Globally, anti-enticement laws were issued by governments in other major near-peripheries, including the Habsburg regions where recruiters sought laborers for the industries of the German Reich.[117] Control over low-wage rural labor was contested. Rural elites wished to retain a subordinated and cheap workforce; urban-industrial employers aimed to recruit workers from near-peripheries; and urban workers attempted to limit entry, most drastically, as we will see below, by imposing immigration restrictions on global flows of migrants, or by imposing internal controls on the movement of rural laborers, as with South Africa's pass system.

Gender and the labor of social reproduction also shaped the migration of workers from low-wage near-peripheries to urban cores. Migration from the countryside to the city disrupted and broke local circuits of social reproduction. This allowed urban cores to profit from the low-wage labor of wage-earning adults without having to support the social reproductive labor of caring for the non-wage-earning young and the elderly who stayed home in the rural periphery. While true of all the young, male migrants who migrated across the uneven economic geography of capitalist development, this was especially visible to observers of African American migrants. As Helen Tucker noted in her 1909 study of African Americans in Pittsburgh, "the children remain in the South, and many of the old people go back there, so that the city of Pittsburgh is under little expense for educating the children and less for caring for the aged."[118] Whether from Europe or the South, young migrant labor in industrial cores could be paid less, since these workers were not directly responsible for the local maintenance of families. The differential demographic impact of migration on local populations can be seen by comparing Sheffield, which received relatively few migrants, to Pittsburgh, which became a major destination for migrants both from the US South and from Europe. At the turn of the century in Sheffield, only 48.9 percent of the male population was in the "productive age group" of 15–44 years old, whereas in Pittsburgh, with its massive immigration, 63.9 percent of men were in this age group.[119] In US cities with large-scale population growth through migration, the cost and labor of social reproduction were outsourced to a global rural periphery, both in the South and across the European countryside. This disruption of local circuits of social reproduction, separating urban productive-age wage workers from the rural social conditions that had enabled them to grow into adults, contributed to depressed wages at the bottom of the production hierarchy where migration substantially shaped the workforce.[120]

Conclusion

A crucial condition for the broad, inclusive growth of the British labor was the success of Irish rural producers in winning access to land. Some connected the success of mass uprisings in the Irish countryside and British cities. According to George Brooks, a British elite deeply disturbed by growing working-class militancy, the "new trade unionism" that emerged from the uprising of 1889 was "the offspring of [the nationalist] movement in Ireland."[121] Migration from low-wage, rural near-peripheries had enduring consequences for workers in urban, industrial labor markets. In the US, the failure of land reform in the 1870s, and the political repression and violent terror experienced by African Americans in the Jim Crow South produced a structurally fractured working class along regional and racial lines, divisions that would encourage employer strikebreaking and white-supremacist exclusions by unions. In contrast to the US, the success of rural mobilizations in Ireland produced a decline in migration and a more integrated labor market across Ireland and Britain. Whereas mass rural struggle supported mass unionization in the UK, the defeat of land reform during Reconstruction in the US created a weakened and divided US working class at its founding moment. It was in this context, in the mid- to late 1880s, that the first great wave of mass inclusive union organizing erupted in both the United States and the United Kingdom.

Parallel Rebellions

THE KNIGHTS OF LABOR AND THE NEW UNIONISM

In 1887, Engels hailed the rise of the Knights of Labor as "an immense association . . . the first national organization created by the American working class as a whole."[1] In the 1880s both the United States and the United Kingdom experienced their first wave of mass labor organizing. While concerns about industrial class conflict had been growing over the course of the nineteenth century, these mass movements put the "Labor Question" front and center in both countries. In the US, the Knights of Labor grew rapidly during the 1880s, peaking in 1886 with widespread enthusiasm for huge railroad strikes that targeted the richest capitalists combined with intense popular pressure for an eight-hour workday. In the UK, partly inspired by Knights, the "New Unionism" gained traction from mass strikes by workers at the bottom of the production hierarchy, in this case the London dockworkers' uprising of 1889. The organizing of the New Unions peaked in 1890, and employers launched an aggressive anti-union counterattack. After their extraordinary peaks, membership in both the Knights and the New Unions dropped precipitously. Both of these movements marked an unprecedented departure from the narrow craft unions that had begun to consolidate national organizations from the 1850s, with signs of institutional stability during the 1870s. Broad organizing that included the masses of workers at the bottom of the production hierarchy was a remarkable, if fragile, achievement.

The dramatic growth and heroic organizing efforts of the 1880s were undeniably important. But of more significance when seen in a comparative perspective is the slow grind for survival during the subsequent decade. In most labor histories, the events surrounding 1886, for the Knights, and 1890, for the New Unions, have understandably captured the most interest. As figure 2.1 suggests, the initial explosion and rapid retreat was broadly similar in the US and UK. Six years after peaking, by 1892 the Knights of Labor had declined to 120,000 members, 19 percent of its maxi-

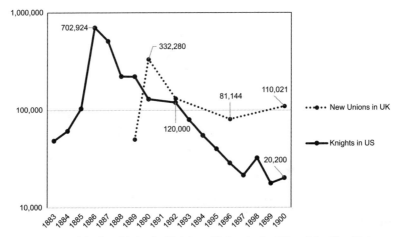

FIGURE 2.1 Membership in the Knights of Labor in the US and the New Unions in the UK. *Sources*: H. A. Clegg et al., *A History of British Trade Unions Since 1889, Vol. 1, 1889–1910* (London: Clarendon Press, 1964), 1:83, table 2; Richard Oestreicher, "A Note on Knights of Labor Membership Statistics," *Labor History* 25, no. 1 (1984): 102–8.

mum; by 1896 the New Unions had fallen to 81,000 members, only 24 percent of their maximum membership. While the Knights did experience a slightly greater decline, their initial peak was also more than twice as high: 700,000 members in the Knights compared to 330,000 members in the New Unions. The rapid retreat of the Knights from 1886 to 1892 seems unremarkable alongside a similar decline for the New Unions. As the next chapter will explore, the important divergence occurred during the 1890s, after the initial rise and retreat. During the 1890s, the New Unions in the UK stabilized at around 100,000 members, while the Knights of Labor retreated to a residual and inconsequential membership of only 20,000 by the start of the twentieth century.

Prior to these bursts of inclusive organizing, from the 1850s to the 1870s unions in the US and the UK had been confined to skilled craft workers, such as puddlers and rollers in steel mills, or locomotive engineers on the railways. The skilled artisans who set type for printers were among the first workers to organize durable craft unions in both countries. Although low-wage, replaceable workers at the bottom of the production hierarchy had often attempted to organize in the mid-nineteenth century, in all cases their efforts proved short-lived and ultimately unsuccessful. Dockworkers, railway laborers, factory operatives, and general laborers had all failed to form durable organizations prior to the 1880s. By far the largest group of wage-earning women in the late nineteenth century worked as domestic servants, although there were also substantial numbers who labored in textile factories and as seamstresses in garment sweatshops. These women workers had found more hostility than solidarity from the men in craft unions. Like their male peers on the docks and the factory floor, they were excluded from the narrow unions of the more secure, and higher-paid, craft workers. Craft workers retained significant control and managerial authority over the production process, and occupied a privileged and powerful position within the broader working class.

The narrow scope of early labor unions caused concern among some sympathetic observers. Offering a remarkably clear assessment, an 1867 editorial in the *Pittsburgh Gazette* observed that "whoever would do something effectually to Protect Labor, must be careful not to narrow his definition, so as to substitute particular kinds of Labor for Labor in general. What are called Skilled Workmen are much less numerous than the classes known as Common Laborers."[2] The *Gazette* highlighted the "open secret" that craft workers were in many cases quite similar to employers, since they hired and paid "what are called Helpers or Common Laborers." Rather than a shared labor solidarity, among "Helpers the impression is universal that the Skilled Workmen are as harsh and grinding in dealing with them" as the capitalist owners.[3] The *Gazette* pointed out the hypocrisy of skilled craftsmen who protested low wages while in turn paying their own helpers far lower wage rates: "If Skilled Men, with the higher wages they always obtain . . . have such deep cause of complaint that they must keep up an outcry, what do they think must be the lot of the Common Laborers? If a Skilled Workman, making from four to eight dollars a day, cannot get along comfortably, what does he think must be the condition of his Helper, to whom he pays from a dollar and a half to two dollars only a day?"[4] The boundary of craft, and the material divide separating the high wages of those on top from the low wages of those on the bottom of the production hierarchy, produced not a unified working class, but one that had intense internal tensions.[5]

Craft unionists largely rejected calls for broader solidarity.[6] In the United States the older craft unions organized their first major convention in 1881, establishing the organizational roots of what would become the American Federation of Labor (AFL). The man who would later lead the AFL, Samuel Gompers, reported against inclusive strategies for the Committee on Organization. Gompers argued that workers should form "a purely trade federation . . . to be composed of 'trades unions' only," indicating a restrictive scope of organization limited to craft workers. Several spoke out against this narrow approach, including one African American worker from Pittsburgh, whose observations succinctly warned against the narrow craft union path ultimately taken by the AFL and the US labor movement. This black worker observed: "We have in the city of Pittsburgh many men in our organization who have no particular trade, but should not be excluded from the Federation. Our object is, as I understand it, to federate the whole laboring element of America."[7] In addition, this delegate warned of the looming threat of strikebreaking by black workers. With "a knowledge of my own people," he warned that it would be "dangerous to skilled mechanics to exclude from this organization the common laborers, who might, in an emergency, be employed in positions they could readily qualify themselves to fill."[8] Locked into low-wage work at the bottom of the production hierarchy by discrimination, African Americans were particularly attuned to the dangers of a narrow craft union organizing strategy. However, in cities like Baltimore, with a long, established community of free African Americans, there were small pockets of African American craft workers. Here too craft boundaries could cut against broader solidarity. At an 1870 meeting of "Colored Mechanics," there "was considerable discussion in regard to admitting the laborers into the association, but without coming to any conclusion about the whole matter."[9] Black craft workers also had concerns about extending solidarity to low-wage common laborers.

In retrospect, craft workers' rejection of broader class solidarity can seem puzzling. But there were several reasons why the early mid-nineteenth century unions in both the US and the UK were narrow craft organizations. In an era before the advances of engineering, chemistry, and industrial science, craft workers' knowledge of the production process gave them considerable bargaining power compared to low-wage workers at the bottom of the production hierarchy; incorporating these low-wage workers was deemed more risky than helpful. Interests were also not fully aligned given that, as mentioned, craft workers often hired, managed, and paid the helpers and laborers who worked alongside them. Last, craft workers often lived in very different social and cultural worlds from low-wage laborers in the mid-nineteenth century. When the Knights and the New Unions built mass, inclusive organizations in the 1880s, it was something radically new in the history of organized labor. For the first time workers at the bottom of the production hierarchy were joining unions, winning strikes, and building durable organizations.

The Knights of Labor in the United States

A group of defeated and frustrated workers organized the Knights of Labor as a fraternal secret society in 1869. The Knights emerged from a meeting

FIGURE 2.2 Railroad monopoly vs. Knights of Labor. On the left, capitalists
cheer on the railroad monopolist with the spear of the corrupt "subsidized press,"
while on the right, workers support beleaguered labor wielding the "strike."
Source: Frierich Graetz, "The Tournament of Today—a set-to between labor
and monopoly," *Puck*, August 1, 1883, centerfold. Library of Congress Prints and
Photographs Division, Washington, DC, USA. https://lccn.loc.gov/2012645501.

to disband an unsuccessful craft union of garment cutters in Philadelphia.
The Knights grew slowly in the 1870s, with most members in the Philadelphia region. However, significant growth came under the leadership
of Terence Powderly in the 1880s, when the organization shed its secre-
tive fraternal roots and became an unprecedented mass movement of all
ranks of workers. Rapid growth was inspired by highly publicized and
successful strikes by railroad workers against the financier and railroad
owner Jay Gould.[10] As figure 2.2 shows, depictions of the Knights were often sympathetic in the mid-1880s. This 1883 cartoon from *Puck* depicts an
overpowered, heavily-armored, train-driven monopolist jousting against
a beleaguered and largely defenseless donkey Knight of Labor; in the background, a private box of millionaires supports the monopolist and a mass
of working-class spectators back the Knights of Labor.

The Noble and Holy Order of the Knights of Labor (to give the organization's full name) was not only a labor union, but also became a political
party and a morally inspired utopian experiment. Adherents envisioned
not just improving wages, but bringing about a post-capitalist cooperative
commonwealth of all producers. Rooted in the traditions of labor republicanism, Knights leadership generally rejected strikes and class conflict in
favor of arbitration, boycotts, and cooperation. Despite these somewhat

unusual features, when considered as a labor union, the Knights offered a plausible path toward a far more inclusive and broad US labor movement committed to organizing all workers and representing their interests in politics.[11]

The 1880s witnessed sustained and remarkable growth in the Order's membership. But progress would come to an abrupt halt in 1886. Several events that year signaled a crisis. First, while the Knights had enjoyed broad public sympathy and support in the mid-1880s, this began to change with the third railroad strike against Gould in March and April of 1886. Second, the Haymarket riots in May created a frenzy of hostility that extended beyond anarchist agitators to target the labor movement more broadly. Third, an escalating conflict over organizational strategy and leadership led to the secession of most of the old craft unions and the formation of the American Federation of Labor in December of 1886 as a separate organization, now deeply hostile to the Knights.[12] Many craft unions had cautiously cooperated with the Knights during their remarkable progress in the mid-1880s, but after the turmoil of 1886, the newly formed AFL turned against the Knights with bitter hostility.

The racially and regionally divided labor markets of the United States immediately posed challenges to the inclusive organizing of the Knights in the 1880s. Despite the structural and political obstacles to solidarity between white and black workers, the Knights made remarkable, and occasionally successful, efforts to bridge the fundamental regional and racial divide in the US working class. In Baltimore, during the surge of Knights organizing in 1886, one of the most remarkable developments "was the fraternization of the two thousand black and white brickmakers" during a parade for the eight-hour workday.[13] In addition to the brickmakers, there were Knights assemblies of wagoners, grain trimmers, and stevedores organized by black workers in Baltimore. However, key leaders in the African American community cautioned against embracing the Knights. A pattern of racist exclusion by white workers made many African Americans suspicious of the labor movement. In a speech at Baltimore's Sharp Street Methodist Church in 1886, one African American leader "advised the colored laborers not to join the white trades union or take part in the present struggle of labor against capital. Until recently, the trades union had refused to receive the colored men in their organizations."[14]

The fragility of the Knights under the pressure of regionally and racially divided labor markets became apparent when organizing black workers in the states of the former Confederacy. The first official statement made by the Knights on black workers was narrowly defensive, rather than welcoming, indicating a keen sense of the threat posed by the low-wage, unorganized, and political disenfranchised African Americans of the South: "Why should workingmen keep out of our organization anyone who might be used as a tool to aid the employer in grinding down wages?"[15] Remarkably, the Knights made substantial progress in organizing African Americans across the South. Although less than 10 percent of the Knights were from the South, between one-third and one-half of these fifty thousand Knights were black workers.[16] After calls for more black organizers in 1885, by the next year, there were four black organizers in Alabama, two in North Carolina, and at least one in most other Southern states.[17] This was an unprecedented level of practical, financial commitment to organizing among low-wage African American workers. Southern whites could brutally punish any attempt at inclusive solidarity. A white Knights organizer working to form assemblies of black workers in South Carolina and Georgia was murdered by local vigilantes. Resistance also erupted from the white majority within the union: white workers refused to work with black organizers, and white organizers refused to support the efforts of black workers.[18]

Predictably, the Knights' attempt at inclusive organizing immediately came under attack. Strikebreaking was always the fundamental barrier to organizing among easily replaceable workers at the bottom of the production hierarchy. In the mining districts of western Maryland, the local assembly of Maryland miners grew to nearly two thousand members in 1882, but effective strikebreaking destroyed the union.[19] The strike started on March 1, 1882, and the Consolidation Coal Company quickly "put up buildings within the stockade at Eckhart Mines to house some 700 strikebreakers and special police."[20] However, it took nearly three months for the strikebreakers to arrive, since the company recruited mostly recently arrived European immigrants.[21] By the end of the summer, the strike had collapsed and workers individually sought re-employment on terms set by the mine operators. As in this case, European immigrants were often mobilized as strikebreakers. But the regionally and racially divided structure of the US labor market made the recruitment of African American workers the cheapest and fastest option for many employers.

Racialized strikebreaking clearly played an important role in undercutting the growth of the Knights in the 1880s. In 1885, the Mallory steamship company in Galveston, Texas, effectively used black strikebreakers against white longshoremen, and despite the Knights' sustained efforts to mediate and build solidarity among black and white workers, the conflict devolved into a bitter and violent "race war" for control of work in the port. Even more prominently, in 1886 black workers from Richmond Virginia, a stronghold of interracial Knights of Labor organizing, were successfully recruited to break a strike of coal miners in western Pennsylvania.[22] In the same year, in the Southern textile industry, which had refused to hire any African American workers, employers in Augusta, Georgia, were able to defeat a strike by threatening to hire black strikebreakers. In 1887, skilled white ironworkers in Birmingham, Alabama, refused to support a strike by their less-skilled black coworkers, forcing the intervention of the Knights' state leadership. Although Knights officials often urged solidarity, over-lapping racial and craft divisions among rank-and-file workers roiled local assemblies.[23]

As a labor union that attempted to organize both white and black workers, the Knights struggled to navigate the internal tensions within their movement. When the Knights held their 1886 General Assembly in Richmond, Virginia, delegates from the New York District Assembly aggressively challenged local segregation. This challenge to Jim Crow mo-bilized a white mob that threatened a lynching, caused outrage in the Southern white press, and won praise from black newspapers across the US. Caught up in a furor, the Richmond General Assembly reaffirmed its theoretical commitment to racial equality, but to ease the anger of South-ern white members and the local white community, the Assembly also clarified that it had "no purpose to interfere with or disrupt the social relations which may exist between the different races in different parts of the country."[24] This defensive statement typifies the class-first/ignore-race strategy taken by organized labor in the US. Many labor leaders have argued that when building class solidarity, racial inequality could and should be set aside to focus on supposedly more "universal" interests, thereby making them, as a recent history of US socialists and race empha-sizes, "tone deaf to the ways in which race shaped social and economic circumstances."[25] A generation later, socialist leader Eugene Debs echoed Powderly in believing there was "no negro problem apart from the gen-eral labor problem," and that socialists had "nothing special to offer the negro."[26] As noted by black radicals such Hubert Harrison who became disillusioned with the Socialist Party, despite rhetorical universality in practice the approach of the AFL and Socialists put the white "race first and class after."[27] The Knights, despite being remarkably successful in or-ganizing black workers, were unable to fully comprehend or specifically address the racial divisions of the US working class. Terence Powderly affirmed this 1886 concession to class over race in his memoirs; it was not necessary, he wrote, to "interfere with the social relations of the races in the south, for it is the industrial, not the race, question we endeavor to solve."[28] In reality, the structural constraints of a racially and regionally divided labor market meant that the "industrial" and "race" question were inextricably intertwined. After the Richmond integration controversy, the Knights became "basically a Black union in the South, and one composed of the economically weakest" sectors of the workforce in the South: rural agricultural labors and urban domestic servants.[29] After Richmond, white Southerners abandoned the Knights. Loyal black members were too economically precarious to sustain an organization on their own.

Even at the height of their power in the mid-1880s, the Knights confronted the racial and regional divides that marked the afterlives of slavery in the United States. Any union of low-wage, easily replaceable workers in the US would have a difficult time surviving, let alone a union of black workers in the Jim Crow South. Maryland's Bureau of Industrial Statistics, formed during the upswing of Knights of Labor organizing, issued its first report as the momentum crested in 1886. "The impulse to organize seems to have possessed the wage-workers of the country," Thomas C. Weeks marveled, noting that in Maryland, "the trades union [had] slowly increased their membership" during the mid-1880s, "but during these few months [in 1886] it is no exaggeration to say they have more than quadrupled their numbers."[30] Weeks correctly perceived the instability of the new organization: "I regard this sudden development as an overgrowth, and believe it will, to an extent, die off."[31] Although the Knights' retreat after 1886 was dramatic, it was also predictable. It was no different in the UK, where the New Unions also retreated at a similar rate after their initial peak. Although the danger of a racially and regionally divided labor market was already clear in the 1880s, the real divergence between the US and UK labor movements came in the 1890s, as mass, often racialized strikebreaking in the US effectively foreclosed the survival of inclusive union organizing.

New Unionism in the United Kingdom

Just as the success of the Knights built on widely publicized and popular railroad strikes, in the United Kingdom prominent and successful strikes played a similar role in the growth of the New Unions. For British workers, the catalyst came from the waterfront. In the summer of 1889, London dockworkers won a significant strike, the focal point of a massive upsurge of unionizing among low-wage workers in the UK. Britain was exceptional in terms of the antiquity of its labor movement. Although the US had a few older craft unions, as Hobsbawm noted, only in the UK "do we find an already established and significant 'old' unionism, rooted in the country's basic industries, to combat, transform and expand."[32] Thus, the "New Unions," to explain their name, emerged alongside established craft unions in the UK. The New Unions organized neglected sectors in Britain, such as rail and water transportation, the lower grades of industries where the craftsmen were already organized (ships, iron and steel, engineering), and regions previously neglected by the main unions, such as parts of the Midlands.[33] Another parallel between the New Unions and the Knights was their treatment by the press. Just as public opinion turned against the Knights in 1886 in the aftermath of the railroad strike and the Haymarket bombing, so too with the New Unionism. Although the London dock strike had enjoyed broad popular support during the summer of 1889, public support in the press began to "waste away during the last weeks of the strike," and the 1890s were marked by "a hostility toward trade unionism in general and new unionism in particular that bordered at times on the hysterical."[34] Thus, quite similar responses faced both the Knights and the New Unions in the late 1880s.

Indeed, the movements were not only parallel, but directly connected. The Knights of Labor played a brief but prominent role in the UK prior to the explosion of the New Unions in 1889. The Knights had established an Assembly in Cardiff in 1883, and in 1884, a group of Liverpool dockworkers organized under the banner of the Order.[35] Michael Davitt, the leader of the Irish Land League, attended the General Assembly of the Knights in Minneapolis in 1887, and in 1888 worked to promote the Order in Britain by speaking at a mass meeting, promising that the union would organize in "skilled industry and unskilled industry, from the agricultural labourer to the scientist in his laboratory."[36] A close friend of Davitt's, Richard McGhee, also spoke at this mass meeting, and served briefly as a Knights organizer in Glasgow, where he built the organization that would eventually become the National Union of Dock Labourers (NUDL), one of the core New Unions in the UK.[37] Knights Local Assembly 443 recruited stevedores in Liverpool in the late 1880s before being driven out of the port by the Dock Labourers union. There was thus both continuity and competition between the Knights and the New Unions in the UK. James Sexton, a Liverpool docker who later became General Secretary of the NUDL, was a member of the Knights of Labor in the 1880s.[38] In the Sheffield area there were at least ten Local Assemblies of the Knights, including nearly 100 members in the iron and steel industry. Among them was Jabez Hall, who would later become a divisional officer of the Iron and Steel Trades Confederation.[39] From promising growth in 1887 to 1888, by the early 1890s the Knights in Britain had largely disappeared. But the British Knights can be credited with having built "up interest in unionism, especially among the unskilled," helping to set the stage for the growth of the New Unionism after 1889.[40]

While labor markets were converging within the UK, both between Ireland and Britain and between different regions in Britain, exposure to cheap, accessible strikebreaking labor still constrained the efforts of the New Unions. As a port, Liverpool was more exposed to strikebreaking by migrant labor from across Europe and later, the broader empire, whereas Sheffield, located in the industrial interior, provided a more secure terrain for the New Unions. Among the first of the New Unions was Havelock Wilson's national seamen's union, formed in the northeast of England in 1887, and quickly expanding to Glasgow and Liverpool. The union eventually claimed a foothold in all the major ports except Liverpool. On Merseyside employers used strikebreakers, resulting in "frequent battles . . . between strikers and 'rats' or blacklegs," with "extra police protection" provided to strikebreakers. The seamen's union was eventually driven from Liverpool.[41] NUDL also encountered fierce resistance in Liverpool. Despite broad sympathy for the 1889 strike in the press, and the efforts of the mayor to mediate, employers imported strikebreakers, and the military was called in to protect the replacement workers.[42] Much as the Knights came to be seen as an African American union in the South after the Richmond crisis of 1886, NUDL was commonly called "the Irish union" since Irish workers played such a prominent role in it.[43] In Sheffield, where less migrant labor was available, the most successful of the New Unions was the National Amalgamated Labourers Union, which "organized workers in steelworks and engineering works, in municipal employ and in the collieries into a strong industrial force in the 1890s and the early years of the twentieth century."[44]

Why did British workers at the bottom of the production hierarchy— dockers, laborers, and others—suddenly succeed in organizing durable unions in the late 1880s? The New Unionism of 1889 was far from the first effort to organize unskilled workers in the UK, but prior efforts had been "localized, small and ineffectual," and these earlier efforts had been "invariably beaten" by employers.[45] Initial scholarship on the New Unions, from Hobsbawm in particular, emphasized the leading role of socialists and an embrace of militant, mass strikes over arbitration. Revisionists have effectively challenged this narrative, suggesting not only increasing moderation by union leaders over the 1890s, but that "the new unions, their rules and their officers were on the side of moderation from their inception." While militant rhetoric was used in the strikes that aimed to establish a foothold, organizationally and strategically the New Unions were quick to turn to routine collective bargaining as a means of conserving resources and capacity.[46] As was also often the case with the Knights, strikes were typically "forced by the rank and file in an *ad hoc* fashion on a usually reluctant leadership."[47] And like the Knights, the New Unions suffered from unreliable leadership, excessively high administrative costs, officers who all too often embezzled union resources, and a substantive lack of internal democracy.[48] Given the success of the revisionists' questioning of the radical politics and tactics of the New Unions, some scholars have come to dismiss the significance of 1889 and the New Unionism altogether, emphasizing a broad, conservative continuity in the British labor movement. But the boundaries of the British labor movement really did expand dramatically after 1889. For "the first time relatively unskilled workers were able to take on and beat their employers in major confrontations and exact significant and lasting improvements in their wages and working conditions." While many of the New Unions suffered the fate of the Knights and ultimately collapsed, several major organizations "became national in scope and proved to be permanent."[49] This was a significant departure that needs to explained.

As with the Knights, efforts to organize low-wage workers in the United Kingdom proved to be highly vulnerable to strikebreaking. Similarly, employers proved to be militantly hostile, and the British state was more than willing to use police and military power to protect strikebreakers. In 1889, immediately after the spectacular success of the London dockworkers, a strike by London gasworkers was met with determined strikebreaking. The employers had ordered "beds and temporary housing" and made prior arrangements with the police to ensure better protection for strikebreakers than had been available on the waterfront. By the time the two thousand strikers turned out, some four thousand replacements had already been contracted to replace them, and the employers quickly prevailed.[50] An even more dramatic confrontation occurred with the gasworkers in Leeds, where hundreds of strikebreakers were imported, protected by "calvary, surrounded by a double file of police, and a file of military" and escorted "by the Mayor and magistrates." This dramatic display of state authority on the side of strikebreaking did not prevent strikers from assaulting the procession, and for several days the town "was like an armed camp," with the military menacing striking gasworkers on the streets.[51] In 1890, as a response to the New Unions, leading waterfront employers and shipowners formed the Shipping Federation to combat the power of the New Unions among dockworkers, sailors, and others. Their first major contest came between December 1890 and February 1891 in London. The Federation had laid careful "plans for the introduction of 'free labour,'" and arranged with the Police Commissioner to have the Metropolitan Police diligently protect strikebreakers instead of the Dock Police, who had proven unable and unwilling to effectively protect strikebreakers in 1889.[52] The Shipping

Federation won an important victory in London. British employers did not hesitate to use state power and highly organized strikebreaking to combat the New Unions, and union leaders could face severe repression. During a strike in Cardiff in 1890, Havelock Wilson was sentenced to six weeks in prison for "unlawful assembly and riot."[53]

Despite the well-organized and militant attacks of employers, why were the New Unions able to survive? Clearly neither employers nor the state provided a benign welcome to the new mass organizing. Scholars have pointed to a number of factors. Skill-based wage differentials began to move in favor of the unskilled in the UK in the 1880s, narrowing the material gap between craft workers and laborers, and increasing the relative bargaining power of workers at the bottom of the production hierarchy.[54] However, the most important factor, as Derek Matthews argues, was the shrinking of the "reserve army of labor" of rural agricultural laborers who could threaten urban workers with low-wage competition and strikebreaking. In the UK, and unlike in the US, there "was a dramatic and consistent (and from the 1880s absolute) decline in the supply of rural labour to unskilled occupations."[55] This shrinking supply limited the ability of employers to undercut urban wages by cheaply and quickly importing strikebreakers from the countryside. Setting the stage for the next chapter, Matthews argues that "up to the 1880s [British] employers of unskilled labour could replace their men with effortless ease and little expense," but after this, "the matter was in doubt especially during peaks in the trade cycle."[56] During the 1890s, 3.1 percent of workers on strike were replaced in the United Kingdom, and in the first decade of the twentieth century, this fell to 2.4 percent; only 0.3 percent of striking workers were replaced during the 1910s.[57] By this point, strikebreaking had disappeared as a meaningful force in British labor history.[58]

Conclusion

When carefully compared, the late 1880s surge of inclusive labor organizing in the US and the UK appear remarkably similar. The retreat of the Knights of Labor after its 1886 peak was unremarkable. The New Unions in the UK experienced a similar decline, driven by a similar employer counterattack. Attempts to organize the easily replaceable workers at the bottom of the production hierarchy were highly vulnerable to strikebreaking, and employers used strikebreakers to considerable effect in both countries. While these similarities need to be stressed, the roots of future divergence were already appearing in the 1880s as the Knights encountered the racially and regionally divided labor markets of the United States. Despite some remarkable achievements in organizing black workers in the US South, racialized strikebreaking and conflict among workers proved immediately destabilizing for the Knights. As the next chapter will explore, the 1890s would be the decisive decade, as US employers were able to use mass strikebreaking to crush inclusive organizing among workers at the bottom of the production hierarchy. Meanwhile, try as they might—and they likely tried harder than their US counterparts—British employers were not able to destroy the New Unions.

Divergence

STRIKEBREAKING AT LABOR'S TURNING POINT

In 1905 Jack London wrote in *War of the Classes* that for capital, the strike-breaker was "by far the most formidable weapon" in the class struggle.[1] Strikebreakers—often called "blacklegs" in the United Kingdom, or "scabs" in the United States—allowed an employer to resume production and defeat the strike, often destroying the union. For low-wage, highly replaceable workers, union organizing was always vulnerable to strikebreaking. Hobsbawm's comments on the threat of strikebreakers to dockworkers can be extended to low-wage workers in general: they were "constantly haunted by the spectre of the blackleg . . . unskilled farm labour flooding" the industry and undercutting wages.[2] Karl Marx's International Workingmen's Association, or First International, was formed to combat the international recruitment of strikebreakers, although during this mid-nineteenth century period, these strikebreakers were mostly skilled craftsmen rather than masses of low-wage common labor.[3]

A comparison of the US and the UK suggests that strikebreaking was the crucial driver of diverging paths for organized labor in the two countries. Strikebreaking, despite its undeniable importance to the balance of power between workers and employers, has received far less attention than many details of working-class life and union organizing.[4] Historians of labor universally acknowledge it, but very rarely is strikebreaking given central interpretative consideration in either local studies or comparative scholarship.[5] As table 3.1 illustrates, the scale of strikebreaking in the US and the UK was vastly different. Although roughly 2.5 million workers went on strike from 1891 to 1899 in both countries, in the US, employers recruited more than three times the number of strikebreakers, meaning that 11.1 percent of strikers were replaced, in contrast to only 3.1 percent in the UK. Joshua Rosenbloom's research has shown how important strike-breaking was for the success of strikes. When strikebreakers were hired, only 27 percent of strikes were at least partially successful for workers in

TABLE 3.1 Strikers and strikebreakers in the US and the UK, 1891–1899

	US	UK
Strikers	2,401,057	2,581,319
Strikebreakers	266,451	80,271
Strikebreakers as a percentage of strikers	11.1%	3.1%

Source: Department of Labor, *Strikes in the United States, 1880–1936*, Bulletin No. 651, August 1937 (Washington, DC: United States Government Printing Office, 1938), 342–43, table V; McIvor, "Strikebreaking in Britain," 12, table 1.

the 1890s; but when employers did not recruit strikebreakers, workers were successful in 73 percent of strikes.[6] Clearly, success or failure, survival or destruction, hung on the use of strikebreakers.

The 1890s were a crucial period of labor movement consolidation. The survival or the destruction of inclusive unionism shaped subsequent efforts to organize, especially during a second major burst of organizing in the years before and during World War I.[7] The New Unions in the UK managed to stabilize at around a hundred thousand members in the 1890s, while the Knights were ground down to only twenty thousand members by the end of the decade, as was seen in the previous chapter. The disappearance of the Knights and the rise of the craft union-based AFL was not as swift as is often assumed. Kim Voss reminds us that the rivalry between the two organizations "was a messy business that lingered for years," and only after seven years, in 1893, did the AFL clearly surpass the membership of the Knights.[8]

Due to a regionally and racially divided labor market, this chapter argues that US employers had far greater access to cheap, quick, and extensive strikebreaking during the 1890s. However, rural near-peripheries were not the only source of cheap, pliable labor. A potentially decisive labor market factor shaping the success of labor organizing is the unemployment rate. Periods of high unemployment provided employers with a large and immediately accessible pool of workers to turn to as strikebreakers. As one scholar has argued, late nineteenth-century "overabundance in the labor market was largely responsible for the success met by the employers in securing scabs locally and also for the widespread weakness of most unions" in the US.[9] However, recent estimates show broadly similar levels of unemployment during the 1890s, as shown in figure 3.1. If anything, the New Unions in the UK faced a more challenging context, with slightly higher unemployment rates. Thus unemployment rates cannot explain the vastly different levels of strikebreaking and union survival in the two cases.

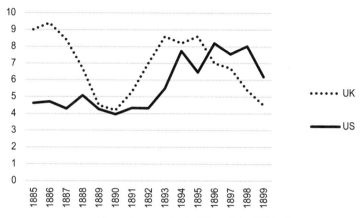

FIGURE 3.1 Unemployment in the US and the UK in the 1890s.
Sources: George R. Boyer and Timothy J. Hatton, "New Estimates of British
Unemployment, 1870–1913," *The Journal of Economic History* 62, no. 3 (2002):
662, table 4; J. R. Vernon, "Unemployment Rates in Postbellum America: 1869–
1899," *Journal of Macroeconomics* 16, no. 4 (September 1994): 710, table 2.

Rather, the broader structural context of rural near-peripheries explains
why the Knights were driven to the margins while the New Unions were
able to survive and stabilize.

It is impossible to know exactly what share of US strikebreakers were
black workers, but substantial evidence points toward them playing a decisive role. Nearly all immigrants from Europe, another unquestionably
important source of strikebreaking labor, had more lucrative, secure, and
appealing routes into Northern labor markets than those available to African American migrants from the South. Two pioneering economists, Sterling D. Spero and Abram Lincoln Harris, suggested the outlines for this
argument in their remarkable 1930 study *The Black Worker*. Spero and Harris argued that black "rural workers, the numerically most important part
of the Negro labor supply, became an industrial reserve" that employers
could use for cheap, effective strikebreaking against organized workers.[10]

During the 1890s, employers in both countries showed similar hostility
to unions, and state authorities in both countries were more than willing to back up employers by providing police and military protection to
strikebreakers. The increasing neutrality of the British state after 1900 was
not the cause, but the result of the consolidation of inclusive unionism in
the UK. By World War I, a clear difference had emerged in how authorities engaged with the labor movement. Confronted with growing trade
union electoral power, the British state refused to protect strikebreakers,
and strikebreaking essentially disappeared; in the US, wherever labor re-

mained politically fractured, the state continued to provide support for large-scale strikebreaking.

Strikebreaking in the UK: The Fading Threat of Irish Migrants

As early as 1736, anti-Irish race riots had erupted in England when imported Irish agricultural laborers attempted to let "themselves out to all sort of labour [in London] considerably cheaper than the English labourers."[11] However, only in the late eighteenth century was there sustained migration of Irish laborers, directed in particular to the industrializing districts of Lancashire and London. By the first decades of the nineteenth century, Irish workers had a clear place at the bottom of the production hierarchy in Britain, taking work that was "dirty, disreputable, or otherwise undesirable" such that "wherever an extensive drain, or canal, or road was to be cut, it was quite usual for nine-tenths of the labourers employed to be Irish."[12] During the years of peak Irish migration to Britain from 1815 to 1870, more affluent Irish migrants could afford to cross the Atlantic to North America.[13] Irish migrants in Britain were thus considerably poorer than those who could make it to the US. Accordingly, Irish strikebreakers became an important tool for British employers to combat efforts to organize workers. Commentary on Irish migration in the mid-nineteenth century UK anticipated the way African American migrants would be discussed by white Northerners in the late nineteenth century. In 1834, William Cobbett, the English radical, defender of trade unions, and advocate for the poor, provided a racialized vision of the different kingdoms of the UK: while the English "had meat and bread and knives and forks," the Irish "had only potatoes and paws."[14] During the famine, English communities petitioned the crown, complaining of a "terrible racial invasion."[15]

British employers were quite explicit about the strategic advantages provided by Irish low-wage competition and strikebreakers. A witness from Manchester testified before commissioners in 1836 that Irish immigration gave manufacturers "an unlimited command of labour," but also expressed reservations about "the effect of the colonization of a barbarous race on the habits of the [local] people."[16] A clergymen from Liverpool complained that "English labourers have unfortunately been taught their rights until they have almost forgotten their duties," but English proletarian haughtiness could be tamed with the "competition of Irish labour," as employers were "very frequently able to put on the screw of Irish competition."[17] A Manchester cotton mill owner made the same point even more directly: "I consider the Irish as a great value as a check on the combination of the English. The moment I have a turn-out and am fast for hands, I send to Ireland for ten, fifteen, or twenty families as the case may be."[18] The most sustained period of violent racialized labor conflict between English and Irish workers occurred from the 1830s to 1860s, coinciding with the peak in Irish migration, with a substantial spike in violence during the railway building "mania" of the 1840s.[19] Initially, during the 1830s, Irish workers were kept out of lucrative railroad work due to "violent opposition from the English labourers."[20] Much like African American migrants a generation later, despite being "channeled into the bottom ranks" of the labor market, Irish migration flowed due to the pull of high wages. As an Irish tenant from Wexford who migrated to become a building laborer in Liverpool reported, "there was a general impression among his countrymen that if they come to England their fortunes would be made, wages are so much higher here."[21] In the 1850s, a major cotton textile strike in Preston was broken through importing Irish strikebreakers.[22] Irish workers' descriptions of their experiences in mid-nineteenth century England foreshadow the experiences of hate strikes directed at African Americans who migrated North later in the nineteenth century: "It is impossible to describe their [the English's] animosity toward us: after abusing us, they often assemble together in large numbers, with all kinds of weapons, to drive us from the work."[23] Irish strikebreakers were "usually shipped in from Ireland for that purpose," and were not typically members of local communities.[24] When employers launched a flurry of legal cases to prevent union pickets from interfering with the importation of strikebreakers, several of the key instances involved the importation of strikebreakers from Ireland.[25]

Writing in 1870, just before the start of the profound transformations of the Irish countryside discussed in chapter 1, Karl Marx offered an assessment of the English working class that centered on the divisions created by low-wage migration from Ireland. Britain's near-periphery had supplied "its own surplus to the English labor market" and thus "force[d] down wages and lower[ed] the moral and material condition of the English working-class." Anticipating the racially bounded working-class formation of the United States, Marx saw in every "industrial and commercial center in England . . . a working class *divided* into two *hostile* camps, English proletarians and Irish proletarians."[26] Marx, however, never extended or generalized this account of geographically structured, racialized class formation.[27] After the 1870s, strikebreaking by Irish workers was increasingly rare. Decreasing rapidly at the same time, by the 1890s Irish migration to Britain had dwindled to a trickle. More favorable access to land in the Irish countryside and converging urban wages meant that migration in general, and the lucrative but risky prospect of strikebreaking wages, would have been less appealing to potential Irish migrants by the 1890s.

Lacking the draw of wage differentials and substantial flows of migration, British employers turned to systematic organization to support aggressive strikebreaking in the 1890s. The Shipping Federation was formed to combat the rising power of the New Unions in 1890, and its organizational efforts in the 1890s far surpassed anything achieved by strikebreaking employers in the US. The Federation maintained three specially fitted ships for housing strikebreakers and controlled a warehouse of bedding, cooking equipment, and other necessities to provide immediate accommodation for up to five thousand strikebreakers during the early 1890s.[28] The most important victory in the employers' counterattack against the New Unions came in Hull, which by 1893 was the best organized port in the UK. The Shipping Federation imported thousands of strikebreakers from across Europe, extra police were deployed to protect them, and the local Poor Law Guardians brazenly acted as recruiters for strikebreakers from among the local unemployed.[29] Gunboats were positioned on the Humber, and riotous street violence and threats of arson escalated tensions.[30] The union was crushed at its strongest port, and Hull became a notoriously anti-union port for years to come. *The Times* of London gloated after the strike that "at Hull as elsewhere, the New Unionism has been defeated."[31] This proved to be somewhat premature, but it reminds us of the widespread ambition, and belief, that British employers could and would destroy the New Unionism. While the impressive organization and aggression of British employers could achieve dramatic victories, these were costly battles, and ultimately the scarce supply of strikebreakers made even disciplined, organized strikebreaking difficult. With Ireland no longer a cheap and reliable supplier of low-wage labor, when the labor market proved to be especially tight, even specialized strikebreaking organizations could fail to provide the necessary strikebreakers.[32]

British employers, despite their benign reputation, were in certain respects more hostile to unionization efforts. British capitalists were certainly far more organized than in the US, and this is particularly apparent in strikebreaking. The Shipping Federation was not the only major centralized strikebreaking organization in the UK. In Liverpool, commercial and shipping interests organized the Employers' Labour Association in 1890 to defend their "absolute and inalienable right" to employ non-union workers.[33] The Liverpool Association had its own offices, labor recruiter, and secretary; accumulated a large fund to support strikebreaking; and established recruiting networks. During its first confrontation with Liverpool dockers in 1890, it imported some ten thousand workers at the enormous expense of £32,000. Backed with these resources, the employers became "more intransigent" during the 1890 dock strike, refused mediation by the Chamber of Commerce, refused all negotiations with the union, and when the workers had been defeated, required all those rehired to sign a contract agreeing to work "harmoniously with non-unionists and importees."[34] The National Association of Master Builders imported strikebreakers from across Europe in the 1890s, and during the 1899 plasterers strike it spent lavishly to arrange for the importation of strikebreakers from Ireland, the US, and continental Europe.[35] British employers developed a specialized array of strikebreaking organizations in the 1890s, including the Free Labour Protection Association, the Association of Non-Unionists, and most prominently, William Collison's National Free Labour Association (NFLA).[36]

After the momentous victory at Hull in 1893, the shipping employers decided to take a less direct approach to strikebreaking, and hand off responsibility to an independent contractor: NFLA. Under Collison's organization, strikebreakers were celebrated as preserving the individual liberty of the worker, whereas direct strikebreaking by an employers' federation had more obvious, self-interested intentions. Collison, a former worker who had become disillusioned after being a member of a union, claimed to respect the narrow "old unions," but railed against the New Unions that relied on mass, coercive picketing under the "tyranny and dictation of Socialistic Trade Union Leaders."[37] At first financially backed by the Shipping Federation and gasworks employers, after 1900 Collison's NFLA increasingly relied on support from British rail companies.[38] The early twentieth century saw a sustained employers' offensive against the railway unions. The NFLA created "a mobile reserve force of railwaymen for breaking strikes wherever they might occur."[39] Although strikebreaking formed the bone and sinew of the NFLA, it also engaged in general "propaganda on behalf of 'free labour' and against new unionism." It lobbied Parliament on labor legislation, campaigned against socialist political candidates, and hosted an annual Free Labor Congress open to the press and attended by prominent Conservatives, where many of the delegates appear to have been fraudulent local hires purportedly representing other places.[40] The NFLA was not just an exceptionally well-organized strikebreaking agency; it was an early and remarkably effective "astroturf" anti-labor organization, claiming to represent grassroots workers who wished to be employed freely without union interference while actually operating on behalf of large employers. Employers in the United States never attempted anything as coordinated or sophisticated as the strikebreaking and anti-union efforts of the Shipping Federation and the NFLA.

Although strikebreaking was most prominent among the large masses of transportation workers on the waterfront and on railways, strikebreakers were also used in the British iron and steel industry. Several relatively small firms effectively crushed unions using strikebreakers. Why did other, larger British steel-producing firms not emulate their example, and the example of the US steel industry?[41] Previous scholars have pointed to hostile attitudes among US employers and an anti-union political establishment. However, given a scarce supply of rapidly accessible strikebreakers, British employers, despite a clear desire to break unions, found it difficult and expensive to do so. US labor historians have often assumed that British employers took a relatively benign view of labor unions.[42] However, a closer look at the evidence suggests an intense, well-organized desire to break unions. The corporate records of several leading Sheffield steel firms show a repeated willingness to turn to strikebreakers. During a fettlers' strike at Edgar Allen, likely around the turn of the century, workers were obtained through Collison's NFLA. The strikebreakers "slept in the top of the building which now comprises the Steel department, the export department, and the Laboratory. These buildings had only just been completed, and were not furnished. Beds were obtained for use by these men, but they stayed a few weeks."[43] During a moulders' strike at John Brown Steel in 1906, the company successfully advertised "for non-Society moulders" and the directors "anticipated [that] we shall obtain all the men we require."[44] The lower rate of strikebreaking in the UK was not because employers were less motivated; the key difference was that strikebreakers were more expensive and difficult to recruit.

If we can discard the notion that British employers were less hostile to organized labor in the 1890s, we must also carefully qualify any assertion that the British state was more favorable to workers than the US authorities. As we have seen, during the 1890s police, army, and naval forces were repeatedly deployed to back up employers and protect strikebreakers in the UK and the US alike. The divergence in state posture came after 1910. After the major burst of organizing in 1911–12, "authorities became increasingly reluctant to provide military and police protection for substitute labour during strikes."[45] This change in state posture toward organized labor was a result of diverging trajectories of labor organizing, not a cause. British workers had become broadly and powerfully organized, and had thus secured important concessions from the state. The Liverpool Employers Association also reversed course, retreating from the "belligerency and uncompromising" stance against unions of the 1890s, and in the period after 1911, recognized the New Unions and established "joint machinery . . . for the more orderly conduct of industrial relations."[46] Strikebreaking essentially disappeared after 1910. Clearly, diverging levels of state repression mattered in the long run, but this divergence occurred well after the crucial period for the survival of inclusive unionism in the 1890s.

Strikebreaking in the US: The Rising Threat of Southern Migrants

US strikebreaking thrived in the 1890s, although success against unions in the US required far less organization and commitment than in the UK. And unlike the UK, where strikebreaking decreased in the first decade of the twentieth century, and then essentially disappeared after 1910, in the United States mass strikebreaking remained a potent force into the 1920s. Despite the Shipping Federation and the NFLA, UK employers mobilized only 80,000 strikebreakers during the 1890s; in the US, despite a lack of similarly centralized and sophisticated strikebreaking organizations, over 265,000 strikebreakers were put to work to defeat organized workers. Was this due to differences in employer motivation? Voss suggests that in the United Kingdom the New Unions survived because they experienced a "less ruthless employers' assault."[47] Similarly, Sanford Jacoby has argued that British employers "rarely . . . seize[d] the antiunion initiative in any concerted or sustained fashion."[48] Recently, Rosemary Feurer and Chad Pearson have concurred in this comparative assessment, arguing that the attack on the Knights of Labor "set the stage for the exceptional nature of employer anti-labor networking in the twentieth century" US.[49] This chapter suggests that British employers' attack was in many ways more ruthless during the 1890s, if we consider the organization and resources devoted to strikebreaking. But despite enormous effort, they were ultimately less successful than employers in the US. Moreover, while British employers' anti-unionism has been downplayed in comparative accounts, in the US, it is important not to view all employers as universally committed to waging war on organized labor. As Thomas Klug suggests, at the turn of the century US employers were often "cautious, hesitant, and uncertain" about strikebreaking, and were "certainly not all open-shop crusaders aching to gamble everything in a war with organized labor."[50] It was not the intention of employers that mattered. In both the US and the UK, employers were hostile to inclusive forms of unionization and attempted to break strikes. Rather, the difference was the underlying structure of a regionally and racially divided labor market in the US that made strikebreaking cheap, easy, and efficient for employers.[51] This gave capitalists in the US a powerful weapon to defeat workers' efforts to organize inclusively.[52]

While broadly more extensive than in the UK, strikebreaking in the

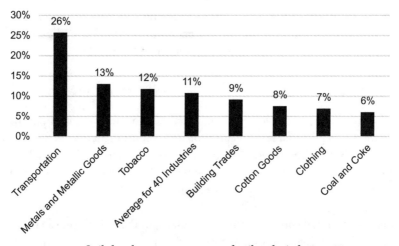

FIGURE 3.2 Strikebreakers as a percentage of strikers by industry, 1881–1900. *Source:* Industries with 100,000 or more strikers. Department of Labor, *Strikes in the United States, 1880–1936*, Bulletin No. 651, August 1937 (Washington, DC: United States Government Printing Office, 1938), 354–55, table VI.

US was also unevenly distributed across sectors. Figure 3.2 shows sectors in which at least one hundred thousand workers went on strike between 1881 and 1900, and the share of those striking workers replaced by strikebreakers. Across the forty sectors considered by the Labor Department, the average rate of replacement of strikers by strikebreakers was 11 percent. The transportation sector, including replaceable workers at the bottom of the production hierarchy such as dockworkers and the lower grades of railroad laborers, saw by far the most strikebreaking, with over a quarter of strikers replaced by strikebreakers. The steel industry fell within the next sector, metals and metallic goods, where 13 percent of strikers were replaced by strikebreakers. At the other end of the strikebreaking spectrum, sectors like clothing (largely women seamstresses) and coal and coke (largely immigrants in remote mining villages) experienced the lowest rates of strikebreaking. The relative lack of strikebreaking in these sectors played a key role in allowing for two of the more inclusive labor unions to emerge in these sectors. Coal and coke (6 percent of strikers replaced) and clothing (7 percent of strikers replaced) were the two exceptional large US sectors where industrial unions were organized before the 1930s. The United Mine Workers started organizing industrially in the 1890s and the Amalgamated Garment Workers in the 1910s, the two most important exceptions to the narrow craft unionism of the AFL, and both later founders of the Congress of Industrial Organizations (CIO) in the 1930s. Conversely, the two industries with the highest levels of replacement of strikers by strikebreakers were two crucial sectors where inclusive organization spectacularly failed in the US: transportation (26 percent of strikers replaced) and metals and metallic goods (13 percent).[53]

It is impossible to know precisely what share of strikebreakers in the United States were African Americans recruited from the South. Newly arrived immigrants from Europe, the local unemployed, and small groups of professional strikebreakers also played an important role. However, while there is a degree of uncertainty as to the precise quantitative scale of strikebreaking by black workers, it seems certain that a regionally and racially divided labor market was crucial in facilitating employer strike-breaking from at least the 1880s to the 1930s. What seems indisputable is that strikebreaking, regardless of which groups of workers were recruited, played a decisive role in shaping the trajectory of US labor organizing.

Several factors facilitated the expansion of strikebreaking by African Americans in the late nineteenth century: the new technologies of the telegraph and eventually telephones, the integration of the South into the national railway system through the adoption of the standard gauge in 1886, and the emergence of professional strikebreaking businesses in the 1890s.[54] Decades ago John Keiser came to a conclusion on racialized strikebreaking that still holds for scholars today: "There were more clashes, and clashes of more significance to contemporaries, than historians generally realize."[55] Despite the lack of precise quantitative data, this chapter argues that black strikebreakers became highly visible and controversial among white workers in the 1860s and 1870s, a substantial presence in the 1880s, and by the 1890s, an established and consequential force in industrial disputes. Racialized strikebreaking emerged in the late nineteenth century not just as a "specter" motivating racial fears among white workers, but as a consequential, strategic force in the balance of power between capital and labor.

The only attempt to systematically track strikebreaking by black workers comes from the economist Warren Whatley, whose compilation of major strikes in which employers recruited African American strikebreakers is presented in figure 3.3. This shows that the 1890s marked a peak for strikebreaking by black workers in terms of the number of individual strikes. If we consider workers rather than strikes, certainly the number of African American strikebreakers was far higher in the larger postwar strikes. Whatley's review of the secondary sources captures the major strikes, but a closer look at primary sources from Pittsburgh and Baltimore suggests that especially prior to World War I, there were many smaller, local strikes in which employers recruited black strikebreakers from the South that did not appear in the major surveys used by Whatley. While the trend in

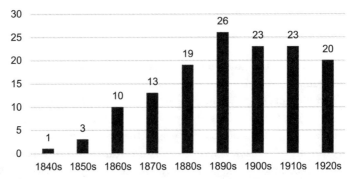

FIGURE 3.3 Major strikes involving African American strikebreakers.
Source: Whatley, "African-American Strikebreaking from the Civil War to the
New Deal," 529–36, table 1.

figure 3.3 is broadly representative, if we consider local, smaller strikes as
well, the numbers for the three decades from 1880 to 1910 likely need to
multiplied by a substantial factor. The local evidence from Pittsburgh and
Baltimore below suggests that Whatley captured only 10 to 20 percent of
the strikes in which black workers were recruited to break strikes.

Factors Driving Racialized Strikebreaking

The pro-business attitudes of a conservative black middle class have sometimes been invoked to explain the prevalence of strikebreaking by African
American workers, but a stronger explanation is rooted in the regionally
and racially divided labor markets entrenched in the United States in the
aftermath of slavery. It is important to consider the differences between
two groups of migrants who US employers could potentially recruit as
strikebreakers: transatlantic migrants from Europe and internal migrants
from the Southern near-periphery. While European immigrants may have
outnumbered African American strikebreakers, there are several reasons
to stress the importance of strikebreakers who could be quickly recruited
from an adjacent near-periphery, who lacked alternative routes into industrial work, and who enjoyed little political protection in Northern cities.

During a strike, timing is all-important. When workers shut down
operations, they have substantial leverage for as long as the employer is
without replacement workers. From the employer's perspective, finding
replacement workers as rapidly as possible during a strike was thus essential. The local unemployed were the quickest and easiest to recruit, but
when unemployment was low (which is when most strikes occurred), or
the strike involved large numbers of workers (increasingly true during the

1880s), these local sources of strikebreakers were quickly exhausted. Near-peripheries were particularly important for industrial conflicts because they could provide strikebreakers rapidly. African Americans recruited from the South were not necessarily the majority among US strikebreakers, but the telegraph, rail transport, and an extensive network of labor recruitment agencies meant that black workers were often the first to arrive. In the 1905 Teamsters strike in Chicago, black strikebreakers only played an important role during the "first three weeks of the strike." As the struggle dragged on, black workers "constituted an ever-decreasing number of strikebreakers."[56] The importance of near-peripheries such as the US South and Ireland was that recruited workers could arrive within days, whereas transatlantic recruitment and transportation would require several weeks and likely at least a month. After the Foran Act in 1885, a law passed in response to transatlantic strikebreaking, it became illegal to arrange transport for workers from Europe under a labor contract. Regardless of the legal barriers, speed and distance made near-peripheries crucial when supplying replacement workers for industrial disputes. In many sectors, a delay of several weeks in resuming operations was unacceptable to capitalists.

A second important difference between European and African American migrants as potential strikebreakers was their position in Northern labor markets. Newly arrived immigrants from Europe enjoyed a far more favorable range of labor market options than black workers at the turn of the century.[57] As will be explored further below, black workers faced extensive discrimination by both employers and workers in Northern labor markets, with many occupations and worksites closed to them by racist hostility. "Times of industrial unrest," a 1905 study of black migrants in Northern cities observed, "have offered him opportunities for work which were before closed."[58] A lack of English-language skills and anti-immigrant hostility certainly impinged upon the options available to recently arrived European immigrants, and the power of nativist boundary-making should not be discounted, but there was far less organized resistance to their employment in particular occupations and jobsites.[59] Most importantly, recently arrived European immigrants already had access to the Northern labor market, eliminating the periphery-core wage differential that provided a crucial structural pull when recruiting strikebreakers.

Last, European and even Asian migrants from abroad had a degree of political protection offered by their country of origin. In contrast, African Americans could rarely secure similar political backing. The importance of this factor became clear during a 1909 strike in the steel town of McKees Rocks, outside of Pittsburgh. The Pressed Steel Car Company had turned to a professional strikebreaker, Pearl Bergoff, who had delivered some six hundred strikebreakers to the plant by the middle of August. However, many of these immigrant strikebreakers had been misled by Bergoff's labor recruiters and then held at the plant. In late August, one strikebreaker escaped from the plant and found his way to Pittsburgh, where he shared his story with representatives from his native land. He "described how he had been mistreated in the plant and retained against his will." This testimony led the Austo-Hungarian vice-consul to submit "peonage affidavits" with the US Commissioner of Immigration for the release of all Austro-Hungarian subjects being held in the plant.[60] Even the beleaguered Chinese state was able to extract $424,367 in reparations from the US government for the violence inflicted on Chinese communities by white mobs in the late nineteenth century.[61] African Americans, though they too were often misled by labor recruiters, held in semi-incarceration while serving as strikebreakers, and brutalized by white mobs, rarely had a supportive government official to whom they could turn for redress.

While a small contribution to the total flow of migrants when compared to European immigration, African Americans could be recruited cheaply and quickly for strikebreaking in Northern industry. Racist discrimination by Northern workers and unions and strikebreaking by African Americans fed upon each other in the closing decades of the nineteenth century. As Susan Bereitzer has argued, white-supremacist exclusion by unions and strikebreaking by black workers became a "vicious circle" of escalating racial hostility.[62] The importance of the South as a near-periphery is especially clear when placed in the comparative framework. While the threat of Irish low-wage competition through migration and strikebreaking receded from the 1870s, allowing the New Unionism to survive the 1890s in the UK, in the US, just as the Knights attempted to launch an inclusive labor mobilization, employers and labor recruiters brought Southern African Americans to Northern cities in increasing numbers as low-wage competitors and strikebreakers.

The Development of Racialized Strikebreaking in the US

Although the 1890s were the pivotal decade shaping the long-term trajectory of the US labor movement, strikebreaking by African Americans had a deeper history reaching back to the antebellum era. The first major strike broken with the widespread recruitment of black workers occurred among New York dockworkers in 1855, foreshadowing the much wider strikebreaking by black workers in 1863 in cities including Buffalo (where three black workers were killed, and a dozen severely beaten), Chicago, Detroit, Cleveland, Albany, New York, Brooklyn, and Boston.[63] In New York, struggles between Irish dockworkers and African American strikebreakers contributed to the tensions unleashed in the horrors of racial terrorism during the 1863 draft riots. Dozens of black workers were killed, with several of the victims lynched and mutilated during the riots.[64] By the 1870s, the recruitment of African American strikebreakers shifted from the Eastern waterfront to the industrial Midwest. African Americans first entered Northern coal mining districts as strikebreakers in 1873–74.[65] In 1875 Pittsburgh steelmakers recruited a group of skilled black puddlers from Richmond, Virginia to break a strike. Spero and Harris found that "almost every labor disturbance between 1878 and the middle eighties saw Negroes used as strike breakers" in the Pittsburgh District, including strikes at the Black Diamond Mill, the Moorhead Mill, the Clark Mills, and most dramatically at the Elba Mills, where the conflict between white unionists and black strikebreakers "precipitated a serious riot."[66] Black workers were among the strikebreakers employed during the railroad uprisings of 1877.[67]

Following these fairly sparse but widely publicized incidents, strikebreaking by black workers became far more widespread in the 1880s. In this decade employers in Pittsburgh "began a more concerted effort to hire black ironworkers during disputes with the overwhelmingly white organizations of iron and steel workers."[68] Some of this was already discussed above in considering the initial rise and retreat of the Knights of Labor. Already at the beginning of the decade, in 1882, the *Pittsburgh Daily Post* reported on the "Labor Troubles" in the region, noting that while the "iron men seem to be on a fair way to arrange their differences, the coal miners and operators are getting wider apart."[69] This was because the miners, when assembled at their convention days before, "demanded as a 'condition precedent' the negroes brought into the mines should be discharged." According to the *Post*, there seemed "to be a concerted effort in the western part of this State to introduce negro labor from the South, in sufficient quantity to displace white miners." On the waterfront, the National Steamship and Old Dominion lines used black strikebreakers to defeat a Knights of Labor strike in New York in 1887.[70] In the same year, black workers replaced strikers from the Amalgamated Association at the Solar Iron Works in Pittsburgh, and two years later, these black puddlers remained at work and broke another strike by the Amalgamated.[71] Crowds of white workers repeatedly threatened and attacked black strikebreakers on the streets of Pittsburgh in the late 1880s.[72] Most strikebreaking by black workers appears to have been concentrated in the industrial Midwest, but as early as 1888 employers recruited black strikebreakers to the distant Pacific Northwest to defeat a mining strike.[73]

The 1890s, as seen in figure 3.3, marked a peak in the number of major strikes involving the recruitment of African American strikebreakers. Widespread racialized strikebreaking in this decade played a leading role in the destruction of the Knights and in driving the AFL into narrow craft boundaries. While there was no centralized strikebreaking operation in the 1890s as formidable as the UK's Shipping Federation or Collison's NFLA, the decade did see the rise of the first major professional "King of the Strikebreakers," Jack Whitehead. Much like Collison, Whitehead had been a union steelworker in Pittsburgh, working as a skilled puddler and roller. A conflict with the union local of the Amalgamated Association led him to leave Pittsburgh and move to Birmingham, Alabama, where he worked in the growing Southern steel industry.[74] However, when the Amalgamated Association struck the Clinton Mills in 1891, Whitehead returned to Pittsburgh with a crew of "forty highly skilled black steelworkers."[75] For the rest of the 1890s, Whitehead made a career of using these "forty thieves," as they were called by defeated union workers, to break strikes throughout the industrial Midwest.[76] Whitehead's strikebreaking crew was, however, rather unusual, both in its professional organization and its provision of skilled craftsmen. Nearly all strikebreaking in the US in the 1890s involved more ad hoc recruitment of strikebreakers to common labor positions at the bottom of the production hierarchy. In the UK, a disappearing reserve army of labor in the countryside meant that organized, centralized strikebreaking agencies were needed to recruit even common, low-wage labor. In contrast, in the US, professional strikebreaking services were largely unnecessary for workers at the bottom of the production hierarchy, and strikebreaking agencies tended to specialize in providing strikers with critical and scarce skills.

The most important strikes of the 1890s—Homestead in 1892 and Pullman in 1894—featured strikebreaking by black workers recruited from the South. In July of 1892, as the Homestead steel strikers of the Pittsburgh District faced an ultimatum to return to work or lose their positions permanently, the report circulated "that a large party of colored laborers who hail from Alabama [were] in the city to take the some of the positions vacated by the locked out workmen at Homestead."[77] By the end of the month, black strikebreakers and white unionists "were engaged in a race war inside the Homestead Steel Works."[78] In August 1892, managers at the Millvale Iron and Steel Company denied rumors circulating among white workers that they "were about to be discharged and their places filled by colored laborers."[79] In September, as the Homestead steel strike was being slowly crushed by effective strikebreaking, the *Pittsburgh Daily Post* reported on the arrival of "60 Italians" who "were shipped to one of the mills" as well as "50 negroes from the South" who "were put to work at the puddling furnaces."[80] In October, the *Pittsburgh Dispatch* noted the arrival of "a carload of 59 colored laborers" who "were brought to the Elba Iron Works" from Chattanooga, Tennessee. Despite being surrounded by "a large crowd of locked-out union men" on arriving, "they were allowed to enter the mill unmolested."[81] The escalating racial hostilities culminated in a massive riot on November 13, 1892. A crowd of two thousand white workers, many of them recent immigrants, attacked the black workers and residences, shouting "Let's lynch the nigger black sheep. Let's hang 'em."[82] Racialized strikebreaking at Homestead provoked comment from the press more broadly. In late 1892 the Democrat-aligned *Baltimore Sun* used the events of the Homestead steel strike to question whether Republicans— who dominated Pittsburgh politics—were truly "better friends of the colored race than democrats."[83] "The general rush at Homestead to kill the colored workers, merely because they were trying to earn a living in a republican State by their labor," the *Sun* noted, would "open many eyes" to the realities of white racism in the North.[84] On the other hand, the African American press heralded the black strikebreakers at Homestead as heroes. A paper in Illinois noted that black workers had "been trying hard to get into the mills since 1887," and the Homestead strike finally opened the door to substantial numbers of black steelworkers.[85] Paul Krause, in his study of the Homestead strike, argues that racialized strikebreaking during the strike "modified the overall quality of ethnic relations" not only in the steel district, but across the region, as white workers increasingly gave voice to "virulent expressions" of racist hostility.[86]

After Homestead in 1892, the second most prominent strike of the 1890s was the Pullman strike of 1894 on the railroads. The Pullman strike was organized by Eugene Debs's American Railway Union (ARU), an industrial union outside the AFL that attempted to break through the narrow craft unions, or "brotherhoods," on the railroads. However, the ARU retained, over Debs's objections, the whites-only membership policies that had been central to previous railroad unions. During the 1894 Pullman strike, the ARU's racially discriminatory membership policy was "generally well known," and many black workers acted as strikebreakers. Some black workers even organized the Anti-Strikers Railway Union. Black strikebreakers often had a clear understanding of the racist policies of organized labor, and this knowledge contributed to their willingness to serve as strikebreakers.[87] Willing Hands, a black miner, explained to his white coworkers why African Americans were so willing to break strikes: "Out of revenge, we the bulk of Afro-Americans go to work for spite."[88] Debs, who would go on to lead the Socialist Party in the early twentieth century, later speculated that if the ARU had admitted black workers, perhaps the union would not have been so vulnerable to the recruitment of black strikebreakers from the South.[89] However, as we will see below, even inclusive union policies did not necessarily prevail against the structural forces of a racially and regionally divided labor market. Even unions with strong egalitarian commitments to the inclusion of all workers regardless of race collapsed under the pressure of racialized strikebreaking.

A review of Pittsburgh newspapers during the 1890s shows extensive coverage of strikebreaking by black workers. The early years of the decade were dominated by the dramatic conflicts of the Homestead strike, already discussed above. In 1894, during a strike in the coke works in the Pittsburgh District, a worker wrote to the *Pittsburgh Daily Post* to clarify that workers were not returning to work. Plants had been restarted "all . . . by imported labor." But according to the worker, the "importation of negro labor into the region" had "only strengthened the strikers" in their resolve to defeat Frick.[90] The next year, "fifty negroes from Knoxville, Tennessee" were brought in to break a strike at the Clinton Mills on the Southside of Pittsburgh, but some of the strikebreakers refused to work since they had been "induced to come from Knoxville by representations that there was not a strike on hand."[91] During a threatened strike in the mining village of Mercer in 1896, north of Pittsburgh, it was "reported that the operators will import negro labor."[92] The next year, in 1897, an editorial from the *Pittsburgh Daily Post* noted a "sensational" report that "a lot of small-pox infected negroes" were being hired "to take the places of the striking white coal miners of the north," and urged that "We don't want them here. . . . The southern negroes brought north to take the places of white men are generally the worst of their race. . . . If the strike cannot be broken without the aid of southern negroes of this class it had better stay unbroken."[93] In July of 1899, a "crowd of 70 negroes, just arrived from the South . . . caused considerable comment" in Pittsburgh. These workers were the "first consignment of 200 men" sent from the "South to work in the mills of the Park Steel Company."[94] Whatley's review of the secondary sources captured only the 1892 Homestead strike as an instance of black strikebreaking in the Pittsburgh District, but local records confirm at least three more instances, and two additional threats to recruit black strikebreakers. The number of minor, local strikes involving the recruitment of black strikebreakers was notably high.

Thanks to oral histories conducted in the 1930s, the perspective of one black steelworker who labored in the Pittsburgh District from the 1880s to the 1920s is available to us.[95] F. J. Amormes recalled that when he entered the Braddock Wire Works in 1887 (later the American Wireworks under US Steel), he was one of only seven African American workers among thousands of whites. More black workers entered during a strike in 1889, bringing the black workforce to several dozen. Amormes noted that "there were no colored who went out on strike in 1892. We stayed in the mill. . . . They maintained what men they had there and kept them in the mill until the strike was settled." By the 1890s, Amormes observed that the steel corporation's recruitment of black strikebreakers was more organized and extensive: "They went over the country and brought colored men here. At the time of the strike they brought a large number of Negroes here from the south. My brother-in-law, Villard, and a white fellow went throughout the South sending Negroes here on transportation. He (brother-in-law) ran a boarding house where the companies boarded some of the Negroes brought here on transportation. They brought about 1200 during the strike in 1899."[96]

Strikebreaking provided no guarantee that recruited replacement workers could retain their employment after the strike was over. It seems that very few black strikebreakers at the turn of the century were able to keep these more desirable jobs after the strike was over. Many, likely the vast majority, returned South, which explains the coexistence of extensive recruitment of African Americans as strikebreakers and the relatively gradual growth in permanent black communities recorded by the census and other surveys in Northern cities around 1900. Amormes recalled that during the 1899 strike, the company "put the colored men on the good jobs" but their loyalty was quickly betrayed since "as soon as the white fellows came back they gave them back their jobs."[97] While some, especially black workers already residing locally, would have hoped to use strikebreaking to gain access to permanent positions previously closed to them, for the black workers recruited from the South the windfall in wages from strikebreaking was more likely to be saved, often in the hope of securing land back in their Southern homes.

In sharp contrast to the disappearance of strikebreaking in the UK, in the United States strikebreaking continued to have a major impact on labor conflict in the first decades of the twentieth century. In Baltimore and Pittsburgh, strikebreaking employers continued to rely on black workers recruited from the South decades after similar practices had largely ceased in the UK. In 1900, the mostly German dockworkers in Baltimore struck, but the strike was defeated by black strikebreakers recruited from Norfolk, Virginia. This marked the re-entry of black workers to the waterfront in

Baltimore after many decades of exclusion.[98] The Baltimore stevedores handling coffee bags went on strike in 1903, but were defeated when "colored men were employed to take the strikers' places."[99] In 1905, truckers employed by the Baltimore & Ohio Railroad at their Locust Point pier went on strike, but "some 75 or 80 negroes" were "brought from Philadelphia to take their places."[100] As noted in the introduction, during strikes by the National Transport Workers Federation in New York and Baltimore in 1912, employers recruited black workers to break the strike.[101] Turning to Pittsburgh, in the steel industry, the Amalgamated pointed to effective strikebreaking and the importation of labor to explain their defeat in 1901 against US Steel.[102] Black union workers in Pittsburgh recalled that for hoisting engineers "Colored men had an organization independent of the Union and competed with the Union on jobs. Whenever Unions would strike this Colored organization would proceed to go on the job and do the work as efficiently as Union men."[103] In 1908 the Pittsburgh Hoisting Engineers made the strategic decision to invite these independently organized black workers to join, and twenty-eight men entered the union. Inclusion left the black Hoisting Engineers powerless, however, and many regretted integration with the white local. After 1908, the local made every effort to prevent additional black members from joining and marginalized the existing black members.[104] In 1909, black strikebreakers were used by the Press Steel Company of McKees Rocks in the Pittsburgh District.[105] In 1912, employers in McKeesport threatened workers at the Fort Pitt Steel Foundry with replacement by "New York Negroes."[106] While transportation from eastern cities was unusual compared to recruitment in the South, in many cases a small but meaningful wage differential also pulled migrants from the relatively labor-abundant ports of immigrant arrival to the comparatively labor-scarce industrial Midwest. In rare instances, white workers also served as strikebreakers against unions of black workers. In 1903, when the predominantly black Building Laborers Union No. 10934 went on strike in Baltimore, "their places were taken by some white men" at one of the larger worksites.[107]

US employers devoted comparatively little organized effort to strikebreaking, but there were a few attempts to systemize the recruitment of strikebreakers. In the early 1900s, two new "Kings" of professional strikebreaking emerged in the US: James Farley and, even more prominently, Pearl Bergoff. Bergoff Brothers Strike Service and Labor Adjustors was launched in 1907. With an office and sales staff and a more professional organization, a decade and a half after the UK the US finally had a strikebreaking agency of some prominence. But even Bergoff's firm failed to match the scope and resources of the UK's Shipping Federation and Collison's NFLA in the 1890s.[108] Chad Pearson has highlighted the work of the National League of Independent Workmen, a supposedly "class neutral project designed to recast" strikebreaking as defending non-unionists' "right to work."[109] But this close analog to the NFLA never achieved the prominence or power of its British predecessor.

The available evidence does not allow firm conclusions about the relative quantitative share of African Americans, European immigrants, and the local unemployed among workers recruited for strikebreaking. Unions and the press certainly exaggerated the numbers of African Americans involved in strikebreaking in many cases. Nevertheless, the broader structure and incentives of the US labor market and the local evidence suggest that, whatever the precise quantitative rate of black strikebreaking may have been, the opportunities of a regionally and racially divided labor market provided a clear and decisive strategic advantage to US employers in their efforts to defeat the growth of inclusive unions during the 1890s. This structural advantage rested both on actual strikebreaking, which gave employers an overwhelming chance of defeating workers, as well as on the threat of racialized strikebreaking, which would have intimidated workers into concessions, limited demands, and suggested the prudence of a narrower approach to organizing.

Northern Reactions to Late Nineteenth-Century Strikebreaking

The scale and visibility of strikebreaking by black workers in the late nineteenth century produced increasingly vehement and more explicitly racist responses. In 1891 a white mineworker wrote to his union journal, explaining growing racial animosity in the North: "Just as long as the colored man allows himself to be shipped around the country in gangs for the purpose of driving white men away from their homes and lowering their wages, just so long will the prejudice and hard feeling exist."[110] A decade later, an editorial in the *Pittsburgh Daily Post* reviewed the arrival of black workers in local industries. The editorial argued that "free trade in negro labor from the Southern States" was "a great deal worse . . . than free and unrestricted alien labor coming to this country by the natural working of immigration. The complaint is made that some parts of Allegheny county are actually terrorized on account of the importation of negroes of desperate character to work in the manufacturing plants in need of labor."[111] However, the editors warned against turning to the tactics of lynching and mob violence that were used to control black workers in the South. Revealingly, already in 1901, the *Pittsburgh Post* instead urged an intensification of racialized policing. The solution to white fears of a growing black population was "the enlargement of the police force. Lynch law will only make matters worse."[112] Here we see the roots of the pervasive racialized policing and punitive incarceration that would prove so destructive to Northern black communities in the twentieth century.

Employers also began to articulate more explicitly racist rationales for their recruitment of black workers in the 1890s. In 1895, one explained why many mine owners employed African American workers. According to the President of the Pinnickinnick Coal Company, "We use negro labor" because in his view it was "not only the most docile, but the best labor in the world." Expressing a racist paternalism that could have been uttered by a Southern planter before emancipation, this coal operator believed that "We need the negroes, and they need us. They look for the white man to take care of them, and we are doing it."[113] The growing presence of black workers and rising competition from migrants from the South sparked genocidal fantasies for some white workers. In 1901 an interview with a white worker on one of Pittsburgh's riverboats offered an unsettling look into white working-class thought at the turn of the century. According to the *Pittsburgh Post*, he proposed "a solution" to the "negro problem which would undoubtedly accomplish results could it be put in force, but as it involves extermination, its employment is somewhat doubtful."[114] Despite their reputation for hostility to labor, state authorities in the North were often receptive to the demands of white workers to prevent employers from recruiting black workers. In 1898, the *Pittsburgh Daily Post* commented approvingly on the violent commitment of the Illinois Governor to confront a train transporting African American strikebreakers "at the State line and shoot it to pieces with Gatling guns" if necessary.[115] While hostility to the Irish in Britain faded at the turn of the century as migration and strikebreaking by Irish workers declined, in the US, racial boundaries hardened.

While labor leaders never advocated racist extermination, by the early twentieth century the racial egalitarianism of midcentury abolitionism and Radical Reconstruction was a distant memory in the US labor movement. The hardening of racial boundaries within the Northern US labor movement during the 1890s had multiple sources, but a leading cause was racialized strikebreaking. In 1891 the United Mine Workers *Journal* published an appeal purportedly addressed to "Our Colored Fellow-Men" that used language more calculated to inflame the racism of rank-and-file miners than to encourage African Americans to reconsider strikebreaking. Despite being addressed to their "Colored Fellow-Men," the mineworkers' journal described black workers as simple tools of capital, "railroaded from the South to the North as labor mercenaries." Capitalists threatened "to hire thousands of them in case the white wage workers make trouble." With "a horde of these darkies, and another horde of Chinese, in the Northern states," capitalists would have all the power and white labor would be defenseless.[116] This insincere effort to dissuade black strikebreakers obviously proved ineffective. John Mitchell, president of the United Mine Workers, testified in 1901 that he knew of "no element that is doing more to create disturbance in mining circles than the system of importing colored labor to take white men's places."[117] Mitchell had direct, biographical experience of racialized strikebreaking. When he was seven, his first contact with African Americans came in 1877 when black strikebreakers were recruited into his hometown of Braidwood, Illinois. The black strikebreakers were "run out of town by force, and returned under the protection of the state militia," only to be frequently attacked by white mobs.[118] Mitchell once again encountered strikebreaking black workers as a young man in Spring Valley, Illinois. Thus, "like other Illinois miners, he used the terms 'scab,' 'strikebreaker,' and "Negro' interchangeably." When white miners in Pana organized a mob that killed seven black men in 1899, Mitchell argued that their violence was justified.

By 1905, Samuel Gompers, the long-serving President of the American Federation of Labor, ominously warned that "if the colored man [by strikebreaking] continues to lend himself to the work of tearing down what the white man has built up," then "caucasian civilization" would have to "serve notice that its uplifting process will not be interfered with in any way," and "a race hatred far worse than any known will result."[119] Although labor leaders certainly whipped up their memberships with horrifying visions of a "horde of these darkies" invading from the South, these fears were not simply imaginary, the fantasies of racist demagogues. The hardening racial boundaries of the 1890s reflected the real terrain of a racially and regionally divided labor market in the US that enabled extensive racialized strikebreaking.

The Great Migration, Strikebreaking, and State Hostility to Unions after World War I

By the World War I era strikebreaking in the UK had disappeared, but in the US, the pause in immigration from Europe due to the war provoked labor shortages in Northern industries, an unprecedented migration of African Americans from the South, rapid membership growth for unions, and an unprecedented escalation of racialized strikebreaking. The Great Migration of hundreds of thousands of African Americans from the South to the North and the importance of racial conflict in the postwar strikes, in particular the 1919 steel strike, are well known. This chapter makes clear that these spectacular conflicts marked the culmination of four decades of migration and strikebreaking across regionally and racially divided labor markets.

The potentially explosive combination of unprecedented migration from the South, rapidly advancing labor organizing, and the recruitment of African American strikebreakers was immediately understood by observers during the war. Southerners feared the mass exodus of rural agricultural labor and stepped up their anti-enticement efforts. In September of 1916, the *Baltimore Sun* reported on an ordinance passed by the Montgomery City Commission in Alabama to make it "an offense punishable by a fine of $100 and sixty days imprisonment to induce any laborer to leave the city."[120] In Pittsburgh, local coverage took note of efforts to preserve "sufficient Negro labor for farm work and other local needs" in the South; in particular, in 1917 the Southern railway operators announced that they would no longer cooperate with Northern labor recruiters in financing transportation of laborers.[121] A few weeks later, the *Pittsburgh Daily Post* reported that "all railroads" were working to "keep Negroes in the South" by refusing to accept the deposits from employment bureaus, as "the industries of that section" were "suffering from lack of laborers."[122]

While Southern employers struggled to retain their cheap labor, white Northerners also raised concerns. The *Sun* warned that the "decline in foreign immigration due to the war" might partially account for the "Colored Exodus from the South." However, the more important factor, according to the *Sun*, was "labor disturbances and the fear of them in industrial Northern centers." The paper argued that "the strong current of colored laborers from the South has been the result of a systematic campaign on the part of business interests in the North" to combat the growing power of organized workers.[123] The Baltimore paper warned Northern employers that racialized strikebreaking would only inflame the class and racial conflicts of the North: "It would be a mistake to use the Southern negro simply as a mercenary in the labor battles of the North," since it would inject racist hostility into "struggles that [were] sufficiently bitter already."[124] By October 1916, the Labor Department reported extensive concern from Northern unions and Southern rural employers over the "unprecedented migration of negro laborers from the South toward the North."[125] Reporting on the AFL convention in 1916, the *Baltimore Afro-American* asserted that the AFL aimed to "Confine Negro to South," noting the resolution of an AFL delegate from Ohio which called for a campaign of education in the South so as to "eliminate the menace to the (white) workers in the northern states."[126] "In a nutshell," the *Afro-American* asserted, the white workers in the AFL were "against the employment of colored men in the North."[127] These efforts to regulate internal migration during the world war, as we will see in chapter 7, paralleled the more encompassing pass laws developed in South Africa during the same years.[128]

The effort to organize the steel industry highlights the unprecedented confidence and growth of the US labor movement during the war, and the defeat and collapse of this effort in 1919 underlines the ongoing vulnerability of unions to racialized strikebreaking. In the months before the strike, the union was strong with the semi-skilled immigrant workers who occupied a growing stratum of work in the middle of the production hierarchy. However, when a strike was called demanding recognition of the union, increased wages, and shorter hours, most of the well-paid, native-born "English-speaking" craft workers remained at work, as did nearly all of the black workers in the steel industry.[129] At the Homestead steel works, of the 1,737 black employees, only 8 joined the union, and only one went on strike; only 6 of the 300 black steelworkers at Clairton joined the strike, and not a single black worker from among 344 at the Duquesne steel works joined.[130] Black welfare workers in the Pittsburgh steel industry noted that reports showed "conclusively that the Negro had not struck." This refusal of solidarity grew from many "years past" during which black workers "had been met with rebuff and refusal of admission" to unions. During the strike, the "Negro workers [felt] this [was] their chance to make their worth known to the employer."[131] From the outset, the 1919 steel strike was undermined by the conjunction of racism and nativism. Black workers remained at work since they had long experienced exclusion and discrimination by the craft unions of the AFL. Native-born white workers in the crucial skilled positions refused to support a union movement dominated by southern and eastern Europeans.

Not only did the black steelworkers already on the job largely refuse to join the union or go on strike, but once the strike was underway some forty thousand black workers were recruited as strikebreakers.[132] This was an extraordinary number. A single strike in the US produced twice the number of strikebreakers as British employers recruited (twenty-three thousand) during the entire decade from 1910–19.[133] During World War I, black welfare officers employed at Jones & Laughlin and Carnegie "frequently went South to secure Black laborers for mills in Western Pennsylvania."[134] According to an interview with an Urban League official, some of these black workers were "men experienced in steel plants" directly recruited by the companies as strikebreakers, including "one group of 300 from Alabama, and another of 65 from Kentucky and Tennessee," but "many more . . . had been drifting in one by one of their own volition, since the word had spread far and wide that there were good jobs to be had in the mills." Exemplifying the drive of Southern African Americans to better their condition through strikebreaking, one man "had walked from Jacksonville" all the way to Pittsburgh and arrived at the Urban League office "ragged and dirty" but hopeful of gaining access to the high wages of the steel industry.[135] While employers made some efforts at recruitment, as was seen before, in the US, with an abundant supply of cheap labor in the near-periphery, sophisticated organization was not necessary to produce abundant strikebreakers. A racially and regionally divided labor market provided ample incentives to bring many African Americans to Pittsburgh and other steel centers during the 1919 strike with little effort from employers.

The scale of strikebreaking in 1919 left a strong impression on the white, immigrant workers who witnessed it. One worker described the Pittsburgh steelmakers' use of black strikebreakers by likening it to chattel slavery: "They used to go down south and buy them bring over here dollar a piece, dollar a head."[136] A Jones & Laughlin immigrant steelworker recalled how the company recruited black strikebreakers and housed them in "shanties" inside the plant: "Used to have a lot of men come in from the South to break those unions. You ought to see the scabs they had working in these shanties."[137] Among the longest-serving black workers in the steel sector, Amormes also recalled extensive strikebreaking by black workers in 1919, when hundreds of men were housed inside the mill.[138] Amormes suggested that some black strikebreakers took advantage of strikebreaking for their own goals: "Some would come and stay two or three days," treating the labor recruiters as a source of free transportation. Amormes believed that company police were used as much to control the black workers as to protect them from white strikers: "The company had to put police to guard the Colored workers back and forth from work so they would not run away." Occasionally, white workers could express sympathy for the precarious position of black workers introduced into the mills as strikebreakers. As one Pittsburgh steelworker recalled of his black coworkers: "They were brought up here by J and L originally from the south and it was pretty tough for them to make a move openly. When it's your life, your family, and your job. . . . I could understand them when they said they couldn't take a chance with their job. They was keeping the family up. You could understand them not coming out in the open" to support the union.[139]

State and employer hostility has been the most prominent explanation for the narrow US labor movement. However, a state that was relatively sympathetic to organized labor was not the cause of the survival of inclusive organizing in the UK in the 1890s, but rather a later result of labor's success in the early twentieth century. This pattern also holds in the United States, as research comparing strikebreaking in sixteen communities during the 1919 strike by Cliff Brown and Terry Boswell shows. Strikebreaking by African Americans was pervasive in 1919, but it was not uniform. Brown and Boswell identify three factors that increased the chance of strikebreaking by black workers: 1) prevalence of recent migrants from the South who were primarily young, single men, 2) a weak local union movement, and 3) a local government that was hostile to organized labor.[140] In localities where workers enjoyed significant influence in local politics, strikebreaking was prevented or mitigated, as in the UK after 1910. In a few cases, such as in Cleveland and Wheeling, racialized strikebreaking was largely prevented and white and black steel workers formed "a cohesive strike force."[141] In Wheeling, the local municipal government was favorable to organized labor, there were relatively few recent black migrants, and the labor movement was strong; in Cleveland, despite a larger group of recent black migrants from the South, the local government attempted to prevent strikebreaking. The Cleveland mayor's refusal of protection proved decisive in "preventing the entry of strikebreakers imported by the mill owners."[142] These examples show that while in some localities US authorities actively supported employers and protected strikebreakers, in other places local government aimed to keep strikebreakers out or harassed and monitored them once they arrived. Certainly, the US state was far more hostile and violent, especially toward the most radical sectors of organized labor. But this was not the cause, but rather the result of narrow, craft, and racially bounded patterns of union organizing the survived the trial of the 1890s.

Large-scale recruitment of strikebreakers from the South continued into the 1920s. Although less prominent than the 1919 steel strike, employers recruited black strikebreakers during several postwar conflicts in Baltimore. During a 1918 strike at Crown Cork & Seal, union officials reported that "no one is working except a few colored men."[143] Southern migrants could also be used against unionized black workers. When unionized black waiters struck in Baltimore, BFL delegates reported that "there was not a single colored man in this city that took their places, but rather the colored men now working were imported from Norfolk."[144] When the municipal laborers employed by Baltimore City went on strike in 1919, the municipality opened the ranks of public employment to African Americans as strikebreakers: "Negroes were employed by the City for the first time to fill the places" of the white workers on strike.[145] In 1924 the *Baltimore Afro-American* feared that a hard-won opening in the building trades would be disrupted by the introduction of black strikebreakers. Italian workers had finally "opened their union to colored men on equal terms in a brotherhood of workers, but the imported colored scabs would not only inject the race issue into the fight, but would undo much of the work recently accomplished here to open the doors of all union crafts to the race."[146] The railroads continued to foster intense racial conflict in the 1920s. In response to the entrenched white supremacy of the railroad brotherhoods, Robert Mays, a dining car waiter, created an industrial union for black railroad workers, the Railway Men's International Benevolent Industrial Association. While it reached a peak of fifteen thousand members after the war, an appeal to the AFL for a charter was rejected because the union violated craft jurisdictions. Rebuffed by the AFL, Mays and the union now took a hostile stance toward white organized labor, encouraging strikebreaking during AFL strikes, and contributing to the defeat of the 1922 shopmen's strike by providing "employers with a welcome supply of strikebreakers."[147] Even as labor retreated in the late 1920s, strikebreaking continued. In 1925 black strikebreakers were employed by the Pittsburgh Coal Company, and F. J. Amormes recalled extensive "'transportation' of colored men into Rankin" in 1926 to break a strike in the brickyard.[148]

With organized labor in a weak and vulnerable position, strikebreaking largely disappeared in the second half of the 1920s before reviving as working-class militancy increased under the protections of Franklin Delano Roosevelt's NRA in the 1930s. However, in 1936, a half century of recruiting African Americans from the South to break strikes in the North came to an end. Roosevelt signed the Byrnes Act making it a felony to transport strikebreakers across state lines for the purpose of interfering with picketing, collective bargaining, or other lawful labor activity.[149] Although replacement workers could still be hired locally, strikebreaking by recruiting in near-peripheries across a regionally and racially divided labor market had come to an end. More importantly, the profound political and economic changes wrought by the New Deal and World War II put the South, at long last, on a path toward economic integration with the rest of the United States.[150]

Conclusion

Strikebreaking, especially during the pivotal 1890s, proved fateful in the divergence between the US and UK labor movements. In the UK the New Unions were able to survive a fierce and exceptionally well-organized assault from employers in the late nineteenth century, in large part because

Irish migrant labor and strikebreakers no longer posed a large-scale threat to British workers. In contrast, in the US, where a regionally and racially divided labor market persisted, African Americans could be quickly and cheaply recruited to break strikes in the North. The experience in the US had parallels in other post-slavery societies, which were also marked by deeply divided economies and labor markets.[151] In Brazil, for instance, strikebreaking by formerly enslaved Afro-Brazilians proved devastatingly effective against attempts to organize workers. Labor market discrimination and a narrow labor movement "created a classic 'reserve' labor force" in Brazil that "could be called up at any time to break strikes, undermine efforts to unionize, and keep wages low." As George Andrews shows in his study of São Paulo, "so limited were opportunities for black workers elsewhere in the economy that sufficient numbers could always be found to respond to employers' appeals for *furagreves* [strikebreakers]."[152] The US experience of migration from low-wage peripheries and racialized strikebreaking was not so exceptional.

As a manager at Carnegie Steel recalled in 1934, "As far as I am concerned, the Negro has been a lifesaver to the steel company. When we have had labor disputes, or when we needed more men for expansion, we have gone to the South and brought up thousands of them. I don't know what this company would have done without the Negroes."[153] Under the structural conditions of a racially and regionally divided labor market, organizing workers inclusively in the US proved to be profoundly challenging. Seen from a high altitude, the structural differences presented so far seem overdetermined. Yet, as we move closer to the ground, there was considerable fluidity and contestation in the late nineteenth century. As the next section will explore, the AFL in the late nineteenth century was an evolving organization. The narrow, racially exclusive, masculinist, and nativist boundaries of the US labor movement formed gradually, with the 1890s marking the key pivot.

PART II

The Pivot of the 1890s

ORGANIZED WORKERS AND THE CONSTRUCTION
OF RACIAL BOUNDARIES

The Negro as a common laborer belonged, therefore, not in but beneath the white American labor movement. Craft and race unions spread. The better-paid, skilled and intelligent American labor formed itself into closed guilds and, in combination with capitalist guild-masters, extorted fair wages which could be raised by negotiation. Foreign born and Negro labor was left outside.

W. E. B. DU BOIS, *Black Reconstruction in America*,
"The Counter Revolution of Property," 596–97

The 1890s were a pivotal decade in the global history of racial boundary-making. In the American context, the rise of this new regime was visibly marked by the consolidation and legal articulation of Jim Crow segregation. This decade also culminated with the passage of the White Australia policy and the rise of a white South African labor movement committed to defending the racial color bar. During this decade, the AFL "became more hostile to black competition at the same time that it embraced more restrictive immigration laws."[1] This parallel was more than coincidental. As Eric Arnesen argues, capitalist transformation came to be understood by white, skilled craft workers as being "under continual threat" from the combined forces of "capital, new immigrants, and African Americans."[2] Immediate labor market competition and racialized strikebreaking did not occur in a static economy, but within the context of a revolutionary reconstruction of capitalism marked by the "second industrial revolution," the rise of the modern corporation, the growth of mass production and consumption, and the consolidation of a new Fordist political economy. Much like their cousins in Australia and South Africa, some British workers also embraced white supremacy to draw boundaries around the labor movement; this became central in British maritime ports as white British workers faced low-wage competition from Asian, African, and Caribbean sailors.

Although white supremacy was the dominant global idiom of racial boundary, the Japanese Empire also produced parallel forms of racialized boundary-making that underline how these processes erupted at the intersection of class, uneven economic geography, and the movement of capital and labor across this terrain. In framing the comparison of the US and the UK, it is essential to avoid the hegemony of US scholarship parochially fixated on the white/black racial boundary and Eurocentric constructions of "white supremacy" that ignore other forms of racial boundary-making not shaped by the familiar markers of skin color that were so dominant in the anglophone world.[3] Chinese migrant workers were described by Japanese nativists as "a different category of people" who took degrading jobs at low wages, as "pigtailed slaves," and as "base people." Japanese newspapers lavished attention on events emphasizing Chinese criminality.[4] Even as the Japanese government protested against the discrimination experienced by settlers in North America, it also issued regulations that "led to the complete exclusion of Chinese from the agricultural sector."[5] Two distinct patterns are exemplary. First, low-wage migrant Korean workers were racialized within Japan, and second, low-wage Chinese migrant workers faced racialization in the Manchurian empire.

After Japan's annexation of Korea in 1910, increasingly substantial numbers of workers migrated from the Korean countryside to labor in mills and mines and build the infrastructure of the Japanese metropole. Their experience was much like the Irish in Britain, or African Americans who moved North: "Koreans tended to receive lower wages than their Japanese counterparts, enjoyed little security of employment, suffered exploitation and intimidation at the hands of labour brokers and employers, were constrained from forming political labour organizations, and received little support from the Japanese trade union movement."[6] As Ken Kawashima shows, "agricultural immiseration" in the rural Korean near-periphery helped produce a "relative surplus population" of migrant laborers who suffered exclusion and discrimination in Japanese labor and housing markets.[7] During the World War I industrial boom, employers at factories and coal mines in Osaka Kobe, Fukuoka, and Hokkaido "turned their eyes to colonial Korea" where they "recruited Korean peasants from the southernmost provinces . . . as cheap, temporary, and non-unionized industrial workers" who earned regulated wages between 30 and 50 percent lower than similar Japanese workers.[8] Echoing British capitalists on Irish labor, and US employers on African Americans, the *Fukuoku Nichi Nichi Shimbun* business newspaper hailed their arrival in 1917 in terms of both cost and power: "The import of Korean workers to Japan holds great promise for capitalists insofar as they reduce production costs and increase profits; moreover, unlike Japanese workers, they are not unionized."[9] However, with the postwar depression, Koreans were the first to be fired from factories and mines. Most Korean workers had to attempt to survive by finding work as casual day laborers, with nearly all "compelled to find erratic and temporary employment as unskilled construction workers." During the 1920s, a racially divided labor market consolidated in which unskilled/ Koreans were subordinated beneath skilled/Japanese workers.[10] Confined to the bottom of the production hierarchy, Koreans also faced widespread housing discrimination and racially motivated evictions.[11] Korean workers attempted to organize in Japan, but their labor organizing efforts were segregated from Japanese workers and politically repressed. In one major coal strike by Korean coal miners, "not a single Japanese worker joined the strike despite repeated appeals for solidarity" to their "Japanese brothers."[12] Rivaling the lynchings of the US and the anti-Jewish pogroms of Russia, Japanese racist hostility toward Koreans took its most horrific turn when, in the aftermath of the Great Kanto Earthquake of 1923, rumors blamed Koreans for looting and fires. This mobilized Japanese mobs, in collaboration with local police authorities, to brutally roam the streets committing the "mass murder of over 6,000 Koreans" in the Tokyo area alone, with countless more killed in other cities.[13]

Outside the Japanese metropole, a distinct regime of racial boundary-making unfolded in Japan's colony in Manchuria in northeast China, where Chinese migrant laborers from Shandong provided a second near-periphery of labor recruitment to mines, factories, and construction projects.[14] Chinese migrant workers were called "coolies," and treated brutally, with the "coolie" label carrying "derogatory and racialized meaning" long after the official "coolie" contract labor system had been banned by Chinese authorities.[15] One Japanese labor recruiting company in Dalian built eighty-nine dormitories capable of housing thirteen thousand migrant laborers that "closely resembled a jail," suggestive of parallels to the carceral compound system in South Africa.[16] In sharp contrast to the housing for Chinese migrants, Japanese workers were provided with the best in modern housing, "outfitted with the latest amenities, such as gas and electric lighting, running water, sewage disposal, and modern heating systems."[17] Chinese workers were believed to be incapable of operating modern machinery, and nearly all Chinese workers were confined to the dirtiest, most dangerous work at the bottom of the production hierarchy. In the rare instances where Japanese and Chinese workers filled the same job, the Chinese laborer earned only a half or a third of their Japanese counterpart.[18]

As one Japanese settler recalled: "When the construction of the levees along the Muling River was carried out . . . almost all the workers were coolies from Shandong. They were housed in shabby huts made from straw mats. [Japanese supervisors] drove them like beasts, whipped them [for punishments] and let many die of malnutrition."[19] Japanese observers developed highly racialized descriptions of these Chinese migrant workers. One visitor to Manchuria in 1923 marveled at "the ability of the Chinese coolie to live on cheap, coarse food—such food as is given to cattle in other lands—the power of physical endurance, of Chinese coolies is the eternal wonder of the Japanese. Beside the Chinese coolies the Japanese workmen are pale and puny."[20] In a rare and valuable comparative study of race and labor, Duncan Money and Lemin Teh compare the mines of Central Africa and Manchuria. They show how low-wage African and Chinese migrant workers launched large-scale, but brief and informal, protests at the mines, whereas the "privileged workers—Japanese and white mineworkers" formed formal "collective organizations and deploy[ed] the imperial ideology to preserve and enhance their position in the racial hierarchy."[21]

Within the uneven geography of global capitalism, whenever capital moved down the development gradient seeking expropriated land, the extraction of natural resources, and less-empowered, low-wage workers, or, especially from the late nineteenth century, when labor moved up the development gradient, seeking higher wages, better conditions, and more political rights, racial boundary-making erupted. As Giovanni Arrighi notes, organized workers across the uneven economic geography of global capitalism have "seized upon or created anew whatever combination of distinctive traits (age, sex, color, assorted geo-historical specificities) they could use to impose on capital some kind of special treatment." Despite ideals of internationalism and universal solidarity, in practice "racism and national chauvinism have been integral to the making of the world labor movement."[22] Rather than being an outlier, the US experience illustrates in compressed, condensed form fundamental, global processes of racial boundary-making in the history of capitalism.

For workers, the structure of labor markets mattered not only in terms of geographical inequalities in wages, but also occupational inequalities as well. While part I explored the importance of regional wage differentials, in part II the analysis focuses in on local structures within urban labor markets—specifically, the wage differential between craft and common labor. Often called the "skill premium," this metric records the difference between the high wages of "skilled" craft workers at the top of the production hierarchy and the lower wages of common laborers at the bottom.

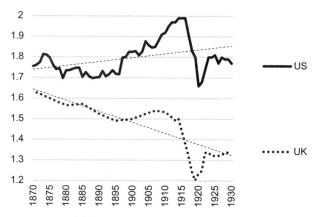

FIGURE P2.1 Wage differential of craft vs. common labor in the US and the UK, 1870–1930. *Source*: Edward Anderson, "Globalisation and Wage Inequalities, 1870–1970," *European Review of Economic History* 5, no. 1 (2001): 94, fig. 1. My thanks to Edward Anderson for sharing his datasets with me.

As seen in figure P2.1, the higher the "skill premium," the larger the gap between the wages of well-paid craft workers at the top of the production hierarchy and low-wage common laborers at the bottom. Migration across regional wage differentials and the scope of local skill premiums were often closely connected. The more exposed an urban workforce was to migration from a low-wage periphery, the higher the wage differential across the skill divide. Migrants typically flooded the bottom of the labor market and depressed the price of common labor. Countries that experienced high rates of immigration—the US, Canada, and Argentina—all had a high craft-laborer wage differential. In contrast, Britain and Australia, where immigration rates were low or heavily regulated, had low wage differentials across the craft divide.

Wage differentials mattered for organized labor because the relative earnings of workers shaped the possibility of shared interests, solidarity, and inclusive collective action. High wage differentials meant that the craft elite and workers at the bottom of the production hierarchy occupied starkly different worlds in terms of their resources and expectations. Building solidarity across such a divide would always be challenging, if not impossible. In contrast, if wage differentials were low, craft workers and those lower in the production hierarchy would have more similar resources and expectations. As figure P2.1 shows, wage differentials in the US started only slightly higher than in the UK in the 1870s, and then increased substantially up to 1914, largely due to the impact of mass immigration. In contrast, in the UK, wage differentials declined in the years leading

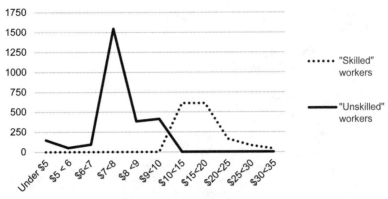

FIGURE P2.2 Distribution of "skilled" and "unskilled" weekly wages at Jones & Laughlin, 1898. *Source*: "Rates of Wages Paid Per Week, December 1898," JLMisc.

up to World War I. The mass mobilization for war provided a major shock to labor markets, but a stark divide remained into the 1920s. Craft workers and common laborers continued to earn vastly unequal wages in the US, while in the UK, wage inequality had decreased substantially. By this point, craftsmen in the UK earned only 30 percent more than a common laborer, but in the US, craftsmen typically earned nearly twice as much as laborers. The material conditions for broad class solidarity were far more promising in the UK.[23]

Wage differentials had a circular, self-reinforcing effect on labor organizing and union strategy. High wage differentials encouraged narrow craft union strategies. Craft unions, fighting for the narrow interests of workers at the top of the production hierarchy, contributed toward even higher wage differentials in the US. In contrast, in the UK, lower wage differentials made inclusive organizing more plausible, and the success of inclusive unions contributed to further reducing the wage differential through bargaining strategies that emphasized wage compression, reducing the gap between the craft elite and common laborers.[24] The structure of the labor market first shaped the kinds of organizing and solidarity that appeared possible and plausible to workers. Narrow or inclusive unions created a feedback loop that reinforced and then amplified initial differences in the labor market.[25]

By the turn of the century, the bifurcated structure of wage-earning in the US and the concentration of union bargaining gains at the top of the production hierarchy were clear. As can be seen in figure P2.2, workers at the bottom and the top of the production hierarchy in the US existed in starkly divided material worlds. Most "unskilled workers" at Jones & Laughlin Steel in 1898 earned between $7 and $8, while the majority of the skilled workers earned more than $15 per week. Building solidarity and organizing workers across such a stark wage differential was extraordinarily challenging. (In South Africa, where wage differentials were even larger, not 2:1 but 10:1, inclusive organizing across the overlapping skill/racial divide was never seriously contemplated.) US unions retreated into a narrow craft strategy of only organizing workers at the top of the production hierarchy. The 1902 report of Maryland's Bureau of Statistics and Information noted that in occupations with a "strong, compact union" there was clear evidence "of the power of organization" to achieve "higher wages, a shorter work-day," and other significant benefits. However, these benefits "all [went] to skilled or well-organized labor. We have yet to hear of any considerable increase in the wages of the unskilled, or common laborer, or the farm hand."[26] Narrow craft unionism was both a result of, and over time, a contributor to working-class wage inequality.

Drawing the Boundaries of Craft

THE CHALLENGE OF INCLUSIVE UNIONISM

The boundary between the craft worker and the common laborer was all-important in the nineteenth century. The craft worker was a man whose skills were rooted in specialized knowledge that gave him substantial control over the production process and a managerial role that gave him command over subordinate helpers and laborers. The gendered "man" is intentional. The craft worker was always a craftsman. Patriarchal forms of familial authority reinforced craftsmen's authority on the shop floor, giving the early labor movement an overwhelming masculine composition despite the preponderance of women and children in the early industrial workforce.[1] Given their immensely stronger bargaining position, craftsmen organized the first durable unions. In contrast, helpers, laborers, factory operatives, women workers, and others at the bottom of the production hierarchy, although they occasionally organized and went on strike, failed to form durable organizations until the 1880s. Yet even with the Knights and the New Unions, craft boundaries proved to be impenetrable in both countries. However, in the United Kingdom, the old craft unions tolerated coexistence with the New Unions, and thus a wide range of workers at the bottom of the production hierarchy—including laborers, helpers, women, and others—joined a far more inclusive British labor movement. In contrast, in the United States, the craft unions of the American Federation of Labor went to war against the Knights of Labor, refusing to tolerate coexistence with more inclusive forms of labor organizing. While women remained a relatively small proportion of the wage labor force in the late nineteenth and early twentieth century, the enfranchisement of women elevated the importance of organized labor's relationship with women workers. In the UK, significant numbers of women workers, organized in unions, provided a grassroots foundation for the Labour Party, whereas in the US, the narrowly masculine craft unions of the AFL lacked these broader ties to women workers and political activists.

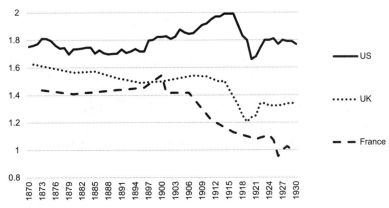

FIGURE 4.1 Craft/common labor wage differentials in the US, UK, and France.
Source: Edward Anderson, "Globalisation and Wage Inequalities, 1870–1970,"
European Review of Economic History 5, no. 1 (2001): 94, fig. 1.

Scholars have disagreed on the role of craft workers in broader labor movements. Were craftsmen reactionary "labor aristocrats," pursuing their narrow self-interest in opposition to the interests of the broader working class, or were they vanguard militants, who used their earlier organization and greater leverage to mobilize a broader working-class movement?[2] While the US seems to generally follow the "labor aristocrat" pattern, scholarship on France has shown that craft workers galvanized broader movements. The roots of these differences can be found in the structural position of craft workers in relation to laborers in the labor market. As can be seen in figure 4.1, the US, UK, and France had quite distinctive wage differential trajectories. France had low and declining wage differentials, while the US had durably high wage differentials. In the US, a material chasm divided craftsmen and laborers, and craft unions functioned primarily as labor aristocracies, committed to their narrow self-interest and indifferent or even hostile to the interests of workers below them. In contrast, in France, craftsmen and laborers shared a much more similar economic position, and radical craftworkers effectively led a broader working-class movement.[3] The UK fits between the narrow conservatism of US craft unions and the inclusive radicalism of French craft unions. In the UK, craft unions generally refused to incorporate lower-paid workers, whose democratic voting power within the union might overpower craftsmen's narrow interests. But UK craft unions tolerated the New Unions that organized inclusively among lower-paid workers. Why was coexistence not possible in the US?

UK Craft Exclusion

Despite the diverging trajectories of the broader labor movements of the United States and the United Kingdom, British craft unions were in many ways quite similar to the AFL craft unions of the US. Like their US counterparts, British craft unions were narrow, conservative organizations that resisted efforts to broaden their memberships to include lower-paid workers at the bottom of the production hierarchy. Despite the initial hopes of the organizers of the New Unionism in the 1880s that the amalgamation of all unions in a sector might create inclusive, united industrial unions, nearly all "attempts to broaden the old craft unions failed."[4] Craft unions objected to the inclusion of more numerous, lower-paid workers who could potentially take control of the organization through their larger numbers and greater voting power. When included, lower-paid workers were denied full membership and voting rights. In the coal, iron, and cotton unions of the UK, helpers occupied a subordinate position within craft unions, with little control over decisions or priorities.[5] In the nineteenth century, the railway workers confined their membership to the most secure and highest paid workers, and several elite crafts seceded to form their own, extremely narrow, sectional organizations.[6] Durable, defensive craft unionism, rather than amalgamation toward industrial unionism characterized most sectors of British organized labor.

In the British steel sector, the leading craft union closely resembled its US counterpart. The Associated Iron and Steel Workers of Great Britain, based in the craft elite of puddlers and rolling mill operators, "remained throughout its existence a complacent and conservative organization" that "ignored the interests of the unskilled."[7] However, unlike in the US, this leading craft union was soon joined by a multitude of other unions that were more inclusive. In the US, tightly policed jurisdictional boundaries ensured that the Amalgamated Iron and Steel Workers was the only major union in the steel sector. In the UK, a second union, the British Steel Smelters Association, emerged in Scotland in 1886 to compete with the Association Iron and Steel Workers. While this was initially also a union of the craft elite, by 1900 the Smelters were organizing the semi-skilled and campaigning against the contract system by which craftsmen hired and paid their subordinate helpers.[8] In addition to these two major unions, there were additional organizations for rolling mill workers, blast furnace men, enginemen, cranemen, and firemen. At the bottom of the production hierarchy, laborers in the steel industry were organized by one of the New Unions, most prominently the dockworkers and gasworkers unions.

This mosaic of competing and overlapping unions produced a pattern of labor organizing that was "complicated and confused in the extreme."[9] When the Steel Smelters Union was formed in Sheffield in 1889, it was "dominated by the first hands," and thus helpers refused to join, limiting membership to around one hundred; the helpers instead joined the Associated Society of Millmen, and quickly gained around four hundred members.[10] The coexistence of multiple, competing, overlapping unions tended to push organizing strategies in a more inclusive direction. This messy framework produced results. Membership in the various organizations increased from thirty thousand in 1897 to over eighty thousand in 1913, by which point unions had a secure foothold in the British steel industry. On the eve of the World War in Sheffield, only 12 percent of skilled steel workers were in unions, compared to some 30 percent of the common laborers.[11] Higher unionization rates among workers at the bottom of the production hierarchy than at the top offered a sharp contrast to the US, where the opposite pattern prevailed.

A few far-sighted British trade union leaders were aware of the challenges that wage differentials posed to solidarity across craft lines. John Hodges of the Steel Smelters union feared that the high wage differentials within the union might weaken solidarity. To bridge the divide among members of the union he led, Hodge attempted to compress wages between the melter craft elite that had founded the union and the helpers that they increasingly represented. While rank-and-file majorities in the branches (where the helpers dominated) approved of his scheme, it was "quietly killed by its opponents on the executive" of the union, where the power of the melter craft elite remained decisive.[12] Nevertheless, while craft workers might object where they had the power to override democratic majorities, the broad, inclusive scope of labor organizing in Britain tended in the early twentieth century to further decrease wage differentials.

The old crafts and the New Unions coexisted in the UK, but it was an uneasy peace. Local tensions often led to the creation of competing, rival city central labor councils. The Liverpool Trades Council (LTC), founded in 1848 and dominated by a craft elite of skilled workers, was highly unrepresentative of the broader working class for most of the nineteenth century. The craft unions in the LTC did not embrace the New Unionism. The relationship between the old and the New Unionism in Liverpool was "never a harmonious one."[13] In 1892, the LTC rejected an effort to demand public works for the unemployed, a measure primarily aimed at helping workers at the bottom of the production hierarchy. This led James Sexton of the dockworkers union (NUDL) to bitterly comment that the craft unions of the LTC were a hindrance to the working-class movement: "The sooner they disband the better."[14] The NUDL disaffiliated from the LTC in 1894 and remained independent for twelve years until rejoining in 1906, but in 1917, the dockworkers once again seceded from the conservative LTC.[15] In the 1920s, a new, rival city central labor council was organized, the Liverpool Trade Council and Labour Party, which aimed to be more representative of the city's working class with less dominance by the narrow interests of the skilled building trades, which had come to dominate the LTC.[16] Craft divisions also proved disruptive in Sheffield. In the steel industry, "divisions between leading hands" and their subordinate helpers and laborers delayed meaningful unionization until the 1890s, by which point wage differentials had already substantially declined.[17] Like Liverpool in the 1920s, Sheffield had two rival trades councils from 1908 to 1920, representing a divide between the old crafts and New Unions in the heavy industries.[18]

Craft boundaries were deeply drawn, and often proved impenetrable. Craft unions in the UK remained jealous of their autonomy and ability to set priorities independently from the influence of the masses of workers below them. It was only under the pressure of World War I that the various craft unions, while retaining their individual autonomy, agreed to cooperate under the Iron and Steel Trades Confederation.[19] However, as significant as these divisions were, they did not compare to the war between the AFL and the Knights in the 1880s and 1890s, or the even more extreme hostilities between the AFL and the Industrial Workers of the World (IWW) in the early twentieth century. While similar tensions existed on both sides of the Atlantic, only in the US did narrow craft unions collaborate with employers and the state to drive their more inclusive competitors out of existence.

US Craft Exclusion

After the decline of the Knights of Labor in the 1890s, the narrow boundaries of the US labor movement consolidated, with organization confined to craft workers at the top of the production hierarchy. As Gary Marks has argued, the AFL became "dominated by relatively closed unions to an extent that was unparalleled in any other major union movement."[20] However, the AFL, despite emerging from the established craft unions in the 1880s, did not ossify into a narrow, rigid craft organization immediately. Rather it was the combined pressures of competition with the Knights of Labor in the 1880s, and then, in the 1890s, the threat of mass strikebreaking, that pushed the AFL to retreat into a rigid, indeed fanatical commitment to narrow craft organization in the early twentieth century as the only secure and successful strategy for labor organizing.

The inclusive tradition of the Knights would survive in industrial unions like the United Mine Workers and the Amalgamated Clothing Workers, but these were exceptions to the dominant pattern. Socialist-led efforts to organize more inclusively, most notably Eugene Debs's American Railway Union (1894) and the IWW were defeated, lacking the stability to offer a sustained challenge to the narrow craft unionism of the AFL. The IWW might appear to have been well-positioned to build a more inclusive US labor movement between 1905 and 1917, before wartime government repression effectively destroyed it. However, even before this assault, the IWW proved mostly incapable of building durable, large-scale locals of workers at the bottom of the production hierarchy. During strikes the IWW could lead and inspire the masses of workers neglected and rejected by AFL, but with a few important exceptions, the IWW did not succeed in building lasting organizations.

Was a narrow US labor movement necessarily weak? While it is true that craft organization tended to orient workers away from political action through an independent workers' party, the refusal of the AFL to launch a labor party in the United States does not mean that craft unions or the AFL were politically powerless. Rather, in terms of the goals they set for themselves, craft unions proved quite powerful both industrially and politically, even if their gains and protections were not broadly enjoyed by the US working class. As Paul Taillon has shown, the four craft railroad brotherhoods (locomotive engineers, conductors, firemen, trainmen) "became the most powerful set of unions in the United States" in the early twentieth century. Their power was marked in particular by their success in securing the eight-hour day through the Adamson Act of 1916 over bitter resistance from the railroad corporations. In the short- to medium-term, craft organization could be remarkably successful, even if this narrow strategy foreclosed broader, more inclusive organizing that could have moved beyond the limited horizons of craft unionism. The railroad brotherhoods also exemplified the racial and craft exclusion of the broader US labor movement. Confined within "rigid craft lines," the railroad brotherhoods "represented less than one-fifth of the railroad workers and were composed more conspicuously of white men of American and rural parentage than any other major North American labor union."[21] The US labor movement was narrow but also powerful and effective for the specific constituencies it served. In addition to the railroad brotherhoods, this was particularly true in the building trades. Here alliances between craft workers and urban political machines provided lucrative construction contracts, political protection, and impressive wage gains for building trades workers and their unions. Rather than experiencing exceptional political repression and employer hostility, the US building trades unions occupied perhaps the most favorable political and economic position of any labor organization in the world in the first decades of the twentieth century.

The steel sector highlights the similarities and differences in organized labor in the two countries. Whereas in the UK steel industry, a variety of organizations eventually organized across craft lines, in the US even the narrow craft unionism of the Amalgamated Association of Iron and Steel Workers proved insufficient for some puddlers who desired an even narrower, more exclusive organization. The Amalgamated earned its name after it combined the various crafts in the iron and steel industry. From only six thousand members in 1885, the Amalgamated reached a peak of over twenty-four thousand members in 1891. However, this numerical strength was shaky since the union was strong in the declining iron industry where craft practices still prevailed, and weak in the expanding steel plants.[22] Paul Kellogg of the Pittsburgh Survey noted in 1914 that the Amalgamated had "paid small heed to the needs of the day laborers in the mills," and that craft unions in general took little interest in issues of broader working-class concern.[23] Already in 1917, two years before the disastrously unsuccessful steel strike, the Amalgamated Association could be dismissed as a "decadent" organization set on a "suicidal" path of self-destruction by remaining entrenched in narrow craft boundaries.[24]

While outside reformers critiqued the Amalgamated for remaining narrow and unrepresentative of a changing working class, the opposite critique emerged from within the union. Puddlers, as elite craftsmen, were becoming troubled by the influence of lower-wage workers. As early as the 1890s, puddlers in the Amalgamated grew concerned that amalgamation with other crafts had been a mistake, since this brought lower-paid and increasingly more numerous workers into the union. Concern became acute when the union voted down a wage scale that would have elevated puddlers' pay. For puddlers, "unionization that failed to defend [their] craft interest was meaningless."[25] In 1907 a group of dissident puddlers seceded from the Amalgamated Association and formed a revived Sons of Vulcan because they felt that the numerous, mid-level finishers had come to dominate the Amalgamated.[26] Illustrating the overlapping of craft and racial boundaries, the Vulcans were also a militantly whites-only union; in addition to craft concerns, its leaders lambasted the Amalgamated for admitting "colored puddlers into full membership" and forcing white union members to work alongside black union members.[27] US craft unions were open to combination with other unions so long as the highest paid craft workers retained "the deciding vote in determining the conditions under which all parties might be called upon to make common cause." But when craft strength was swamped by lower-wage workers, secession movements were attempted, and were often successful.[28]

The rigid craft unionism of the AFL emerged over time. The 1890s marked the key pivot away from flexible collaboration toward narrow craft boundaries. Collaboration with the Knights up to 1886 suggests the early flexibility of craft unions. In 1888, reflecting a growing concern about the inadequacy of traditional craft jurisdictions in emerging Fordist mass production, Samuel Gompers tentatively suggested "a scheme whereby direct representation in the [AFL] convention would be transferred to 'industrial divisions,'" rather than the craft unions.[29] This would have revolutionized the AFL's structure. But this tentative flexibility in the late 1880s was quickly forgotten in the decade that followed. The bitter experience of strikebreaking, rising wage differentials, mass immigration, and hardening racial boundaries produced an absolute commitment to narrow craft unionism by the start of the twentieth century. In 1901 the AFL recommitted to craft organization in the Scranton Declaration. This AFL policy statement declared that while the violation of craft boundaries by the United Mine Workers would be tolerated, this was allowed only as a unique exception. The broader principle was an unequivocal endorsement of craft unionism. The Scranton Declaration asserted, "the magnificent growth of the A.F. of L. is conceded by all students of economic thought to be the result of organization on trade lines."[30] In 1903 Gompers doubled down on this strategy despite left-wing pressure to adopt a more inclusive organizing approach. He warned that while "industrial organization is pervasive in the history of the labor movement, [it] runs counter to the best conception of the toilers' interest now, and is sure to lead to the confusion which precedes dissolution and disruption."[31] Collaboration across craft boundaries still seemed possible in the late 1880s, but by the early twentieth century, the Scranton Declaration of strict craft-only organization became holy writ for a generation of AFL leaders who would dominate the US labor movement until the 1930s.[32]

Although the narrowing of wage differentials during World War I opened new possibilities of broader solidarity, the US labor movement remained confined within narrow craft boundaries. During the postwar surge of labor organizing, a few activists attempted to shift the Baltimore Federation of Labor away from its narrow craft boundaries. In September 1920, a delegate to the BFL "suggested that the Federation go out and organize the unorganized," a suggestion that met with a muted response from the leadership.[33] In 1923, another BFL delegate introduced a resolution "calling on the American Federation of Labor to institute proceedings calculated to bring about the amalgamation of workers along industrial lines," but after the resolution was sent out for consideration, all unions reported as strongly opposed, with the notable exception of the Lady Garment Workers Union, which reported two-thirds in support of industrial amalgamation.[34]

Despite the survival of a few, exceptional unions with more inclusive organizing strategies, at the heart of the US labor movement was the narrow craft union. In particular, the dominant position of the building trades crafts and their deep alliances with urban political machines was a distinctive feature of the US labor movement.[35] In the UK, building trades workers were no better organized than other sectors.[36] In the US, lucrative building contracts were doled out by urban political machines in return for the electoral support provided by building trades members. Although building trades workers represented less than 8 percent of the US workforce throughout this period, building trades unions constituted 15 percent of AFL union membership in 1897, rising to 23 percent in 1910, and reaching an astounding 27 percent of union members in 1929.[37] US building trades workers were likely the most powerful, influential, and affluent workers in the world. In Pittsburgh the building trades had successfully "forced their daily rates of wages higher than those of any other men in the District" and won the eight-hour day by 1902, with the unions representing "perhaps 75 percent of all the men working in these trades."[38] In 1923 the Secretary of the Baltimore Building Trades Council and the President of the Baltimore Federation felt entitled to demand that the Maryland governor explain why "non-union Plumbers" were being employed on a government building project.[39] An obliging Governor Ritchie promised to "look into the matter at once."[40] The Merchants and Manufacturers Association of Baltimore took note of the power of the building trades in the city. The "question of pay of skilled labor in the building trades" required attention, as the power of "Labor Organizations" could prevent building and would "practically mean stagnation" in the local real estate market.[41] Far from experiencing hostility or repression, the building trades enjoyed an amicable, and indeed, lucrative relationship with the municipal state in the US. Tied closely to urban political machines, the building trades enjoyed remarkable power and protection. By contrast, the British building trades unions struggled to consolidate central, national authority, and local branches frequently "broke ranks in what amounted to a free for all," with twenty-five distinct building trades federations in different urban regions.[42]

Through the apprenticeship system, the building trade crafts controlled access to high-wage positions by channeling access to family members, creating unusually homogenous unions that were heavily reinforced by kinship ties and racial boundaries. Rather than exclude black workers altogether, the building trades offered a place to black workers at the bottom of the production hierarchy, working under white craftsmen as unskilled workers in the hod carriers and laborers union. Substantial numbers of black workers were organized in this subordinate position and enjoyed relatively high wages when compared to other laborers, but modest ones when compared to the white craftsmen at the top of the building trades. Already in 1886 Baltimore's hod carriers, numbering "about 600" and nearly all African Americans, were "a thoroughly organized body of labor" who enforced the union card showing good standing.[43] African American workers in the building trades found a position within organized labor, albeit a subordinate position that purposefully segregated black workers into the most backbreaking, lowest-paid work. To the extent that US craft unions had a place for black workers and others confined to the bottom of the production hierarchy, the hod carriers in the building trades typified their position: separated, segregated, and subordinated to white craft workers above them.

Coexistence or Conflict: Craft and Inclusive Unions

Why did the craft unions coexist with the New Unions in the UK while in the US craft unions launched a bitter assault on the Knights of Labor and later attempts at inclusive organizing? Two structural factors stand out: the extent of strikebreaking and the level of wage differentials. Given the higher wage differentials in the US, bridging the gap between craft workers and laborers was a greater challenge. Kim Voss finds that the Knights were able to do "relatively well . . . so long as wage differentials were not too high and resources were not spread too thin by organizational proliferation of less-skilled workers' assemblies in a single industry."[44] In addition, strikebreaking mattered for organizational strategy. In the UK, where strikebreaking was far less extensive, it was possible for a union to survive even though it recruited its membership exclusively from workers toward the bottom of the production hierarchy. In contrast, in the US, where strikebreaking was three times as common during the 1890s, a union composed solely of non-craft workers would face certain destruction under the pressures of strikebreaking. In the UK the New Unions organized around and under the crafts, avoiding direct confrontations with the jurisdictional claims of the craft unions. As Eric Hobsbawm has argued, the "fact that workers [in Britain] on both sides of the skill gap kept to their proper stations as 'artisans' and 'labourers' proved to be of considerable advantage to the general unions in their formative period," since this prevented the destructive "competition with the 'crafts' which wrecked the Knights of Labor" in the US.[45] Extensive strikebreaking explains why laborers in the US could not organize and survive within their own unions. In order to survive, the Knights needed to incorporate more secure craft workers into a mixed organization, the typical mixed Local Assembly. These mixed organizations aimed to leverage the relative power of more secure craft workers to bolster the position of more vulnerable, replaceable laborers at the bottom of the production hierarchy.[46] Conell and Voss's study of the Knights in the iron and steel industry shows that tensions across the craft line were essential. The prior existence of a craft local prevented industrial patterns of organizing, and instead "channeled less-skilled workers' assemblies" into separate organizations so that the more numerous laborers could not overrule the craft elite within a combined, mixed organization.[47] The Knights' cross-craft organizational strategy, made necessary by the extent of strikebreaking in the US, essentially subordinated the interests of craft workers to support a project of broader solidarity. Unsurprisingly, craft workers in the US were resistant to such a sacrificial, solidaristic strategy, especially as wage differentials grew.

Craft Boundaries and Gender Boundaries

The survival of the New Unions in the United Kingdom and the collapse of the Knights in the United States had lasting implications for gender boundaries in the labor movement. In the UK, far more women were organized in unions, with the National Union of Teachers (NUT) becoming one of the largest and most powerful unions in the UK by the 1920s. In contrast, the retreat to rigid craft boundaries in the US left nearly all women workers outside the ranks of organized labor. The overlapping of the gender and craft boundary had important consequences for labor politics. The heavily masculinist craft unions of the AFL generally kept the broad range of women-led, urban welfare reform movements at arm's length, whereas in the UK, trade-union women played a crucial role in bringing together labor politics and urban reform politics within the Labour Party.[48] By the 1920s, women were a substantial 16.5 percent of union members in the UK, whereas in the US, only in the 1950s did women come to compose a similar share of union members.[49]

Although the Knights demonstrated a remarkable early commitment to organizing women workers and a degree of feminist egalitarianism, the consolidation of the craft unionism of the AFL produced a deeply masculinist US labor movement. During the 1880s, Leonora Barry served in national leadership of the Knights of Labor and used her position of power to raise awareness of sexual harassment; all district assemblies were called upon to set up a sub-committee of "three active and intelligent women" who could investigate "any abuse existing which a female worker would be delicate in mentioning to the General Executive Board."[50] The Knights were committed to equal pay for equal work, woman suffrage, and temperance, and these issues made the Knights "particularly appealing to women."[51] Substantial numbers of women workers from the textile factories and clothing workshops joined the order. Most remarkably, the Knights also organized domestic workers, including servants, while also recognizing married women's domestic labor as vital, productive work. As one woman from the Chicago Knights argued, it required "as much hard work to keep a house successfully as to build a house successfully," thus putting the often invisible, uncompensated labor of social reproduction on par with the labor of well-paid craftsmen in the building trades.[52]

However, the hardening of craft boundaries in the 1890s was a gendered process that sidelined feminists and women workers within the US labor movement. While early data is limited, a detailed breakdown of union workers in New York suggests that women as share of union members declined from 4.8 percent in 1894 to only 2.9 percent in 1908.[53] According to a study in 1912, women supposedly lacked "the courage and aggressiveness necessary for encountering employers, and for demanding any desired measure."[54] As Ileen DeVault has shown, the craft unionism of the AFL "came to be read as 'male' perhaps even more so than they were read as 'white,'" and as craft unions consolidated in the 1890s, AFL craft unions marked their jurisdictions through "a series of trade-specific definitions of skill and economic power that ultimately relied on gender as a key element."[55] Although less common than racial membership restrictions, several unions explicitly banned women workers in an effort to forestall the feminization of the labor market, including the Barbers, Watchcase Engravers, and the (railroad) Switchmen. In 1907 the Iron Molders Union launched a campaign to prevent any further entry of women into the trade, and resolved to impose a fifty-dollar fine or expulsion on any union man who "gives instruction to female laborers in any branch of the trade." Several unions, such as the Potters, Upholsterers, and Paper Makers, admitted women, but imposed rules that confined women members to peripheral positions and the bottom of the production hierarchy.[56] Given a masculinist and patriarchal foundation, many craft unions in the AFL were hostile to women's growing political influence in the early twentieth century. As late as September 1920, when the 19th Amendment was already ratified, the craft unions of the BFL repeatedly stated their opposition to woman suffrage.[57]

As with the Knights, the New Unionism organized unprecedented numbers of women workers. In particular, the growth of the New Unions brought increasing numbers of women who worked in white-collar office work and the public sector into the labor movement. Most importantly, organized teachers became major force in the UK labor movement and articulated a decisively feminist labor politics that in the US was forced into retreat after the collapse of the Knights. The NUT became one of the largest unions in the UK by the early twentieth century.[58] This massive union fostered a number of important internal caucuses. The Equal Pay League, founded in 1904, became the National Federation of Women Teachers in 1907, a caucus within the NUT that worked to "promote a feminist agenda."[59] Within the NUT, assistant teachers, women teachers, married women teachers, and head teachers all had caucuses to represent their interests within the broader union.[60] This large-scale organization of women workers proved crucial in building solidarity between the Labour Party and unions. The statist, redistributive politics of the Labour Party did not come from the traditional craft unions. Rather, women activists provided the grassroots foundation for statist reform programs aimed at community health and social welfare. The Women Labour League, organized in 1906, played a crucial role in expanding the Labour Party from a focus on narrow trade union politics concerned with collective bargaining rights toward broader issues of working-class concern that resonated with a broader community of voters.[61] Exemplifying this mediating role, the reunification of the moderate and the socialist wings of the Sheffield labor movement in the 1920s occurred under the presidency of Gertrude Wilkinson, a leader of the Sheffield Women's Trade Union League, secretary for the Fabian Society, and a representative for the Sheffield District Teachers Association on the city council.[62] In contrast, most teachers in the US organized much later, often outside the labor movement. In the 1920s, the American Federation of Teachers was dominated by men high school teachers who minimized the importance of women and feminist politics.[63] While the British labor movement was undeniably marked by masculinist, craft commitments, there were also powerful feminist countercurrents that found practical expression in unions like the NUT and in the municipal welfare politics of the local Labour Party.

Conclusion

A craft boundary divided the working class in both the US and the UK. In both countries, craft workers at the top of the production hierarchy resisted efforts to expand their organizations to include lower-paid workers whose interests and voting power might threaten the position of elite craftsmen. However, the significance of craft depended on material conditions. In the US, an initially higher wage differential was pushed even higher by mass immigration and by narrow craft organizing. In the UK, a lower wage differential was further reduced by the force of inclusive unions that more broadly represented all workers. The 1890s were a key pivot for the hardening of craft boundaries. While the AFL initially appeared open to collaborative forms of organization, by 1901 the Scranton Declaration made narrow, rigid craft organizing official union dogma in the US. Gender boundaries within the working class reinforced the craft boundary. In parallel to these craft and gender boundaries, during the pivot of the 1890s racial boundaries and anti-immigrant nativist boundaries also consolidated in the US labor movement.

Black Workers and the Boundaries of White Supremacy in the United States

In 1901 an African American magazine argued that the "trade and labor unions are the greatest enemies of the Negro in America and are doing more to foster and encourage race hatred and caste spirit than any other agency we know of."[1] This dark assessment of organized labor's role was all too apt at the start of the twentieth century. Yet, a decade earlier, a far different relationship seemed possible between African Americans and the labor movement in the United States. The Knights of Labor had won acclaim from African Americans for organizing large numbers of black workers and challenging Southern segregation at the 1886 Richmond Assembly. Even the American Federation of Labor took a strong, principled stand against racist whites-only membership policies in the early 1890s. The subsequent years, however, witnessed a clear hardening of both craft and racial boundaries. As parallel reinforcing processes, craft and racial exclusion were driven by the same causes. Narrow craft unionism and white supremacy in the labor movement were responses to the pressure of strikebreakers, and most visibly to black strikebreakers recruited from the South. The leaders of the AFL craft unions, rather than attempting to replicate the Knights' inclusive organizing, increasingly concluded by the early twentieth century that the only stable and durable way to organize was to limit union membership to white craft workers.

According to journalist Ray Stannard Baker, in the early twentieth century both white and black residents of "every large city" reported that "race feeling and discrimination were rapidly increasing."[2] With the escalation of racialized strikebreaking as a crucial driver, the 1890s marked a grim turning point in the longer history of racism in America. Ever since C. Vann Woodward challenged assumptions about the timeless antiquity of Jim Crow white supremacy in *The Strange Career*, scholars have debated the degree of continuity vs. change in the Southern racial order after slavery.[3]

This chapter contributes to scholarship that emphasizes the importance of changes in the late nineteenth century, with the 1890s marking the transition between a period of flexibility, uncertainty, and possible collaboration across racial boundaries to the early twentieth century when racial boundaries hardened and black political and social rights had eroded. Glenda Gilmore argues that "the late 1890s represented cataclysmic ruptures in the fabric of black civil rights, not simply the institutionalization of repression."[4] Most powerfully, Tera Hunter's study of black women workers in Atlanta traces changing racial boundaries and the terrain of resistance, starting from the possibilities suggested by black washerwomen's militant strikes in 1881, followed by a reaction to these efforts in the 1890s when "blacks were met with systematic encroachments on their civil and human rights" and "political disenfranchisement, vigilante violence, and *de jure* segregation intensified . . . to tip the scales of justice decidedly in the favor of whites."[5] Crucially, a massive hate strike by white women textile workers in 1897, in which white strikers demanded, "We want all them niggers out of there, and that's what we are going to have," marked a key turning point, leading to an "unprecedented invigoration of white organized labor in the city" while decisively closing the era in which "black and white workers in Atlanta had formed brief political and trade union alliances," most prominently under the Knights of Labor in the mid-1880s.[6] From an "apogee of hope" in the 1880s Atlanta reached a "nadir of despair" in 1906 when increasing urban migration, intensified labor market competition, and a vitriolic gubernatorial campaign that articulated the fears of white workers unleashed a riot that killed dozens and injured hundreds of black Atlantans.[7] Had land reform been far-reaching after emancipation, a very different terrain of struggle might have been opened up in the late nineteenth century, but with black workers landless and disenfranchised, the century closed with white supremacy triumphant.

While the 1890s marked a crucial pivot, white supremacy among organized workers had a longer history. The argument is not that working-class white supremacy did not exist prior to the 1890s, but rather that this decade led to an intensification and hardening of racial boundaries. Efforts to bar African Americans from skilled work went back to the antebellum era, when white mechanics and artisans pressured state legislatures to bar the enslaved from apprenticeships and skilled crafts.[8] Early emancipation in the North set the stage for the early emergence of a working-class, populist racism. In Northern cities such as Cincinnati and Philadelphia, as Du Bois noted, as "groups of laborers fighting for bread and butter" competed, tensions erupted "into race riots" and full on "race war."[9] During the Civil War, black caulkers were driven out the shipbuilding industry in

Baltimore, Chicago butchers struck against any employer who hired black labor, in Cincinnati black workers were driven off the waterfront, and the New York draft riots were entangled with the effort to drive black workers from the docks.[10] When the National Labor Union held its first convention in Baltimore in 1866, the Committee on Colored Labor, chaired by a Carpenter and Joiners delegate whose union only admitted white workers, was unable to come to a position on admitting black workers to the labor movement.[11] At the next convention, William Sylvis warned that "the time will come when the Negro will take possession of the shops if we have not taken possession of the Negro."[12] So soon after emancipation, the ominous implications of white organized labor taking "possession of the Negro" could not have been lost on union delegates. This was among the first of many repeated instances, as Bruce Nelson has noted, in which white unionists cast African Americans "not as fellow workers but as instruments in the hands of others."[13] When the Negro Labor Association met in 1869, they condemned "the exclusion of colored men and apprentices from the right to labor in any department of industry or workshop . . . by what is known as 'trades' unions,'" calling the US labor movement's racial boundaries "an insult to God, injury to us, and a disgrace to humanity."[14] In the revolutionary atmosphere of the Civil War and Reconstruction, underpinned by the material upheaval of emancipation, it seemed possible that these entrenched racial boundaries might ease. However, as Du Bois noted, "American labor refused, in the main, to envisage black labor as part of its problem."[15] When faced with growing migration, low-wage competition, and strikebreaking, rather than extending inclusion and solidarity, "white American labor almost unanimously turned" to protective racial boundaries around the best paid jobs, anticipating the struggle of white South African workers to maintain the color bar.[16]

Abolitionist Egalitarianism in the 1870s and 1880s

In the 1870s and 1880s, some union leaders, inspired by the egalitarian possibilities of abolitionism and Radical Reconstruction, produced union constitutions and formal declarations that committed their organizations to racial equality. This was new and remarkable. As David Roediger notes, "the very idea that Black-white labor unity was desirable and important . . . was essentially a post-Civil War innovation."[17] Yet these few "idealistic craftsmen" who opposed racial discrimination were "always in the minority at national conventions."[18] During the 1870s, the cigarmakers union eliminated a constitutional clause requiring that members be "white practical cigar makers," and the bricklayers and carpenters also eliminated whites-only membership policies. But many craft unions, including the puddlers in the Sons of Vulcan and the railroad brotherhoods, retained whites-only membership clauses.[19] Whatever claims of racial equality might be made in constitutions, conventions, or by union officers, weak central union executives in the 1870s and 1880s were neither willing nor able to risk the integrity of their fragile, emerging unions "by attempting to force the idealism of the few upon the intolerant and apathetic many."[20] Terence Powderly, the leader of the Knights in the 1880s, was deeply shaped by his mother, whom he described as "a pronounced abolitionist." From his position in the national executive he "lectured, scolded, and sanctioned white members of the Knights who resisted the rules of equal treatment for black members."[21] When an organizer from Pittsburgh, Gilbert Rockwood, suggested "quietly" rejecting black union members while officially following the "letter of the law" on inclusion, Powderly rejected such subterfuge and demanded that the egalitarian principle of inclusion be rigorously enforced.[22]

Even if national unions rejected overt exclusion, until the 1890s national executives were weak and most power remained with locals. Despite the fact the national bricklayers union rejected racial discrimination, the Maryland local imposed a fifty-dollar fine on any member who worked alongside black workers.[23] In 1874, Baltimore displayed the uncertain racial boundaries of the emerging labor movement. Although an integrated crowd of black and white oyster shuckers marched to demand better wages, a few weeks later, white men in prison suits and blackface paraded to protest competition from convict labor, thus reinforcing the division between respectable, free, white labor and unfree, criminal, black workers.[24] Despite the fact that whites-only clauses were common, when the craft trades first federated in 1881, unions that wished to affiliate were required to pledge to "never discriminate against a fellow worker on account of color, creed or nationality."[25] When the craft unions seceded from the Knights in 1886 and established the AFL, the new federation had to untangle a mass of contradictory policies on whether membership in craft unions would be open to all, regardless of race, or confined to white workers only.

The AFL initially showed a powerful commitment to enforcing the principles of racial equality in the early 1890s. At its 1890 convention, the AFL reaffirmed its opposition to "trades unions having provision in their constitutions which exclude from membership on account of race or color."[26] In these early years, AFL delegates repeatedly voted to reject the appointment of an organizer to support the machinists union due to the union's whites-only membership clause. When Gompers spoke at the machinists' convention later in 1890, he urged the union to drop their racist membership policy and thereby gain entrance to the AFL as an affiliated union. When the machinists failed to honor their promise to revise their constitution the next year, not only did the AFL refuse to admit the machinists, the Federation went on the offensive by organizing a rival, competing union "based upon the principles which recognize the equality of all men working at our trade regardless of religion, race, or color."[27] A similarly aggressive and interventionist policy was taken with the Brotherhood of Boiler Makers and Iron Shipbuilders, whose effort to affiliate with the AFL was also rejected in 1893 due to a whites-only membership clause. Here too, the AFL went on the offensive by chartering a rival union open to black workers.[28] Given the AFL's fundamental commitment to autonomy for organized trades, this heavy-handed intervention by the national federation in the internal policies of the machinists and boilermakers was extraordinary.[29]

Racist Retreat under the Pressure of Strikebreaking

Before the outbreak of World War I, the South African white supremacist Maurice S. Evans toured the United States, and felt vindicated when he found that even among former "abolitionists" racial hostility had "grown perceptibly." He found that this "change [was] reflected in the attitude of the average citizen, and especially the employer and working man, in the gradual closing of many branches of labour to the Negro."[30] The pressure of racialized strikebreaking in the 1890s resolved the contradiction of egalitarian commitments alongside widespread racial exclusion by pushing US labor leaders toward white supremacy. By the mid-1890s, earlier commitments to racial equality were crumbling. In 1895, the AFL leadership informed the machinists that they could remove the whites-only clause from their constitution while still retaining a whites-only membership. As the AFL president wrote to the machinists, "many crafts refused to admit a colored man without having any such provision in their constitution, the matter being left absolutely with the local unions."[31] Following this guidance from the AFL, the machinists removed the whites-only clause from their constitution and replaced it with a membership ritual that pledged members to only recruit white men to the union. The boilermakers, and a year later the blacksmiths, quickly copied the machinists and gained admittance to the AFL using the same maneuver.[32] In 1896, Gompers attempted to bring the powerful Brotherhood of Locomotive Firemen into the AFL by encouraging them to follow the machinists' example. However, the Firemen refused to hide their commitment to white supremacy. The Brotherhood responded that its members would "not care to belong to an organization that is not honest enough to make public its qualification for membership."[33]

The deception involved shows an uneasiness about overtly embracing white supremacy, but this too would quickly fade. By the end of the decade, even blatant, constitutionally explicit whites-only policies were no longer a barrier to affiliation with the AFL. In 1899 and 1900, two smaller railroad brotherhoods, the Telegraphers and the Trackmen, were permitted to join the AFL with constitutions that specified whites-only membership in an obvious violation of the AFL's official non-discrimination policy. In 1902, the Stationary Engineers, a union already affiliated with the AFL, amended its constitution to add a whites-only constitutional clause, without any comment or rebuke from AFL leadership.[34] The culmination of this sad trajectory came in 1910, when the AFL admitted the Brotherhood of Railway Carmen, a union with a whites-only constitutional clause, and shortly thereafter revoked the charter of the competing International Association of Car Workers, a more inclusive union with black members that refused amalgamation with the Brotherhood because of its whites-only constitution.[35] Whereas in the early 1890s, the AFL had aggressively used its affiliation and chartering powers to pursue more egalitarian membership policies with the machinists and boilermakers, by 1910 it was doing the opposite: welcoming a racist whites-only union and revoking recognition from a competing union that aimed to organize all workers regardless of race.

A leading cause for this shift in orientation was the prominence and power of racialized strikebreaking in the 1890s. Philip Foner pinpoints the 1890s as "the decade in which the policy of Negro-white unity . . . retrogressed" in the labor movement, as white trade unionists came to see African Americas as "natural strikebreakers."[36] At the end of the decade, Gompers argued that black workers, by serving as strikebreakers, had "so conducted themselves as to be a continuous convenient whip placed in the hands of employers."[37] As the egalitarian possibilities of abolitionism and radical republicanism faded in the late nineteenth century, the AFL accepted, and increasingly embraced, white supremacy. In the late 1890s, Gompers cautioned that the "temperament" necessary for "the modern trade union" seemed to be "particular to most of the Caucasian race."[38] In the early twentieth century, Gompers and Mitchell both pointed to strikebreaking as the key driver of growing racial tensions.[39] As Gompers stated in 1905, "caucasians . . . are not going to let their standard of living be destroyed by negroes, Chinamen, Japs, or any others."[40]

The AFL was not alone in retreating from racial equality during the 1890s. The Knights of Labor, although beset by racial tensions and threatened by racialized strikebreaking, had maintained a commitment to equality and the inclusion of black workers during the 1880s and early 1890s. As the black worker who introduced Powderly at the 1886 Richmond Convention had proudly asserted, "one of the objects of our order is the abolition of those distinctions which are maintained by creed or color. . . . We have worked so far successfully for the extinction of those regrettable distinctions."[41] This egalitarian commitment crumbled in the 1890s. After a poll of white locals in 1894 showed overwhelming support for the idea, the Knights of Labor announced that the only solution to the "race problem" in the United States was to use government funds to deport African Americans to Liberia, the Congo, "or some other parts of Africa."[42] The Knights had retreated to the antebellum racist fantasy of making black Americans disappear through deportation to Africa.

Alongside the retreat of the AFL and Knights from earlier egalitarian commitments, the 1890s also marked a failure to break with the whites-only membership that dominated the railway unions. When dissidents from the railroad brotherhoods organized the industrial American Railway Union (ARU) in 1893, a debate erupted over whether to maintain the previous whites-only policy of the brotherhoods. The union, led by the socialist Eugene Debs, seemed poised to challenge the narrow craft and racial boundaries of the railway unions. At the ARU's founding convention, Debs argued for opening the new union to black workers: "I am not here to advocate association with the Negro, but I will stand side by side with him, take his hand in mine and help whatever is in my power."[43] However, another delegate responded that the new union would "lose 5,000 members in the West if the colored men were allowed to become members," and the convention upheld whites-only membership in a closely divided vote.[44] The American Railway Union was defeated in the 1894 Pullman strike, while the craft railway brotherhoods survived, and ultimately thrived within their narrow boundaries. In 1898, the president of the Firemen promised "a campaign in advocacy of white supremacy in the railway service," so that "every locomotive in the country would be fired by a white man."[45] While the AFL retained a superficial, rhetorical commitment to racial inclusion and organizing black workers, the railroad brotherhoods paralleled white unions in South Africa. They proudly celebrated their commitment to white supremacy. The railroad brotherhoods were by the 1910s both the "most racially exclusive, as well as the most powerful, unions in America."[46]

The steel sector shows the winding path of white supremacy in US unions. The Sons of Vulcan, the first durable union in the sector, was organized by the highly skilled puddlers in the 1870s and restricted membership to white men. However, the Vulcans' successor, the Amalgamated Association of Iron and Steel Workers, changed course in 1881 and allowed "colored lodges" to join with full membership rights. These included the African American puddlers in Garfield Lodge No. 92 at the Black Diamond Steelworks in Pittsburgh.[47] Despite some early efforts at inclusion, however, black union workers never gained a secure place, or respect, within the Amalgamated. At the 1888 Amalgamated Convention a faction of white workers attempted to re-insert "white" into the membership clause of the union's constitution, and in 1890, several locals protested against the hiring of black workers in unionized plants.[48] Largely excluded from the predominantly white unions, African Americans in the Pittsburgh District organized the "Colored Laboring Men's Protective Association" in 1889.[49] As F. J. Amormes recalled of the 1890s, the "Amalgamated did not bother with the Negroes in the unions. . . . The colored were doing mostly labor work, they did all the heavy work. They never got anything easy."[50] In 1893, the *Pittsburgh Daily Post* offered a sweeping and pessimistic assessment of the state of the Northern labor market and union movement:

> That negro mechanics do not have a fair show at the north is apparent from the fact that we find so few engaged in mechanical occupations on an equality with the whites. Negro labor at the north is almost entirely driven to menial occupations or the crudest forms of unskilled labor. The labor unions will not accept colored workmen as members, and the large numbers who have come here from the south are largely driven to idleness. . . . [T]he conclusion was reached that it was the natural course of events for the white workingmen, especially where organized, to exclude the blacks from employment whenever they were able to do so. . . . We do not believe that it is right. . . . [A]ll testimony goes to show the negro mechanic has better opportunities in the old slave states than in the north.[51]

The intertwined process of racial boundary-making and racialized strike-breaking thus comes into focus. Since both unions and rank-and-file white workers aimed to keep black workers out of Northern industrial jobs, the only means of accessing these jobs for many black workers was through strikebreaking.

In 1901, as the Amalgamated Iron and Steel Workers attempted to negotiate a contract with US Steel, black workers feared that "the unionizing of all the mills will leave them completely out," and thus plans were made for "a National negro labor union" to counter the effort of white workers to exclude them from the industry.[52] In August of 1901, the *Post* reported that black workers, long denied membership in the Amalgamated, were not likely to be moved by eleventh-hour appeals for solidarity:

> The negro laborers of McKeesport held a mass meeting last night in the Bethlehem Baptist Church. A resolution was passed in which the negro workmen state they will not organize and will have nothing to do with the Amalgamated Association. Application will be made at once for positions in the local mills. The colored men are bitter against the Amalgamated. Many of them in the past few years have made application for membership in the association, but in every instance were refused admittance. Recently organizers of the association have been about attempting to form an organization of colored workmen, but the offer has been refused and the colored laborers say that now that the Amalgamated is in trouble it need not look for any assistance from them.[53]

A 1902 resolution from the annual convention of the Amalgamated called for renewed efforts to organize black workers. However, the real aim of inclusion in this instance was to control black workers and prevent them from gaining access to skilled jobs higher in the production hierarchy.[54] White workers in the Amalgamated organized hate strikes against the employment of black workers. In 1906, an Amalgamated strike by a local in Alabama ended when the company agreed to the local union's demand to "discharge all niggers."[55] When the decimated Amalgamated signaled a belated willingness to organize black workers in 1907, there was little reason to believe that the leadership's commitment could counter rank-and-file opposition to cooperation with black workers.[56] These tensions produced the whites-only secession of the puddler elite in a revived Sons of Vulcan in 1907.[57] R. R. Wright wrote for the Pittsburgh Survey in 1914 that the "general opinion of the Negro men I talked with was that the unions were a hindrance rather than a help to them."[58] The "whole history of unionism in the Pittsburgh steel industry as far as the Negroes are concerned has been the attempt on the part of the white workingmen to use the [black workers] to their advantage, without giving any corresponding advantage to them." According to Wright, many "intelligent Negro workmen" were in "a quandary," since they believed "most fervently in the ideals of labor unions," but experience had taught them to keep their distance from predominantly white unions.[59]

Beyond the steel industry, Pittsburgh reveals broader patterns of racial discrimination by AFL craft unions, and, where black workers were allowed to join, clear efforts to keep them subordinated to white leadership. Unions played a key role in enforcing occupational bars. A bricklayer from Virginia became a porter and a carpenter from North Carolina became a janitor after the local unions in Pittsburgh refused them membership. A printer from Baltimore was allowed entry to the local union in Pittsburgh, but found it impossible to secure employment since white workers refused to work alongside him.[60] During a 1918 "Meeting of Mechanics" among African American union men in Pittsburgh, a black cement mason observed that "no Negroes have been taken into the Union as cement masons during the last three years," despite applications from "several . . . well qualified" men. This cement mason remained convinced "Negroes should go into the Unions but that the white Unions absolutely are opposed to taking Negroes."[61]

Rather than integration into unions as powerless subordinates, black workers often demanded separate locals that would provide more direct leadership and influence. In Pittsburgh the white plasterers local insisted that black plasterers join the white local "as individuals," but the black workers refused since they believed that as part of the white local they would "not be given the opportunity to work the same jobs with white plasterers and the Union [would] handicap them instead of helping."[62] A study in 1924 found that the Brotherhood of Carpenters had twenty-five locals and 5,200 members in the Pittsburgh District, but there were only fifteen African Americans carpenters among this number.[63] A 1929 report argued that the "city federation of unions" functioned by "driving black men from their jobs by merely threatening them or the owner" with a strike across the building trades.[64] The Bricklayers constitution provided for disciplinary measures against racist members, but as the report noted, "discrimination [was] easy to experience but most difficult to prove."[65]

Waterfront work was one of the few areas in which a significant number of black workers joined AFL unions in the early twentieth century as part of the International Longshoremen's Association (ILA). But black workers were generally deeply dissatisfied with their subordinate position within the ILA. In Baltimore, after the black workers in integrated ILA locals felt controlled by their white fellow unionists, they applied to the international for a separate charter. However, the white Baltimore members attempted to block this, demanding the international issue a separate charter to the black workers only for "dock men," which would have confined the black workers to the most irregular and lowest-paid work in the port.[66] The ILA overruled the local white workers and issued a new charter for Baltimore's black longshoremen in Local 858. Much like the plasterers in Pittsburgh, black longshoremen in Baltimore preferred their own segregated local due to the hostile treatment they experienced at the hands of their fellow white unionists.

Hate Strikes and Rank-and-File White Supremacy

Was working-class racism a top-down process, imposed from above by elites, or a bottom-up, grassroots process, tied to workers' everyday experiences getting work, protecting their jobs, and fighting for better conditions? While capitalist managers were certainly eager to exploit racial divisions, from the late nineteenth century forward the construction of racial boundaries was primarily driven by processes of working-class formation. Increasingly, white supremacy permeated the US labor movement not through the top-down policies of officials, but through the bottom-up pressure of workers. As a report from the Pittsburgh Urban League concluded, regardless of what labor leaders or constitutions might say in favor of equality, there was a powerful "sentiment against the negro in the rank and file of the white workers."[67] White railroad workers were particularly outspoken in their commitment to white supremacy. As one union carmen explained in 1905, "I was born with an abolitionist father; but when the time does come that I must sit down in social equality with the Negro . . . I want to be carried away to the nearest insane asylum."[68] Even within unions that organized substantial numbers of black workers, such as the ILA, white racism was potent. On the New York waterside in the 1920s, informal committees of white longshoremen "went from pier to pier asking the stevedores to give preference to white labor," and while this action was officially "frowned on" by the union, when the president of the local representing black workers complained to the international, "white officials . . . refused to have anything to do with him."[69] To justify their hesitance to hire black workers, employers pointed to the opposition of their white workers. In the early 1920s, Baltimore employers offered ten reasons for not hiring black workers, many of which (italicized) centered on the opposition of white workers:

1. Traditional policy of the plant not to employ Negroes.
2. *Fear of racial difficulties if whites and Negroes are introduced into the same plant.*
3. *Fear of the objection of white workers and the resultant labor difficulties.*
4. Traditional beliefs about the Negro which concern their mentality and character. . . .
5. Fear of bringing negroes into contact with white women workers.
6. Lack of training of Negroes for certain jobs.
7. Unsatisfactory experience with Negro workers in the past.
8. *Advocacy of certain jobs as belonging exclusively to the white race.*

9. Expense that would be involved in making alterations in the building to accommodate white and Negro workers separately.

10. *Objection of labor unions.*[70]

Decision-making in hiring was clearly shaped by the anticipated reactions of white workers. As the *Baltimore Afro-American* reported: "Employers tell us that they do not object to the employment of Negroes but their workers do (meaning their white workers.)"[71] The pronouncements of labor leaders, union constitutions, and local membership policies have received substantial attention; at the foundation of all these was vehement racial boundary enforcement by ordinary white workers.

By the first decade of twentieth of the century, growing African American migration to large cities, and their visibility as strikebreakers, motivated white workers to draw racial boundaries and defend their favorable position in the labor market. However, intense hostility and exclusion was not universal, but reactive to migration from the countryside, expanding black populations, and the visibility of racialized strikebreaking. In 1908, journalist Ray Stannard Baker found that in in small Northern towns, with a small, stable African American population, "discrimination is hardly noticeable," and black workers were allowed to "enter the trades, find places in the shops, or even follow competitive business callings" without provoking white hostility. However, in larger industrial centers, where African American migration centered, there were only "places for the coloured man at the bottom," since "many labor unions, especially in the skilled trades, [were] hostile to Negroes," and the "feeling among union labour men has undoubtedly grown more intense in the last few years owing to the common use of Negroes as strike breakers."[72] W. P. Livingston, an avowed white supremacist who saw racial hatred as a "sentinel keeping watch and ward over the evolutionary process," was also attentive to economic forces driving racial boundary-making at the turn of the century. In Northern cities "where there has been an increase in the coloured community the avenues in which they make a living have been steadily closed."[73] Pittsburgh illustrates the narrowing of occupational opportunities for black workers as the size of the African American community increased in the late nineteenth century. The percentage of employed black men working as laborers at the bottom of the production hierarchy increased from 30.9 percent in 1870 to 53.2 percent in 1900. The impact of narrowing occupational boundaries can best be illustrated by focusing on the stable, local black workers in Pittsburgh who had been born in Pennsylvania. For these non-migrant African Americans, the range of occupational options also narrowed: the share working as laborers increased from 21.6 percent in 1870 to 36.7 percent in 1900, and the share working in crafts declined from 6.5 percent in 1870 to only 4.4 percent in 1900.[74]

Behind the narrowing occupational options for black workers, hate strikes manifested the appalling power of rank-and-file white supremacy. Hate strikes were pervasive in the 1890s. These were usually informal strikes by white workers that aimed to drive black workers out of particular jobs or off specific worksites. Although hate strikes during the 1940s have been widely studied, there has been comparatively little attention to the longer history of hate strikes by white workers.[75] The struggle between white and black workers for the control of desirable jobs has a history deep into the antebellum era. The caulker riots of 1858 and 1859 in Baltimore saw gangs of white workers drive black workers out of this relatively skilled arena of craft work on the eve of the Civil War.[76] In 1865, white ship-caulkers in Ohio went on strike to "maintain the superiority of white men."[77] In his 1902 study of the black working class, W. E. B. Du Bois highlighted the importance of hate strikes in the prior decade, and noted that one of the largest hate strikes on record occurred in Pittsburgh in 1890 and involved some four hundred white workers who went on strike for eight months against the employment of black workers.[78] Throughout the 1890s, informal crowds of Irish and Welsh workers were reported to have "employed 'Direct Action' . . . with a vengeance in keeping Negroes out of the crowds of job seekers at steel mill gates" in Pittsburgh.[79]

Hate strikes imposed boundaries on access to jobs, and in conjunction with unions' exclusionary policies drove black workers to become eager strikebreakers. When the Amalgamated attempted to relocate three black union workers on strike to a non-striking steel plant in another district during the 1901 steel strike, the white Amalgamated members in the non-striking plant refused to work alongside the relocated black union members. This threatened hate strike against fellow unionists convinced the disillusioned black workers to return to Pittsburgh, denounce the racism of their fellow white Amalgamated members, and encourage other black workers to return to work and break the strike.[80] In Baltimore, "a large number of bricklayers went out" on strike in 1903 "because negro laborers were employed to fill in some concrete foundations" in a major building project for the Naval Academy.[81] Workers were not the only ones who could go on hate strikes. During the 1905 Teamsters strike in Chicago, over two thousand white elementary school students went on hate strike by walking out of their classes after black strikebreakers delivered coal to their schools, leading to the arrest of two eleven-year-old girls accused of being ringleaders.[82]

As figure 5.1 shows, hate strikes accounted for between 4 and 10 percent of all strikes between 1881 and 1905. Leah Boustan's impressive study

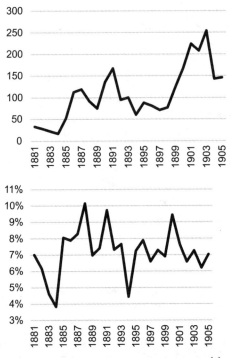

FIGURES 5.1A AND B Hate strikes in the US, 1881–1905. (a) number of hate strikes; (b) hate strikes as a percentage of all strikes. *Source: Twenty-First Annual Report of the Commissioner of Labor, 1906: Strikes and Lockouts* (Washington, DC: Government Printing Office, 1907), 580–614.

of migration and labor markets, while attentive to employer discrimination, passes over hate strikes as "rare," and thus misses the importance of grassroots, rank-and-file white supremacy in shaping the North's occupational structure.[83] In its report, the US Labor Commissioner delicately described these as "strikes against certain persons," but as an explanatory note clarified, they were in fact largely rooted in white workers' "objections against working with negroes or foreigners, etc."[84] Although the statistics are merely suggestive, they indicate a sizable and sustained role for hate strikes in the late nineteenth century, targeting primarily black workers, but also immigrant workers, and in certain cases, women workers as well.

The Baltimore Federation of Labor routinely investigated informal outbreaks that erupted when white workers felt that racial boundaries had been violated. In support of the Painters' union, the BFL's grievance committee confronted a building site manager where "several members had seen the colored porter painting on the outside of the building."[85] In 1925, a delegate for Carpenters Local 101 reported with alarm that "colored laborers are doing carpenters work on the new Knights of Columbus Building" in Baltimore.[86] In 1929, two hundred men working on Baltimore's port development program struck against a contractor who was "engaging Negro laborers and other common labor to string wires for electrical construction," thus trespassing on the craft boundaries of white workers.[87] Although hate strikes primarily targeted black workers, other non-white workers were also targeted. When two hundred Puerto Ricans arrived at the Sparrows Point steel plant on December 18, 1918 "to be utilized on laboring work, 5,000 employees walked out" in a massive hate strike by the white workforce.[88] In 1919 the BFL appointed a Special Committee to investigate "the Porto Rican labor question at Sparrows Pt.," but the labor officials were unable to determine "who was responsible for the presence of these men in this country."[89] The most horrific hate strikes of the 1920s occurred on the railroads. Throughout the early twentieth century, railroad workers organized multiple large hate strikes against the employment of black workers.[90] In an effort to preserve skilled positions in the operating crews for white workers, disguised assailants killed or wounded sixteen African Americans on the Illinois Central system during 1921. Horace Hurd, murdered in 1921, was found with a note pinned to his mangled corpse: "Let this be a lessen to all nigger brakemen."[91] This vigilante pressure by white workers contributed to a 26 percent reduction in the share of trainmen positions held by black workers in the South during the 1920s.[92]

Conflicts in the labor market over who had access to what jobs were at the center of working-class white supremacy, but racial boundaries were reinforced by experiences in the broader Jim Crow structures that consolidated in the early twentieth century. As the minutes of the Baltimore Federation of Labor suggest, Jim Crow practices in the broader community caused tensions within the local labor movement. A delegate from Baltimore's Longshoremen Local 858, a union of black dockworkers, noted that there were "no accommodations at Capt. Logan's Hospital [available] for colored people," and thus he questioned the BFL's financial support for the institution. Delegates from Local 858 also complained that during a recent BFL mass meeting held at a local theater, the "colored men" were required to "go to one section of the theatre."[93] The *Baltimore Afro-American* was not impressed by the BFL's excuses for this incident of segregation, claiming that the president "tried to pour oil on the troubled waters" by refusing to acknowledge the racism of the theater.[94] These experiences led the head of Local 858 to say that he "found it distasteful" to participate in a broader labor movement that tolerated Jim Crow practices and where many unions continued to ban black workers.[95] In 1924, a black union delegate for Laborers 644 in Baltimore "complained of the treatment of colored people at Riverview," a park, during the Federation's Labor Day festivities. Again the BFL officials deflected by claiming that "it was the Riverview Park employees and not the Federation who protested the attendance of the colored people at the park." Indicating the disinterest of the white unionists in hearing the concerns of the black workers in the laborers local, a motion to send the complaint to the grievance committee was overruled by a motion to table the issue, killing further discussion.[96] These protests seem to have had little impact on how the white unions of the BFL planned social events. In 1925 the union's "Vagabond Players" performed a racist skit with the title "Mixed Marriages."[97] That any black workers remained within these racist AFL unions seems extraordinary.

African Americans and the Labor Movement in the 1920s

From the era of the American Revolution to the present, African Americans developed a radical political tradition that has provided the backbone of the drive for egalitarian democracy in the United States. Despite the racial boundary-making of organized white workers, a remarkable number of African Americans remained committed to the principle of labor solidarity. Despite a white labor movement that gave little reason for optimism, the democratic tradition of African American politics supported a vision of an inclusive, unified working-class struggle that transcended racial boundaries.

Typical of this commitment was the *Baltimore Afro-American*, a leading black paper that proclaimed on its masthead its vision of inclusive, industrial unionism. The *Afro-American* provides insight into how parts of the black community viewed the AFL and organized labor in the aftermath of World War I. Acknowledging the centrality of racialized strikebreaking, the paper observed that there was "prejudice against and fear of colored workers due to their frequent and recently conspicuous use as strike-breakers."[98] Rather than celebrate strikebreaking, however, the *Afro-American* suggested the power of organized labor to its readers: "There was a time when the coal miner and the railroad worker were at the bottom of the list. They were the lowest-paid laborers. Where are they now? At the top. How did they get there? Labor unions."[99] In June of 1919, the *Afro-American* covered the Atlantic Coast District convention of the ILA, noting that some "forty colored delegates" were hosted by two black dockworkers from Baltimore who served on the welcoming committee.[100] According to the African American ILA delegates, "In recent years, men of our race have been actively engaged in the movement to get our people into the ranks of organized labor."[101] While generally critical of the Federation, the paper was willing to praise the BFL when it acted with justice toward the black community. In February 1920, the *Afro-American* was impressed that the Baltimore Federation of Labor, "without a dissenting vote," had gone "on record . . . as favoring the same pay for colored teachers in county schools as whites receive." According to a BFL delegate, there "was no color line with labor people," and the *Afro-American* admitted that while this was clearly an exaggeration, the "Federation has shown that [this] rings true in a number of instances."[102]

While the *Afro-American* was willing to give the BFL credit when it opposed racist inequality, it also promoted potentially more egalitarian forms of organizing outside the AFL. Black workers were urged to "Join Big Union of 'Pick and Shovel' Men" as part of the independent Labor Union of America that organized under the motto: "no segregation, no limitation as to creed or color." The nature of this ephemeral organization is somewhat unclear, but it appears to be one of the many independent, black unions organized in the early twentieth century. The Labor Union of America claimed to have five hundred members in Baltimore, and one representative "declared it to be the only Union for colored working men." Organizers made a point to stress that "we are independent of the Federation of Labor."[103] The *Afro-American* also provided space in 1920 for a long article by Ben Fletcher, a leading IWW organizer and longshoremen from Philadelphia. Fletcher condemned the AFL on two points: its outdated craft organization and its racism. Fletcher wrote that the AFL had "completely divorced" the black worker and left him "ignored by the trade unions." According to Fletcher, the "leaders of the American Federation of Labor [were] bitterly opposed to the Negro worker becoming a factor in the affairs of the labor movement." In contrast, the IWW organized industrially and was founded on the principle that "race prejudice must not and will not be permitted" in the organization.[104]

The immediate postwar years appeared to be hopeful. Perhaps the AFL unions would change, or perhaps a rival organization would spring up to organize inclusively. By the end of the decade, this early optimism had faded. As William Jones noted in the *Afro-American* in 1928, the "liberal pronouncements of labor leaders" had little importance since "the Negro in the long run is controlled by his daily experiences with organized white labor." Given that "the main function of craft unions is to control jobs so as to control wages," the reality of the labor movement as experienced by African Americans was that "unions limit the employment of Negro workers in favor of the white members."[105] By the end of the 1920s, African Americans had come to an accurate if bleak understanding of the US labor movement: since craft and racial boundaries reinforced each other, the craft unions of the AFL served white workers while harming black workers.

Among black observers, one union was often held up as an exception to the exclusionary patterns of the AFL: the United Mine Workers (UMW), the only major industrial union in the American Federation of Labor. The UMW would go on to break from the AFL in the 1930s to create the Congress of Industrial Organizations (CIO). That black workers joined the CIO in such large numbers in the 1930s was in large part due to the favorable reputation gained by the UMW among black workers in the 1920s. In 1916, the *Baltimore Afro-American*, while warning that "the American Federation of Labor has never concerned itself about the welfare of the great mass of colored labor in this country," observed that the "United Mineworkers Union is a notable instance where the colored workmen have received a fair show."[106] The UMW had fifty thousand members in the Pittsburgh District in 1924, and roughly one-sixth (eight thousand) were African Americans. A survey of the unionized black miners around Pittsburgh reported that there were no limits on the jobs black workers could occupy, and the pay was attractive.[107] A researcher for the Pittsburgh Urban League found that "Negro members of the United Mine Workers seem quite happy in being affiliated with the organization," and reported the words of one black worker: "It is the greatest labor organization in the world and the only one affiliated with the American Federation of Labor which is concerned about the Negro workers and gives him a fair deal."[108] Abram Lincoln Harris, as a graduate student summer intern at the Urban League in 1924, offered a sharp contrast between the miners and the craft unions of the AFL. The UMW appealed to black workers on the basis of class solidarity, while the American Federation of Labor was dominated by a "white constituency possessed of the traditional American color psychosis."[109] By the 1920s, African American observers had a clear understanding of the US labor movement. Strikebreaking and union discrimination had created a vicious feedback loop in which the boundaries of white supremacy and craft reinforced each other.

Conclusion

White supremacy, for all its durability in US history, has also been malleable, continuously transformed by underlying terrains of inequality and domination. The 1890s were a key pivot during which both craft and racial boundaries hardened in the United States. The Knights of Labor and the AFL entered the 1890s officially committed to egalitarian racial inclusion, but the mass mobilization of racialized strikebreaking in the 1890s pressured organized labor into a defensive, racist retreat. Certainly a variety of factors drove the consolidation of Jim Crow white supremacy more broadly in the 1890s, but for organized labor, a regionally and racially divided labor market, increasing competition for desirable jobs, and racialized strikebreaking played a leading role in this decisive hardening of racial boundaries.

Even a union fundamentally committed to anti-racism and careful to protect the interests of black and white workers in an egalitarian fashion crumbled under the pressure of entrenched working-class white supremacy. Peter Cole's history of the remarkably heroic IWW longshoremen's union in Philadelphia highlights the achievements and ultimately the stark limits of a union with deep egalitarian commitments. Faced with a lockout in 1922, the IWW local was crushed by strikebreakers, many of them African Americans from the South, others sent by the International Longshoremen's Association of New York. Cole concludes, "Despite its radical, mixed-race leadership, large black membership, and proven commitment to racial equality, Local 8 still suffered from racial divisions, exacerbated by the Great Migration and rising segregation. The lockout indicates just how difficult it was to maintain an interracial union in this era."[110]

National Boundaries

IMMIGRATION RESTRICTION IN
THE SHADOW OF SLAVERY

As workers became increasingly mobile in the late nineteenth century, labor movements had to confront the movement of labor. Riots erupted across France in the 1890s to protest the hiring of low-wage migrant workers from Italy and Belgium. French socialists severely limited the number of immigrants who could be hired on municipal public works. In Germany's Ruhr industrial district, migrant Polish mineworkers were dismissed as "a less educated race" and nativist regulations were issued requiring proficiency in the German language to work in the mines.[1] Working-class nativism was global, but in certain cases, such as Australia and the United States, immigration restriction became a central strategy of the organized working class. Just as with craft and racial boundaries, the 1890s marked a shift by American organized labor on the question of European immigration. At the beginning of the 1890s the AFL had rejected anti-immigrant legislation. However, by the end of the decade, the AFL had become the leading organized force supporting European immigration restriction in the US. The pivot of the 1890s placed the US labor movement on a path of anti-immigrant nativist politics that would endure throughout the twentieth century, with the AFL-CIO only shifting course in 2002, rejecting previous efforts to harden the border and limit entry, and instead expressing solidarity and support for newly arrived immigrants.[2] Nativist racial boundary-making erupted in the 1890s not only because of workers' increased mobility across capitalism's uneven economic geography, but also due to the increasing material salience of citizenship status. An emerging welfare state made it increasingly important to distinguish eligible residents from ineligible outsiders for redistributive welfare programs.[3] As workers embraced nativist restriction, governments in the late nineteenth century devised the first guest worker programs, which "aimed to give employers access to foreign workers who nativists sought to ban."[4]

The nativist reaction against immigrant workers in the United States must be understood in the context of the longer history of slavery, which left all workers at the bottom of the production hierarchy, both enslaved and wage laborers, in a precariously unprotected position. By the 1890s, organized workers had long been vehemently opposed to Chinese immigration. The 1870s witnessed the rise of the California Workingmen's Party, an anti-capitalist, racist, and anti-immigrant political movement that stormed to power on the West Coast with a critique of Chinese migrant labor deeply rooted in the anti-slavery politics of the Civil War era.[5] The success of the Workingmen's Party pushed the national parties to adopt the Chinese Exclusion Act in 1882. The subordination, hostility, and violence experienced by immigrant workers in the US was in part the legacy of antebellum production structures that accepted violence and brutality toward replaceable laborers. Most directly, slavery and immigration restriction were linked because internal migration within the US and transatlantic migration were understood as interlinked threats of low-wage, compliant labor that capitalists could use to crush native-born, white workers. The 1890s was a period of both intensified strikebreaking and unprecedented mass migration. The smaller, highly visible, and consequential movement of African Americans leaving the near-periphery of the US South and the massive flood of impoverished Europeans leaving southern and eastern Europe were similarly understood by workers in the 1890s as connected, combined threats to native-born white workers. Mass migration did not always result in nativist hostility, however. The racially and regionally divided labor market in the US can be compared to Argentina, which experienced nearly double the rate of immigration as the US, but whose labor movement did not turn to nativist protection or embrace racialized craft boundaries. As the closing section of this chapter will show, mass immigration alone cannot explain the potent combination of racism, craft protection, and nativism in the US. Rather, regionally and racially divided labor markets, high wage differentials, and distinct immigrant groups hierarchically positioned within the occupational structure produced a labor movement that turned decisively to racist nativism in the 1890s.

The importance of nativism has not been missed by scholars of US labor history, and the reinforcing boundaries of craft and nativism has drawn substantial attention. Gwendolyn Mink noted the "admixture of race consciousness and job consciousness within the AFL," and argued that given this narrow craft structure, the "very job consciousness that first made unionists out of workers then made unionists into exclusionists."[6] Craft organization and nativism shared an approach to managing the labor market based on restriction and exclusion. During the 1897 debate where the AFL resoundingly endorsed a literacy test to restrict immigration, delegates explicitly connected craft restriction and immigration restriction. As one representative of the Cigar Makers stated: "If trade-unions have a moral right to restrict the number of apprentices . . . then they have a right to ask for legislation to restrict immigration."[7] Scholars have likewise recognized that the 1890s were pivotal for the AFL, marked by a shift from an internationalist commitment to welcoming all (white) workers at the start of the decade to a militant commitment to immigration restriction by its close. David Brian Robertson notes that in the 1890s, "a coalition of workers and other interests gradually formed around further immigration restriction." After President Cleveland vetoed a literacy test passed by Congress in 1897, the AFL "took a much stronger anti-immigration stand than it had before." Previous divisions over immigration restriction disappeared, and the AFL "grew increasingly supportive of strict immigration limits" in the early twentieth century.[8] The turn to racist nativism in the 1890s must be understood not in isolation, as is often the case in studies of migration, but in the broader context of the legacies of slavery, in particular a racially and regionally divided labor market that left workers at the bottom of the production hierarchy exceptionally vulnerable.

Workers Divided: Native Craftsmen and Immigrant Laborers

Since the Jacksonian era, artisans, journeymen, and mechanics have understood themselves in opposition not only to employers, but equally, if not more so, in contrast to laborers and helpers who were totally subordinated to a proprietor's power: in the most extreme case, the slave, but also the common laborer. Low-wage labor at the bottom of the production hierarchy in the United States, when not done by slaves, was akin to slavery, and was outside the house of honorable white labor as it was understood by nineteenth-century craft workers.[9] The proximity of slavery during the nineteenth century meant that the boundary between the independent artisan and the common laborer was reinforced by the boundary between freedom and enslavement. This division between craft workers and common laborers persisted after emancipation and channeled poor, newly arrived immigrants into vulnerable positions at the bottom of the production hierarchy.

The segregated and racialized arrangement of the occupational hierarchy can be clearly seen in table 6.1. Typical low-wage workers, such as steel laborers, longshoremen, or railway laborers, were a group dominated by immigrants and African Americans. Building laborers provide a telling exception, reflecting the remarkable power of the building trades unions'

TABLE 6.1 Stratification of US occupations by nativity and race in 1910

Bottom of the production hierarchy	Total	Percentage		
		Native white	Foreign born	African American
Steel laborers	194,329	22.9%	69.6%	6.9%
Longshoremen	51,841	21.1%	56.3%	22.4%
Railroad laborers	453,925	32.1%	50.3%	15.4%
*Building laborers	856,004	50.5%	29.3%	17.4%
Top of the production hierarchy				
Steel crafts	31,223	63.5%	32.1%	2.5%
Locomotive engineers	96,229	89.1%	10.5%	0.4%
Locomotive firemen	76,381	84.8%	8.4%	6.8%
Carpenters	682,490	71.7%	24.0%	4.4%

Source: United States Census, 1910, Volume 4, Statistics of Occupations, table VI, "Total Persons Ten Years of Age and Over Engaged in Specified Occupations in Each Industry or Service Group, Classified by Age Periods, Color or Race, Nativity, and Parentage, and Sex."

alliance with urban political machines. Building laborers earned far more than other laborers, were often unionized in conjunction with the local building crafts, and here alone were native-born white workers in the majority. The most elevated of the craft labor aristocrats were the railway locomotive engineers, whose union was not only fiercely committed to white supremacy, but also composed almost entirely of native-born white men. The locomotive firemen, a stepping-stone position to engineer, were similar, but here, Southern railroads had effectively used black firemen as strikebreakers, creating a small workforce of black firemen (6.8 percent) compared to the negligible number of black locomotive engineers (0.4 percent). The carpenters, by far the largest craft occupation in the early twentieth century, were dominated by native white workers. The steel crafts (molders, puddlers, rollers, roughers, finishers, and heaters) were similar, with roughly two-thirds white native-born workers, one-third immigrants, and a negligible number of African American workers.

Immigrants entered urban labor markets on terms set in part by the agrarian conditions in their homelands. Immigrants in jobs at the top of the production hierarchy were usually workers who arrived under more favorable circumstances. They came from more prosperous, less oppressive agrarian regimes: English-speaking workers from Britain, and more broadly, independent farmers from Germany and Scandinavia. In contrast, the immigrants in jobs at the bottom of the production hierarchy were generally workers who arrived under more desperate circumstances: southern and eastern European peasants who had lost access to land, as well as large numbers of Jews fleeing racist pogroms. Occupational stratification among immigrants is typically understood in terms of cultural, ethnic, and religious differences. However, their hierarchical positioning in the US labor market was also shaped by the structural position of the rural peripheries from which they migrated. The fallback position provided by rural origin points shaped decision-making in the urban labor markets where immigrants moved. Those migrating from regions where rural producers had greater access to land and political rights (northern Europe) could be selective and strategic when entering the US labor market. Those pushed to leave by lost access to land and political repression and violence (eastern and southern Europe) were more often forced into accepting the most immediately available options.

Marked as expendable by the shadow of slavery, immigrants at the bottom of the production hierarchy in the United States occupied a dangerous position: they were far more likely than native-born workers to be killed in industrial accidents. As W. E. B Du Bois wrote, "in no country in the civilized world did human life become so cheap."[10] As the Pittsburgh Survey noted in 1914, Slavic workers were "the greatest sufferers from accidents in the Pittsburgh region, for to their lot falls the heaviest and most dangerous work."[11] In describing victims of industrial accidents, a Pittsburgh steel foreman at the turn of the century recorded deaths for "five men and twelve hunkies," explicitly racializing the most vulnerable section of his workforce.[12] David Brody describes an "unbridgeable gulf" separating, in the parlance of the Pittsburgh District, "the 'Hunky' and 'English-speaking' workmen."[13] One native-born steelworker complained of being surrounded by "these Hunkies": "They don't seem like men to me hardly."[14] If US employers were distinctive, the main reason was that many employers had been enslavers up to 1865. This unquestionably left an enduring imprint on the outlook of the broader ruling class. As Gavin Wright has suggested, perhaps "the most enduring legacy of slavery . . . was the persistence of a bifurcated society in which economic elites did not identify with or internalize the well-being of the majority of the population."[15]

Given that full human standing was denied to immigrant workers, it was not surprising that a shocking death toll ensued. From 1906 to 1910 at one Pittsburgh steel plant, records indicate the disproportion of industrial harm: 4,936 immigrants suffered serious workplace injuries, as compared to only 761 native-born workers.[16] Underpinned by the disposability of racialized low-wage workers, the vulnerability of laborers at the bottom of the production hierarchy meant that the US was, and remains, an extremely dangerous place to work. In the late nineteenth century, US railway workers were more than twice as likely to be killed at work (one in every 357 employees) compared to English railway workers (one in 875).[17] In the early twentieth century, the rate of fatalities in US coal mines, where immigrants and black workers predominated, was three times as high as in the UK, and twice as high as in Prussia.[18] An appalled German trade union leader who visited the US prior to the outbreak of war in 1914 commented that "human life on the other side of the big pond [in America] is apparently given little value."[19] Governments "count what counts" to them; it is thus revealing that while the UK began to keep detailed and accurate statistics of workplace fatalities in the mid-nineteenth century, it was not until the 1970s that the US developed a reliable national system of tracking occupational deaths.[20] The disproportionate violence and death experienced by those at the bottom of the production hierarchy has endured to the present. As reports of undocumented immigrants killed at construction worksites remind us on a nearly daily basis, poor, newly arrived migrants continue to live under the shadow of slavery, their health and lives treated as expendable by employers and fellow workers.[21] A comparison of workplace fatalities in the US and the UK in recent years found that compared to the UK, manufacturing workers in the US were twice as likely to be killed at work and construction workers were three times as likely to be killed while working.[22]

Scholars have debated the significance of repressive violence during strikes in the US, but general statements about US workers as a whole are not possible. Crucially, as seen in table 6.2, violence during strikes was not evenly distributed. As Rick Halpern points out, "racial and ethnic stratification" fundamentally shaped how workers in the United States experienced repression and violence at the hands of employers and the state.[23] Some, in particular white, native-born craftsmen, especially those in the building trades, enjoyed extensive government protections. In contrast, immigrants and African Americans did not enjoy these protections and were particularly vulnerable to violence. Table 6.2 shows that the exceptionally high level of violence during strikes in the US was concentrated in specific sectors and among particular groups of workers. Fatalities during strikes were closely correlated with the share of immigrants in the sector. Mining had both the highest percentage of foreign-born workers and by far the highest rate of fatalities in strikes, followed closely by the steel industry. Unsurprisingly, given close alliances with urban political machines, very few workers were killed in building trades strikes. Elites did not hesitate to openly endorse violence against immigrant workers.

TABLE 6.2 Labor violence and foreign-born workers by industry in the US

	Fatalities in strikes per million workers, 1890–1909	Foreign-born workers in 1900
Railways	1.7	22.3%
Building	0.5	28.2%
Steel	5.6	35.8%
Mining	12.8	44.3%

Source: Data on strike mortality from Price Fishback, "An Alternative View of Violence in Labor Disputes in the Early 1900s: The Bituminous Coal Industry, 1890–1930," Labor History 36, no. 3 (1995): 429, table 12.1. United States Census, Part VII, General Tables, table 2, "Total Persons 10 Years of Age and Over Engaged in Each of 150 Groups," 10–12.

During the Pullman strike in 1894, Frederic Remington praised the cavalry and contrasted the "real American striker" who could be reasoned with against the "foreign trash" who required violent repression: "Eventually this unlicked mob will have to be shot up a little."[24]

The violence unleashed on immigrants, both as expendable bodies at work and as vulnerable protesters when striking, must be understood in conjunction with the broader vulnerability of racialized low-wage workers at the bottom of the production hierarchy. Those most subjected to violence, even after emancipation, were African American workers. While native-born white workers and their unions often enjoyed amicable relationships with state authorities, black workers were exceptionally susceptible to harsh and punitive policing. Generally discriminatory policing could be particularly punitive when black workers attempted to organize. When the black drivers in Baltimore quit work, one of the men who "used profane language" toward his employer "was arrested and committed to jail for thirty days."[25] Most horrifically, the lynching of African Americans provided the background for the widespread toleration of violence against immigrants at the turn of the century. Post-Redemption lynching was often rooted in economic struggles among black workers, sharecroppers, and landlords.[26]

Organized Labor's Pivot to Nativism in the 1890s

Before the 1890s, organized workers had expressed commitments to international solidarity and the importance of the United States as a refuge for the world's oppressed. In the 1880s, Terence Powderly rejected nativism since the Knights were "internationalist" and restricting immigration could be "construed as opposing [a] portion of humanity."[27] The AFL repeatedly debated immigration restriction in the early 1890s, and the organization repeatedly refused to support such restrictions. During these "sharply divided" debates, defenders of immigration argued that "the brotherhood allows no diminution in the measure of its love. . . . Before all else it sets universality, solidarity."[28] But in 1892, the Knights committed to a literacy test, and in 1897 the AFL also put its weight behind a nativist literacy test that would have severely limited the entry of southern and eastern Europeans.[29]

Why did organized workers pivot to nativist immigration restriction in the 1890s? In the late nineteenth century, hostility to internal migration by African Americans and transatlantic migration by southern and eastern Europeans became conjoined. In the partisan politics of the 1880s, tariff protection for industry could be extended by analogy to labor protection through restrictions on immigration. Democrats, banging their white-supremacist drum, pilloried Republicans for protecting capital with tariffs while leaving labor unprotected. According to Thompson Murch (D-ME), described by the *Pittsburgh Daily Post* as "the leading labor representative" in Congress in 1880, while the "corporations and big capitalists" enjoyed tariff protection, they "don't want labor protected" since "the practice of some of our manufacturers" was to make profits by "importing pauper labor from Europe, negro labor from the South, and Coolie labor from China."[30] After the 1880 election, the *Pittsburgh Daily Post* observed that "workingmen" had learned to distrust the promises of Republicans to protect labor, since recently "some of [the] Republican humanitarians" had imported "low price negro labor from the South" and turned "white men adrift and fill[ed] their places with cheap and brutal negroes."[31] This charge was again repeated in 1882, with the claim that Republican manufacturers who campaigned to "protect" workers through the tariff had in fact "imported cheap negro labor from the South and pauper labor from Europe to take the place of white workingmen."[32] And yet again in 1884, Republicans were charged with having "imported cheap foreign labor from Europe, and cheap negro labor from the South."[33] In 1891, during a debate in the Pennsylvania Senate on a "provision prohibiting the employment of unnaturalized persons" on road construction for state highways, Senator William Flinn, a leading Pittsburgh building contractor, stated that he "would be glad to see our immigration laws changed so as to shut out the Italian and other cheap laborers," since if "this were done the colored laborers of the South . . . would come North, where their labor was needed."[34] Flinn, who had already gained some notoriety for recruiting black workers from the South, seemed to suggest that nativist hopes were futile, since one supply of cheap labor could be substituted for another. A letter to the editor by a Pittsburgh worker blamed the declining position of the craft worker on "the cheaper foreign and negro labor imported by the Steel Trust and its subsidiaries."[35] As was typical, it was not static competition within the labor market that workers rejected, but rather how migrants appeared to shift the balance of power in favor of capital and transform the nature of work.

In the 1890s the American Protective Association (APA) exploded as a mass, anti-Catholic political movement. The literacy test, inspired by disenfranchisement efforts in the Jim Crow South, gained significant political traction after 1893 as a means of reducing low-wage labor immigration from southern and eastern Europe.[36] Over the mid-1890s, the anti-Catholic APA became a mass movement and a significant force in US politics, a parallel to the working-class Protestant Orangeism that was so powerful in Liverpool during the nineteenth century.[37] Union leaders were extremely wary of conflict between Protestants and Catholics within the labor movement. Protestants still dominated the craft unions of the labor movement, but there was a sizable minority of Irish Catholics as well. In 1894 a report to the AFL convention warned that "the greatest need of the day was the abolition" of the APA.[38] Nevertheless, the APA enjoyed considerable support among rank-and-file union members, and many unions turned to anti-immigrant advocacy at the local level.[39]

The nativist APA had a complex relationship with the labor movement in the 1890s, denouncing inclusive unions that incorporated large numbers of immigrant, Catholic workers while remaining neutral toward the AFL craft unions that remained predominantly native-born and Protestant. The APA manifesto committed the organization to the "protection of our citizen laborers."[40] The APA was a relentless antagonist of the Knights in particular (Powderly was a Catholic) and inclusive unionism in general: Debs as leader of the American Railway Union was accused of secretly being a "Romanist."[41] The APA's *Patriot* newspaper described Debs as the "grand steerer of Micks, the Huns, the Slavs and the Dagos in their mission of misrule, anarchy, and revolution."[42] In 1887, Cardinal Gibbons of Baltimore had traveled to Rome to counsel the Catholic Church against condemning Henry George and the Knights of Labor, since many Catholics had joined these movements. This plea was seized upon by the APA as proof of "favoritism among Catholics for the 'socialism' of George and the 'anarchism' of the Knights of Labor."[43] While the APA was intensely hostile to the Knights of Labor and to Debs's American Railway Union, the association took a more neutral position toward Gompers and the AFL.[44] Although the APA enjoyed only a brief efflorescence in the

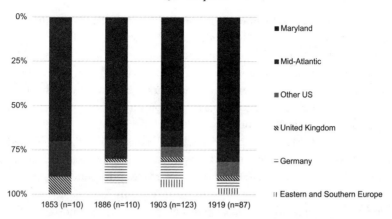

FIGURE 6.1 Birthplace of union officials in the Baltimore labor movement. *Sources:* Labor leaders identified in the *Baltimore Sun and Daily Record* for 1853 and from official state reports. Thomas C. Weeks, *First Biennial Report of the Bureau of Industrial Statistics and Information of Maryland, 1884–1885* (Baltimore: Guggenheimer, Weil & Co., 1886); *Twelfth Annual Report of the Bureau of Statistics and Information of Maryland 1903* (Baltimore: The Sun Book and Job Printing, 1904), "Labor Organizations in Maryland," foldout between pages 65 and 66; *Twenty-Eighth Annual Report of the Maryland State Board of Labor and Statistics 1919* (Baltimore: [n.p.], 1920), 228–40. Birthplace established through identifying matches in the manuscript censuses from 1850, 1880, 1900, and 1920 on Ancestry.com. Compiled with research assistance from Nicole Ramirez. Full "Baltimore Labor Leaders" dataset available at https://www.rudibatzell.com/data-sets.

mid-1890s, it left a deep mark on the US labor movement by consolidating rank-and-file anti-immigrant sentiment and attacking inclusive forms of labor organizing as dangerous and un-American. In part because of the political terrain that the APA had helped to consolidate, labor support for immigration restriction after 1897 was constant.[45]

In addition, the ease with which the US labor movement embraced nativism was in part the result of a leadership that was often largely native born, as seen in the profile of Baltimore's labor leadership given in figure 6.1. In Baltimore, the officials of local unions were highly unrepresentative of the local working class. At four points of relative strength for organized labor in Baltimore, the manuscript census was used to explore the background of Baltimore labor leaders and union officials. Even as a massive wave of immigration transformed the United States in the late nineteenth and early twentieth century, there was little reflection of this transformation in the leadership of Baltimore's unions, with between 80 and 90 percent of union officials born in the United States, most of them locally in the state of Maryland. In both 1903 and 1919, only two African

American union officials could be identified: in 1903, Joseph Kane of the Teamsters and James Johnson of the Hod Carriers Union; in 1919, George Bell of the Colored Waiters Unions No. 836 and David J. Brown of the Ship Yard Laborers No. 15980. While migration transformed the composition of the working class, the leadership of the labor movement in Baltimore remained essentially unchanged.

During the 1890s, many local labor unions became fixated on the threat of immigration. The District Council (DC) of Carpenters in Western Pennsylvania became preoccupied with immigration in early 1894. In January, the DC received complaints from a laborers' local against the "methods of those in Power in Furnishing employment in the Parks to Unnaturalized residents in Preference to citizens and taxpayers of the city."[46] The next month the DC endorsed a "Bill for the better Protection of American Labor," and the "various local unions" of the Carpenters were urged to take action in favor of immigration restriction.[47] In March of 1894, in response to an inquiry from the US Senate Finance Committee, the DC argued that the solution to the labor problem was "restriction of Imigration [sic] and less hours of labor," explaining that "Immigration has been the means of displacing thousands of men from regular employment."[48] In 1895, to protect the jobs of native-born building trades workers, Pennsylvania passed a law "providing that none but citizens of the United States shall be employed in any capacity in the erection, enlargement, or improvement of any public building or public work within the Commonwealth."[49] The United Mine Workers, despite being a largely immigrant union, was led by "white English speaking" officials who saw immigrants and black workers as inherently "immoral, careless, and unskilled."[50] Mass meetings of miners called for a complete closure of US borders, and in 1897, the mineworkers union secured a state law that taxed companies for each non-naturalized worker hired. Although soon declared unconstitutional, before the ruling came down nineteen immigrant miners were massacred by a sheriff's posse in Lattimer, Pennsylvania, while protesting this nativist "alien tax."[51] Pennsylvania also passed laws banning the foreign-born from receiving liquor licenses, hunting on public lands, or owning a gun. According to the Pennsylvania Department of Labor, "a definite change of attitude on the part of the State toward the foreign born" occurred in 1895, when the legislature passed a resolution decrying "the constant influx of an ignorant and vicious class of immigrants as a great and growing evil, highly injurious to American workingmen and dangerous to American institutions."[52] A decade later, a combination of nativism and racism motivated a rare effort in Baltimore by unions to organize an independent political movement. In 1906, the Baltimore Federation of

Labor launched the Workingmen's Political League after both major parties had failed to follow through on the passage of the "Dawkins Bill," a measure that would have restricted work on all public projects in Baltimore to registered voters, thereby eliminating competition from immigrants and recently arrived migrants from the South.[53]

The turn to nativism was driven by white workers, but anti-immigrant sentiment also resonated among black workers. In the 1882 washerwomen's strike in Atlanta, the strikers attacked both the mechanized steam laundries and their Chinese rivals, who were told to leave the city within fifteen days. The African American washerwomen issued an open letter that melded labor militance and anti-Chinese nativist violence: "Mr. Slam Sling Chinamen you better sling your shirt short cause we mean what we say, cause your time is growing old.... [W]e expect to sail through bloody seas and we will die for our company. Miss Brooks is ready to shoulder her rifle, Miss Sillese her sharp shooter."[54] For African Americans, mass immigration highlighted the injustices of white supremacy. As a Pittsburgh minister lamented in 1891, as a black man and citizen, "he hadn't as much right as the ignorant foreigner who had only been here a few months."[55] According to one black steelworker who had worked in the Pittsburgh District since the 1880s, when it came to racism toward African Americans, the "foreigners [were] worse than the true Americans."[56] Susan R. Breitzer suggests that "anti-immigrant rhetoric" by African Americans should be seen in part as an effort to encourage the AFL to organize black workers in the early twentieth century.[57] Signaling the early rise of black/brown tensions that would gain greater prominence in the second half of the twentieth century, in 1928 the *Pittsburgh Courier*, a leading African American paper, expressed approval for extending restrictive immigration quotas to Mexicans.[58] Despite sharing a common, racialized position at the bottom of the labor market, black and immigrant workers have long struggled to find common ground.

The Limits and Consequences of a Nativist Labor Movement

From the perspective of international working-class solidarity, organized labor's turn to nativist politics in the United States was a tragedy. But in terms of practical impact on union efforts, the turn to nativism had more complex consequences. The AFL's nativism damaged efforts to organize more inclusively in industries with large numbers of recent immigrants. However, given the hardening of craft boundaries after the 1890s, the AFL was never deeply committed to pursuing more inclusive organizing strategies. On the other hand, the AFL's success in implementing immigration restriction after World War I was likely labor's most significant political victory of the early twentieth century.

The AFL's nativism complicated efforts to organize immigrant workers. Efforts to organize steel workers in 1909–10 were "fatally corrupted by the craftsmen's nativism."[59] This was even more visible in the steel strike of 1919. In Pittsburgh the refusal of most of the well-paid native-born craft workers to join the strike, in combination with large-scale strikebreaking by black workers recruited from the South, proved fatal to the strike's success. Interviews with the "wives and mothers of American and Scotch [Irish Protestant] workers who had not gone on strike" revealed an attitude of "extreme contempt for the whole movement on the ground that it was made of ignorant 'foreigners' with whom their husbands and sons of course would have nothing to do."[60] During the steel strike, a union organizer spoke in Polish to a group of immigrant men to promote the AFL's anti-immigration politics: "The American Federation of Labor had worked for the past six years in order to shut off the influx of immigrants from Europe into this country" and the labor movement "had finally succeeded in having the United States Government put an embargo on foreign immigration for a period of four years, which he held as a great factor," since it prevented the "steel corporation" from buying "ocean going ships and bring[ing] labor from Europe" to break the strike.[61] While immigrant workers proved the most committed during the 1919 strike, the effort of the AFL to use restriction as an appeal to recently arrived immigrants was likely counterproductive to sustaining their organizing effort. As Claudia Goldin has argued, immigrant groups that were still actively migrating in large numbers, such as these Polish workers, generally desired to keep borders open, while "old immigrant" groups whose migration had decreased—the Irish, Germans, Scandinavians, and British—embraced immigration restriction during this period.[62] The AFL's nativism thus reflected the most organized segments of the working class. The International Ladies' Garment Workers' Union (ILGWU), a union led by Jewish socialists, was the only major exception to the nativist orientation of the US labor movement. It remained resolutely internationalist, and in 1912 its convention condemned restriction legislation since it "intensifies national and race hatred" and would "prevent victims of political, religious, or economic oppressions from finding a place of refuge in the United States."[63] Given their historical confinement within the Russian Pale of Settlement and late nineteenth-century flight from the violence of pogroms, Jewish workers in the early twentieth century were uniquely and acutely aware of the dangers of closed borders.[64]

The Immigration Act of 1924 was both an abhorrent example of American racism and one of organized labor's most important political victories. In the terms that organized craft workers in the US set for themselves, the implementation of broad, permanent, peace-time immigration restriction in 1924 was understood as a major victory for labor against capital. The 1924 quotas were the culmination of a renewed campaign for restriction alongside the mass mobilization of the nativist, antisemitic, and white-supremacist Ku Klux Klan.[65] The origins of immigration restriction in 1924 went back to 1897, when the AFL endorsed and Congress first passed the literacy test, only to be defeated by a presidential veto more than a dozen times. In 1917, Congress finally succeeded in passing the literacy test over the veto. However, by this time the literacy test "was not as restrictive a measure as when it was first proposed because literacy rose rapidly in Europe" between 1897 and 1917.[66] While some restrictionists called for complete exclusion of European immigrants, on the model of the Chinese Exclusion Act, a quota system was instead used in the 1921 Emergency Immigration Act, which set annual immigration quotas at 3 percent of the 1910 population for each national immigrant group. This emergency act was revised, making it permanent and more restrictive, in 1924. Quotas were now based on the 1890 US population, a point before most southern and eastern European immigrants had arrived. In addition, the permissible annual quota was reduced from 3 percent to 2 percent of the 1890 population for each national immigrant group. Immigration had peaked in 1907, when 1.3 million immigrants entered the United States, and these acts drastically reduced this flow of migration. The 1921 Act reduced the permissible number of southern and eastern European immigrants to 156,000 annually, and the 1924 Act restricted this number to only 20,000, an insignificant trickle compared to the flood prior to World War I.[67] Organized workers had succeeded in drawing a powerful, racialized boundary around the national labor market.

While a number of patrician, Anglo-Saxon reactionaries certainly supported restriction, the struggle over immigration after World War I was largely between unions that demanded restriction and employers who wanted to keep borders open. In 1920, District Lodge 12 of the Machinists wrote to urge all members of the BFL to support "the enactment of legislation stopping all immigration for the present, and for four years after the peace has been declared."[68] In 1921, the AFL responded to employers' Open Shop Drive by blaming immigration. Unions had been weakened by "the condition of unemployment" which had "been accentuated by keeping open the floodgates of immigration, which has added to the confusion and given employers an additional weapon."[69] In 1922, the Baltimore Federation warned that immigration restriction was under threat since Congress was "showing signs of giving way to employing interests anxious for cheap, alien labor."[70] Indeed, capital organized a robust resistance to the imposition of immigration restriction. When President Wilson vetoed the literacy test passed by Congress in 1917, he had the full backing of the US Chamber of Commerce.[71] In addition, when Congress was exploring the introduction of a quota system in 1923 for the restriction of immigration, the Chamber opposed the "three percent immigration law" because it was "not adaptable to changing conditions" in the labor market.[72] Instead, employers favored a flexible system in which permissible rates of immigration would increase when unemployment was low and wages were rising.[73] Major manufacturers, including the Bethlehem Steel Company, testified in 1923 against immigration restriction and for the free movement of immigrant labor.[74] All the major representatives of capital, including the US Chamber and the National Association of Manufacturers, opposed the 1921 quota law, and the even more restrictive 1924 legislation.[75] Judge Elbert Gary, president of United States Steel, led what the *New York Times* characterized as "general attack by capitalists" on restriction legislation, and described immigration restriction to US Steel stockholders as "one of the worst things this country has ever done for itself economically."[76] Broadly popular with the US electorate, however, the nativism of the AFL scored a victory over capital in 1924.

Even as organized labor secured a long-delayed restriction of European immigration, attention turned to the southern border with Mexico, highlighting the arena of immigration policy that would remain the most contentious for the rest of the twentieth century. Gompers had argued for the inclusion of the Americas in the 1917 literacy legislation, after migration from Mexico into industrial centers increased during the war. Once again, during the debate on the 1924 quota Act, Gompers pressured the bill's sponsor to include Mexico and Canada in the restrictive quota system.[77] The 1924 act, however, exempted the Americas, as had the literacy test of 1917, thus leaving migration from Mexico unrestricted at the behest of Southern agricultural employers in California and Florida who were "particularly powerful, relentless, united, and vocal in the opposition" to any restrictions on migration from Mexico.[78] For a brief period in the 1920s, the AFL attempted to cooperate with Mexican unions in reducing migration across the southern border, but in 1929, this position was rejected in favor of pressuring Congress to include Mexico in the restrictive quota system.[79] In 1930, the Pittsburgh Central Labor Union passed a resolution expressing "keen interest" by "members of organized labor" in legislation providing for the "Restriction of Immigration from Mexico, Filipino, and other Latin-American countries now before Congress," claiming that this immigration was "breeding a dangerous, festering sore, murders, and riot conditions."[80] Offering a racist nativism that would continue to reso-nate among white workers up to the present, according to the Pittsburgh Central Labor Union, "American citizens, skilled workers [were] being crowded out by mixed breeds of aliens," and "settled citizens, men with families" were being "discriminated against" by the steel companies in favor of recently arrived Mexican workers.[81]

Immigration restriction points to an uncomfortable continuity be-tween the 1920s and the rise of more inclusive, industrial unionism in the 1930s. As Beverly Silver has argued, the "U.S. labor movement's suc-cess in having open immigration outlawed in the 1920s set the stage for the stabilization of the US working class and contributed to the subse-quent CIO . . . victories in the 1930s."[82] Nativism was often constitutive of successful labor movements. As the next chapter will show, the most powerful, broad labor movement of the early twentieth century was built behind the racial boundaries of the White Australia policy. The drastic reduction in immigration changed working-class communities. After 1930, far fewer newly arrived immigrants put downward pressure on the labor market, wage differentials moderated, and the cultural and social distance between the immigrant and the native-born worker decreased.[83] While certainly not the only cause, the success of nativist immigration restriction in the 1920s "explains much of the turbulent labor history of the 1930s."[84] By drawing restrictive boundaries around the national labor market, the narrow, nativist, and racist politics of the AFL in the 1920s helped to create the conditions that allowed for the broad and inclusive CIO to grow and survive in the 1930s.

Argentina: Mass Immigration without Racist Working-Class Nativism

The United States and Argentina were the two countries that received by far the largest share of immigrants crossing the Atlantic in the late nine-teenth and early twentieth centuries.[85] While workers in the US mobilized to secure racialized nativist boundaries, the labor movement in Argentina did not. Both countries were major recipients of "new immigrants"—in the case of Argentina, primarily from Italy and Spain, whereas the US received more eastern European migrants.[86] Much like the US, at the turn of the century, Argentina's most successful unions remained within craft boundaries.[87] However, despite some broad similarities, narrow craft boundaries did not become entrenched as a rigid policy, nor did Argen-tine workers turn to nativist immigration restriction. As Hobsbawm has noted, although immigration tends to produce fractures in the working class, in some cases, such as Argentina, "highly unified working classes with a powerful class consciousness have been forged."[88] Despite levels of immigration double those in the US, Argentine unions "never related the wage level to massive immigration," and unlike in the US, Blanca Sánchez-Alonso points out, "unions never acted as a pressure group pushing the government to close the door to foreign workers."[89] What explains this divergence?

While both countries experienced mass immigration, these immigrants entered and shaped very different labor markets and occupational structures. Most fundamentally, in Argentina the boundaries of craft, native birth, and race never aligned in a reinforcing process. Declining craft-laborer wage differentials in Argentina suggest that craft workers could increasingly build bridges with workers below them on the production hierarchy.[90] As we have seen, in the US, craft work was dominated by native-born white workers, while immigrants and African Americans were relegated to the bottom of the production hierarchy. No such stark divides marked the Argentine social structure.[91] Immigrants were 82 percent of common laborers and 71 percent of craft workers in Buenos Aires in 1914.[92] This contrasts sharply with table 6.1 above, which shows an occupational structure far more deeply marked by immigrant status. Given how slavery's legacies placed immigrants in a vulnerable (if comparatively lucrative) position in the United States, different kinds of workers chose Argentina and the US as their destination. Fernando Devoto argues that migrants selected Argentina if they had "a longer time horizon" and "prioritized having better jobs and living in a society that was less discriminatory," whereas they chose the United States if they "expected to return soon, and aspired to maximize their income in the shortest possible time."[93] In addition, whereas in the US the "old immigrants" from northern Europe and the "new immigrants" from southern and eastern Europe occupied distinct, stratified positions in the occupational hierarchy, this was not the case in Argentina.[94] Jeremy Adelman points out that when Argentine immigrants arrived late in the nineteenth century, there was no "early generation of craftsmen immigrants" who formed defensive alliances rooted in overlapping bonds of craft and "ethnic solidarity."[95] Craft, ethnic, and racial boundaries did not align in Argentina. Building from these very different labor market structures, organized labor did not turn to racialized nativist boundary-making.

It might seem plausible that immigrants were too politically powerful in Argentina to make immigration restriction viable. Immigrants reached a peak of around 30 percent of the Argentine population, twice the proportion in the United States. But this did not equate to substantial political power. Despite easy access to citizenship, astonishingly few Argentine immigrants became naturalized and secured their rights to participate in politics. Only 0.25 percent of immigrants were naturalized in 1895, rising to 2.25 percent in 1914.[96] Argentine immigrants joined unions and took strike action, but they showed relatively little interest in politics, unlike in the United States, where urban political machines quickly mobilized immigrant communities into partisan politics.[97] There was no powerful immigrant lobby fighting to prevent restriction in Argentina. Rather, Argentine workers simply never mobilized to draw a nativist boundary around their national labor market.

Elites contested Argentina's commitment to open borders, but without a mass movement of organized workers demanding restriction, only minor, individually targeted restrictions were implemented. Forming an important part of Argentine political culture, freedom of movement was enshrined in Article 25 of Argentina's 1853 Constitution, guaranteeing entry to any immigrant willing to work. The Immigration Law of 1876, which remained in force until 1932, provided only two criteria for exclusion: health and old age.[98] When legislation restricting immigration was passed in Argentina, the political debate focused on the danger of anarchist radicals and made no reference to racial or ethnic categories.[99] When racial categories were invoked, it was by those "who depicted European workers as of intrinsically greater utility than indigenous labour."[100] The prominence of Italian and Spanish workers in early trade unions and radical politics at the turn of the century led to some elites questioning the established notion of European migrants as "agents of civilization." Migrants were now seen as potentially dangerous, and the new laws enabled the executive to "expeditiously expel 'undesirable' foreigners."[101] A few legislators proposed a literacy test for restriction, based on the US model, but these proposals never gained traction or mass support, due in large part to the profound political power of large landowners fiercely committed to unrestricted immigration.[102]

Just as in the United States, the pause in migration during World War I enabled the Argentine labor movement to dramatically expand. The importance of immigration to the relative bargaining power of Argentine workers became especially clear during World War I, when migration came to a halt and shifted to net emigration, with more people leaving the country than entering it. As the labor market tightened, a wave of labor mobilization from 1916 to 1921 made organized workers a major force in the nation for the first time. However, in 1921 a dockworkers' strike in Buenos Aires was crushed with organized ultra-right strikebreakers, and after this defeat, organized labor in Argentina collapsed as mass immigration resumed. Membership fell from a high of one hundred thousand immediately after the war to only twenty-two thousand members by 1925.[103] The wartime era did produce some new immigration restrictions, but these came not at the behest of organized labor, but as a result of the unprecedented militancy of workers in 1919. A new administrative decree in that year aimed to slow and control immigration through the burden of bureaucracy and paperwork, requiring all immigrants to supply a photo identification, and three additional certificates: one showing a lack of a criminal record, a second an absence of begging, and a third testifying to mental health.[104]

Given how profoundly the wartime pause in immigration boosted labor organization, and how quickly the labor movement retreated once mass immigration resumed in the 1920s, it is particularly remarkable that Argentine politicians and unions did not embrace restriction in the 1920s. In 1919, the Museo Social Argentino convened a survey and discussion of expert opinion aimed at revising Argentina's immigration law.[105] During the 1910s, Argentine elites had developed a broad consensus on the need to "select immigrants before their entry into the country," with people of Asian, African, and Slavic descent seen as particularly worthy of restriction.[106] Alejandro E. Bunge, in summarizing their findings, observed that "most advocate for some measures to select immigration, and additionally, to restrict it."[107] While sectors of the Argentine ruling class were open to embracing racialized restriction, their project found no mass support.

In addition, this apparent elite consensus was disrupted in the 1919 Museo Social survey with a remarkable note of dissent. Emilio Frers, a lawyer, writer, politician, and longtime advocate for rural interests, offered a stirring defense of open immigration. Frers commended the 1853 constitution for requiring open borders and giving the federal government "a constitutional duty to promote European immigration."[108] On the "Question of Races," Frers argued that "this country must abandon all racial prejudice," citing Jean Finot's "admirable book" which he believed had conclusively demonstrated that "it is neither possible nor permissible to speak of racial disparities, let alone inferior races. . . . The human species is one, and all its varieties are equally perfectible; it is a matter of environment and education. Indigenous peoples of America, Africans and Oceanians, Malays or Mongols [can all] transform, adapt, and eventually rise to the common level of Europeans."[109] Building from Frers's bold rejection of racial hierarchies, he offered a remarkable reframing of nativist racial exclusion gaining traction in other countries. Europeans were "generally inferior to all others in terms of sobriety," and this weakness had produced in the US, Canada, and Australia "an entire economic-social system whose purposes include excluding competitors, monopolizing work for white men, and enjoying the privilege of occupying specific zones or regions of the world." These protective racial boundaries, Frers asserted in an unexpected inversion of Social Darwinist logic, "amounted to a confession of inferiority in the struggle for life."[110] Frers admitted that Argentina's open immigration had served to "provide abundant and cheap labor for a numerous proletarian reserve army," but rather than producing a nativist boundary within the occupational structure, he saw immigrants and native workers sharing a similar predicament: "Large foreign corporations . . . treat our exploited population, both native and immigrant, as a colonial people."[111]

The Radical Party, the Argentine trade unions, and the Socialist Party all failed to make a nativist "defense of Argentine workers against foreigners."[112] One exceptional nativist voice was a Socialist Party representative in the Chamber of Deputies, Enrique Dickman, who repeatedly denounced Argentina's open immigration policy between 1919 and 1922. Targeting the entry of "Hindus" and "Chinese" in particular, he warned that "the racial struggle, in essence, is nothing more than the struggle for wages."[113] Yet when, in 1923, acting under the influence of the emerging quota system in the US, the government brought a restrictive immigration reform law to Parliament, the bill sparked such an intense political and media backlash that the government quickly withdrew the measure.[114] Given a vastly different configuration of labor markets and occupational hierarchies, the Argentine labor movement did not turn to nativist boundary-making, and there was no mass support for restriction. Clearly, in the 1920s, many Argentinians continued to share Frers's strong commitment to the ideals of open migration enshrined in the 1853 constitution.

Argentina shows that mass immigration did not automatically produce a nativist labor movement. More than the rate of immigration, the ways in which immigrants entered and shaped the labor market were decisive. But broader patterns of labor nativism could not be forestalled indefinitely. When the Peronists came to power in the 1940s, ministers from a business background favored further open immigration, but those from a labor background increasingly supported restriction. In particular, the ministers of the Interior and Foreign Affairs expressed fears about the "competition that immigrants would exert in the labor market," and argued for restriction as part of a "labor and socialist tradition of defending local workers."[115] Yet rather than being a local inheritance, this nativist "tradition" had been incorporated from broader, global patterns of racialized working-class formation that had developed outside of Argentina.

Conclusion

By the 1920s, the US working class was profoundly fractured along lines of craft, race, and nativity. The mass popularity of the Klan of the 1920s among midwestern, native-born, Protestant workers and the simultaneous mass popularity of Marcus Garvey's Universal Negro Improvement Association among African Americans suggests the power of these divisions. In Aliquippa, the Jones & Laughlin steel town in the Pittsburgh District, a black steelworker organized a chapter of the UNIA in "response to the rise of the Klan" in Western Pennsylvania. While the Klan's vigilantism went largely unpunished, the organizing work of the UNIA was closely surveilled. As the UNIA gained mass popularity in the Pittsburgh area, J&L fired any black workers identified as UNIA members.[116] US organized labor was unprecedently powerful in the 1920s, a power registered most clearly in winning immigration restriction over the objections and resistance of capitalists. Yet the working class was at the same time fundamentally fractured.

In 1926, the British trade unionist and secretary for the International Federation of Trade Unions John W. Brown reported on the tensions revealed at the World Migration Congress. Supported by unions and labor parties, "the rapid growth of restriction of migration" had "intensified the already existing inequalities" that "prevail on different parts of the earth's surface," "inequalities [which] constitute one of the most acute dangers of the present world situation."[117] Despite egalitarian commitments, worker's movements were increasingly implicated in entrenching the inequalities between capitalism's Global North and South. While organized labor in the US has in recent years scaled back its anti-immigrant political commitments, across the Global North anti-immigrant populism remains a powerful force motivating working-class electorates. As regrettable as it may be for those who value international working-class solidarity, the passage of widespread, racially motivated immigration restriction must be seen, in terms of the goals that organized workers set for themselves, as one of the US labor movement's most significant political accomplishments. Against opposition from capitalists, who wished to maintain an open flow of low-wage labor from Europe, the AFL succeeded in imposing nativist boundaries around the national labor market. While it may be ethically appealing to "assert that migrant workers don't suppress wages, bosses and borders do," the empirical record suggests that nativist immigration restrictions are effective in raising the wages for those at the bottom of the production hierarchy.[118] Those committed to global labor solidarity must honestly confront the necessarily painful tradeoffs between the diverging interests of different groups of workers across capitalism's uneven economic geography. Vernon Briggs, a labor scholar outraged by the AFL-CIO's twenty-first century departure from its prior nativist commitments, calls the modern, pro-immigrant US labor movement "the friend of the self-serving immigrant advocacy groups" but "no longer . . . a champion of American workers."[119] But Briggs's retreat to nativist chauvinism only perpetuates global structures of racialized inequality. Unions must give consideration to the immediate material interests of their members, and this requires reckoning with the impact of migration on labor markets. Yet, as Argentina reveals, mass immigration does not necessarily provoke a nativist backlash if migrants are not confined within segmented structural positions in the labor market. One must hope that the ideals of broader working-class solidarity can find space to shine through. At a time when the "racist and nativist beliefs that fueled the immigration restriction movement . . . a century ago remain a crucial dimension of mainstream American politics," that light of inclusive solidarity seems dim indeed.[120]

Drawing the Boundaries of White Supremacy in the British Empire

Speaking to the Liverpool Trades Council in March 1914, a white South African union leader observed: "The nigger in South Africa was just as much a slave as the niggers used to be in America, and perhaps even more so."[1] Although he suggested that black workers "were entitled to better conditions," he made no mention of his own union's role in preserving the occupational color bar that placed white workers in well-paying jobs and confined black South Africans to dangerous, low-wage work. The South African labor leaders arrived in Liverpool as part of a tour of England to protest their deportation from South Africa after leading a general strike in Johannesburg. Their initial arrival in London had elicited what Jonathan Hyslop describes as the "biggest British labour demonstration of the early twentieth century."[2] While protesting the arbitrary deportations of the labor leaders by the South African government, the broader demonstration gave implicit support to the cause of white workers and white supremacy in South Africa. Nine trade union leaders had been deported from South Africa after two general strikes led by unions that demanded the exclusion of non-white workers from skilled jobs. The massive rally in 1914, and the tour of England that followed, aimed to support these deported leaders and the white-supremacist unions they led. Hyslop argues that across the British Empire, the working classes of various regions were "bound together into an imperial working class that produced and disseminated a common ideology of White Labourism." In Hyslop's account, the rise of working-class racism in Britain, the "White Australia" policy, and the beginning of South African industrial segregation were elements of a unified process of racialized imperial class formation. While this imperial perspective is useful, it also risks flattening out variations. Racial boundary-making happened in distinct ways, always shaped by local material forces. Thus when comparing how labor movements turned to racial boundary-making, it would be a mistake to restrict our view to the

British metropole.[3] The United States as a continental empire should be compared not just to the United Kingdom, but to the larger British settler-colonial maritime empire, with particular attention to the self-governing dominions of Australia and South Africa. While white supremacy was undoubtedly pervasive across the British Empire in the early twentieth century, the construction of racial boundaries by workers occurred in historically evolving local contexts.

The decline in racial hostility that British workers directed toward migrants from Ireland at the end of the nineteenth century shifted the terrain of racial boundary-making. With land reform improving conditions in the Irish countryside, and with wages converging between the British and Irish isles, the material conditions underpinning racialized hostility against the Irish faded. At the same time, in the British maritime sector, white supremacy and the exclusion of non-white labor became a central concern for workers and unions in the early twentieth century. Only among seamen and their unions was racial boundary-making in Britain similar to patterns in the US. But when we turn to the broader maritime empire, the British imperial experience offers striking parallels to the US. With its campaign for restrictive immigration policy, the union movement in Australia drew deep racial boundaries around its labor market, limiting wage differentials across the craft divide and producing the most well-organized labor movement of the early twentieth century. South Africa parallels the US in the centrality of racial boundaries that reinforced the craft divide. White craft workers organized militant craft unions in South Africa that excluded black workers from membership and fought to protect the industrial color bar that preserved well-paid work at the top of the production hierarchy for white workers. A "white labourism" was certainly pervasive throughout the British Empire, but it operated in distinct ways depending on local material and political conditions. The reception of South African labor struggles in Liverpool and Sheffield suggests that distant racial formations were recognized quite unevenly.[4] The South African experience was far more legible in Liverpool, a maritime port with a long history of racial boundary-making, than it was in Sheffield, an industrial city where workers remained largely isolated from flows of low-wage migrant labor.

Anti-Irish Racial Boundaries Fade

In 1870, Karl Marx described a deeply divided working class in his adopted home in Britain. English workers, Marx argued, viewed the Irish "the same as . . . the 'poor whites' [saw] the 'niggers' in the former slave states of the U.S.A.," and this "antagonism [was] the secret impotence of the English working-class."[5] While hostility to the Irish in Britain was intense in the mid-nineteenth century, it faded rapidly thereafter, and by the early twentieth century, had largely disappeared. Liverpool was a leading site of these hostilities, and the comparatively delayed emergence of the Labour Party on the Mersey registers the divisions in the Liverpool working class between native Protestants and migrant Catholics. As Eric Hobsbawm observes, the "relatively smooth integration" of Irish workers into the British labor movement at the turn of the century was "all the more striking when we recall that grassroots anti-Catholic and anti-Irish sentiments were powerful and sometimes savage in Britain."[6]

Religion and culture, stressing the Protestant/Catholic divide, articulated the structural division between low-wage Irish migrants and English natives. This has led to some uncertainty about whether to describe the Irish experience in mid-nineteenth century Britain as racism.[7] But racism does not necessarily need to be marked in terms of skin color, ancestry, or biology; it can be articulated in terms of any social markers that differentiate the vulnerable outsider/migrant from the empowered insider/ native. From the 1840s to the 1870s, "public discourse about the Irish" was "inflected with the language of race," depicting them as "intemperate, emotional, sentimental, predisposed toward violence . . . fit for service when closely controlled."[8] A materialist approach less entangled with language, culture, and ideas makes it clear that poor Irish Catholic labor migrants were racialized by English Protestant workers in nineteenth century Britain. While the parallels are striking, there were some key differences with the experience of African Americans in the postemancipation United States. The racialization of the Irish in mid-nineteenth century Britain was brief and uneven in comparison to the durable structures of white supremacy across the Atlantic. The boundaries of anti-Irish racial hostility were always more porous. Unlike poor Irish laborers, more affluent Irish, especially Protestants, experienced little hostility in Britain.[9] Last, compared to a baseline of white supremacy reproduced over centuries of chattel slavery in the US, the period of intense, bottom-up working-class hostility toward Irish labor migrants endured no more than a generation.

During the mid-nineteenth century, English workers regularly mobilized hate strikes against the employment of Irish workers. The *Sheffield Independent* reported that in nearby Lincoln, native "labourers [were] threatening gross assaults on the Irishmen, and still worse on the farmers who engage them."[10] In Rotherham, adjacent to Sheffield, special constables were required in 1838 to protect "the poor Irish from the aggressions of their English fellow-labourers."[11] Even with extra law enforcement, however, it was "impossible to reconcile the English to work again along with the Irish, and they peremptorily declare, that if the Irish again come to work, they will strike." The English workers had destroyed the food and clothing of the Irish workers, and driven them off the job. Several of the Irish workers protested in language of common citizenship and shared military service that echoed the terms on which African Americans protested racist exclusion in the US. The Irish argued that since they "did not fail to take their full share in the defence of the country . . . it was most unjust that they should be debarred from peacefully labouring side by side with Englishmen." Two years later, trouble again flared up around Sheffield, near Eckington on the North Midland Railway. A crowd had "riotously assembled . . . with spades, hammer-shafts, and hedge-stakes" and "attacked the Irish labourers. . . . and forced them to leave their work."[12] Similarly, on a building project outside of Liverpool, "considerable jealousy" existed among the English and Irish workers on the Chester & Birkenhead Railway. The English workers protested that the Irish "flocked too numerously to this country" and worked for "a rate of wages below the English standard."[13] Despite the prevalence of hate strikes, Irish workers enjoyed considerably greater personal and political security within Britain than did black workers in the US. When one of the sub-contractors agreed to hire only English workers, "the Irish labourers assembled [and attempted] to beat them off, in which they succeeded, by superior numbers, and the employment of dangerous weapons."[14] Few African American workers would have felt politically secure enough to make such a violent challenge to white workers. In the coal mines and railroads outside of Birmingham, in the town of Walsall, a crowd of 1,500 to 1,800 English workers attempted to "drive the poor Irishmen, with their wives and families, from the town" by "threatening violence to all who would oppose them."[15] Near Wolverhampton, a thousand English miners had met, and agreed to drive "every Irishman from this employment," attacking those who resisted "with sticks and. . . . volleys of stones."[16] Just as white workers in the US attempted to prevent black workers from working alongside them, so too in the UK, English Protestant workers mobilized violently against the employment of Irish Catholics migrants as low-wage competition.

After erupting at midcentury, by the 1870s hostility and discrimination against Irish workers in the UK was on the decline, although anti-Irish sentiment was evident into the early twentieth century, especially in places like Liverpool.[17] During the midcentury peak in migration, English workers had maintained racialized boundaries in the production hierarchy that "channeled [Irish laborers] into the bottom ranks" of the labor market, but these began to ease after 1870.[18] In coal mining, Irish workers had been confined to lower-paid surface work while native-born English craft workers maintained a "stranglehold on hewing."[19] On visiting British coal mines in 1872, a visitor noted that "not so long since . . . English 'pitmen' refused to permit the Irishmen to work in the mines, but now. . . . differences of nationality rarely occasion a dispute, and prejudice" no longer "shut out the Irishmen from sharing in the mining labour of the district."[20] These divisions also constrained the early growth of unions in areas where Irish migration was particularly predominant. Up to the 1870s, "problems of ethnic and sectarian bigotry, accentuated by immigration" from Ireland prevented sustained organizing among Liverpool workers.[21] It was only in the 1870s that Irish workers became substantially involved in the broader British trade union movement, and the rise of the New Unions after 1889 marked general incorporation of Irish workers into the British labor movement.[22]

Liverpool was one of the places in the United Kingdom where anti-Irish hostility registered more deeply and persisted longer. Racialized boundaries shaped the occupational and production hierarchy in Liverpool into the early twentieth century.[23] The massive 1909 battles between crowds of Irish and Protestant rioters underlines the persistence of these divisions. The 1909 riots were the "the most serious sectarian strife seen in a British mainland city" since the Gordon Riots of 1780.[24] The riots followed a summer of provocation by the militant Protestant preacher George Wise, and after a number of Protestant carters were assaulted, with one killed, mobs of rioters from both Catholic and Protestant neighborhoods attacked workplaces and homes, purging the minority group and establishing more sharply demarcated neighborhood and occupational boundaries in the city.[25] As one historian describes the 1909 riots: "Gangs consolidated denominational uniformity, street by street, workplace by workplace."[26] This was the last major riot that pitted Irish Catholics against English Protestants. As we will see below, when riots erupted across Britain in 1919, Irish/English differences had faded and rioters targeted workers of African and Asian descent in the maritime sector.

On the Liverpool waterfront, a sharp divide separated the relatively well-paid Protestant carters and the low-wage, casual labor of the largely Irish dockworkers. Much like US craft unions, the carters' union started as a deeply Protestant organization, closely tied to working-class Orangeism and the populist sectors of the Conservative Party in the city. Founded in 1889, the carters' union functioned as "an integral part of Liverpool's ethnically divided labour market."[27] Two years after its founding, the union's assets consisted of "one reed band and two fife and drum bands," the essential marching paraphernalia of "Orange working-class culture" that mobilized many Protestant workers in Liverpool.[28] Competing Protestant and Catholic marching bands, and associated neighborhood gangs, routinely fought for control of the streets of the city in the late nineteenth century. The union grew from this social world. The officials appointed to represent the union in the 1890s were prominent local Conservatives and Orangemen. When the mostly Irish dockworkers went on strike in 1890, the carters overwhelming voted against joining in solidarity. Suggesting a narrow craft perspective, union representatives explained that "as a union we have never interfered in trade quarrels outside our immediate calling."[29] However, this narrow exclusiveness proved temporary in Liverpool. By the early twentieth century, the Protestant carters had established a working relationship with the predominantly Irish National Union of Dock Labourers (NUDL). The carters' union joined the industrial coalition of the National Transport Workers Federation in 1911 and demonstrated sustained, inclusive solidarity during the 1911 transport strike. Whereas in the US, craft boundaries hardened over the 1890s, in Liverpool the carters moved toward "a broader conception of trade unionism."[30] By the 1911 transport strike, Irish workers had been recruited to the union in substantial numbers, even if they remained a minority in a Protestant-dominated occupation.[31] In 1919, the carters elected a Catholic as General Secretary, a remarkable shift for an organization with deep roots in working-class Protestant Orangeism.[32] While the craft unions of the AFL remained largely all-white organizations, and the color bar was fiercely defended in South Africa, English and Irish workers who had once violently battled in the streets of Liverpool were able to join in durable solidarity.

The gradual easing of the Protestant boundaries of the Liverpool carters' union highlights the increasing incorporation of Irish workers into the Liverpool working class. An even more striking illustration of this process comes from the juxtaposition of intense working-class divisions during the 1909 riots and broad working-class solidarity during the 1911 transport strike. Coming just two years after the 1909 riots, the Liverpool transport strike revealed that while sectarian tensions persisted, collaboration and solidarity between Protestant and Catholic workers was increasingly possible.[33] Prominent, symbolic demonstrations of Protestant/Catholic solidarity occurred during the strike. For instance, sectarian marching bands, whose parades and provocations had incited street violence for half a century in Liverpool, now marched together in solidarity with the strike. One Liverpool neighborhood integrated their Protestant and Catholic bands to form one, unified working-class marching band. This remarkable band was symbolically led by a drum major who "proudly whirled his sceptre twined with Orange and Green ribbons as he proudly led his contingent band, half out of the Roman Catholic, half out of the local Orange band."[34] The 1911 transport strike also marked unprecedented solidarity across the craft divide in the port.[35] The Shipping Federation, which "had been breaking strikes for over twenty years," was overwhelmed by the inclusive scale of the strike.[36] The 1911 strike marked a fundamental transition for organized labor in Liverpool. Prior to the strike, the NUDL had represented only eight thousand dockers, a small and vulnerable fraction of the urban working class. After the strike, membership grew to thirty-one thousand, and the union had become broadly representative of the waterfront workers and an undeniable social and political power in the city.[37] That this leap forward in class solidarity and labor organizing came just two years after massive sectarian rioting was all the more remarkable.

While divisions within the Liverpool working class were easing, and common interests could be recognized and acted on during strikes, the boundaries between Protestant and Catholic workers had not disappeared. Protestant Orangeism and Irish Catholic Nationalism remained powerful political commitments for workers in Liverpool. In 1912, the Liverpool Working Men's Conservative Association rallied tens of thousands — estimates varied from twenty-five to two hundred and fifty thousand — for militaristic anti-Home Rule speeches promoting Britain's continued colonial domination of Ireland. Masses of Protestant workers cheered speakers who warned that "10,000 young men of Liverpool" were ready to be armed and sent as vigilantes to Ireland to defend Protestant and imperial interests against the threat of Irish autonomy.[38] By the early twentieth century, Liverpool Irish were mostly second- or third-generation immigrants, and while they remained loyal to Irish Nationalist politicians, practically their politics aligned with Liverpool's still weak Labour Party.[39] The creation of the Irish Free State in 1922 opened the door for former Irish Nationalists to become Labour Party members. By the 1920s workers of Irish descent were "playing a significant role" in the city's increasingly powerful Labour Party.[40] Working-class Protestants remained loyal to the Conservatives much longer. Still, the creation of the Irish Free State also required a reorientation of the Protestant working-class. The Orange ideology of working-class Protestantism in Liverpool shifted in the twentieth century from hostility to Catholics to a more general "fear of foreign workers both inside and outside Britain," and in Liverpool a deep "distrust and suspicion over control of areas of the job market remained up until World War Two."[41]

As low-wage migrants from an impoverished agrarian periphery to prosperous metropolitan core, Irish workers in mid-nineteenth century Britain experienced racialized hostility and violence. However, as wages converged between Ireland and Britain, as migration and strikebreaking declined, and as land reform and enfranchisement enhanced the economic and political position of Irish rural producers, hostility to the Irish faded. Irish workers became integrated into an increasingly cohesive British working class in the early twentieth century. Even if the racialization of the Irish was relatively brief and partial, their escape from this subordinate position is instructive. It was not a cultural process of increasingly tolerant beliefs, but material and political changes—land redistribution, converging wages, and enfranchisement—that underpinned the erosion of previously enforced racial boundaries.

Racial Boundaries in the British Merchant Marine

For the most part, British workers observed racial boundary-making at a distance. During the 1890s the Trade Union Congress (TUC) protested the use of "foreign pauper labour," and after the Boer War, the TUC argued that British lives should not have been lost so that "white labour in the Transvaal should be ousted and replaced by yellow slave labour" in South Africa.[42] However, in one crucial sector, racial boundary-making by organized workers was intense and immediate. In the maritime sector, among seamen in port cities, competition from Asian, African, and Caribbean sailors provoked sustained racial boundary-making in the early twentieth century. Anti-immigrant politics gained traction primarily in port cities like Liverpool in the early twentieth century.[43] In Liverpool, both Conservatives and Labour, aiming to win working-class voters, blamed foreigners "whether Irish, Jews, or Chinese" for "disease, housing shortages, unemployment, and national decline." In Liverpool's working-class politics, imperial questions of "class, commerce, and culture were rewritten in a racial shorthand to ease political expression."[44] More broadly, as Laura Tabili argues, racial hierarchies in Britain were "constructed by the political economy of a declining maritime empire."[45] However, the broader British labor movement only occasionally registered the racial divisions in the maritime sector. Outside of port cities, in industrial centers like Sheffield, British workers experienced racial boundary-making only faintly in the early twentieth century.

Far more than anywhere else in Britain, white supremacy and racial boundaries became entrenched in the maritime sector among sailors. As Martin Daunton has observed, the racial conflicts that "formed a barrier to union organization" in the United States also in appear in Britain, but only "with respect to seamen."[46] Competition from foreign labor in general, but especially from the non-white Lascars of South Asia, Chinese, and black workers from Africa and the Caribbean motivated white British seamen's hostility. South Asian Lascars had been an important part of the British merchant marine since the eighteenth century, drawing on the impressive skills developed by the maritime traditions of the Indian Ocean. Already in 1823, Parliament enacted strict and explicitly racist laws governing Lascar labor in the British merchant marine, largely confining it to the Indian Ocean.[47] All Lascar contracts had to terminate in India, and Lascars could be forced to accept any contract that did so.[48] As early as 1879, sailors had marched in Cardiff chanting "Send out your blacks and we'll murder every one of them," and a year later a riot erupted that "resulted in a colored seamen being seriously wounded."[49] The "rough equality" of seamen on sailing ships was replaced from the 1870s by a new "industrial division of labor, reinforced by colonial racial hierarchies" on steamships, with dangerous, hot, and dirty work assigned to low-wage, non-European workers.[50] The percentage of foreigners on British ships increased from 14.6 percent in 1890 to 21.1 percent in 1900, and racial tensions increased substantially in the first decades of the twentieth century, with growing hostility to sailors of Greek, Arab, and African descent. During 1905 and 1906, an explicitly racist union seceded from the seamen's union and rallied workers with the slogan "British Crews for British Ships," a close parallel to the white-supremacist Sons of Vulcan in the US steel industry during the same years.[51] Proto-fascist groups such as the British Brothers League campaigned against immigration and joined with the sailors' union to "agitate against the loss of 'British heritage'" in the merchant marine.[52] Prior to World War I, hate strikes in Liverpool by white sailors targeted the employment of workers of Asian and African descent, and for black workers driven off the ships, pervasive local discrimination made finding new employment extremely difficult.[53]

Struggles over the labor force of the British merchant marine brought global processes of racial boundary-making home to British ports. In 1907, the *Liverpool Daily Post* highlighted a resolution on the "manning of British ships" introduced at the annual conference of Havelock Wilson's seamen's union: "Having noticed the continuous increases of Lascars and Asiatics, from 1897 to 1907, in the British mercantile marine," the union was called upon to "enter an emphatic protest against this system, seeing that it supplants British white labour."[54] The resolution urged the Labour Party to "frame a bill to compel all British vessels having British mails to employ British white labour in each and all departments" and all merchant ships "to employ 75 per cent British white labour."[55] While embracing the defense of white labor, the union's leadership criticized the resolution primarily on the grounds that it specified *British* labor, thereby undercutting the white "internationalism" that had been fostered in recent years between maritime workers in British, Dutch, and German ports. The resolution was referred to committee for reconsideration. White internationalism and white supremacy coexisted here as an early preview of a unified "social fortress" Europe.[56]

In addition to efforts by local seamen, the Liverpool press devoted substantial attention to efforts by Australia and New Zealand to protect the employment of white crews on their ships.[57] In 1911, Australia, New Zealand, and Canada all demanded more legislative authority to regulate the racial composition of shipping crews in their ports as self-governing dominions. As the Secretary of the Colonies warned in response: "if there was any question which seemed to threaten not only the well-being, but the actual existence of the empire, it was the difficulty between the white and native races." Tensions were escalating due to "a rivalry of cheap labour" and the desire to preserve "the colour bar."[58] British imperial officials had to balance the demands of their white settler dominions for racial exclusion and nativist boundaries with the demands of South Asians for fuller rights and protections as subjects of the British Empire. Joseph Ward, the prime minister of New Zealand, in urging "their duty to protect . . . the white crews" in South Pacific shipping, envisioned this as a step toward a global, imperial apartheid: "They ought to urge upon all nations the policy of 'Every colour going back to its own zone.'"[59] As a global, governing race, European settlers were implicitly exempted from this expectation of races being confined within their proper geographical zones.

The growing strength of the sailors' union and increasing protective legislation deepened tensions between white British sailors and their non-European competitors. The 1894 Merchant Shipping Act, in a concession to the sailors' union, required English fluency to serve on British ships, but over the union's objections this requirement was waived for "Lascars and British inhabitants of British protectorates." In addition, improved crew space and rations were required by the Act, but this only widened the differential in the cost of white British compared to Lascar labor. The shipping companies continued to hire more Lascars and displace white British workers. By 1911, one-quarter of seamen on steam vessels were Lascars.[60] In response to growing organizational power and legislative protection for British sailors, shipping employers looked toward cheaper, less protected labor sources. In 1908, the trade journal of UK shippers offered a picture and commentary on "The Yellow Man as Sailor," and observed that while many "hard things have been said of the Chinese," the owners of vessels in Asian waters had "found them almost model employees, being contented and well behaved," with an "intelligence . . . distinctly in their favour."[61] In the years before the First World War, Chinese and

South Asian sailors came under attack from the sailors' union as "inferior Asiatics" who would "herd together like pigs," surviving on meager rations.[62] The seamen's union fought the Indian Merchant Shipping Act since it permitted "the employment of Lascars on inferior terms to those of British seamen."[63] While superficially calling for equal wages, the union in fact "consistently stood for policies of racial exclusion," often cloaking these proposals in seemingly egalitarian rhetoric.[64] The union's expectation was that if equal wages were mandated, employers would only hire white British workers. In a pamphlet in 1913, the seamen's union warned a wider working-class audience that if "the employment of Asiatics can be justified on board British ships, competing with our people in our own country, then justification exists for thousands of Chinese to be imported into this country to compete with the miners, railwaymen, fishermen and all other classes of shore workers."[65] From 1900 to 1930, as much as one-third of the workforce of the British merchant marine comprised non-European workers of extraordinarily diverse origins, but most were hired at colonial ports in Africa, Asia, and the Caribbean for two-year contracts that paid wages of one-third to one-fifth of those earned by white British seamen.[66] After World War I, the seamen's union shifted its concern over racial boundaries from Asian Lascars to black sailors; a few black British sailors were resident in British ports, but many more were hired in the West Indies and British territories in Africa during World War I.[67] Diane Frost argues that West African Kru sailors, like African Americans in the US, were "a 'reserve army of labour' that could be wheeled in and out of the British economy as conditions dictated."[68] These parallels in the labor market also produced parallels in racial violence.

Much as the Great Migration provoked race riots across the industrial Midwest, the unprecedented entry of African and Caribbean workers into the British merchant marine during the World War incited race riots that erupted in nine major British ports in 1919. Although widespread, the level of violence was low compared to the US, and marginal compared to the six thousand Korean migrant workers massacred in Japan in 1923. Only five individuals lost their lives in these riots (three white, two black), whereas in the US the death toll from the postwar riots was at least fifty, nearly all black victims.[69] In June of 1919, the *Liverpool Courier* made plain the racism festering in the city: "One of the chief reasons of popular anger behind the present disturbances lies in the fact that the average negro is nearer an animal than the average white man."[70] In Liverpool the riots erupted when a black Bermudan ran from the police, fell into the Queens Dock, and died as a crowd of white workers shouted, "Let him drown."[71] White mobs began attacking black Liverpool residents, "savagely attacking, beating and stabbing every Negro they could find in the street."[72] After the riots in Liverpool, white workers at several large factories launched hate strikes against black coworkers, many of whom were long-standing employees; one estimate suggested that some 120 black Liverpudlians lost their jobs in these hate strikes.[73] After the 1919 race riots in Cardiff, the League of Coloured People complained of the occupational barriers erected against non-white workers: "The trade unions, the police and the shipowners appear to cooperate smoothly in barring colonial seamen" from getting work.[74]

White supremacy hardened in ports like Liverpool during the 1920s. In 1925, in response to the postwar slump in shipping demand, the Maritime Joint Supply Office, a collaboration between the Shipping Federation and Havelock Wilson's union, agreed to restrict maritime jobs to those who had fully-paid-up union cards, thereby finally excluding most South Asian Lascars and non-white workers from maritime employment.[75] During the 1920s and 1930s, local unions and the Labour Party aimed to "prevent the engagement at the port of black seafarers living in Liverpool."[76] Unsurprisingly, Liverpool produced Britain's most racist politician in the early twentieth century. David G. Logan, Irish Nationalist and later Labour MP for Liverpool, was "probably the most vociferous racist in Parliament" after he arrived in Westminster in 1929. Logan's racial hostility had developed over a long political career representing the Irish working-class wards on the Liverpool City Council.

Nativism and Working-Class Power in White Australia

Soon after the six Australian colonies united in 1901, the now self-governing dominion became home to the world's most powerful labor movement, a labor movement organized within the boundaries of the racist, nativist protection of "White Australia" immigration restriction. Seen globally as the "white workingman's paradise" and the "hope of the labour world," Australia's nativist boundaries provided an inspiration for white workers and a caution to capitalists.[77] As in the United States, anti-Chinese restriction prevailed first. However, while East Asia's relative proximity always made the competition of Chinese labor particularly visible in the South Pacific, Australian unions also became concerned about European labor migrants. Measures were also taken to stop strikebreakers from being recruited from New Zealand and Britain, and when Italian migration increased in the 1920s, Australian workers mobilized against the threat of low-wage European migration.

The restriction of migration by organized Australian workers created a distinctive labor market in terms of wage differentials across the craft

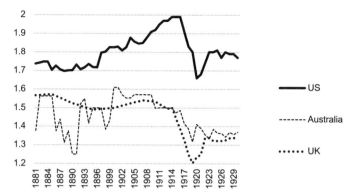

FIGURE 7.1 Wage differentials across the craft divide in the US, UK, and Australia. *Source:* Edward Anderson, "Globalisation and Wage Inequalities, 1870–1970," *European Review of Economic History* 5, no. 1 (2001): 94, fig. 1.

divide. While most settler societies such as the US, Canada, and Argentina had relatively high wage differentials, due to mass immigration pushing down wages at the bottom of the production hierarchy, Australia had strikingly low wage inequality. The relatively high cost of travel from Europe to Australia meant that only a relatively small number of more prosperous migrants arrived. At the same time, the closure of Australian borders to Asian migrants under the "White Australia" policy eliminated the possibility of mass migration of low-wage workers from East or South Asia. As seen in figure 7.1, limited low-wage migration produced modest wage differentials across the craft divide in Australia, creating favorable material conditions for the mass organization of an inclusive labor movement behind the racial boundaries of a closed national labor market.

Mass migration to the US and highly constrained migration to Australia shaped the labor market in very different ways. Between 1877 and 1913, different populations of workers migrated to the two countries. In the US, unskilled immigrants (52 percent) far outnumbered skilled immigrants (17 percent). In Australia, the opposite was true: skilled immigrants (29 percent) outnumbered unskilled immigrants (25 percent) in this period.[78] Although the US and Australia shared a parallel, intertwined history of nativism, the outcome was quite different. While the US had deeply divided labor markets, the "White Australia policy made viable a wage floor and slowed the growth of segmented labour markets."[79] Similar commitments to racial boundaries around the national labor market produced strikingly different outcomes in the two countries. As Gary Cross neatly summarizes, "A racism that defined citizenship in Australia created a divided citizenry in the United States."[80]

The White Australia policy and the rise of organized labor were inter-twined in the late nineteenth century. While the 1850s Gold Rush had provoked a range of anti-Chinese measures including restrictive licenses, taxes, and fees, as well as riots and violence against Chinese miners, out-right exclusion was not immediately implemented. In the 1860s the Chinese population in the Australian colonies declined by 40 percent and several colonies actually repealed their anti-Chinese measures.[81] The more direct origins of the White Australia policy came in 1878, during a strike of white Australian sailors protesting the employment of Chinese work-ers by the Australian Steam Navigation Company on several of its Pacific routes.[82] The prior year, in 1877, the recently organized Sydney Trades and Labour Council had gained political experience by leading the agitation against British financial subsidies for migration to Australia. In 1878, they launched a renewed effort to restrict Chinese immigration.[83] After the steamship company replaced European crews with Chinese workers on eight of its ships, the strike began in November 1878. Tensions escalated when the company attempted to replace the striking white workers with newly arrived Chinese strikebreakers.[84] The steamship company tele-graphed Hong Kong for three hundred more strikebreakers. However, the strike continued to prevent the company's operations, as "the extra Chinese [strikebreakers] would take some time to arrive."[85] A month later, news arrived in Australia that the ship carrying the Chinese strikebreakers had been wrecked at sea, foreclosing any chance that replacement workers could be swiftly secured.[86] Immediately thereafter the strike ended. The company agreed to a settlement that limited the number of Chinese sailors that could be employed.[87] Much like the racial violence that accompanied strikes in the US and South Africa, during the conflict workers attempted to burn down Chinese businesses and white mobs assaulted Chinese res-idents on the streets.[88] While the strike was a victory for organized white workers, they met resistance from business interests. Large Australian employers argued that "all immigration served to bring down the price of labour, and that Chinese immigration would be especially useful in this respect."[89] But with continuing agitation by organized labor and a smallpox outbreak that was blamed on Chinese immigrants, anti-Chinese legislation was passed in 1881, one year before the US passed the Chinese Exclusion Act.

Like the US and the UK, Australian unions first attempted large-scale, inclusive organizing in the late 1880s. Sheep grazing and wool exports were central to Australia's economy, and much of this new inclusive organizing was led by the Australian Shearers Union (ASU), reorganized as the Aus-tralian Workers Union (AWU) in 1894.[90] As elsewhere, however, this effort to organize inclusively at the bottom of the production hierarchy proved fragile and vulnerable to strikebreaking.[91] In the 1891 Queensland Shearers Strike, employers organized extensive strikebreaking by importing workers and "police and military forces moved into the district" to intimidate strikers and protect strikebreakers.[92] Sheep farmers, coal operators, and steamship companies all organized formidable employers' associations to resist the growth of inclusive unions.[93] Australian employers turned to the most convenient near-periphery for strikebreakers.[94] Restrictive legislation from the 1880s foreclosed the use of Chinese strikebreakers in the 1890s, but there were alternatives closer to home. During the strike "a great part of the so-called free labour employed was procured in New Zealand," and it was felt that "while the shearing labor remains unorganized [in New Zealand], it is a standing menace" to unions in Australia.[95] The *New Zealand Times* complained that Australian unions resorted to "lynching, lies, and legislation" to prevent New Zealand workers from gaining employment in Australia.[96] However, tensions quickly eased. The growing power of unions in New Zealand eliminated easy access to strikebreakers. During the mid-1890s, New Zealand unions even sent organizers on ships carrying strikebreakers to attempt to dissuade workers from scabbing.[97] Ultimately, the pool of labor available in New Zealand was small, wage differentials were marginal, and advancing organization on both sides of the Tasman Sea prevented further strikebreaking. While the threat of New Zealand as a near-periphery from which strikebreakers could be recruited passed, the bitter defeats of the 1890s would inform the rise of the Australian Labor Party, as workers turned to compulsory arbitration to force employers to recognize unions.

The unification of the six independent Australian colonies in 1901 led to the creation of a distinctive "national settlement" in which workers would be protected from low-wage competition by the White Australia policy, industrial capital would be protected by tariffs, and the state would provide compulsory arbitration that would centralize and bureaucratize collective bargaining.[98] The strike defeats of the 1890s led to the formation of Labor Parties in each of the Australian colonies. These Labor Parties were quickly able to gain influence by holding the balance of power between free traders and protectionists at the regional and national level.[99] This "national settlement" of racist immigration restriction, tariff protection, and compulsory arbitration proved exceptionally favorable to organized labor. By 1910 Australia had the highest union density in the world.[100]

The cornerstone of this settlement was the White Australia Policy. Perhaps surprisingly, the 1901 Restriction Act avoided any explicitly racial language. In fact, the origins of this racist legislation with race-neutral language tie together the histories of racial boundary-making in the United States, South Africa, and Australia. Due to treaties with Japan and China, British officials pressured Australian legislators to avoid overtly racial language when implementing restrictive immigration legislation. Thus, in the 1901 Act restriction was based on a discretionary dictation test in which an entrant could be required to write out a passage dictated to them in any European language.[101] The convoluted procedure of the 1901 Australian law "had its genesis in American immigration legislation," specifically the 1896 literacy test passed by Congress. Restriction legislation in the US, as noted above, drew inspiration from the Jim Crow disenfranchisement laws spreading across the US South that relied on literacy tests to provide superficially non-racial mechanisms of disenfranchising African Americas.[102] However, the example of US legislation would not arrive in Australia directly. The 1896 literacy test in the US, which required immigrants to transcribe a passage in their native language, directly inspired Natal officials in South Africa to implement a dictation test in 1897 to restrict migration from South Asia while avoiding any explicitly racial language that could cause delays and complications with British imperial officials. However, rather than allowing South Asian languages, the 1897 Natal Act required the passage to be written in a European language of the immigration officer's choice. This South African legislation became the direct model for the legislation adopted in Australia in 1901. The circuitous construction of this legislation, from Jim Crow disenfranchisement, to anti-immigrant literacy test, first in the US, then in South Africa, and finally in Australia, exemplifies the flows of knowledge that reinforced racial boundary-making globally. US white supremacists, working under the constraints of the 14th and 15th Amendments, taught racist nativists around the world how to achieve racial restriction while avoiding explicitly racist legislative language.

Australian unions, organizing behind closed borders, were industrially inclusive while also vehemently racist. Soon after its founding in the 1880s, the ASU adopted membership rules that excluded Asians and Pacific Islanders.[103] The Queensland Shearers Union demanded that its members refuse to work alongside Chinese workers. It even refused affiliation with the broader ASU in the 1890s due to "perceived softness over the race issue."[104] In contrast to South Africa, where native Africans were uniformly barred from the labor movement, in Australia the small population of aboriginals were welcomed into the AWU. Aboriginals did not represent substantial labor market competition for Australian workers; despite profound cultural hostility toward aboriginals, unions did not feel compelled to draw a racial boundary. In fact one aboriginal shearer,

William Ferguson, served as an AWU organizer in the 1890s and went on to a career in the Australian Labor Party.[105] During the 1920s, the AWU reaffirmed its commitment to white supremacy. The union refused to affiliate with the Australian Council of Trade Unions since this federation, based on its connection to the Soviet-sponsored Pan Pacific Trade Union Secretariat, refused to endorse the White Australia policy.[106] The Council of Trade Unions, according to the AWU president, offered "an open door for the coloured hordes of the North Pacific."[107] However, the Soviet influence declined, and two years later the Australian Council of Trade Unions endorsed the White Australia policy.

While organized Australian workers were primarily fixated on the possibility of large-scale migration from China and India, the threat of strikebreaking and low-wage competition from Europe also motivated the nativism of the labor movement. In the lead-up to the passage of the 1901 Immigration Restriction Act, the Australian Labor Party successfully added an amendment prohibiting the importation of labor under contract to employers modeled on the 1885 Foran Act in the United States. According to Australian Labor Party representatives, imported contract labor from Europe had been used to "break up the unions" in the US.[108] Even British migration did not go uncontested. Nationalist politicians who hoped to bolster Australia's military and economic capacity were keen to promote large-scale migration from Britain, but Australian unions and the Labor Party were wary of immigration's impact on the labor market. In response to plans for subsidized migration from Britain in 1907, AWU union delegates condemned attempts to "crowd the streets of our cities with poor men and women" who could be used to "bring down the standard of wages all around."[109] During the 1920s, two-thirds of the British migrants who arrived in Australia traveled with government assistance.[110] The Australian Labor Party condemned assisted migration at its 1924 conference. Assisted migration from Britain served "Capitalist Governments . . . flooding the Australian labor market, reducing Australian working-class standards."[111] After 1921, when the closure of US borders redirected some Italian migrants to Australia, workers organized to limit European migration more broadly.[112] In 1924 the AWU convention decried the growing "Southern European menace."[113] Despite the cries of alarm from unions and the Labor Party, the number of Italian migrants was minuscule by global standards. Only twenty-five thousand immigrants left Italy for Australia between 1922 and 1930.[114] Unassisted migration to the South Pacific remained prohibitively expensive, especially for relatively poor workers from eastern and southern Europe.

While the White Australia policy was a painful repudiation of the ideals of international labor solidarity, it was undeniably effective in achieving the goals of organized white workers. The combination of racist immigration restriction and distance from Europe allowed Australian workers to forge a protected national labor market with low wage differentials. These material conditions supported inclusive unions that grew rapidly and held decisive political power. According to an Australian socialist writing to *The Clarion* in 1912, only "the white race" was "far advanced enough in mental evolution to be successful democrats," and thus Australia was uniquely destined to be "a great land" as the "only all-white continent."[115] In South Africa, organized white workers struggled to build parallel, but distinct racial boundaries. The most important boundaries in the gold mines of the Witwatersrand and across South Africa were internal to the labor market, dividing white workers at the top from African natives below.

The Color Bar in the South African Production Hierarchy

In 1919, a labor adviser to the South African Chamber of Mines toured the United States while attending the International Labor Conference in Washington, DC. He came away impressed with US capital's power to defeat organized workers. In a report on "World Labour Conditions" circulated to leading South African mine managers and industrialists, the adviser identified three models: the European path, which had been shaped by the immediate threat of communism; the British path, in which a working-class democratic majority was able to wield power; and the US path, in which a divided working class kept organized labor weak. In pointing to high wage differentials and the lack of solidarity across the craft divide, this admiring South African pinpointed the sources of narrow unions in the US: "The existence of large bodies of unskilled labour . . . possessing little sense of comradeship with the skilled workers, [has] tended to limit the influence of organised labour."[116] For the Chamber of Mines, this was an appealing model that South Africa could emulate.

In South Africa, the basic divide within the working class was between highly paid white workers and the masses of native African laborers who worked as short-term contract migrants under oppressive and coercive conditions.[117] Other racialized groups were positioned between these two extremes on South Africa's stratified production hierarchy. "Coloured" workers, those of mixed European, African, and Asian descent, occupied a distinctive intermediate position, earning more than native Africans but less than white workers. In the building trades, where African labor was entirely excluded, the color bar was drawn between white workers and these "coloured" workers.[118] In addition, contract workers from South

Asia labored in the cane fields, and for a brief period, Chinese contract workers were recruited to the gold mines.

The South African countryside was an inverted mirror image of the experience of rural producers in Ireland. Whereas the Irish rural poor gained the franchise in the 1880s and won extensive land redistribution around the turn of the century, in South Africa, native rural producers were gradually disenfranchised from the 1880s onwards and were pushed off the land into overcrowded reservations. This political and economic transformation of the South African countryside ensured an abundant supply of low-wage workers to the mining industry.[119] The contradictory tendencies of British policy in Ireland and South Africa were highlighted by a Liverpool Methodist preacher in 1914: "While we pursue land reform at home we dare not sanction agrarian crime across the seas. In the South African Union the blacks outnumber the whites four to one, but they have legal tenure of only one-fifteenth of the soil. . . . The black man is to be tolerated on his own continent only as a labourer, and the moment he seeks to rise above his servitude he is treated as a public peril."[120] With its steeply stratified wage structure and racialized production hierarchy, South Africa illustrates most dramatically the links between access to land in the countryside and how migrants entered urban production hierarchies.[121]

The development of the industrial color bar and the recruitment of low-wage migrant labor from the South African countryside were intertwined processes. Mining capitalists in the Witwatersrand (Rand) district of the Transvaal held extraordinary power. But the construction of the industrial color bar was fundamentally driven forward by the resistance and mobilization of workers, most decisively, by white workers who demanded and defended it, much like many craft unions in the US. The process was also shaped by African migrants refusing to be recruited and Chinese contract laborers rebelling against their conditions. In South Africa's all-important mining sector, the first legally-binding structure of occupational racial segregation was drawn up by a mining engineer who believed that safety could be promoted by removing black workers from dangerous underground work. While initially promulgated from above in 1892, the early craft unions of white workers eagerly embraced regulations that reserved skilled jobs for white workers.[122] Unions drove the extension of the color bar to skilled workers above ground in the mid-1890s, and by the end of the decade, the defense of the color bar became a central concern for organized white mine workers in South Africa.[123]

While skilled, experienced miners from Britain were at the top of the production hierarchy, at the bottom were masses of African migrant laborers who worked on six- to nine-month contracts. From the 1890s onwards, mining capitalists represented by the Chamber of Mines had attempted to push a larger share of the African population into wage labor in the mines. In 1911, the president of the Chamber explained the struggle of mining capitalists to recruit African labor: "The tendency of the native is to be an agriculturalist, who reluctantly offers himself or one of his family as an industrial worker. . . . He cares nothing if industries pine for want of labour when his crops and home-brewed drink are plentiful."[124] A small class of African landowners who profited from the growth of commercial agriculture caused concern, but even more troubling to employers was the larger group white South Africans called "squatters": African cultivators who lived on white- or government-owned land, either as rent-paying tenants or sharecroppers. These "squatters" had too much independence, in the eyes of white South African employers, since they could refrain from selling their labor for wages. While white commercial farmers received generous government subsidies, infrastructure investment, preferential credit access, and tax relief, African rural producers were harried and constrained by discriminatory taxes, fees, and regulations that aimed at "translating independent squatter peasants into wage-labourers."[125] African Americans had fought an unsuccessful battle to secure access to land during Reconstruction, and in South Africa, black natives fought a long, losing battle to retain access to their land.

The Boer War (1899–1902) severely disrupted the recruitment of African labor to the mines, both by weakening the administrative and coercive capacity of the state, and by offering African workers unprecedently high wages in the tight wartime labor market. In a parallel to the freedpeople's occupation of abandoned Confederate plantations during the US Civil War, during the Boer War, perhaps as many as a hundred thousand Africans "simply settled . . . upon land vacated by 56,000 whites." These black settlers believed "that after a British victory" they would secure access to the land of defeated Dutch landowners. This expectation was quickly frustrated, causing "restlessness and unusual excitement."[126] The prospect of land redistribution, and the experience of high wages during the war, raised expectations among Africans. Thus when wages were reduced for minework in 1902, Africans refused to be recruited. A crisis loomed for the mining industry. African rural producers still had sufficient access to subsistence in the countryside. They could launch a "general strike" against minework. As white authorities complained: "The native method of striking is very simple. . . . [H]e is always going home, and if he is not satisfied with the conditions of employment, he simply does not come out again."[127]

To meet this crisis, the mining industry would need to find an alternative source of low-wage, vulnerable labor. An American observer suggested recruiting African Americans. However, as a South African mining engineer explained, given the democratic and egalitarian political tradition that African Americans had developed, this would be a dangerous proposition:

> With regard to American niggers they would be the very worst thing that could be introduced. Aside from the fact that we require cheaper labor than they would provide, there is the much greater objection that they would tend to awake a spirit of insubordination among the ordinary natives. The nigger at home [in the US] is always looking for an opportunity to emphasize his idea of his equality with the whites, and when he comes out here, as I have had occasion to note, [he] becomes a great nuisance by reason of the distorted American ideas of liberty and equality. . . .[128]

While wages were a crucial index of relative positions of power, political traditions and perceived capacity for collective action were also important to employers when recruiting workers. Thus, rather than to the Americas, the Chamber of Mines looked to the East. To mine managers, "Chinese labor promised a measure of control and coercion that had been . . . impossible to impose directly upon African workers."[129] In response to employer demands, the British government negotiated an agreement to import tens of thousands of Chinese indentured workers. Reports of the poor working conditions in South Africa meant that labor recruiters were refused access to Guangdong province in South China where most labor recruitment happened; nearly all the Chinese workers who came to South Africa came from Northern China, drawn to sign indenture contracts by wages five times the rate prevailing locally.[130] Crucially for the formal institutionalization of the color bar in South Africa, in order to overcome widespread resistance by organized white workers, the 1904 Labour Importation Ordinance provided a detailed list of the jobs at the top of the production hierarchy that would be exclusively reserved to white workers.[131] Some sixty thousand Chinese indentured laborers were eventually recruited to work in South African gold mines, but South African capitalists had gravely miscalculated in their racialized expectations of a docile workforce. The militant resistance of these Chinese workers to harsh conditions, and the violent, punitive policies used to control them, quickly undermined the project.[132] Alarmed by reports of abuse and violence against Chinese workers, political opposition consolidated in Britain. The 1906 election of a Liberal government in the UK, and the election of the Dutch nationalist Het Volk (People's) party in the Transvaal signaled the end to the importation of Chinese workers to the gold mines.

It was in this context that white South African workers organized their first major strike in 1907, marking the decisive starting point of a long struggle to enforce and defend the color bar. The immediate cause of the strike was management's demand at the Knight's Deep mine that white miners oversee three rather than two drills operated by black laborers.[133] Had this practice become general, the share of mine labor done by white miners would have been substantially reduced, and the employment of African laborers would have expanded. This issue had previously caused small disruptions in 1897 and 1902, but by 1907, it had taken on a more serious form, since "the growing proficiency of African miners threatened the privileged position of white miners." In 1902 one in six mine workers had been white, but by the time of the strike, this number was only one in ten.[134] Another important change had also reshaped the composition of the white workforce. At the time of the strike, British immigrants were 90 percent of the skilled craftsmen who worked on the surface. Only 10 percent of these desirable jobs were held by native-born, Dutch-speaking Afrikaners. In contrast, in underground work, the previous monopoly of British miners had been broken; the share of Afrikaners had risen to 40 percent of the white workforce in the dangerous, underground mining work by the time of the strike.[135] Afrikaners were paid considerably less than the experienced British miners, and when the union went on strike in 1907, thousands of rural Afrikaners proved to be eager strikebreakers.[136] In addition, the fact that "much of the actual mining expertise" was increasingly held by African laborers allowed for inexperienced Afrikaner strikebreakers to be hired as replacement white supervisors.[137] Structural labor market divisions between Dutch Afrikaners and British immigrants initially fractured white solidarity in South Africa.

Faced with disruptive white workers and the loss of Chinese labor in 1907, mine employers carefully considered an even more aggressive expansion of the African workforce. Ultimately, the need for a political accommodation with Het Volk, the ruling party in the Transvaal, dissuaded mining employers from attempting a major breach of the color bar after defeating the union in 1907.[138] On the other side, Het Volk briefly flirted with the "whites-only" employment policy promoted by H. F. Creswell, a mine manager who soon became the leader of the South African Labour Party. The possibility of a "whites-only" labor policy caused considerable anxiety among mine managers. Rather than expanding the employment of white workers (as Creswell and the South African Labour Party demanded) or black workers (as many mine managers desired), the color bar remained in place as an uneasy truce that received further legal sanction in 1911 with the Mines and Works Act.

In recognition of industry's concession in observing the color bar, the South African state worked to secure an increasing supply of black wage laborers without the incentive of increased wages. In the Cape, the Locations Act of 1909 raised taxes and fees on black tenants and sharecroppers, and in the Transvaal, the 1908 Natives Tax Act similarly incentivized landowners to evict independent black tenants in favor of hiring wage laborers.[139] Two decades of pressure on rural African producers crystallized in the Natives Land Act of 1913, which forbid Africans from purchasing land in "white areas," left only 13 percent of the country as Native Reserves, and redefined the terms of rural tenure to reduce "rent-paying squatters and sharecroppers to the level of labour tenants."[140]

The Natives Land Act aimed to stabilize agrarian change in black areas, where individual landholding was limited to very small plots. These regulated rural sectors enabled low-cost social reproduction of the African migrant workforce, in particular care for the young and elderly in rural communities, while the pressure of poverty meant that households were motivated to secure wage income from migrant workers recruited to the mines.[141] This spatial separation of migrant low-wage labor from its geographical site of social reproduction was a general feature of capitalism's uneven geography, as has been discussed above, but nowhere did it become as sustained and systemic as in South Africa. By 1910, some two hundred thousand migrant black workers arrived annually to work labor contracts of six to nine months in the gold mines.[142] The culmination of a long process of rural dispossession, the Natives Land Act of 1913 stabilized a politically and economically vulnerable workforce that was neither fully divorced from the land nor able to survive without supplemental income from wage labor. In addition, pass laws strictly regulated movement and a monopsonistic state-supervised recruitment agency suppressed wages and placed black workers in carefully surveilled compounds.[143] Systematic violence against black mineworkers by white supervisors was rooted in these labor market structures. Wages were suppressed through artificially set maximums for black mineworkers; thus routine violence was necessary to elicit productivity.[144] Migration from the US South, while a function of a variety of oppressive practices, lacked the depth of systemic coercion deployed against the black inhabitants of South Africa.[145]

The tight labor markets and labor militancy of World War I also challenged the color bar in South African mining. Black workers launched unprecedented efforts at labor organizing and organized white workers recommitted to a militant defense of white supremacy. After decades in industry, black workers in South Africa were gaining familiarity and confidence with new industrial organizing strategies.[146] During the 1910s and 1920s, Africans forged a mass politics for the first time in which "African men from across . . . linguistic and ethnic differences addressed each other as confederates and equals for the first time."[147] Eastern European Jewish syndicalists associated with the International Socialist League (ISL) helped initiate labor organizing among black workers. But the radicals in the ISL remained deeply isolated from the white South African labor movement.[148] Early 1919 was "marked by widespread strikes, pass burnings, and riots by African workers," and a few months later the Transvaal Native Congress launched a campaign for higher wages and for the abolition of the pass laws that controlled internal migration.[149] The culmination of growing African politicization and organization came in February 1920, when some seventy thousand black workers participated in a massive strike against the gold mines, one of the "most sustained and complex worker protests in South African history."[150] After ten days, the mining companies granted substantial wage increases and promised improved outlet stores that could provide affordable necessities like food and clothing.[151] After these victories, African workers who continued to resist were forced back into the mines with extraordinary violence.[152]

Even after postwar labor militancy retreated, black South Africans continued to challenge their subordinate position during the 1920s. The most important organization of black workers in the 1920s was the Industrial and Commercial Workers Union (ICU), which melded the ideas of Marcus Garvey's Pan-African nationalism with the syndicalism of the Industrial Workers of the World. This remarkable, if unstable, organization was founded in 1919 and grew to at least a hundred thousand members by 1927. The ICU was initially led by "poorly educated, full-time wage earners," but as racial boundaries hardened in the 1920s, significant numbers of middle-class, educated black South Africans joined the organization and transformed it from a "trade union to a mass movement fighting against white supremacy."[153] Internal factionalism and political repression destroyed the ICU in the late 1920s.[154]

White workers observed this growing militancy with concern. The 1922 Rand Revolt, the defining moment in South Africa's labor history, had its roots in the destabilization of racial boundaries during World War I, when labor scarcity in the white workforce had forced mine operators to move experienced African workers into a small number of semi-skilled positions legally reserved for white workers. To preserve industrial peace, and to stabilize racial boundaries within the production hierarchy, a 1918

"Status Quo Agreement" had enumerated the jobs assigned to white and black workers at each mine. By the summer of 1921, the president of South Africa's Institute of Engineers dismissed the "sentimental colour bar" imposed by the agreement, and called for the widespread substitution of African for white labor.[155] In December 1921, the South African Chamber of Mines announced that it would no longer respect the Status Quo Agreement, and that some two thousand white workers would be replaced with lower-paid African workers.[156] White miners went on strike in January, but met with little success. After several months, on March 6 the white unions announced an escalation of the conflict into a general strike; the next day, crowds of white men and women began attacking and murdering Africans in working-class neighborhoods.[157] White strikers not only shot and killed black residents, and mutilated black bodies, but also threatened to burn down autonomous black neighborhood institutions, including a school and a stable.[158] The eruption of racial terrorism and murder during the 1922 strike was part of the racialized "spatial organization of the urban environment" that culminated in the national policy of legalized segregation under the Native Urban Areas Act of 1923.[159]

The white strikers were eventually brutally crushed using modern warplanes and heavy weaponry. But while white workers might have lost the industrial battle in the 1922 Rand Revolt, they won the larger war over the color bar. The passage of the Industrial Conciliation Act early in 1924 established a legal framework through which white unions could have their demands met while explicitly excluding all African workers from any protections or legal recognition.[160] This exclusion parallels the 1935 National Labor Relations (Wagner) Act in the United States, which excluded from its protections agricultural laborers and domestic servants, both groups dominated by African Americans.[161] In addition, a Labor-Nationalist Pact government was elected in 1924 that "legislated preferential employment and wage increases for white workers."[162] As an alliance of Dutch Afrikaner nationalists and English-speaking trade unionists this "Pact" government resolved the divisions that had initially pitted British craft unionists against poor Afrikaner strikebreakers in 1907.[163] White South African workers overcame internal divisions while engaged in a decades-long struggle to construct and entrench the color bar.

White Laborism in Britain: Receptions of South Africa in Liverpool and Sheffield

For many British workers, the struggle to enforce the color bar had a limited resonance in the early twentieth century. Of course, fifty years earlier workers in Britain had organized a "religious bar" to keep Irish workers at the bottom of the production hierarchy, but these parallels were either not remembered or conveniently forgotten by the early twentieth century. A study of Hull has suggested that British workers' perception of South Africa reflected an "absent-minded racism," since while organized workers in the city "knew perfectly well about the inferior status of black workers in South Africa," they "were not keen on placing that issue at the fore."[164] In Sheffield, the details of the South African experience landed very faintly. By contrast, the struggle of white workers in South Africa resonated more clearly in Liverpool, a port city with a far more direct, material experience of racialized struggle over access to jobs. British port cities, as we have seen, had direct experiences of racialized competition and conflict among low-wage maritime workers.[165] For white Liverpool workers who rioted in 1919 and engaged in hate strikes against the employment of black factory workers, the struggle of white South Africans to preserve the color bar resonated with local material conditions. This was far less true in Sheffield. In Britain's industrial interior, white South African struggles were met first with silence, and later with considerable skepticism.

The Liverpool press offered a remarkably clear account of the South African labor situation. In 1902, the *Liverpool Daily Post* covered the refusal of African workers to labor in the mines after the war, noting the "unwillingness of natives who obtained good wages from the military authorities to re-engage themselves" and a general "new spirit of independence caused by contact with soldiers."[166] In the ensuing debate in Parliament on the importation of Chinese workers to South Africa, a Liverpool MP prioritized the employment of white workers by suggesting that four thousand unemployed casual dockworkers from his city could be sent to South Africa to be employed in the mines.[167] While the suggestion was not made seriously, it still suggested a conceptual connection between British and imperial labor markets. The Liverpool press also covered the 1907 miners' strike in detail, noting the use of Afrikaner strikebreakers, efforts to recruit African laborers, and the precipitating issue of expanded African drill operators.[168] Both the *Liverpool Echo* and the *Liverpool Daily Post* clearly grasped the stakes of the 1907 strike.[169] The *Post*, in an article titled "Shall White Labour be Eliminated?," took note of the views of *The South African News*, which had "published a remarkable article, in which it says that the strike was founded on a well-grounded fear that the magnates were inaugurating a policy of slowly eliminating white labour, and that the mineowners desire an extension of semi-skilled labour under white supervision.... The whole question as affecting South Africa is whether the field of white employment shall contract or expand."[170] This, of course, was the same question for white British sailors as they faced growing competition from Asian, African, and Caribbean seamen. A letter from a Cornish investor in South African mines published shortly after the 1907 strike gave Liverpool readers a sweeping account of the South African labor situation. He emphasized the shifting division of labor between British, Afrikaner, and native labor, the steep wage differentials of the labor market, and the importance of coercive measures in the countryside to produce an adequate supply of black African laborers.[171]

In contrast, coverage of labor issues in South Africa was far sparser in both the *Sheffield Independent* and the *Sheffield Daily Telegraph*. News items were usually confined to a few words from the wire services.[172] Strikingly, on the same day that the *Liverpool Daily Press* published "Shall White Labour be Eliminated," both the *Independent* and the *Telegraph* in Sheffield published a Press Association Foreign Special newswire article with a very different emphasis.[173] Here "the action of the mine-owners in endeavouring to reduce the number of whites employed" was noted, but the most prominently featured perspective, from "a Labour member of the Legislature," argued that the mine owners were "fanning the flames of race hatred by introducing the Dutch, for the Dutchmen were inexperienced, and they might as well have introduced monkeys." In the Sheffield papers, white solidarity fades into the background against the racialization of low-wage Afrikaner strikebreakers. In Liverpool, where white maritime workers were mobilizing against low-wage competition from non-European sailors, the struggle for white supremacy in the production hierarchy registered clearly. In Sheffield, perhaps informed by the city's central role in armaments production during the Boer War, the racialized hostility of British workers against their low-wage Dutch competitors appeared as the central lesson of the 1907 strike. White racial boundaries were not invisible in Sheffield. The Conservative *Daily Telegraph* noted a Labour MP's call to "assist the starving white men in the Transvaal, who were unable to get work through the determination of the mine-owners to oust white labour." But once again, this seemingly broader "white" solidarity was narrowed to British craftsmen "who were anxious to return to England."[174]

In the years after the 1907 strike, South Africa appeared prominently at three moments in the Liverpool and Sheffield press: South African independence in 1910; reviews of *The Real South Africa*, published in 1913; and the arrival of the deported South African trade union leaders in 1914. In 1910, Britain approved self-rule for the Union of South Africa, thereby uniting the formerly separate colonies under an autonomous government. Black South Africans had been granted a limited and diminishing right to vote in the British colonies, but in the former Dutch colonies, Africans had never had access to the franchise. Union in 1910 raised the question of the future of black civil and voting rights. In 1909, the *Liverpool Daily Post* took note of Labour Party efforts to amend the South African Union bill in order that "the native franchise shall be retained" in the Cape and Natal.[175] In Sheffield, the *Independent* gave more sympathetic coverage to Labour Party efforts to protect African voting rights under the union. In Parliament, Ramsay MacDonald, leader of the Labour Party, admitted that this issue put him in opposition to the South African Labour Party: "It was with the greatest grief and sorrow that he opposed friends of his own who occupied positions of political responsibility in South Africa."[176] MacDonald was "convinced however, that this [political] colour bar was meant to be final, and that the intention was that never, so far as man could secure, should a native or a coloured man sit in the Parliament of United South Africa. He could not share the belief that opinion in South Africa was improving in this respect. On the contrary, his melancholy belief was that racial antipathy was becoming more marked, and therefore it was that he stood and appealed to the Government to do more than they had done to protect the rights of the natives."[177] In addition, the *Sheffield Independent* noted that the Methodist Synod had expressed "its disapproval of the colour bar in the South African Union Bill."[178] Liverpool papers appear to have taken no notice of this protest. While debate over the South African Union was noted in both cities, critical coverage of the emerging racial order in South Africa was far more pronounced in Sheffield.

In Sheffield, the local labor movement also spoke directly to the 1910 South African Union Bill. Although Liverpool, with its fractured working class, did not have the resources to support an independent Labour and Trade Union newspaper in the early twentieth century, in Sheffield trade union leaders published their own paper, the *Sheffield Guardian*. Sheffield's labor leaders argued that "all lovers of freedom" should celebrate the Labour Party for its "fight . . . on the South African Bill, for the recognition of the rights of the natives."[179] The permanent disenfranchisement of black South Africans was "revolting" since it used "colour" to subjugate "a man. . . . as an inferior being." While the Parliamentary Labour Party's struggle was in vain, the Sheffield trade unionists claimed that "South African politicians at least know how repugnant the restriction is to the whole British nation." While Sheffield labor leaders claimed to speak for the British nation, white Liverpool workers more directly exposed to competition low-wage workers from Africa, Asia, and the Caribbean obviously did not share this clear, if abstract, egalitarianism.

In considering the reception of South African developments in Britain, the reviews of Ambrose Pratt's *The Real South Africa* in the two cities offer a second point of comparison.[180] Pratt, an Australian, aimed to dissuade British emigrants from making South Africa their destination. The book warned that black workers were quickly becoming "skilled and dexterous craftsmen."[181] According to Pratt, the "market for skilled labor [was] strictly limited and the negro encroaches on it more and more as time proceeds," while work at the bottom of the production hierarchy belonged "wholly to the blacks: it is ensured to them by the cheapness of their labor."[182] Only a few "highly trained craftsmen" might have a chance at success in South Africa, while the average worker would "only increase his poverty" by selecting South Africa for emigration.[183] At a time of increasing interest in overseas emigration to British settler-colonial dominions, Pratt's denunciation of South Africa, and implicit endorsement of Australia as a white workingman's paradise where all could prosper, appears to have generated substantial local interest.[184] Both the *Sheffield Daily Telegraph* and the *Liverpool Daily Post* published detailed reviews of the book. The Sheffield paper described a "Vivid Book on the Black Menace," and noted the growing entry of black workers into the skilled trades: "Mr. Pratt's conclusion is that . . . South Africa . . . can never be the home of a great white people until the tide is turned, and white labour is given entrance to, and secured in the position of the entire field of industry."[185] In Liverpool, the *Daily Post* offered a more critical assessment of the book, arguing that it painted an overly negative and one-sided picture.[186] For the Liverpool reviewer, growing black political aspirations were particularly notable: The "blessed words 'constitution' and 'a vote' [had] stirred their imagination. . . . [T]he craving for a vote seems . . . an obsession." A result of this growing black political and economic advance in South Africa would be to "compel the white man, whether Dutch, or British, or Jewish descent, to draw together." While the Sheffield review rejected South Africa as a suitable destination for emigration, in Liverpool, the reviewer offered a more positive assessment, perceptively predicting growing white solidarity in the face of rising aspirations from the black majority.

Beyond Pratt, the Liverpool press was far more attentive to publications exploring the South African experience. The *Liverpool Daily Post* reviewed Walter Meakin's *The Life of An Empire* in 1907, which suggested that "Johannesburg, like the North in the United States, will be the backbone of the whites," but for this to succeed, "more work must be reserved exclusively for white men."[187] Four years later the paper reviewed H. Mortimer Durand's *A Holiday in South Africa*, which suggested the need for a "settled policy" for "the treatment and control of the black and coloured society." Without objection, the review noted that "caste" in the form of an "industrial wall . . . raised between black and white" had "succeeded slavery" in organizing South African production hierarchies. This more detailed coverage suggests that Liverpool readers were more intimately familiar with the conditions and struggles unfolding in South Africa.

By contrast, in Sheffield the *Weekly Telegraph* published a remarkable article, "The Briton Abroad: White and Black in South Africa," with the assumption that its readers were not well-informed and needed a forthright lesson on South African racial and production hierarchies. The first lesson for Sheffield readers was that "it cannot be made to clear enough to the intending emigrant that there is absolutely no white unskilled labour in South Africa."[188] The Sheffielder who landed in South Africa would find "himself in charge of a gang of natives who carry on the purely manual part of the work, while the white man superintends." The white overseer needed to be "a little autocrat in his own particular sphere," the paper explained to Sheffield workers who might emigrate. The *Weekly Telegraph* also felt compelled to warn Sheffield workers against naïve racial egalitarianism. In Yorkshire, most workers had only encountered "gentlemen of colour" in the form of an African Bishop, the Liberian Prime Minister, or the "bejewelled black pugilist driving costly motor-cars." Given this limited experience, the Sheffield worker's "ideas as to the colour line, if he holds any at all, [were] somewhat peculiar" from a South African perspective. Such imperfect racial knowledge would "delude him, when a greenhorn at the Cape, into treating the primitive, untutored members of his gang more or less on the 'man and brother' system," as fellow workers deserving respect. Sooner or later, the British emigrant in South Africa would see the "error of his ways" and come to understand that when in charge of "a gang of niggers" it would be necessary to punish slacking and "high jinks" with a "vigorous reprimand, both vocal and physical." The *Weekly Telegraph* clearly suspected that potential emigrants from Sheffield would be unprepared for South Africa. The column closed with a final dictate for Sheffield workers in preparation for potential emigration: "it is absolutely necessary that the supremacy of the white man should be firmly asserted and maintained even in the minor matters of everyday life." Whereas in Liverpool, maritime and port workers would have had direct experiences with racialized struggle for control over work, in Sheffield, the emigrant "greenhorn" had to be warned away from the delusion that black workers might be treated as a "man and brother."

The most direct British engagement with the South African labor movement came in 1914 after nine deported trade union leaders arrived in London in late February. Despite a sustained tour during April and March, for the most part the connection with South African experiences

was quite shallow, and local leaders repurposed the South African controversy to meet more immediate, local concerns. The centrality of the color
bar and the racialized struggle for control over jobs to the original conflict
was mostly ignored.[189] In particular, South Africa was reflected in an Irish
mirror, since the Home Rule controversy dominated British politics at the
time. For the Tory *Sheffield Daily Telegraph*, South African developments
were reframed in terms of the protection of Protestants under proposals
for Home Rule in Ireland. For Conservatives, the inability of Parliament
to interfere with South Africa's deportation of the union leaders called
into question commitments for the protection of Protestants in a self-
governed, Catholic-majority Ireland.[190] In Derby, the local Labour MP ran
with the logic of these Tory arguments, suggesting that if "Ulster was justified in using force to gain their demands, it was the duty of railway men"
in England as in South Africa "to anticipate the refusal of the companies to
grant their demands by organizing armed forced at once."[191] On the other
hand, the Liberal *Independent* in Sheffield also connected South African
developments to the more pressing concerns in Ireland, but in this case,
as part of larger struggle for land reform. In April, as the deported South
African union leaders toured England, Sheffield's Liberal paper hailed
the victory of the South African Labour Party in the Transvaal provincial
elections—"welcomed by progressives the world over." Since the South
African Labour Party supported a land value tax, the "path will be clear
for an attack upon monopoly."[192] In this peculiar, partisan reading from
afar, the "land valuation taxation issue" and not the occupational color bar
was the key to "counteract[ing] the mine owners' intent to extirpate the
white community." While the racial stakes of the South African struggle
registered, the terrain of conflict was shifted to one more familiar to English Liberals: policies promoting land reform.

For British labor leaders, the tour of the South African labor leaders
spurred discussion of labor movement tactics, in particular the syndicalist,
revolutionary general strike as opposed to more incremental political elec-
toralism. To British labor leaders, faced with syndicalist challenges from
below, the lesson drawn from the deportations was that South Africans
had mistakenly pursued an industrial, syndicalist strategy without building sufficient political power. As the president of the Electrical Trades
Union in Sheffield argued at his union's annual dinner, "a lesson to learn
from the deportation of the labour leaders from South Africa" was that
while "some placed their faith in industrial action, and some in political
action . . . both were necessary."[193] Philip Snowden, a Labour Party MP,
wrote in the *Sheffield Guardian* that the South African labor movement
highlighted the dangers of syndicalism such as that of the Irish radical

James Larkin: British workers did not "desire more influences of that sort of trade unionism."[194]

During the 1914 tour of the deported leaders, the racial occupational boundary at stake in South Africa was never acknowledged in the Sheffield coverage. Between January and March of 1914, the *Guardian*, as the official paper of the Sheffield labor movement, carried eight stories covering the strike, the deportation of the labor leaders, and the tour of England. The racial dimensions of the South African labor movement were never acknowledged by the local trade union paper. Initially, the *Guardian* used the repression of the strike in South Africa to highlight that this use of state power against labor leaders could encourage English employers in local strikebreaking efforts.[195] The next week the paper highlighted divisions between the English and Dutch-speaking South Africans: "Not long since" a "war between Briton and Boer took place," and now the "same Boers" were "assisting the British Government to crush Trade Unionism."[196] Once again, in Sheffield coverage stressed British-Boer divisions and ignored broader black/white conflict. In addition, the trade unionists' paper used the events to urge electoral support for the Labour Party in Britain. The repression in South Africa proved that the Liberals were no friend of the working class. The events would require "those people who still believe that the Liberal Government is really in love with the working classes" to reconsider; or as another article bluntly stated, "Liberalism is the enemy. Toryism is the enemy. Democracy must find its own foot soldiers" in the Labour Party.[197] Another prominent theme in the *Guardian* emphasized that an attack on the rights of workers anywhere in the British Empire was a threat to workers in England. The deportation of the labor leaders under martial law without trial required a united defense of "the common rights of the whole people of Great and Greater Britain," whether these rights were threatened in "South Africa, or Ireland, or India or anywhere else."[198] Snowden agreed, arguing that the "only permanent basis" for the British Empire was "the recognition throughout its length and breadth of these great principles of civil liberty for which our forefathers have fought."[199] Unanswered in this bold declaration was the most important question: who were the "the whole people of Great and Greater Britain"? In discussing the South African experience, Snowden, like the Labour movement in Sheffield more generally, remained silent on whether these "great principles of civil liberty" extended to the non-European subjects of the British Empire in India, South Africa, and elsewhere.

For maritime workers in Liverpool, such an immediately pressing question could not be ignored. In contrast to the silence from Sheffield, concerns about racial boundaries resonated clearly in Liverpool. In February, the *Liverpool Echo*, a paper loosely aligned with the rising local Labour Party, took note of a "startling statement" from the South African Mine Managers' Association, that the "real cause of the industrial unrest . . . was the advancing skill of the natives, many of whom are now able to do the white man's work."[200] In a direct attack on the color bar, the manager argued that mine owners "must give equal opportunities to the whites and the blacks." While acknowledging employers' desire to abrogate the color bar, the Liverpool press also took note of white workers' defense of these racial boundaries. In Liverpool, a speech by H. J. Poutsma, one of the deported union leaders, explaining the racial struggle over jobs, was covered in detail: "Now that the Kaffir [native African] was somewhat skilled and so much cheaper," South African capitalists and politicians "were beginning to weed out all the white men from the mines and put the natives in their place. It was only natural that the white labourers endeavoured to maintain their wage and status."[201] When J. T. Bain, another of the deported leaders, arrived in Liverpool a week later, he made a more implicit racial argument. Under "proper management South Africa should become the world's great farm," more attractive to white settlers "than even Canada or Australia."[202] Given the comparison to these white settler colonies, implicit in this "proper management" was the maintenance of white supremacy and the industrial color bar. At the same Liverpool meeting, another deported leader made the comments with which this chapter opened, observing that the "nigger in South Africa was just as much a slave as the niggers used to be in America, and perhaps even more so."[203] While discussions of race were completely absent in the Sheffield coverage, issues of racial hierarchy were clearly recognized in Liverpool.[204]

A decade later, by the time of the 1922 Rand uprising, the racialized occupational boundaries central to the struggles of organized white workers in South Africa registered far more clearly in both cities.[205] In November 1921, before the start of the strike, the *Sheffield Daily Telegraph* observed that the "proposed change in policy in regard to coloured labour threatens trouble in the South African gold mines."[206] In January, as the strike began, the *Telegraph* offered the perspective of a South African "industrial expert": "Behind it all is the question of racial equality. . . . Hitherto in South Africa the native and the half caste worker, no matter how highly educated or skilled, has been precluded from engaging in skilled tasks, these being regarded as the close preserve of the white worker."[207] The *Liverpool Echo* described a "movement, which began with a strike following on the Rand mineowners' plan to increase the amount of native labour."[208] After the outbreak of racial killing with the declaration of the general strike, the *Liverpool Daily Post* observed that British readers might "think it strange that the strikers are shooting down the natives wantonly. But it should be remembered that the use of native labour in certain circumstances is among their grievances."[209] The *Liverpool Echo* prominently featured a comparison of "whites" and "natives" killed during the racial rioting, and offered unsettling details of the racial terror: "The spectacle was to be seen of strikers . . . sometimes even accompanied by women and children, chasing natives and coloured people and emptying their revolvers at their terrified victims." Even in Liverpool, where the 1919 race riots were a fresh memory, the reporter appeared shocked at reports of a man within view of a police station "firing deliberately into a crowd of coloured people."[210] If in 1914 the discussion of racial boundaries was uneven and muted in Britain, by 1922, the centrality of white supremacy in South African labor struggles was abundantly evident. Yet coverage of the 1922 strike suggests more disgust than enthusiasm or solidarity from British observers.

In Sheffield, the trade union press simply ignored the Rand revolt, perhaps suggesting a choice to withhold solidarity. Indeed, the broader coverage of the 1922 strike in Sheffield suggests a substantial degree of direct opposition to the white supremacy of organized South African workers. Most strikingly, a long article titled "The Riddle of the Rand: Psychology of the South African Miner by One Who Knows Him" in the *Sheffield Independent* made it clear that some viewed white South African workers as unusual, clearly distinct from the British working class.[211] Seemingly written by a Sheffield resident who had lived in South Africa, the article opened by making this differentiation clear: "The extraordinary acts of violence, intimidation, and sabotage recently committed by the Rand rebels can only be explained in one way. The miner in South Africa is not the ordinary type of Colonial, but a kind of dangerous leaven in the Commonwealth." White South Africans were thus set apart from "ordinary" white British colonial subjects. Familiar antisemitic tropes appeared to inform how this Sheffielder characterized South Africans as a "dangerous leaven." South African miners were "without roots," and came "from all over Europe . . . with a strong Slav element." They came "to make money and get away." Unlike other British settler-colonial dominions, "nobody thinks of going to live in Johannesburg as one might consider settling down in Winnipeg or Melbourne." The author argued that white miners developed their racism in South Africa, rather than carrying it with them from Europe: "Although a miner may only propose to work in Joburg for a few years, he quickly picks up the colour prejudice. He has no difficulty in accepting the legend that the black is naturally incapable of doing his work." Yet the growing skill of African workers, who could now "use the drill as efficiently as the European," meant that white workers' jobs were under threat. This challenge to the "colour bar," the author argued, explained "the extreme bitterness and strength of the race hatred which has been shown by the rebels" during the strike. Whereas in 1914, the *Weekly Telegraph* had urged Sheffield emigrant "greenhorns" to quickly adopt the prevailing racism of the South African industrial hierarchy, by 1922, the *Independent* offered the perspective of a returned South African emigrant who had found the racism of white South African workers alien and disturbing.

Additional coverage from Sheffield suggests deepening hostility to South African white supremacy. Intriguingly, Arthur Guttery, a Primitive Methodist preacher from Liverpool, found an audience for his views on South Africa not in the local Merseyside press, but in Sheffield, where working-class religious dissent had strong roots.[212] Guttery offered a clear assessment of the South African situation, and a moving vision of working-class solidarity: "This compulsory divorce from the land [after the 1913 Natives Land Act] produces an industrial servitude without hope. Trade unionism is forbidden [to black workers], the very name is regarded as treason. He has no vote, no land, no friends, only his naked labour which the white capitalist will secure on the cheapest terms. . . . Labour must take up the black man's cause, for where the negro is practically a slave, the white worker will not remain long free."

Within Sheffield, partisan divides between Tories and Liberals shaped coverage of South Africa, while the Labour press chose to ignore the South African experience entirely. The Liberal *Sheffield Independent* offered sympathetic coverage of the struggles of black South Africans.[213] By contrast, the Tory *Sheffield Daily Telegraph*, while acknowledging increased black mobilization, urged sympathy for white South Africans: "It is easy at this distance to forget that these South African white men are living on the brink of a volcano. . . . [T]he ascendancy of white people in South Africa . . . exercised firmly but humanely, [was] absolutely essential to the existence of South Africa as a civilized State."[214] In 1921 both Sheffield papers covered a lecture by a South African educator on "Problems of Race and Labour in South Africa" at Sheffield University.[215] The lecturer, from the Tiger Kloof Training Institute in the Cape, argued that "the black races were feeling the colour bar which prevented them from attaining to responsible positions. They were not always going to be content to be hewers of wood and drawers of water." The suggestion of "eliminating the colour bar so that black and white may compete on their merits" was met with "applause" from the audience at Sheffield University, according to the Liberal *Independent*. Notably, the Tory *Daily Telegraph*, more inclined to defend imperial white supremacy, did not record this signal of the crowd's approbation.[216]

While Sheffield's labor movement paper remained silent on South Africa, throughout the 1920s the *Sheffield Independent* offered clear sympathy with the plight of black South Africans, often from the perspective of religious dissent. Basil Matthews, preaching "Christian brotherhood," pointed to the "exclusion of the negro from the possession of his ancestral land" and the "will of white labour to create and maintain a virtual monopoly of skilled and highly paid occupations" as the two profound injustices at the root of black discontent in South Africa.[217] Rejecting the biological and cultural racism of his era, Matthews suggested that racial conflict arose from "disturbing economic, social and political conditions." In 1929, the Sheffield professionals at the local Rotary Club discussed South Africa after a visiting speaker argued that it "was a mistake . . . to segregate the blacks."[218] In the Liverpool press, similar criticism of South Africa's regime of white supremacy was entirely absent. Instead, the *Journal of Commerce* continued to promote South Africa as a desirable destination for white settlers, noting in 1925 that "nobody wants to see white labour in competition with black or Asiatic" workers, and commending the "authorities" who had "taken steps to regulate coloured labour . . . so that the white man will have an infinitely better chance."[219] The South African experience met with a complicated, uneven reception across Britain, profoundly shaped by local material conditions and filtered through partisan lenses.

Conclusion

"White laborism" stitched together an imperial working class within the British Empire, but these stitches were thin and fragile in places like Sheffield, even as they were thick and binding in Australia, South Africa, and maritime ports such as Liverpool. The direction and content of racial boundaries varied significantly, depending on the material conditions of local labor markets. South African labor struggles resonated far more clearly in Liverpool, where shipowners could relate to the desire of colonial gold miners to replace expensive white workers with cheaper, non-European replacements, and where white maritime workers threatened by competition from Lascars, Chinese, and black sailors could understand the struggle of white South African workers to protect their jobs through a racial color bar. In Liverpool, and in port cities around Britain, racialized boundary-making was not a distant abstraction, but a direct experience rooted in local labor markets. In contrast, in Sheffield, the white laborism of the empire resonated only faintly, and in a few cases, was actively disavowed.

PART III

Homes, Sports, and the Rise of Unions

SOLIDARITY AND SEGREGATION IN WORKERS' SOCIAL WORLDS

They were given public deference and titles of courtesy because they were white. They were admitted freely with all classes of white people to public functions, public parks, and the best schools. The police were drawn from their ranks, and the courts, dependent upon their votes, treated them with such leniency as to encourage lawlessness. Their vote selected public officials. . . . White schoolhouses were the best in the community, and conspicuously placed. . . . The newspapers specialized on news that flattered the poor whites and almost utterly ignored the Negro except in crime and ridicule.

> W. E. B. DU BOIS, *Black Reconstruction in America*,
> "Back Toward Slavery," 700–701

In 1915 Alfred Williams wrote, in his autobiography of working-class life, that "every hour spent outside the factory is a precious addition to life." A worker who accepted longer hours was "guilty of the highest folly and negligence." He was "the forger of fetters for himself and his children after him."[1] Working-class formation was rooted in experiences both at work and at leisure. Yet it seems clear that most workers valued their time outside of work far more than their time on the clock. The rise of mass-production Fordism from the 1890s transformed work: craft power declined, "semi-skilled" labor expanded, and managers exerted increasing control and authority over the shop floor. These changes destabilized the old dichotomy of white over black and craftsmen over laborer.[2] Fordist mass production tended to blur previously sharp craft and racial divisions in the production hierarchy, but the working-class social worlds that consolidated around these new plants in the twentieth century were also crucial sites for racialized boundary-making. Homes, schools, leisure, sports, and the social life of their families and communities were increasingly important to workers. Yet, as Du Bois suggests, these were also arenas where racial boundaries divided white workers who enjoyed status, respect, political influence, and superior public amenities from black workers who were publicly ignored "except in crime and ridicule."[3]

The previous two sections of this book have explored the large-scale structures of land, labor markets, and global inequality, and from this context, the processes of racialized boundary-making that consolidated in different settings. Here we turn to the everyday experiences of workers themselves, how they lived and how they engaged in collective action. Between the 1890s and 1920s, the social worlds of working people in both the United States and the United Kingdom were remade, leading to the formation of a new kind of working class that organized in new ways and made new demands.[4] Although the two countries are usually studied in isolation, a comparative perspective reveals that parallel changes in housing, neighborhoods, leisure, and sports had strikingly opposite results. In the US, white and black workers became more deeply divided, while in the UK, previous divides within the working class receded.

This transformation started at home. Developers, corporations, and governments produced improved and expanded working-class housing in new Fordist suburbs that moved to the outskirts of cities alongside the relocation of new mass-production plants. This was an uneven process, but already underway beginning in the 1860s, and gathering momentum after the 1880s.[5] Homes became increasingly important sites for working-class leisure, and reduced hours and increased earnings created new expectations of mass participation in the emerging market for consumer durables. While new homes became an anchor of working-class social worlds, much of the transformation of working-class social life occurred beyond the home. From the 1870s to the 1920s, drinking declined and new forms of organized, commercial leisure expanded. Working-class social worlds were remade as previously informal, unregulated pastimes were transformed into commercial, regulated, bureaucratic channels. Nowhere was this more visible than in the rise of organized sports. Youth played sports on school and club teams, workers played on factory and amateur club teams, and most of all, sports spectatorship, commentary, and betting became central to working-class Fordist masculinity in the early twentieth century.

Workers' social lives in their homes, leisure, and sports were all transformed in similar ways in these years in the US and the UK, but the resulting patterns of class formation were profoundly different in the two countries. In the UK, these transformations bridged divides within the working class, drawing craftworkers and laborers, Protestants and Catholics closer together. The remaking of working-class social worlds had the opposite effect in the US. Working-class neighborhoods, schools, commercial leisure, and sports were all racially segregated, deepening the fundamental fracture that split the US working class. It was not just distinct material positions in the labor market that undercut inclusive solidarity between white and black workers in the US; it was also the fact that workers lived, raised children, and relaxed in separate, segregated social worlds.

Fractured or not, these transformed social worlds created a working class that turned to a new form of collective mobilization: the modern bureaucratic labor union. In the nineteenth century, working-class collective action had erupted in a tumultuous street politics of rioting. From the 1880s to the 1920s, increasingly centralized, bureaucratic, and durable labor unions coordinated and disciplined working-class collective action, redirecting workers from spontaneous crowd politics toward strategically planned and centrally coordinated strikes and collective bargaining. Workers not only mobilized in new ways; they made different demands. Rather than the "honor of the trade," they fought for a "living wage."[6] While autonomy had been a central demand of workers in the nineteenth century, in the twentieth century, workers reoriented toward demands for redistribution: more money for less time worked on the job from employers, and political programs that taxed the rich and provided state-funded services to the community.

Racial boundaries were key to the remaking of working-class social worlds and politics. Since the rise of mass bureaucratic unionism was rooted in transformed working-class social worlds, racial segregation in neighborhoods, leisure, and sports impinged upon the possibilities of inclusive working-class organization. If workers returned to segregated and unequal homes, neighborhoods, and leisure networks, whatever solidarities might be forged on the shop floor would be exceedingly thin. In addition, the reorientation toward statist, redistributive politics increased the significance of racial boundaries in defining state welfare policies: who was a citizen and who was an ineligible alien, who was deemed worthy and deserving and who was excluded and denied access?[7] By the 1920s, racial boundary-making, while still rooted in racially and regionally divided labor markets, was also increasingly driven by new material structures: unequal access to housing and constrained eligibility for statist welfare benefits.

Solidarity and Segregation in the Industrial Suburb

In an address to the American Bankers' Association in 1919, a business-man promoted home ownership as "the savior of the nation" since "men who own their own homes do not think of Bolshevism, I.W.Wism and kindred diseases which are spreading over the country."[1] While working-class homes were seen as an antidote to revolutionary radicalism, working-class householders (and the many more workers who aspired to live in a modern home) turned out to be keen union members. Ironically, despite the hopes of some businessmen, homes may have been a spur to more im-mediate, if less radical, forms of working-class militancy. Fears stoked by the growing power of organized labor during World War I and the global shockwaves of the Russian Revolution led governments in both the United States and the United Kingdom to build housing for workers to avert so-cial unrest and manage the wartime labor market. In the UK, this led to a massive public building program of new council estates; in the US, after a brief period of government-built housing during the war, state efforts shifted to subsidizing private home ownership among workers. In both countries, the right to a modern home as a site of consumer abundance had become a key part of working-class politics by the 1920s; but in the US, expanding white working-class homeownership was understood in terms of racial boundaries and segregated neighborhoods.[2]

Although the world war marked a key turning point, the new impor-tance of housing reflected a much longer shift in working-class residence from city centers to industrial suburbs. Alongside the growth of mod-ern, mass-production factories from the 1880s, a new kind of working-class industrial suburb spread at the outskirts of major cities, such as the public council estates of Liverpool and the industrial suburb of Dundalk in Baltimore. In Liverpool, the rearrangement of working-class house-holds as they migrated to council estates diminished long-standing and bitter hostilities between Irish Catholics and English Protestants in the city, producing integration and solidarity on the new suburban council estates that made them unusual early bastions of Labour Party support in Liverpool. In contrast, in Baltimore, the industrial suburbs around the Sparrows Point steel plant were strictly segregated, and a powerful white working-class homeowner identity consolidated based on the exclusion of African American workers from these desirable new neighborhoods. The rehousing of workers provided new bonds of solidarity, but in the UK, these ties were encompassing, overcoming prior divisions among workers, whereas in the US, new housing provided a new material foundation for working-class white supremacy. Yet these local developments were part of global shifts. As Carl Nightingale has argued, Baltimore's infamous attempt to impose formal residential apartheid in 1910 was part of a "planet-wide proliferation of residentially segregated cities designed to uphold racial hierarchies" in the early twentieth century.[3]

Thus housing emerged as a central material underpinning for racial inequality and racialized boundary-making in the early twentieth century. While land continues to matter for rural producers across the Global South, within urbanized settings housing has replaced agricultural land as the material asset shaping workers' fallback position in the labor market. Workers from households who owned homes would be able to navigate entry into the labor market with more choices and options since they had a relatively favorable and secure fallback position. Workers from households denied access to homeownership, as were most US black families in the twentieth century, would be pressured to enter the labor market immediately, slotting in to whatever positions were open. Housing was consequential for multiple reasons: it meant wealth and access to better schools and other public amenities, but also, and often overlooked, it was a form of security shaping labor-market decision-making. As Gabriel Winant has shown, working-class housing functioned "as private group insurance to shelter extended family units against episodic distress."[4] Contemporary patterns of racial inequality in American housing have their roots in the turn-of-the-century rise of industrial suburbs. Today in the US, while 64 percent of white working-class households own homes, only 36 percent of black working-class households are homeowners.[5]

Fordist Factories and Industrial Suburbs

In the US, the reinforcing consolidation of craft and racial boundaries in the labor movement in the 1890s coincided with the beginnings of the spatial relocation of production and working-class housing. The racial boundaries drawn through the labor movement and the production hierarchy were also drawn through working-class neighborhoods during the early twentieth century. Mid-nineteenth-century cities had limited "segregation along economic, ethnic, and racial lines," with mixed-income neighborhoods producing a landscape of "residential heterogeneity." It was only in the late nineteenth century that "patterning by ethnicity and race" became entrenched in the urban landscape.[6] Working-class industrial suburbs grew alongside the spatial relocation of capitalist production with the rise of Fordist mass production. Some moves began in the 1860s, but the major relocations of plant and housing from city centers to industrial suburbs occurred after 1880.[7] In Pittsburgh the "major reorganization of production under corporate capitalism" after 1880 "drove the spatial extension of development far beyond the traditional urban core," creating the greater Pittsburgh District stretching roughly forty miles from downtown.[8] Companies that had emerged within the urban core relocated to new industrial suburbs dispersed along the vital transportation network provided by the three major rivers: the Allegheny, Monongahela, and the Ohio.[9] Carnegie's Edgar Thomson Works in Braddock was the first major suburban plant, commencing production in 1875, but others soon followed. In the 1890s, Westinghouse relocated several major plants upstream along the Allegheny River, giving the Turtle Creek region the name "Electric Valley." A similar suburban development occurred in Aliquippa, which was built by Jones & Laughlin in 1905 to house workers for its new integrated steel plant.[10] Similarly, the typical Baltimore rowhouses built in the early twentieth century reflected a shift in capitalist production to "mass, machine production." Rowhouses in a typical working-class industrial suburb were occupied by skilled workers (27 percent) and operatives (27 percent), with a substantial group of white-collar workers in clerical positions (20 percent) and sales (13 percent). Residents typically worked for large employers such as Baltimore & Ohio Railroad, Baltimore Gas & Electric, Potomac Telephone, Baltimore Transit, and the Post Office. Only a few worked for small companies, mostly in the building trades. Laborers and African Americans were absent and excluded from this new residential neighborhood.[11]

In both the US and the UK, investments in new industrial plants often required relocating to new, suburban factories, and this posed challenges for housing and retaining a workforce. At US Steel's Duquesne Works, the personnel director warned in 1921 that the housing "conditions in McKeesport affecting our mill men are bad beyond description," and urged the company to tackle "rent profiteering" and "speed up the construction of houses" so that "unscrupulous property owners" could no longer take advantage of their employees.[12] As this suggests, the managers of large

FIGURE 8.1 Workers' homes built by Jones & Laughlin Steel Company. During the construction of the Aliquippa Works from 1906 to 1913, the Woodlawn Land Company, a subsidiary of the steel company, built modern homes for Jones & Laughlin steel workers. *Source*: "Jones & Laughlin Steel Corporation Mill and Coke Ovens," Jones & Laughlin Steel Corporation Collection Photographs, 1864–1953, MSP33.B008.F01.I01. Detre Library and Archives, Sen. John Heinz History Center.

plants were willing to sacrifice the interests of the petty landlords who rented poorly constructed houses as a short-term, speculative venture. To displace small, private landlords, large corporations built quality houses to rent, and increasingly to sell. The companies accepted a loss on building these residences with the goal of a stable workforce with predictable levels of rent.[13] Most housing was developed for workers at the top of the production hierarchy, whose stronger position in the labor market meant that if they found local housing conditions unacceptable, they could easily move to find work elsewhere. As seen in figure 8.1, when Jones & Laughlin built their new suburban steel works at Aliquippa in the first decade of the twentieth century, the company spent $140,748 building "dwelling houses" for workers, more than 10 percent of the general construction costs of the new plant up to 1907.[14] By 1909, Jones & Laughlin had contracts in place for the construction of 430 more houses, which would bring the total to 610.[15] When Sheffield's John Brown steel company was building their new suburban steel plant at Scunthorpe, managers debated how best to develop housing.[16] The manager of the new Scunthorpe plant warned that better housing was "absolutely essential" for retaining the services of skilled workers such as "the better class of moulders" who "would not consider remaining in the semi-permanent houses such as we have at present."[17] By November 1920, John Brown & Co. had confirmed plans for constructing 144 houses, including 71 "small concrete Bungalows," 30 "large concrete bungalows," 39 "brick cottages," and 4 "Brick Bungalows for Staff."[18] More rarely, employers could be pressured to build housing for workers lower on the production hierarchy. In 1922, the *Pittsburgh Press* reported that the Duquesne Light Company was building "28 dwellings . . . with every convenience for the comfort and well-being" of the residents, the homes to be "occupied by the unskilled workers at the Colfax plant of the company."[19] While only a fraction of the working class had secured the most modern, updated homes by the 1920s, these homes had become a universal aspiration and expectation.

In the US, companies had to manage the racial segregation in their workforce both on the job, and when building housing. US employers were eager to employ African American workers from the South as low-wage laborers and strikebreakers. When these workers were retained, the refusal of local white landlords and property owners to offer housing to black families meant company housing was often the only option. Discrimination in Northern housing markets was long-standing. In 1891, the Non-Denominational Colored Ministers Council of Human Rights of Pittsburgh and Allegheny denounced the "cruel distinctions as are practiced by real estate brokers and other business men." In denouncing the real estate industry, these ministers declared that "the Afro-American race" would no longer "submit to the brutal impositions of evil-disposed white people."[20] When Jones & Laughlin built the Aliquippa works, housing for its workforce was divided into twelve distinct "Plans," with "Plan 6" reserved for plant managers and foremen, and "Plan 12" reserved for English-speaking workers.[21] At the bottom of the production hierarchy, Italians were concentrated in Plan 11, and black workers in the Plan 11 extension.[22] Several steel workers who later became union leaders described purchasing a company-built home. George Alex Dominic recalled: "Dad bought a house up on plan 7 on Oakwood Avenue. 105. We lived there for quite a while, til '37."[23] Clark Cobb, an African American steelworker, recalled his family moving into a house on Spalding street in Plan 11. The company "was just building houses like, just throwing them up you know. Because they were short" of housing for workers.[24] Cobb remembered many black families buying houses in Aliquippa in the early 1920s: "Houses was cheap then." Despite segregation, company-built housing was often the only new, modern housing stock available to African American families. In the early 1920s, the Pittsburgh Urban League noted with concern that new housing built by "Negro Building concerns" was located on "cheap land on a high hill" far from any transportation. The more favorable development for black workers in the Pittsburgh District was the fact that "industrial concerns in the suburbs" were also "building and planning to build cheaper houses for Negro workmen."[25] In the US, although private builders and real estate agents played leading roles in developing and segregating the new working-class industrial suburbs, both the government and large employers also played important roles in determining what kinds of workers would live where and under what conditions. While there were more parallels than often appreciated, ultimately the far larger role played by the state in developing working-class housing in the UK had an enduring impact on British working-class social worlds.

Working-Class Integration on the British Council Estate

The same underlying processes of capitalist reconstruction during the Second Industrial Revolution drove the relocation of factories to suburbs in the US and the UK, but ultimately the process of rehousing workers unfolded along a radically different trajectory in Britain. In the UK, the state played a central and decisive role in building housing, and while the construction of new industrial suburbs entrenched racial divisions in the US, in the UK publicly built council housing undercut the divisions that had divided working-class communities in the nineteenth century. Had divisions between Irish and British workers remained as intense before World War I as they were in the mid-nineteenth century, the British state would not have provided such a broad, universal program of home building. In turn, the leading role of the state further eased the remaining divisions between Irish Catholic and British Protestant workers. Whereas in the US, the state only played a brief role as builder during World War I, in the UK, government-built housing was central.[26] Roughly a quarter of British urban working-class households moved to the suburbs during the interwar period, with 13 percent of all workers moving into public council housing, 9 percent making private purchases with mortgages, and 3 percent renting in private developments.[27] In the years after World War I, workers moved "to new suburban communities of semi-detached private or municipal housing," creating not only a new spatial configuration of working-class life, but as Peter Scott has argued, a new working-class disposition rooted in cleanliness, privacy, and increasing participation in the consumer economy.[28]

In 1919 Parliament passed the Housing and Town Planning Act, which required local municipal authorities to implement plans to provide needed housing in each locality. In addition, private builders were incentivized with a lump-sum subsidy for houses constructed that met the Health Ministry's standards.[29] Although 500,000 new municipal houses were initially planned in 1919, by 1920 receding "fears of Bolshevik revolution" and a decline in the power of unions from a wartime peak led the government to roll back ambitions, limiting the number of houses built to 170,000.[30] However, the election in 1924 of Britain's first Labour government led to additional public building, with the Wheatley Act of 1924 providing expanded subsidies for municipal building. The Labour government also brokered a "gentlemen's agreement" with the building trades unions, offering increased work on public projects in return for a relaxation of craft boundaries and concessions on the entry of apprentices into the trade.[31] Most importantly, the new council houses provided working-class people with "hot running water, bathrooms, gas, electricity, and substantial gardens, creating aspirations" for many in the 1920s that by the 1930s "had become expectations."[32] As the wife of a railway labourer recalled on moving to a Liverpool council estate: "I loved it. Everything was new. We had a bath to ourselves, hot water and lots of space. I can remember the range in the kitchen. All the neighbours used to polish it to see who could get the steel edges the cleanest. We were very proud of our new houses."[33]

In the UK, this remaking of working-class neighborhoods contributed to the easing of tensions between Protestant and Catholic workers. The construction of new suburban developments disrupted the local networks that had both bound workers together and deeply divided them in their previous neighborhoods in the old urban core. The dense housing of the mid-nineteenth century was intensely communal, with family and social life unfolding in public on the streets. As a sociologist studying Sheffield in 1929 noted, the old crowded slums in the city center produced "an extraordinary sense of neighbourliness and social intimacy," with births, deaths, and the "details of everyday life" shared with neighbors.[34] In moving to the modern council estates in the suburbs, working-class families gained access to the amenities of a modern home and the aspirations of a consumer economy, but also lost direct contact with sectarian networks of mutual support.[35] While materially beneficial, the move to the suburbs was also disruptive.

In places with deep divisions within the working class, such as Liverpool, this disruption opened the possibility of broader solidarities. As one Liverpool resident recalled, the move to the Woolfall Heath council estate eased the deep religious hostilities that had long divided Catholics and Protestants in the city: "Where we came from, down Scotland Road way, Catholics and Protestants only came together to fight. The Catholics lived in certain streets, Protestants in others, and no one mixed. Out here, though, the Corporation forced us all to mix because all the children, at first, had to go to the Council schools. Well, when people start to mix, a lot of the old hatreds start to go and out here the Orangemen and the Catholics never fought like back down town."[36] In cities like Liverpool, the relocation of the working class to the suburbs enabled new kinds of solidarity. As we have seen, as late as 1909, violent and extensive sectarian rioting had driven Catholic and Protestant minorities out of particular neighborhoods.[37] Ultimately, the spatial remaking of workers' social worlds also had political significance. In a city where religious and ethnic divisions stymied the growth of the Labour Party, Liverpool's new suburban, working-class wards in the council estates became early, exceptional Labour strongholds after 1921.[38] The council estates turned Irish nationalists and working-class Tories into Labour Party voters. Workers who remained in the older urban core remained loyal to their established political ties through the 1940s, but those who moved to the new, integrated suburbs overwhelmingly became Labour voters by the 1920s.

Working-Class Segregation in the US

In the US, relocation to new working-class suburbs also created social worlds that supported different patterns of class formation and a new kind of politics. But rather than a politics of class solidarity, as in the UK, the workers in the US who moved to improved housing in the early twentieth century forged a defensive white racial solidarity that aimed to maintain segregated neighborhoods. As in the UK, working-class suburbanization eased tensions between native Protestants and immigrant Catholics, producing a more inclusive and more sharply bounded white working class. Yet above all housing came to underpin the core fracture between white and black workers. Leading interpretations of housing and racial segregation in the United States stress the period of the Great Depression, New Deal, and World War II as the era during which the federal government became centrally involved in redlining, the mortgage market, and fostering both housebuilding and racial segregation in the United States, as well as the period in which white working-class families came to expect secure, segregated access to housing as a social right.[39] While the post–World War II era certainly marked the culmination of these processes, their origins lie in the transition to Fordist capitalism at the turn of the century. The large-scale housebuilding of the Emergency Fleet Corporation during World

War I reconfigured and expanded the role of government in providing housing. This government role helped create new expectations of housing as a political right for white workers. Although the 1940s and 1950s greatly extended working-class housing developments and patterns of segregation, already in the 1920s white working-class families were mobilizing politically to draw overlapping racial and spatial boundaries around segregated industrial suburbs.

Baltimore provides an ideal setting in which to trace the overlapping of state, employer, and private developers in the early construction of racially segregated working-class housing. The Emergency Fleet Corporation built one of its largest projects for the Bethlehem Steel Company, just to the southeast of Baltimore at Sparrows Point. This was an ideal steel-making location with access to deep-water ports for iron ore and coal. The plant was part of the late nineteenth-century process of industrial suburbanization. The plant first cast steel in 1889, and in the 1890s, the Maryland Steel Company built a company town in Dundalk where workers rented houses along a grid that segregated residents by race and position in the mill.[40] In 1916 Bethlehem Steel bought the plant to take advantage of war production, and during the war, the Emergency Fleet Corporation lent $3.2 million to the Liberty Housing Company, Bethlehem Steel's housing subsidiary, to fund house-building projects at Dundalk and St. Helena, adjacent to Sparrows Point.[41] By August of 1918, three thousand workers were completing a house every three hours, as the Emergency Fleet Corporation aimed to rapidly complete 827 residential units.[42]

As seen in figure 8.2, when the government-built homes went on sale in November of 1919, Dundalk was described as "the last word in modern industrial village building," with "maple trees rising" and "housewives rolling baby carriages on the cement sidewalks that seem endless."[43] Dundalk, according to the *Sun*, had "given mechanics modern homes with bathrooms, electric light and gas, hot and cold water, little front porches . . . and plenty of fresh air." Most importantly, these homes could be purchased "on monthly installments about the same as present rental rates . . . in the city." However, a few weeks later, the Dundalk company clarified that it was "not interested in the sale of any houses in Dundalk to outsiders," since Bethlehem Steel needed "every one of them for our own men, and a great many more."[44] The steel company's housing subsidiary also expressed gratification that Frank Novak, a leading Baltimore developer and the "king of the two-story rowhouse," planned "to build 450 homes" privately at Biddle Street station, where workers could easily commute by train to Sparrows Point.

As working-class housing expanded and improved, racial segregation

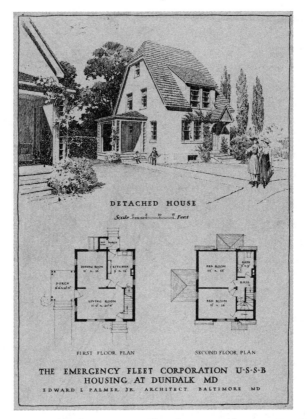

FIGURE 8.2 Plans for Emergency Fleet Corporation houses at Dundalk. Government-built housing for workers during World War I provided a foundation for growing expectations of political and government support for working-class access to improved, modern homes. *Source*: Plans for Emergency Fleet Corporation Houses at Dundalk. Unidentified Artist, Housing, Government: United States. Maryland. Dundalk: Governmental Agencies of House Construction. US Shipping Board, Emergency Fleet Corporation: Detached House: The Emergency Fleet Corporation U-S-S-B Housing at Dundalk, MD. Edward L. Palmer Jr., Architect. Harvard Art Museums/Fogg Museum, Transfer from the Carpenter Center for the Visual Arts, Social Museum Collection, Photo © President and Fellows of Harvard College, 3.2002.2013.

gained greater political significance. In 1910 the Baltimore city council passed a series of pioneering racial zoning ordinances meant to lock in neighborhood boundaries and keep black homebuyers out of majority-white neighborhoods. This residential apartheid law was widely copied across the United States, and drew interest from as far away as the US Occupation Authorities in the Philippines.[45] As Elizabeth Herbin-Traint argues, these experiments with formal racial segregation in the early twentieth century were driven by populist mobilizations of the insecure "middling sorts," including home-owning craft workers. The *Baltimore Afro-American* pointed to the "wails of whites of moderate station in life" as the force behind the segregation ordinance. In contrast, large employers, who hoped to recruit African American workers as cheap labor, resisted attempts to legislate racially exclusive neighborhoods.[46] After a black attorney purchased a house in Baltimore's Eutaw Place, police had to be deployed to defend his house from the violence of white mobs. Thousands signed a petition to the mayor and city council calling for "measures to restrain the colored people from locating in a white community, and proscribe a limit beyond which it shall be unlawful for them to go."[47] Racial segregation was understood in the 1910s as part of an effort to bring rational, scientific planning to the city. It was not a staunch reactionary who implemented racially segregated urban planning in Baltimore, but J. Barry Mahool, a mayor "known as an earnest advocate of good government, women's suffrage, and social justice."[48] These ordinances were passed despite their obvious violation of the 14th Amendment. Unsurprisingly, in *Buchanan v. Warley* (1917), a Louisville segregation law modeled on Baltimore's was struck down. With this law defeated in the courts, equally effective but less overt measures were soon implemented to secure racial boundaries in the city. *Buchanan v. Warley* provides an early illustration of the futility of court decisions against the material underpinnings of racial inequality.

Following on its early but unsuccessful attempts to create a regulated urban apartheid, Baltimore was also a leader in institutionalizing the use of racially restrictive covenants to keep neighborhoods segregated in the 1920s. As Paige Glotzer has shown, Edward Bouton of the Roland Park Company pioneered the use of racially restrictive covenants to exclude African American and Jewish residents in his upscale, private housing developments in suburban Baltimore.[49] When Bethlehem Steel planned Dundalk, Bouton was hired as a consultant, and he copied the racially restrictive covenants from his upper-class suburbs to the working-class industrial suburb of Dundalk. These restrictive covenants were retained by the Emergency Fleet Corporation, and became a crucial part of how homes were advertised to white, working-class buyers. When Dundalk's houses were being marketed in 1922, the "Own Your Own Home" brochure issued by the company emphasized that the restrictive covenants "keep up neighborhood standards and . . . maintain property values" by excluding undesirable residents. The brochure also explicitly connected Dundalk's restrictive covenants to those of wealthier suburbs: "With all of its advantages and conveniences, with all of its value-building restrictions,

[Dundalk's] homes and homesites are most moderately priced. In fact, it is the only moderate-priced development around Baltimore having all the restrictions of the high-priced developments."[50] As Christopher Niedt argues in his study of Dundalk, by the 1920s "the legality of employment and housing discrimination [had] enabled Bethlehem [Steel] to play an active role in producing new white expectations of privilege (the covenant) and reproducing old ones (job segregation)."[51] The embattled craft/racial boundary in the production hierarchy was thus reinforced by the increasingly powerful boundary of racial segregation in new working-class suburbs.

Around Sparrows Point, Bethlehem Steel confined African American workers to residences in the Turner's Station area, while white laborers were placed in homes in St. Helena. A range of operatives, craftsmen, and white-collar workers lived in Dundalk, creating a carefully graded residential segregation by both occupation and race.[52] Bethlehem steel financed the construction of black workers' homes in Turner Station, but even as their numbers grew from 1500 in 1920 to close to 6,000 in 1930, segregation, job discrimination, and restrictive covenants kept black workers out of desirable, all-white neighborhoods and at the bottom of the production hierarchy.[53] The more secure, well-paid white workers of Dundalk were also hostile to poorer white migrants from the South, who were accused of spreading crime from "Hill Billy Heights."[54] Already in the 1920s, the categories white, worker, and homeowner had been fused together in industrial suburbs such as Dundalk, creating new racialized working-class social worlds that animated an enduring white political commitment to segregated neighborhoods.

Even though government building was relatively brief during World War I, many working-class families came to understand access to good housing as a political question during these years. In 1919 the *Baltimore Sun* reported on legislation from the Department of Labor for "a system under which nationally controlled banks would lend money on easy terms to individual home builders or purchasers, just as the farm loan banks advance money to farmers."[55] Although federal mortgage subsidies would be enacted later, World War I had already created momentum toward government-subsidized private homeownership. In 1922 the United States Chamber of Commerce (USCC) balloted its members on various proposals in Congress for supporting broader homeownership, including "a system of loans available to all citizens and others limited in their benefits to ex-service men."[56] USCC members voted 1023 in favor of "legislation and appropriations to enable ex-servicemen to build homes," over 677 who voted in opposition. Housing, in the early 1920s, was clearly an emerging political concern. Thus in 1921, as the postwar boom went bust, unemployment created a crisis for Dundalk's new homeowners, and the residents petitioned the Emergency Fleet Corporation, demanding a grace period for mortgage payments and a retroactive reduction in home prices.[57] The white homeowners of Dundalk won support from local politicians, in particular Senator Joseph Irwin France, who pushed President Harding to intervene in January of 1922. Under political pressure, the Dundalk Company, a Bethlehem subsidiary, ultimately agreed to purchase the mortgages and provided a 22 percent discount on original home prices.[58] Thus by the 1920s white working-class homeowners had come to see the federal government as a key alley in advancing and protecting their interests.

By the 1920s, the skilled, white craft workers of the Baltimore Federation of Labor thought of themselves as current or aspiring homeowners. The President of the Baltimore Federation of Labor reported on his participation in "an exposition relative to home building and home furnishing" aimed at working-class consumers.[59] Building trades unions reminded delegates that if houses for workers were "built by Union labor they would be much better" than non-union built homes.[60] Baltimore building trades delegates also urged union members to "get in touch" with the Carpenters local "when they needed repairs to their homes."[61] The labor movement also supported various efforts to finance home purchases. One Baltimore building society met at Carpenters' Hall and was controlled by men who were all members of Carpenters Local 101.[62] In addition, several locals in the Baltimore Federation of Labor subscribed capital funds to a "Labor Bank" in 1925 to support the financing of union members' homes.[63] Trade union members also mobilized politically to defend their growing investment in homes. In 1924 the Baltimore Federation of Labor backed a bill in the Maryland Legislature that exempted "$1,000 from taxation on homes up to $7,000."[64] Writing in the AFL's *American Federationist* in 1926, urban planner Clarence S. Stein asserted that "every worker has his ideal home" in the form of "a free-standing house with plenty of space around in which the youngsters can play."[65]

The centrality of homeownership for white workers was also notable in Pittsburgh, although in the steel city we can also see that for many eastern Europeans the full "American" amalgamation of white/worker/ homeowner remained incomplete. A 1929 study of a working-class ward in Pittsburgh found that a "large proportion of people own their homes."[66] The Irish, many second- or third-generation immigrants, were the largest group of homeowners. Years earlier, in the nineteenth century, when many Irish were still impoverished laborers, Protestant-Catholic rivalries between Welsh and Irish bands (much like in Liverpool) had resulted in the "occasional fisticuff between the two groups." But by 1929, economic divisions between the Welsh and the Irish had faded as an encompassing white solidarity eased former rivalries. In contrast to Irish laborers, the Welsh had arrived as experienced puddlers, powerful skilled craftsmen, and by the late 1920s had moved from the smoky and dirty flood plains to the nearby hilltops. There, the study reported, "at least half of Welsh families own their own homes, many of which have been acquired through the Building and Loan societies." The investigator estimated that between 60 and 75 percent of Germans owned their own homes. New immigrants, the "slavs" and Italians, were less likely to be homeowners. Bodnar, Simon, and Weber's later study of Pittsburgh demonstrates that at the bottom of the production hierarchy, African Americans were worse off than new immigrants by 1930. By comparing two typical working-class neighborhoods for each group, the authors are able to precisely identify the growing gap in homeownership in the 1920s. African Americans rarely owned homes (0.5 percent and 12.5 percent were homeowners), while Polish immigrants had more success (21 percent and 39 percent were homeowners), and Italians did best of all (31 percent and 45 percent were homeowners).[67] Here, in the 1920s, we see the foundations of the enduring racial wealth gap that continues to materially fracture the US working class.

While the black/white racial boundary was paramount, there was also extensive hostility toward others at the bottom of the production hierarchy at this time: Italians and eastern European immigrants. In an investigation of the 1919 steel strike, one investigator noted that the divisions among workers were reflected in their homes: "The Hunky," as many eastern Europeans were pejoratively labeled, was not welcome in "the 'better' saloons and movies," and was confined to "Hunky Town," which the "'Americans' refer to [with] contempt."[68] In contrast, "upon the hill" lived the Northern European immigrants, often described as "Americans" since they could speak English, with a "spacious well-kept home, wide veranda, a lawn and trees, and nicely paved streets." African Americans in this ward, a report ten years later noted, were "scattered . . . in several small colonies," and their presence had been vehemently resisted.[69] In one area of black residence, the "Irish-American element [had] fanatically opposed the presence of the Negro. . . . Sharp clashes occurred in the early days after the arrival of the first Negroes. One or two colored men were shot in fights at that time. . . . The Slavs, Italians, and other newcomers tend to curry credit with the 'Americans' by out Americaning them on this race issue, so that they are at times as rabid as the 'Americans.'" While division between "Americans" and new-immigrant "Hunkies" certainly marked recognized spatial boundaries in the Pittsburgh District, all workers of European descent were quick to unite against the incursion of black workers into their neighborhoods.

As white workers mobilized to defend the racial boundaries of increasingly segregated neighborhoods in the early twentieth century, it is unsurprising that housing segregation was a leading concern for African American activists. The Pittsburgh Urban League urged support for "any movement which tends to increase the number of houses available to Negroes," and their advocacy resulted in a report on race and housing by Pennsylvania in 1926.[70] As this survey noted, while there was no "segregation . . . in Pennsylvania by law, a very effective residential segregation of Negroes by force of public opinion occurs in many communities in the Commonwealth."[71] Spatial boundaries had significantly hardened in the early twentieth century: "Years ago it was not as difficult for Negroes to obtain good housing accommodations as it is today." Already in 1926, this survey pinpointed the central mechanisms that would preserve and expand racial segregation through the rest of the twentieth century. White homeowners feared that a "Negro Invasion" would lead to "a depreciation in realty values," and this "theory has been frequently used in Pennsylvania by real estate men as an excuse for refusing to sell houses to Negroes." Despite these obstacles, the survey observed that "nowhere is the desire for homeownership more pronounced than among Negroes." For instance, the number of black-controlled Building and Loan associations in Pennsylvania grew from eight societies with a capital of $150,000 in 1910 to thirty-four with a capital of $5 million in 1925. Meanwhile, a letter in the *Baltimore Afro-American* called on Baltimore's mothers to unite to fight for better houses: "We want better homes to live in—demand them— fight for them, if need be, and in the end get them."[72] In an article on the refusal of the School Board to build a school in a black neighborhood, the *Afro-American* bitterly and sarcastically observed that "the best solution we have for the problem is to get in touch with Frank Novak or some other builders who build new houses in the suburbs and get them to build more rapidly and probably when all the whites have moved" to the suburbs, the School Board would finally agree to build a new school.[73] This sarcastic commentary proved to be tragically prescient. Anticipating white flight and the transformation of Baltimore into a predominantly African American city, the *Afro-American* bleakly concluded in 1923 that only when all the white people had left for the suburbs would the School Board provide the needed buildings. Working-class housing became an issue of working-class politics: white workers organized to preserve their control of new neighborhoods, black leaders mobilized to gain access to housing. When the National Negro Business League convened in 1930, the assembled black leaders called "on the President of the United States to consider . . . the difficulties of the Negro in acquiring homes."[74] African Americans, just like white workers, looked to the government to help them secure their aspirations for well-built, affordable, modern homes.

Geography has always been central for inequality in the history of capitalism, from the global scale, where the rise of capitalism bound industrial cores together with slave-labor plantation peripheries, to the most local scale, where the relatively affluent and empowered built boundaries against perceived threats from poorer, less-secure neighbors. These local boundaries were particularly consequential in the United States, where craft, racial, and neighborhood boundaries reinforced each other in the early twentieth century. Segregation was also pursued in the United Kingdom, although class and status rather than race defined the hierarchies built into the spatial configuration of cities. In several instances, the slightly more affluent residents of privately built suburban developments attempted to prevent the construction of nearby government-built council estates. When private owners failed to stop government construction, private homeowners built walls blocking the streets between the working-class council housing and their own private developments. The most notorious examples of this segregation were the walls constructed around the Downham estate in London in 1926, topped with broken glass, and the Cutteslow estate in Oxford, as seen in figure 8.3, topped with rotating spikes. These walls became an "iconic symbol of middle-/working-class divisions" in the UK, even though the actual class compositions of the neighboring suburbs were only marginally different.[75] Slightly more secure, better-paid British workers were eager to draw imposing boundaries against those who were more precarious and lower on the production hierarchy. Even without the added fuel of racist antagonism, more secure sections of the working class in the UK also aimed to distance themselves from poorer neighbors. These British segregation walls were revealing, but relatively isolated practices in the UK. In the US, residential segregation resulted in a pattern of working-class formation in which secure, white workers at the top of the production hierarchy became homeowners, and vehemently defended their whites-only neighborhoods, while African Americans were confined to the lowest-paying jobs and prevented from securing homes.

Working-Class Leisure in the Industrial Neighborhood

Homes in the new industrial suburbs anchored new leisure practices, both within the home, often oriented toward new consumer goods, and outside

FIGURE 8.3 Segregation in the UK: Cutteslowe estate wall. More affluent
residents of a private development in Oxford had a brick wall topped with rotating
spikes built to segregate themselves from the less secure workers of adjacent
government-built council housing. *Source*: John Peacock, "Cuttleslowe Wall,"
photograph film negative, 35mm, POX0218563,WG:8847/26. Oxfordshire County
Council—Oxfordshire History Centre.

the home, in municipal spaces like parks, and in commercial venues such
as movie theaters and dance halls. New working-class homes were at the
center of a new configuration of working-class leisure that was increasingly privatized, regulated, and commercialized. In the mid-nineteenth
century, few workers enjoyed much leisure staying at home. Old city center working-class residences were typically cramped and uncomfortable.
However, the rise of industrial suburbs transformed the working-class
home into an increasingly important and meaningful site for leisure and
recreation. Of course, spacious homes had long been important for elite
social life, but from the late nineteenth century the social and cultural
meaning of the working-class home was transformed. Home holidays such
as the celebration of a child's birthday gained traction in the late nineteenth
century, and by the 1920s, when the song "Happy Birthday" appeared,
"children's birthday celebrations had become a fairly standard practice"
across social groups in the US.[76] Christmas, as a domestic celebration
centered on consumption and gift-giving, followed a similar trajectory
of late nineteenth-century growth and nearly universal acceptance by the

1920s.[77] Two practices with particular resonance and enduring importance for working-class leisure are examined here: gardening and a broad array of "do-it-yourself" home improvement activities. The growing importance of home life for workers thus paralleled and reinforced consolidating patterns of residential racial segregation. As Elizabeth Herbin-Traint writes, in the new Fordist industrial suburbs, as workers' homes became more important to them, homes came to represent "an extension of the self, and for many whites, that self could not be interracial."[78]

A survey of life among Pittsburgh steel workers after they secured the eight-hour day in 1924 offers a striking picture of the expanded domestic sociability of working-class families: at "one house a man stood swinging two children in a hammock, talking and laughing with them. . . . Another one was playing ball with his youngster. A third was out in his garden pulling up weeds under the supervision of his wife. A fourth was building an addition to the house. A fifth was mixing cement for the floor of his garage."[79] This vignette captures the home-based aspirations of working-class domestic leisure and family sociability that have continued to drive working-class demands for shorter hours and more pay for the past century. While Pittsburgh steelworkers were close to the global apex of industrial wage earners, similar desires for materially improved homes also motivated even the most desperate sectors of the global working class. In South Africa in the 1920s, a leader of the black community explained the growing discontent with low wages in terms of rising consumer aspirations: "The native of olden times used to live largely on sour milk and mealies," but today he "must have his coffee and sugar at least once a day" and "bread also as often as he can. . . . [T]he natives of today are ambitious to have beds, even in their kraals, whereas in the past they had mats. The storekeepers are selling these things in large numbers, and you find these things in even the rawest native huts."[80] When workers left the countryside to earn wages in the nineteenth century, migrants often hoped that their earnings would enable them to purchase land and reestablish their families in the agricultural world. But by the early twentieth century, visions of a return to the land were fading. Wage-earning now supported aspirations for a domestic material abundance that became substantially real for those at the top of global production hierarchies, and tantalizingly possible on a future horizon for all. Samuel Gompers, for all the failures of narrow craft unionism, clearly grasped the materialistic orientation of the remade working class in these years. Speaking in 1899, Gompers argued that workers wanted "more leisure, more rest, more opportunity . . . for going to the parks, of having better homes, of reading books, of creating more desires."[81]

In the nineteenth century, alcohol and informal leisure had spilled into the streets in masculine working-class social worlds. Unregulated traditional fairs and games faded during the mid-nineteenth century, and most importantly, alcohol consumption declined dramatically. From a peak in the 1870s, the volume of alcohol consumed per capita declined substantially in both the US and the UK.[82] The percentage of UK consumer expenditure on alcoholic drinks fell by nearly half, from 15 percent in the 1870s to just over 8 percent by the 1910s.[83] In 1889, the leader of the British Steel Smelters Union reported that 55 percent of the union's branch meetings took place in pubs. Only fifteen years later the share of meetings held in pubs had declined to only 6 percent.[84] Workers drank less largely because they had more money and more attractive options for spending it. While Bible lessons and the moralizing lectures of temperance reformers had failed to divert workers from the saloon, social workers took a more practical approach in the early twentieth century and promoted organized sports as a healthful diversion from drink. In Sheffield, amateur footballers could compete against teams organized by both the Bible Class League and by local publicans.[85] Although the pub and saloon remained important in working-class life, in the late nineteenth century drinking "lost its all-embracing importance" in workers' social worlds.[86] A social worker observed in 1905, "The cheap piano in the home, the baseball game, and the ten, twenty, or thirty shows are the only influences which rival the temptation of the saloon."[87] A journalist investigating the new "saloonless conditions" of the 1920s United States found that rather than drinking, workers increasingly turned to "neighborhood athletics" and "the movie."[88] By volume consumed, by time spent, and by value of money expended, drinking in 1910, even before wartime restrictions, was significantly less important than for workers in the late nineteenth century.

Among the most important home-based leisure activities that reshaped working-class social worlds in the early twentieth century was amateur gardening. Alfred Williams recalled in his 1915 autobiography that when winter turned to spring, workers "who have a couple of square yards of land, a small back-yard, or a box of earth on the window sill, prepared for the task of husbandry—the general talk in the spare moments now will be of peas, beans, onions, and potatoes."[89] The plant magazine of the Edgar Allen steel works noted the "great number of workmen who exhibit the produce of their gardens" at the Sheffield Horticultural Show.[90] In the 1920s, newspapers offered columns with helpful tips for urban amateur gardeners.[91] As a Pittsburgh steelworker explained, with the expanded leisure time after the eight-hour day he was "growin' a garden. The kids think I'm crazy spendin' so much time in it, but I don't care.... They want me to get a car. I'm thinking about it. . . . I guess I want to stick around home for a while and see how my garden grows."[92] In the UK, the growth of working-class suburban housing, both on council estates and in private developments, produced some "four million new gardens" during the interwar period.[93] As an early migrant to Liverpool's Larkhill council estate in the 1920s recalled: "Arthur loved the garden. I hardly saw him the first year we moved in, he was out in the garden all hours. You see, our generation had never had gardens, before the First World War, everyone came from a terrace house with just a little back yard."[94] In surveys of council housing tenants in the UK, gardens ranked "highest on the positive features of new housing."[95] While gardening was certainly among the most important and most visible of home-based working-class leisure activities, a wide variety of other hobbies also reshaped workers' leisure hours.

Auto and motorcycle repair, model building, and DIY home improvement had all become important domestic activities for working-class men by the 1920s. This growth of home-based hobbies and improvement projects was connected to broader transformations of capitalist work and production. On the one hand, more spacious homes in industrial suburbs provided an attractive and appealing setting to pursue projects; on the other hand, the elimination of traditional, autonomous craftsmanship from industrial work with the rise of Fordist mass production left workers seeking meaningful, creative engagement in other arenas. The growth of hobbies from the 1890s marked a "a reembracing of preindustrial labor, a re-creation of the world of the yeoman, artisan, and independent merchant" within the household.[96] One steelworker's wife noted that after the eight-hour day, her husband was often getting in her "way, wanting to know what I am doing and what he can do," and while at first this was disconcerting for the wife, she soon became thankful that her husband and steelworker sons had "done so many things for me to make the place more attractive."[97] Ship model-building was an important home-based hobby, and in promoting a local competition, the *Liverpool Echo* encouraged participation by observing that "a well-finished model will be an ornament to your house."[98] Home improvement could involve creative DIY projects, but also refashioning interiors with new consumer goods. In 1903, a budget study in Baltimore profiled a machinist whose family made substantial investments in home improvement through purchasing $82 (roughly $2,500 today) worth of new furniture.[99] The Bureau noted that "those things which were luxuries a few years ago, are today necessities."

While husbands and wives might cooperate in making their homes more attractive, the garage and automobiles emerged as an important adjunct to the house and a central site of working-class masculine leisure.

In the US, although not yet in the UK, automobile ownership became a widespread aspiration—and for a relatively affluent section of the working class, a reality—in the 1920s. Motorcycle ownership was more common among workers in the UK, many purchasing and gradually fixing broken machines.[100] A Carnegie Steel worker admitted that before the 1919 steel strike "he got 'auto crazy' and bought a car for $300," selling all his Liberty Bonds for the purpose. During the 1919 strike, he regretted "having done it, but he [did] not want to sell unless he [was] obliged to."[101] Automobile ownership appears to have been common among Baltimore Federation of Labor members by the mid-1920s.[102] With the eight-hour day in 1924, one steelworker used his leisure time as an amateur mechanic. As his wife observed: "He putters about the old car. He's building a garage right now. That's a good thing that saves money. If he were working the long shift, he couldn't do it, of course. Wouldn't have the time to. Lots of men are building garages."[103]

The new working-class social world anchored around the home in the industrial suburb also reshaped gender, creating the foundation for the modern invention of the "traditional family."[104] During the 1919 steel strike, the long hours in the steel mills were one of the primary complaints. As one investigator noted, "real family life" with twelve-hour shifts was "impossible," and the "women feel this lack keenly and are eager for a shorter work day." If their husbands had more time at home, they would "have a chance to really enjoy life," according to one Pittsburgh woman.[105] "Old Pat," a Pittsburgh steelworker, recalled that before the eight-hour day, when he came home he could "think of nothing but bed." He acknowledged the injustice to his wife, saying, "A woman at home wants more of a man than to feed his face and hear him snore. . . . A wife has a right to a husband."[106] As Steven Gelber has argued, home-based hobbies created a new "domestic masculinity": "The metamorphosis of the restrained and distant Victorian father into the engaged and present suburban dad was one of the more significant changes in the structure of the modern family."[107] In 1924 a steelworker was asked if his wife enjoyed having him home after the eight-hour workday was implemented. "You bet," he answered. "We're getting acquainted all over again."[108] With more time for home-based leisure, men had become not just "breadwinners," but were "now considered social members of the family."[109] As one steelworker explained of the changes brought about by shorter hours, "I like going home to the wife and kids. I like putterin' around the house."[110] In new industrial suburbs, the home provided the site in which working-class family life took on new meaning and significance. This amplified the social meaning of homes and neighborhoods. When white workers in the US defended racial boundaries around their segregated neighborhoods, they felt they were defending not just their property values, but the spaces in which they had come to define themselves as men, women, and working-class families.

The broader working-class neighborhood also provided expanded recreational spaces in the early twentieth century. Cities built parks that spatially confined, organized, and regulated working-class outdoor leisure. The growth of municipal parks and the public provision of leisure activities transformed the relationship between municipal authorities and working-class revelers. Rather than police attempting to repress workers' often unruly use of streets and public space, as was common in the nineteenth century, public provision of leisure spaces aimed to channel and regulate how workers spent their free time.[111] With the growth of municipal parks, "social activities became contained within specialized spaces where they could be regulated," and working class social life moved from the streets, vacant lots, and open fields — the "interstices of the urban form" — to designated municipal and commercial venues such as football stadiums and public parks.[112] As Martin Daunton has argued, the relocation of urban leisure into "specialist spaces which were controlled and regulated by their owners, whether commercial or municipal" strongly curtailed the "communal, *ad hoc* and participatory life" of the mid-nineteenth century.[113] The late nineteenth century saw the transformation of unevenly policed vacant spaces into fenced, ruled, and regulated parks and sports facilities, and cities became major investors and providers of regulated public space.[114] In 1875 the Sheffield Town Council purchased its first park for public use, and by the end of the century the city managed 277 acres of parks and 47 acres of recreation grounds.[115] In Baltimore, mayor Ferdinand C. Latrobe drove a reformed Parks Commission to spend over $1.4 million on land purchases between 1875 and 1900, bringing over 1,000 acres under municipal control in Baltimore by the early twentieth century.[116] Liverpool saw a major expansion of public provision in the 1920s. During the decade 18 new football fields were built, tennis courts expanded from 172 to 400, and golf courses from 1 to 5 within the city park system.[117]

As park systems expanded, cities did far more to both provide and control the activities in their parks. Baltimore claimed the title of being the "Cradle of Municipal Music." The city had funded the first municipal band in the United States in 1912, and officials also claimed that it was the "first city to have out door community singing, and the first city to have an Orchestra of real symphonic dimensions, under exclusive Municipal administration and at the public expense."[118] For community singing, words were projected on a screen for mass sing-a-longs with thousands of participants, and during the summer, Baltimore's municipal band performed nearly every night in the parks. During the music, "open-air street dancing [proved] to be a popular feature" on the "large expanses of asphalt paving."[119] Pittsburgh followed Baltimore's example and organized its own municipal band in 1918, but the organizers from the Bureau of Recreation reassured the public that they would be "programming only high-class music"—that is, music from white people. Thus "jazz" got the "razz" and only "classics" that improved "the tastes of Pittsburgh audiences" were permitted in the Pittsburgh parks.[120] In 1920, promoters of "orderly, scientific, comprehensive" urban planning in Pittsburgh noted that "only in the past generation has recreation assumed its prominent place as one of the primary functions of government."[121] The planners urged that further expansions were urgently needed, since Pittsburgh ranked "twenty-fifth in number of baseball diamonds" in the country, and thus "athletic fields" were "one of Pittsburgh's greatest needs." By 1929 Pittsburgh's Bureau of Recreation was running seventy-eight municipal facilities across the city.[122] Public parks had become a vital part of working-class social worlds by the 1920s, providing unprecedented levels of resources and regulations to manage previously informal outdoor leisure.

The importance of parks to working-class social worlds meant that the struggle to draw racial boundaries for control over these spaces was ferocious, and repeatedly instigated race riots in the US. From the 1890s, black Baltimoreans found that both old, and the growing number of new parks were "entirely closed to them or offered separate entrances and facilities."[123] African Americans were banned from most of Baltimore's public parks (over a hundred) with only a handful of exceptions. Tennis courts were fully segregated in 1910, as were baseball and football fields. These racial boundaries were carefully monitored. In 1915 Baltimore's city comptroller complained that baseball games were being played in Druid Hill park between "white and colored boys" in violation of the city's segregation regulations.[124] During the 1920s, the *Afro-American* and black community leaders pressured the Park Board to develop playgrounds in black neighborhoods, and an auxiliary committee was formed to negotiate with the mayor and Park Board.[125] Pittsburgh lacked Baltimore's explicit system of racial regulation, but its parks were in practice largely segregated.[126] As figure 8.4 illustrates, unregulated play on the streets often brought black and white children together, while public parks, and swimming pools in particular, provided regulated, racially segregated environments. In Pittsburgh "recreation centers, playgrounds and swimming pools," despite being "publicly owned," routinely "denied access" to black residents.[127] For black children in largely white schools, the vigilant

FIGURES 8.4A AND B Racially integrated crowd on the street and all-white swimming pool in Pittsburgh. Informal socialization in the streets often brought white and black children together, but as authorities expanded recreational areas, such as the Ormsby Park Pool, racial segregation deepened as white residents claimed exclusive rights to improved neighborhood amenities. *Sources*: Pittsburgh City Photographer, "Crowd of Children on the Street," June 8, 1931, Mt. Washington Roadway from Monor Street, 715.3114241.CP, Pittsburgh City Photography Collection, University of Pittsburgh; Pittsburgh City Photographer, "Ormsby Park Swimming Pool," August 4, 1916, 715.16907.CP, Pittsburgh City Photography Collections, University of Pittsburgh.

policing of racial boundaries around parks could cause problems during school trips. The Urban League repeatedly complained to the Pittsburgh Board of Education of "the policy of Kennywood Park Management of not permitting Colored children, in connection with school picnics, to enter the swimming pool."[128]

In the realm of neighborhood commercial leisure, the most significant change in this era was the rise of the cinema, especially for young women. Movies offered a standardized cultural product that played a key role in the "formation of a sense of national [rather than] urban identity."[129] The cinema was most popular with young, working-class women, with survey evidence suggesting that audiences, especially during matinees, were overwhelmingly women.[130] Pittsburgh offered the very first "Nickelodeon" in 1905, launching a citywide, and soon international, phenomenon of cheap, accessible movies for working-class audiences.[131] Social workers at Pittsburgh's Woods Run Settlement illustrated the desire of workers for "economic freedom" in terms of their consuming power at theaters: freedom meant "making ends meet and still hav[ing] a nickel to spare for the nickelodeon."[132] The inexpensive nickelodeon was one of the most accessible entries to the world of "going out" and downtown commercial leisure for workers at the bottom of the production hierarchy. The extraordinary rates of attendance at theaters in the first decades of the twentieth century speaks to the insatiable desire of workers for this new form of mass entertainment.[133] The experience of going out, and the uniform content of films themselves, tended to bridge working-class divides, and brought workers at the bottom of the production hierarchy into a new mass cultural mainstream.[134] Labor organizers aimed to use the appeal of cinema to attract workers to their movement. Delegates to the Baltimore Federation of Labor were "urged . . . to invite unorganized workers to attend" a screening of "the motion picture 'Labor's Reward.'"[135] While the on-screen product may have been standardized, in the US, of course, audiences were segregated. Jim Crow predictably prevailed in Baltimore's theaters, and in Pittsburgh too, theaters were segregated or refused black customers entirely.[136] The Urban League's director noted that with the arrival of more African Americans in Pittsburgh, there "were growing limitations set against Negroes in our theaters."[137] Nevertheless, even if racial boundaries extended to theaters, the mass consumption of standardized cultural products meant that nearly all workers had a topic of conversation at hand, and discussion of popular films filled working-class social worlds. The only topic that perhaps demanded more attention, especially among men, was sports.

Alfred Williams, an autodidact craft worker who taught himself Greek and botany in his spare hours, looked down on the cinema as offering "little real value to the workman," since the "pictures serve only to indulge the craving for the novel and sensational." But he could not deny their massive popularity with his fellow workers.[138] Young workers especially, Williams complained, had minds so full "of blood and thunder, crime, and mawkish love dramas" from the cinema, that they were "quite incapable of imbibing sound and useful knowledge." Even if traditionalists like Williams complained, cinema achieved something unprecedented among workers: a shared national, even transnational set of cultural products circulated and became a routine and intensely felt part of working-class lives. The fact that so many workers now had broadly shared cultural references contributed in part toward more inclusive, geographically dispersed networks of working-class solidarity required for participation in the emerging mass bureaucratic unions.

Conclusion

The rise of corporate capitalism and Fordist mass production created new, improved working-class housing in industrial suburbs, and fostered new working-class social worlds shaped by their homes and neighborhoods. In the UK, these transformations bridged previous divides, bringing Irish Catholic and English Protestant workers together and providing the social foundations for a new politics of class solidarity. In the US, neighborhood social worlds also provided the foundations for a new kind of working-class politics, with white workers drawing racial boundaries to protect their segregated neighborhoods. Although struggles over neighborhood racial boundaries would erupt most spectacularly after World War II, the social foundations for these struggles were securely in place by the 1920s. Just as the turn of the century marked the intertwined hardening of racial and craft boundaries in the US labor movement, so too in working-class neighborhoods, the growth of Fordist industrial suburbs marked the rise of new patterns of urban segregation. Housing provided the foundation for the reproduction of the working-class racial wealth gap in the twentieth century, a durable inequality at the root of contemporary structures of racial inequality.

Fordist Masculinity

WORKERS ORGANIZED IN
THE SPORTS BUREAUCRACY

For observers in the early twentieth century, the importance of sports in remaking workers' social worlds was clear. Jane Addams wrote in 1907 that the "young athlete . . . rushing to join his baseball team" would pass by more destructive forms of leisure such as the saloon and the gambling booth, and on the field "his participation" was "not that of the drilled and mechanical soldier of an autocracy, not the hypnotic performance of a stereotyped part, but the conscious participation of the citizen in the life and feeling of the whole."[1] In contrast to Addams's democratic emphasis, another social worker, Sidney S. Pexotta, took a more authoritarian position in his evaluation of youth baseball, a game that required "order, quiet, team work and the implicit reliance on the leadership of the officers of the team."[2] Pexotta aimed to use sports to "bust up" the youth gangs of the neighborhood, and claimed that youth gambling on street corners had disappeared since baseball had been organized in the neighborhood.[3] As another social worker put it, baseball taught "team play and quick obedience to authority" in the form of the umpire.[4] "If a young man were asked to name the leading influence of his early life," another social worker claimed, he would most likely point to "the moulding power of sports."[5] While social workers could emphasize either the authoritarian or democratic potentialities of sports, the managers of factories also understood youth sports in terms of producing healthy, productive bodies, and cooperative workers who would be good team players. The personnel manager at US Steel's Duquesne Works urged that the directors give attention to the experiences of youth: "The boys of today are the mill men of tomorrow and we feel any assistance given in Playgrounds, YMCA, Boy Scouts . . . will come back to the plant in a few years as new assets."[6]

The phenomenal growth of organized sports—youth sports, amateur clubs sports, and of course, professional sports—during this era is well known to historians of sports. But sports is a field often neglected by labor historians, especially in the United States.[7] Cinema, dance halls, radio, vaudeville, music halls, and other areas of expanding commercial leisure have all received extensive attention. But organized sports deserve similar focus. Sports played a central role in the construction of a new Fordist working-class masculinity. The experience of participating in and following organized sports forged new masculine dispositions and habits among rank-and-file workers that prepared them for membership in centralized, bureaucratic unions. In addition, the world of sports was one of the most visible and spectacular sites where racial boundaries were staged and debated.

The sports bureaucracy and the labor bureaucracy shared many practical experiences: dues paying, formal rules given in by-laws and constitutions, coordinated planned activity, structured leadership, and ranked position in a larger hierarchy of locals, districts, and national organizations. As Ross McKibbin has written, the "English industrial class was neither politically nor culturally homogenous, but love of football united them almost more than anything else."[8] Early social surveys found that even informal youth football teams "were usually quite well organized and democratic in structure; some even elected secretaries by secret ballot."[9] This suggests that overlapping dispositions and practices guided workers through both organized sports and organized labor.[10] As Ralph Milliband suggested in *Marxism and Politics*, while sports were certainly "very strongly pervaded by commercialism," it should not be dismissed as "bread and circuses." A "deep interest in the fortunes of . . . Leeds United Football club" was clearly compatible "with militant trade unionism and the pursuit of class struggle."[11] Indeed, it was not only compatible, but the masculinity forged in the world of organized sports was a crucial underpinning for the rise of mass bureaucratic unions. By the late nineteenth century, "working-class men found a meaningful context for their life in cities through the socialization and communal identity provided through sport."[12] In Sheffield's East End district surrounding the steel mills, workers in the late nineteenth century were drawn not to the "Mechanics' Institution, or even the trade union or friendly society," but rather to "the football ground."[13]

Organized sports provided crucial nodes for the new, Fordist working class networks. Job searches were rooted in personal ties and social networks. As a Polish immigrant in Pittsburgh explained, alongside family and kin, organized sports were crucial for these networks: "The only way you got a job [was] through somebody at work who got you in. I mean this application, that's a big joke. . . . [T]o get a job with the railroad, my brother-in-law got it for me. My job at the hospital, my dad got it for me.

I got the job at the meat place . . . the boy I used to play ball with, he got it for me."[14] Rank-and-file trade union leaders often first emerged as leaders in the world of organized sports. As Eric Hobsbawm describes in his profile of Herbert Smith, leader of the miners' union in the 1920s, he was a "slow, hard, reliable man, keener on cricket and Barnsley Football Club whose matches he attended religiously, than on ideas."[15] If the British miners were among the most powerful unions in the Global North, similar patterns also appeared among the Industrial and Commercial Workers Union in South Africa, an extremely vulnerable organization in the Global South. Here, Charles Kumalo was elected as a shop steward "to the Estcourt Executive in Natal due largely to his prowess as a soccer player."[16] Countless future shop stewards and local presidents secured their first experiences of working-class leadership in the world of organized sports by being elected captains or "secretaries" of their local baseball or football team. Fordist masculinity, the bureaucratic world of organized sports, and the consolidating labor bureaucracy were closely woven together. As Elizabeth Faue has suggested, by "employing metaphors of sports and struggle, the labor press portrayed workers and work as male."[17]

The new centrality of organized sports in workers' social worlds provided experiences with formal rules, written regulations, procedural mechanisms, quantitative assessment, and capacious, diffuse loyalty that prepared workers for membership in and leadership of the new bureaucratic unions. Organized sports shaped the dispositions of workers, helping to forge working-class men whose interests could be channeled into centralized collective bargaining in the early twentieth century. Organized youth sports at schools and neighborhood clubs were the starting point for many men who went on to organize and lead unions. Organized sports also worked to draw racial boundaries across the US working class, with segregation at schools, local clubs, and professional teams all reinforcing the racial divide that fractured the US working class. While girls and women participated in organized sports at higher levels than one might expect, for boys and men, organized sports were central in constructing a new Fordist masculinity.

The Expansion of Schools and Organized Youth Sports

In the mid-nineteenth century, elites had feared the consequences of allowing working-class children to be shaped by an informal education on the streets. To keep children off the streets, and to train them to become good workers and responsible citizens, elites were willing to invest in increasingly large and expensive school systems after the 1870s. With their bells, schedules, formal hierarchies, and written regulations, schools provided an introduction to the bureaucratic authority of the mass-production firm.[18] Interpretations that stress schools as a form of social control, however, while certainly grasping an important part of working-class education, often miss the area of school life to which working-class youth, boys in particular, attached the greatest significance: youth sports.

Schools were a central institution for directing children into the world of organized sports, and the reach of schooling expanded dramatically around the turn of the century. While children may have been ambivalent about their classroom lessons, their sporting experiences were a vital part of working-class childhood. From the 1870s to the 1920s, the amount of time working-class youths spent in schools increased dramatically. More students attended more regularly for longer periods of time. In Sheffield, average attendance in elementary schools increased from 70 percent in 1877, to over 86 percent in 1902, while in Pittsburgh, attendance rose from around 83 percent in 1879 to around 90 percent by 1912.[19] Attendance officers were vigilant in attempting to enforce compulsory attendance requirements, with school officials in Pittsburgh conducting over fifty thousand investigative visits in 1913.[20] Among the working-class parents prosecuted by the Sheffield School Board for failing to send their children to school were a labourer, a furnaceman, a washerwoman, a carter, a widow, a forgeman, and a miner.[21] The youth gangs that had fiercely patrolled mid-nineteenth-century neighborhoods showed the imprint of the expanding force of school life. Rather than identifying with a particular street or leader, youthful crews at the turn of the century instead identified with particular schools or sports teams.[22] As schooling left a deeper imprint on working-class children, the school experience was often equated with sports participation. When profiling the "office boys," the plant magazine of the Edgar Allen steel works noted their school backgrounds and athletic interests. For instance, Samuel Bates of the Foundry Order Department had "commenced his education at the Meadow Hall Road Council School, and finished it at the Kimberworth Higher Education Standard School," was a "a very enthusiastic member of the Boy Scouts," and "excels . . . at cricket, his specialty being fast bowling."[23] Similarly, William Marshall, who worked in the laboratory department, "commenced his education at the Mexbro' National School" and during "the latter part of his school he was goalkeeper for the school team." What subjects these boys studied was not mentioned, but their cricket and football accomplishments were carefully publicized.

While broadly similar, the expansion of schools had opposite effects on workers' social worlds in the US and the UK. In the UK, for the generation

FIGURE 9.1 Sheffield schoolchildren performing at Empire Day at Bramall Lane
Stadium, 1906. *Source*: "Empire Day Pageant at Bramall Lane," Picture Sheffield
s02847, Sheffield City Council Archive and Local Studies Library.

of young people who came of age in the early twentieth century, schools
"gather[ed] the children of all sections of the working class together" and
provided "an increasingly uniform experience," in particular easing "the
older barriers between skilled and unskilled" workers.[24] In Liverpool, delays in Catholic school building produced integrated schooling on the new
council estates of the 1920s, contributing to smoothing divisions between
Protestants and Catholics.[25] The regulated mass experience provided by
schools was dramatically captured during events such as the Sheffield
school system's Empire Day Pageant in 1906. As can be seen in figure 9.1,
thousands of children dressed and marched to form the Union Jack and
the English and Scottish flags, giving symbolic expression to the role of
schools in constructing broader, more abstract national and imperial solidarities of Britishness.

Meanwhile, in the United States schools helped to integrate native-
born and immigrant Europeans into a more cohesive white working class
while at the same time deepening the racial boundary between white and
black children. Baltimore's explicitly segregated and unequal schools never
offered the opportunity for bridging the chasm dividing white and black

workers in the United States.[26] In Baltimore, black leaders fought relent-
lessly for the provision of better school buildings, equitable teacher pay,
and more resources for the segregated schools serving African American
children.[27] In Pittsburgh, although schools were not formally segregated,
African American students in the 1920s were highly concentrated in only
four schools.[28] As in Baltimore, Pittsburgh's black community leaders understood the importance of education. Pittsburgh's Urban League champi-
oned education for African Americans in the city with their "Go to High
School—Go to College" campaign, pointing to education as a means to
collectively "help defend and protect" the community and "the Race."[29]
As schooling became a more important part of working-class life trajectories at the turn of the century, expanding educational access contributed to
a more integrated working class in the UK and a more segregated working
class in the US.[30]

While much of the school curriculum may have been received indif-
ferently, working-class youth showed a remarkable enthusiasm for sports.
Organized youth sports were practically non-existent in the 1870s, but by
the 1920s they had become central to working-class life. Alfred Williams, in
his 1915 biography of work in a UK railway shed, recalled that the boys who
worked at the firm were "always ready for some game or other," especially
football, and would often get locked out by "overstaying at football" on
the recreation field during the mid-day meal break. Far from exhausted
at the end of the day, the boys would "in the evening . . . race home to tea
and afterwards go out again while it is daylight, never seeming too tired
for sport and play."[31] Sheffield was a pioneer among British cities in the
provision of organized youth sports. The Sheffield Elementary Schools
Football Association was founded in 1889 by the teachers of the district
and regularly featured fifty-team tournaments. Important youth matches
attracted thousands of spectators.[32] Winners of the "Clegg Shield" championship, depicted in figure 9.2, drew particular interest to youth football
in Sheffield, as did the inter-city matches between a select Sheffield team
and rivals from London, Manchester, Liverpool, and other cities.[33] Foot-
balling youths came from households with wage earners employed across
the production hierarchy, from skilled craftsmen to laborers. Based on a
review of the family backgrounds of thirty-three Sheffield youth footballers from 1890–1904, the occupations of cohabiting fathers and brothers
fell mostly into laboring and craftsman categories (sixteen craftsmen and
fourteen laborers), with twelve youths with family members in white-
collar work, and six whose families were small proprietors.[34]

In Baltimore, a main event in the youth sports calendar was the football game between the city's two leading high schools, City College and

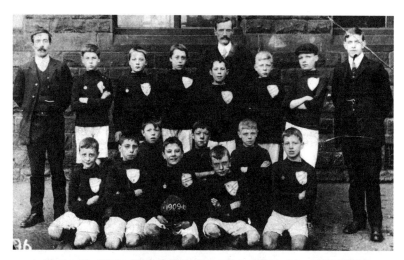

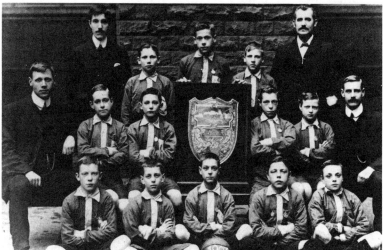

FIGURES 9.2A AND B Duchess Road and Bugoyne Road school football teams, 1909–1910. School football became popular in Sheffield, with teams competing for the Clegg Shield and adopting modern uniform conventions. Youth sports became a crucial site for the formation of a new Fordist working-class masculinity in the early twentieth century. *Sources*: "Burgoyne Road School football team," 1907, Picture Sheffield s00128; "Duchess Road Senior School Football Club," 1909–1910, Sheffield St. Mary's, Picture Sheffield s09316. Both from Sheffield City Council Archive and Local Studies Library.

Polytechnic, with the game attracting thousands of spectators.[35] In Pittsburgh, the Woods Run Settlement house supported a wide variety of sports connected to local schools. For girls they helped organize "swimming, hiking, scouting . . . and athletics," and for boys, "hand soccer, football, mush ball . . . swimming," a "bowling league," and baseball teams for a tournament organized by the *Pittsburgh Press*.[36] The settlement described how local baseball diamonds had become overcrowded with youth teams: "One evening there were four teams of older boys (eighteen and over) using the field north of the house, two teams taking their turns at a time. On the south side a team of boys 14 to 16 years old were going through their batting practice while the girls were completing their game. . . . This condition exists five nights a week."[37] Powerfully underlining the importance of sports-based social ties for working-class youth, when nine-year-old Clarence Thomason, the son of Lithuanian immigrants, was killed in the steel mill, his football teammates provided flowers and served as his pallbearers at his funeral.[38]

Labor unions were eager to play a role in organizing youth recreation. In Baltimore, the Labor Federation actively promoted the Pioneer Youth Camp.[39] The Pioneer Youth was a trade union rival to the Communist Young Pioneers. By 1928, 162 local labor unions across the United States participated in the Pioneer Youth summer camps, and the effort had received backing from nine international unions, most importantly the two major garment workers unions, the ILGWU and the ACWA.[40] The Baltimore Federation of Labor helped organize a local branch of the Pioneer Youth Summer Camp in 1927. When the effort was first introduced, the Federation's President described it as "a union scout organization," offering a workers' alternative to the militaristic Boy Scouts.[41] Over the coming weeks, BFL delegates were encouraged to "view a film on the work of the Pioneer Youth," to purchase "tickets for a Pioneer Youth benefit," and received speakers who encouraged participation and financial support.[42] At the end of June, the BFL President reassured anxious union parents that "a capable doctor [was] in constant attendance" at the summer camp.[43] The energetic recruitment bore fruit; fifty-one children attended Baltimore's first Pioneer Youth Summer Camp, with growth expected to encourage more "games, baseball" and "athletic work," as well as camp counselors from the Federation of Labor who could "explain to the children the tenets of organized labor."[44] Although funded primarily by private donors committed to progressive labor politics in Baltimore, several unions also made substantial contributions to the camp, including Carpenters Local 101, Painters No. 1, and Steamfitters 438.[45]

In the US, youth sports followed the segregated boundaries established by schools and the settlement houses. In Liverpool, the Protestant/Catholic divide initially fractured youth sports. Protestant schools and teachers had popularized football in Liverpool, but during the initial popularity of the sport in the 1890s, "Protestant schools were unwilling to compete or cooperate with their Catholic counterparts."[46] This led to the creation of a segregated Catholic Schools Athletic Association in 1899, and a Catholic Schools Football League shortly after.[47] However, by the 1920s, especially among those working-class families who relocated to suburban council estates, schools and youth sports became increasingly integrated across religious boundaries. Despite the declining significance of anti-Irish hostility in Britain in the early twentieth century, religious boundaries in sports could be remarkably durable. Only in 1973 did the Liverpool Catholic Schools Football League amalgamate with the Liverpool School Football Association.[48]

Organized Sports and Working-Class Amateurs

The clearest sign of the enduring mark that sports left on youth was the multitude of workers' amateur teams. In parallel with the rise of youth sports, organized amateur sports became an important part of working-class masculinity in the late nineteenth century. Both employers and unions attempted to harness this grassroots enthusiasm, but it was workers themselves who displayed a remarkable commitment to getting organized for sports. From the 1890s, Liverpool had several amateur football leagues, with most deeply rooted in working-class neighborhoods. Most amateur teams were composed of workers, ranging from laborers, to craftsmen, to significant numbers of white-collar staff. John Preston has meticulously tracked the growth of amateur football in Liverpool, with participation expanding from twelve leagues in 1898, rising to eighteen leagues in 1901, twenty-one in 1905, and a remarkable forty-one leagues by 1909.[49] If each team had at least eleven players, and if an average league had ten teams, this suggests at least 4,500 organized amateurs in Liverpool, the vast majority of whom were workers. Team names suggest five typical origins for these amateur football clubs: plant-based teams, church teams, volunteer military brigades, pub teams, and local neighborhood/park teams.[50] A representative match, reported in Sheffield in 1884, was that between the Attercliffe Church Choir Boys and the Atlas Works team of John Brown & Co.[51]

Unsurprisingly, workplace social ties often formed the basis for amateur sports, and employers were eager to support plant-based teams, as seen in figure 9.3, depicting footballers from the Machine Shop Department at

FIGURE 9.3 Machine shop team, Firths 1903. With support from emerging personnel and welfare department, workers carried their enthusiasm for sports into the workplace, organizing departmental and company-wide teams. *Source:* "Finalists in the Atlas and Norfolk Departmental Football Competition," 1903. *The Bombshell: A Monthly Journal Devoted to the Interests of Employees of Thomas Firth and Sons,* 3 (September 1919): 367. Local Studies Library 052.74 S, Picture Sheffield y04702, Sheffield City Council Archive and Local Studies Library.

Firth's Steel in Sheffield. Companies sponsored plant-based teams, such as Bibby's United (of the shipping company) and Johnson's Dyeworks (chemical manufacturer), whose contests were organized in the North Liverpool and District League.[52] In 1895, the White Star Wanderers (of the shipping company) played the Prescott amateur club at Goodison Park for the amateur championship before an appreciative crowd of three thousand spectators.[53] By the 1920s, Liverpool had a separate "Steamship League" with teams from White Star, Coast, Canada Pacific Railway, Cunard, Leyland, Elder-Dempster, Clao, and Houston steamship companies.[54] By the 1920s, Sheffield's Works League had two divisions and eighteen teams representing all the major steel and engineering companies in the district.[55] At Edgar Allen Steel in Sheffield, the "Works Knock-Out Competition" featured eight football teams drawn from precisely demarcated occupational groups within the firm:

1. Finishers and Fettlers
2. Foundry Moulders and Labourers
3. Electricians, Construction Department and Fitters
4. Machine Shop

5. Staff
6. No. 2 Fettlers
7. Yard and Machinery Departments
8. Steel and Smith's Departments.[56]

As a report to the Works Committee of John Brown Steel in 1919 indicates, workers at the company were "conversant with the arrangements which have been made in recent years in the Sports Clubs of other firms," and while John Brown had been "pioneers of Works Sports Clubs," they were now "behind the others in accommodation and conveniences."[57] For instance, when the John Brown team played against "Cammells in all classes of sport, and when visiting their grounds," workers were "able to have a bath" and enjoyed better facilities. Thus the Works Manager urged the directors "to make the ground and club house at least equal to those connected with other firms."[58] Even smaller companies like Balfour's steel felt compelled to make substantial investments in providing a "sports ground" with a "pavilion" for their employees by the end of the 1920s.[59]

In the United States, where corporate welfare and personnel policies were pioneered, employers also played a leading role in organizing amateur sports. In Baltimore, over one thousand spectators came out to see amateur baseball between teams from the city's two largest companies: the Baltimore & Ohio Railroad and the Sparrows Point steel plant.[60] Of all of the B & O's welfare programs, athletics was by far the most successful: in contrast to educational and cultural offerings, "men liked sports without being told that they should."[61] Employees themselves organized the first teams, but the creation of the Welfare Bureau provided corporate support for an "elaborate network of teams and local leagues" across the rail network. The B & O organized a championship tournament between the major divisions of the railroad, with the final game played at the Homewood stadium of Johns Hopkins University in Baltimore.[62] In Pittsburgh, the Carnegie Steel Company by 1915 had built "numerous playgrounds, baseball fields, and tennis courts at its various plants," including three baseball fields at the Homestead Works, three tennis courts and a swimming pool at the Farrell Works, and baseball diamonds at Clairton, Etna, and Duquesne works.[63] A report from the Personnel Department of the US Steel Duquesne Works provides a sense of the variety of organized leisure offered to workers at the plant. First in importance was the "Industrial Baseball League," with an Upper and Lower Division. It was organized with assistance from the YMCA, and matched Duquesne Works employees against baseball teams from other plants across the Pittsburgh District.[64] Second came the plant's internal "Vinegar League," with baseball teams organized by the plant's departments including the steel works, skelp mills, lap mill, electrical department, and the plant railroad. Employees from the company also competed in an industrial basketball and industrial volleyball league. A variety of bowling leagues were also popular with workers. In the Pig Iron League, teams from within the Duquesne Works competed, while in the electrical department, skelp mills, and galvanizing department, bowling proved so popular that workers organized their own internal department leagues.

Labor leaders were not content to leave amateur sports in the hands of employers.[65] A 1928 report on recreational programs organized by US unions noted that "among sports, baseball and bowling easily hold first place, although other forms of athletics" were occasionally sponsored by unions, including "tennis, golf, basketball, hockey, football, boxing, hikes, swimming, and even a team of sharpshooters."[66] Union baseball teams were credited with "interesting the younger members in outdoor sports" and also with promoting "greater social intercourse between the members and the families of members." In Pittsburgh, the Typographical Union appears to have been particularly active, "holding monthly euchres and dances" to support visiting professional "National Baseball Teams." During the summer, the Typographical Union organized baseball and golf tournaments for the local labor movement.[67] In Baltimore, the Pipefitters, Sheetmetal Workers, Plumbers, and Electrical Workers all organized baseball teams, and the Elevator Constructors organized a bowling league that "meets every Saturday night."[68] These were not just informal pickup games among union members; the Electrical Workers Local 28 and Plumbers Local 48 in Baltimore "placed uniformed ball teams on the field," and BFL delegates urged other unions to follow their example by organizing uniformed and competitive teams for local trade union baseball competition.[69]

As with other dimensions of working-class social worlds, in the US amateur sports was racially segregated. As Rob Ruck has noted of steelworkers in the Pittsburgh District, "blacks might have sipped and dined with whites in Homestead's commercial district and worked alongside them in the mill, but when it came to the company's recreational program, Jim Crow was the rule."[70] In response to the exclusion of black workers from company teams, Pittsburgh's Urban League, in conjunction with its committee of African American welfare workers and employment managers, set up a parallel Industrial Baseball League for black workers.[71] The enthusiasm of black workers for baseball was made clear when a group of workers at Homestead who "were not satisfied with the selection of the first team" at the plant, decided to "organize a second" rival black baseball team.[72] The seriousness of the competition among black amateur baseball teams in Pittsburgh was also illustrated when one team brought an allegation of "ringers" to the organizers, alleging that the black team from Clairton "used outside pitchers" who were not employees of the company.[73] Pittsburgh's black employment managers saw organized, amateur sports as part of a project of race uplift, aiming "to train our people to work in organizations."[74] While the didactic dreams of managers did not necessarily transmit to workers, the experience of organized sports in formal leagues with officials, rules, and regulations contributed to the construction of a new kind of working-class masculinity in the early twentieth century.

Working-Class Masculinity and the Transformation of Pugilism into Boxing

Informal fighting had been a defining ritual of working-class masculinity in the nineteenth century, and while fighting remained popular with working-class audiences in the 1920s, instead of bare-knuckle battles on the streets and fields surrounding their cities, boxing now occurred under official rules and regulations, with official sanction, staged in respectable rings at the heart of the city. Because fighting was the most popular working-class sport in the early twentieth century, it offers perhaps the most direct insight into changes in working-class masculinity. During the mid-nineteenth century in both the US and UK, fights were legally prohibited. Yet pugilism flourished, ranging from spontaneous contests of strength and valor to more organized spectacles.[75] What seemed like a riotous brawl to bourgeois observers was often loosely organized pugilistic sport. A challenge would be issued, a crowd would assemble, the men would strip off their shirts, and the fight would commence.

Mid-nineteenth-century spontaneous street pugilism was occasionally reported in some detail. In Pittsburgh, the *Gazette* detailed a "mill" on Fifth street: "The first round C—made a pass at M—and got a 'stunner' on his nose; M—returned it handsomely with a 'left hander,' which took effect under C—'s ear, and ended the round," and so on until a knockout ended the match in the fifth round.[76] Workers took pride in competing in these matches. A miner recalled a pitman who "always gave himself an extra clean wash on pay Friday, because he wanted to look 'decent' when he put off his shirt to fight."[77] After a "jostle" on the street in Pittsburgh, James Munn, a thirty-four-year-old teamster at a glass works, and Charles Carson, a twenty-two-year-old glass blower, faced off in "fair fighting," with "Munn pull[ing] off his coat" and facing Carson.[78] A street fight in

Sheffield between Thomas Gannon, a table-blade forger, and Patrick Brannon, a plasterers' laborer, was a typical pugilistic contest. Thomas Collins, an awl blade maker, and Thomas Duckett were "aiding and abetting" the fighters as seconds.[79]

While any street or open lot could be turned into a venue for this kind of boxing, in some cases matches were larger, planned affairs. However, despite fighting's popularity, these larger mid-nineteenth-century contests were relegated to remote districts away from the surveillance of urban police. In Pittsburgh, a contest between the rival cities on either side of the Allegheny River matched Darby McDonough, a thirty-year-old day laborer from Pittsburgh, against a pugilist from Allegheny. The fight was held on Gazzam's Hill above Soho, "where eleven rounds were fought, McDonough coming out of the mill the winner . . . with a 'smashed bugle.'"[80] Another "noted pugilist" of Pittsburgh, "Young" Sullivan, issued an open challenge to a fighter from Washington, DC, as well as several "noted buffers."[81] Thomas Barnes, a pocket-blade maker, was a fixture in the boxing scene around Sheffield. His contest with James Parsons, both described as "young men, prize-fighters," drew a large crowd in December 1866.[82] The police had "received information that a prize-fight was about to come off," and on arriving on the outskirts of the city where the fight was taking place, the authorities discovered "about two-thousand people . . . form[ing] a ring in a field." The police in Liverpool learned that a fight was underway in an abandoned lot.[83] In this "waste ground" claimed by the people of Liverpool for their entertainment, "about 400 or 500 people" had gathered, "watching two men, who were stripped to the waist, fighting."

After the 1880s, informal street pugilism was reformed, regulated, and transformed into the modern sport of boxing. The Queensberry Rules, issued in 1866, were widely observed in practice in the 1880s, and only became dominant in the 1890s in both the US and the UK. Rather than local custom and masculine honor regulating fights, the new rules marked the beginning of the transition. Drawing on this formalization of the rules, in the 1880s courts began to distinguish between legitimate "sparring," which could be a legal exhibition of skill, and violent prize fighting, which remained illegal.[84] The transition from informal pugilism to regulated boxing involved the creation of standardized weight divisions, increasing regulation by "a complex set of formal written rules," a fixed number of rounds, the use of sparring gloves, and control by a trained expert as referee.[85] The last heavyweight fight with bare knuckles occurred in 1885 in the UK and in 1889 in the US.[86] By the turn of the century, the reformed sport of boxing had gained commercial success, public recognition, and official sanction.

In the early twentieth century, Pittsburgh police detectives began monitoring and regulating matches, observing the crowd but also stepping in to force contestants to "refrain from . . . fighting" that violated the new, official rules of the sport.[87] Promoters downplayed the raw violence and instead emphasized "the scientific and strategic aspects of the sport," such as precise footwork, the angles of arms and shoulders, and the technical delivery of blows.[88] In the early twentieth century, respectable athletic clubs took over organizing fights, and bouts were no longer consigned to outlying wastelands, but were staged at prominent, central locations such as Pittsburgh's old City Hall, the Exposition Hall, the Grand Opera House, and above all, the Duquesne Gardens, the city's premier indoor arena, with a capacity of up to eight thousand.[89] Signaling official acceptance, in 1910 a steel town in the Pittsburgh District organized a prize fight to pay off the Fire Department's mortgage on a new hose house, and during World War I, the army used boxing to encourage fitness for the troops.[90] In 1910, the largest boxing crowd in more than two decades assembled in Baltimore, but instead of occurring in some unregulated space on the outskirts of the city, the match was held in Oriole Park Stadium under the formal auspices of the Armory Athletic Club, which was praised for its orderly administration of the event.[91] As seen in figure 9.4, in the 1920s the YMCA staged amateur boxing matches in Pittsburgh's public parks, a remarkable sign of the sport's new organizational control and formal acceptance.

Far from its nineteenth-century outlaw roots, by the 1920s professional boxing in the US was sanctioned and regulated by state athletic commissions. After the war, Pennsylvania fully legalized boxing with the McBride Act of 1923 and created an Athletic Commission to regulate the sport; in Britain, although boxing never received official legal recognition, the British Boxing Board of Control became the permanent, semi-official sanctioning body for the sport in 1919.[92] This bureaucratic control of the sport can be seen in Maryland, where the State Commissioners licensed "clubs theaters and individuals" who planned to "hold boxing and wrestling exhibitions."[93] However, it was not only promoters and organizers who were subject to state regulation. The Maryland Commissioners suspended boxers for "Faking," "not giving the best effort," and "poor showing," disciplined referees for "inefficiency," and sanctioned managers for "ungentlemanly conduct."[94] Boxing had become a recognized and respected professional and amateur sport, with a sizable bureaucratic apparatus of formal rules, trained officials, licensed promoters, and state regulators.

Racial segregation in boxing was especially sensitive, since the spectacle of white and black men engaged in brutal physical violence, with the possibility of victory for the boxer of the supposedly inferior race,

FIGURE 9.4 Amateur boxing sponsored by the Pittsburgh YMCA in 1921. The YMCA's involvement in boxing matches underlines the sport's new status. *Source*: Pittsburgh City Photographer, "Boo Ryan and Chuck Schuering Boxing," YMCA Field Meeting Lawrence Park, September 10, 1921, 715.211702.CP, Pittsburgh City Photography Collection, 1901–2000, University of Pittsburgh.

was deeply unsettling to the expectations of white supremacy, both in the US and in the UK. In the early 1920s the UK's Home Office, likely with the 1919 race riots across British ports in mind, prohibited the British heavyweight champion, Joe Beckett, from boxing against a black man from French Senegal—Louis Mbarick Fall, known as "Battling Siki"—on the grounds "the colour issue might awaken grave partisan passion and animosities among the spectators."[95] The issue of racial segregation in boxing was far more pressing in the United States. While authorities aimed to impose segregation, audiences also clearly showed a desire to see racially staged fights between white and black boxers, and profit-hungry promoters were eager to serve audience demand. Up until 1925, Pennsylvania's State Athletic Commission banned "mixed boxing matches" between black and white athletes.[96] New York, California, and Wisconsin also had state bans on boxing matches between black and white fighters.[97] In the US, the "color line" in heavyweight boxing was drawn in the 1890s when John L. Sullivan, the white heavyweight champion, refused to fight Peter Jackson, a legendary black challenger, and subsequent white heavyweight champions followed suit, although in the lower-prestige, lower-weight

categories white and black boxers occasionally battled.[98] Fights between
white and black boxers were not meant to foster integration, but were
staged and promoted as "battles for racial superiority," giving racial boundaries spectacular, violent display.[99]

Filmmakers were drawn to the mass audience that boxing attracted,
and fight films were an important early genre at the turn of the century.
Remarkably, nearly half of boxing films produced in the early twentieth
century featured fights between white and black boxers, and this popularity led to widespread efforts to censor and suppress boxing films.[100]
This was especially true after 1908 when John Arthur "Jack" Johnson, an
African American boxer, broke the color line and became the national
heavyweight champion in the US. Two years later, Jim Jeffries came out of
retirement, as he explained, "for the sole purpose of proving that a white
man is better than a negro."[101] This attempt to restore white supremacy in
the boxing ring failed spectacularly, as Jeffries was easily defeated. While
African Americans in Pittsburgh "took to the streets in jubilation," many
Southerners were deeply alarmed at this spectacular inversion of Jim Crow
white supremacy.[102] Alarming authorities across the US, a film was made
of Johnson's triumph over Jeffries. In response to Johnson's victories over
white challengers, Congress enacted legislation banning fight films.[103]
This convergence of film, the modern sport of boxing, and racial segregation in the US neatly captures the transformation of working-class social
worlds and the racial fracture that divided the US working class.

The Workers' Game: From Riotous Crowds to Orderly Masses

Even more popular than boxing, at least by the 1920s, were the new professional sports that became national pastimes: baseball in the US and
association football in the UK (known in the US as soccer). Similar to
boxing, changes in these "workers' games" help us chart a transformation
in working-class masculinity: declining violence, formalization of rules,
venues, and regulations, and the expanding importance of bureaucratic
organization. Baseball in the US and football in the UK followed parallel
trajectories: early popularity in the 1870s, growing organization and professionalization during the next two decades, and by the turn of the century, massive, new, and recognizably modern concrete and steel stadiums
that loomed over the urban landscape to accommodate the increasingly
orderly masses of working-class spectators.[104] Both sports had roots in
informal folk games, but the late nineteenth century marked a series of
connected changes: teams moved from informal play in parks and open
lots to official stadiums of increasing size and specialization, paid pro-

fessional players replaced amateurs, and crowd sizes grew exponentially. Rules were codified and play increasingly conformed to these regulations.

Creating, codifying, and enforcing formal written rules created a new form of bureaucratically regulated sports. When teams from Sheffield and London met at Brammal Lane in 1872, there was considerable confusion over the rules, since each team was accustomed to different local traditions.[105] A review of reported "football oddities" from 1862 to 1880 found that the frequency of accepted play not conforming to standard rules decreased substantially by 1880.[106] Qualitative assessments of temperament or brawn were supplemented by new quantitative metrics such as winning percentages, batting averages, rankings in league tables, and the heights and weights of players. Professional sports in the early twentieth century was a novel bureaucratic and quantitative spectacle, and these practices and procedures shaped a new kind of masculinity, creating working-class dispositions familiar with navigating the nuances of written rules, quantitative assessment, and bureaucratic adjudication.

Workers' enthusiasm for professional sports grew slowly at first, but by the turn of the century, crowds of spectators had reached enormous proportions.[107] Suggesting the humble origins and slow initial growth, in the summer of 1883 only two hundred spectators attended a baseball game at Baltimore's Oriole Park.[108] By the 1890s, crowds of thousands were common, and sometimes tens of thousands. As an article from the *Sheffield Daily Telegraph* in 1892 observed, there was "something amazingly seductive about modern football. It grips the fancy of sexagenarians who never played the game in their youth," and women, too were moved to shout "'Well done!' with a lustiness the thought of which subsequently brings flushes to their cheeks."[109] Local rivalries and holidays often produced large and enthusiastic crowds. When baseball teams from Washington, DC, and Baltimore met at Oriole Park on the Fourth of July in 1890, more than five thousand spectators turned out.[110] In the UK, Boxing Day became a football holiday. As the *Sheffield Daily Telegraph* reported in 1895, Boxing Day had become "essentially a holiday for outdoor sports," and twenty-six thousand spectators were reported to have watched crosstown rivals Sheffield United play Sheffield Wednesday at Brammal Lane stadium.[111] In Liverpool, the local rival clubs of Liverpool and Everton played on Christmas Day in 1897, attracting "fully 30,000 spectators" to Goodison park.[112] Workers dominated the composition of these crowds, although white-collar workers and professionals also attended in large numbers.[113] Figure 9.5 illustrates the arrival of other distinctive feature of sports culture: night games under the floodlights and commercial memorabilia and collectibles, in this case a drinking cup celebrating Sheffield's

FIGURES 9.5A AND B Floodlight match (1878) and championship commemorative jug (1896). Key markers of modern sports spectatorship emerged in the late nineteenth century. Workers could enjoy the spectacle of an evening game under innovation of artificial electrical lights. Championships were celebrated through commercial souvenirs such as Sheffield Wednesday's 1896 drinking jug. *Sources:* "Artists impression of a floodlit football match, Bramall Lane probably the first ever played under floodlights, the match was played between Blues and Reds," 1878, Picture Sheffield t05148; Sheffield Newspapers, Ltd., "Commemorative jug. Sheffield Wednesday Winners of the English Cup," April 18, 1896, Picture Sheffield, s02506. Both from Sheffield City Council Archive and Local Studies Library.

championship in 1895. By the turn of the century, the *Sheffield Daily Telegraph* observed that "every Saturday in this city some two thousand boys and men" were playing football in amateur leagues, while "some thirty thousand people [were] watching the various games" played by professionals.[114] Organized sports, both amateur and professional, had become an unprecedented mass experience.

The new importance of sports to workers reshaped urban social worlds. A new, dramatic visual and reporting style is evident in the papers, including photographs of the players in action and extensive coverage using sports slang and jargon.[115] The percentage of newspaper coverage devoted to sports more than quadrupled in just over three decades, rising from 4 percent in 1890 to 17 percent in 1923.[116] In the UK, socialists were alarmed by the growing mania for football. As one Independent Labour Party editor wrote in 1908: "Difficult though the task may be to push football out of the heads and push Socialism in, the task must be undertaken, for just as surely as football doesn't matter, Socialism matters a great deal."[117] Labour Party newspapers had to wrestle over the inclusion of sports coverage and betting tips, since these topics were popular with working-class audiences but frowned upon by socialist political organizers. Socialist editors usually found working-class leisure preferences for football and the cinema distasteful, but movement papers failed if they refused to offer sports coverage and betting tips.[118] Alfred Williams, a craft worker who assiduously studied Latin and Greek while tending his furnace, did not share the enthusiasm of his fellow workers for sports. In his 1915 autobiography, Williams wrote that "the love of" football as a "pastime has come to be almost a disease of late years — old and young, male and female, of every rank and condition, are afflicted with it."[119] Younger workers spent their free time "kicking about something or other" and "from week's end to another they are brimful of the fortunes of the local football team." Williams recalled that workers even boasted of having foregone a "Sunday dinner in order to find the money necessary for him to attend Saturday's [football] match." Williams, like the editors of socialist newspapers, wished to discuss more serious subjects with his workmates, but sports was the only topic that could arouse interest from his fellow workers. All else "must yield to the supreme fascination and excitement of football." By 1909 over one million spectators attended football games in the UK over the season, giving an average attendance of sixteen thousand per match. By the early twentieth century, "popular civic identity was more generally created and sustained by the successes of sports teams than by any other factor."[120] Opening day for the baseball season became a major civic occasion in Baltimore, with "a parade, a brass band concert, a flag raising" and official ceremonies.[121]

Local dignitaries attended the opening game, including the mayor, governor, and the US Secretary of State.[122]

The reorientation of working-class collective action from riotous street politics in the nineteenth century to bureaucratic labor unions in the twentieth century was underpinned by a broader transformation in workers' social worlds. This was made particularly visible in crowd behavior at sporting events. Riots by spectators were relatively common in the 1880s and 1890s but had become relatively rare by the twentieth century. In 1882, at least ten umpires were attacked by rioting mobs at baseball games, and the Boston stadium went so far as to install barbed wire around the field to restrain its spectators.[123] Likewise in Sheffield, the "field of play" at the Brammal Lane stadium had to be "strongly barricaded" for the 1891 Football Cup competition to "prevent any encroachment such as took place" two years prior when the venue had hosted a championship match.[124] Organizers struggled to keep fans off the field, but also failed to stop those who "availed themselves of free entry by scaling the wall" around the park, where "checktakers at the stands" could be "overpowered. . . . and in consequence the stands were invaded."[125] Fans clearly expected to see the best show from the competing teams. In 1890, when the Blackburn Rovers sent out their backup squad to play, the assembled football fans were incensed and tore down the seating and goalposts.[126] In response to these disturbances, the Football Association deployed its growing disciplinary apparatus. After a referee had ordered several Sheffield Wednesday players off the field for fouls in a cup tie match in 1892, the crowd "threatened to assault" him and the referee "had mud thrown at him," making a police escort necessary.[127] Although the Football Association found Sheffield Wednesday as an organization blameless, the club was punished for the unruly behavior of its fans. During a match between Sheffield Wednesday and Sunderland in 1903, home fans hurled oranges at the referee, and "at the close of the match the Sheffield Wednesday team and officials . . . were stoned by the unruly section of the spectators." The Football Association convened a commission of investigation in Manchester, and after hearing evidence, punished the Sunderland club by ordering the closure of their stadium for a week.[128] Amateur matches could also inspire unruly crowds, as when the Sheffield Strollers played the Doncaster Rovers, and a crowd assaulted and stoned the referee.[129] Even youth football could inspire riotous behavior, as in 1896 when spectators invaded the field of play for the Cheshire Junior Cup and drove off the referee ten minutes before the end of the game.[130] Baltimore also witnessed several baseball riots in the early twentieth century. In 1904, rotten eggs were thrown at an umpire deemed incompetent by the crowd, and police were forced to escort the umpire from Oriole Park. In 1908, when another umpire made a controversial ninth-inning call, "the majority of the 3,500 spectators made a wild rush" and "might have done [the umpire] bodily harm had not a corps of policemen formed a cordon around him and escorted him to the box office."[131]

While rioting eventually declined, working-class sporting crowds were increasingly likely to be described in terms of unprecedented public order at stadiums. In the nineteenth century, any sizable assembly of working-class people had been viewed by authorities as potentially riotous and disorderly. Yet, when Sheffield Wednesday won the 1896 Football Cup Championship, observers were astonished by the size and order of the crowd that welcomed the returning team. The *Sheffield Daily Telegraph* marveled that the crowd exceeded a royal visit, and estimated that "close upon a hundred thousand people" thronged the streets "to welcome the victorious team and to have a glimpse at the glittering trophy."[132] In 1894, a reporter for the *Liverpool Mercury* decided to "study" the crowd drawn to Goodison Park for the Football Cup championship, noting that while "packed together in their thousands" the "crowd [was] very even tempered" if a "bit excited."[133] As Rollin Hartt noted in *People at Play*, his exploration of American leisure from 1909, baseball fans were "progressing, however slowly, toward that commendable attitude of morality" in which crowds no longer tied "tin cans to" the umpire's coat-tails, or chased "him up trees, bedecking him with tar and feathers, or forcing him to seek asylum in the town jail." These riotous practices had faded, and baseball crowds "now harry this martyr with rhetoric—accusations of perjury, piracy, and grand larceny, for the most part, and now and then a promise of annihilation."[134]

Enthusiastic fans, arrayed as orderly masses, came to be seen not as dangerous, but as displaying a kind of intelligence and solidarity. Hartt suggested that the "whooping and bawling" of the crowd, which many upper-class observers dismissed as animalistic passion, in fact "reflects intelligence, intelligence finer and higher than we are wont to believe the proletarians possessed of." This working-class intelligence arose from long study: "Having played baseball, watched baseball, talked baseball, read baseball, dreamed baseball, and devoted little earnest cogitation to anything but baseball ever since he was able to lift a bat, [as a spectator] he takes in each move as swiftly as it occurs, and knows by lifelong experience what it portends." Similarly, in 1892, when Wednesday and United, the hometown rivals, played in Sheffield, the *Telegraph* noted the "educational effect of competition" on the crowd, which had "grown so wonderfully impartial."[135] Instead of roaring "in wild disgust," the Sheffield spectators "would impress all and sundry with the depths of their acquaintance with

the science" of the sport. Most directly suggesting a link between organized professional sports and the rise of organized labor, Jane Addams
emphasized the experience of solidarity created by masses of spectators.
While attending a baseball game, workers were "lifted out of their individual affairs and so fused together that a man cannot tell whether it is his
own shout or another's that fills his ears. . . . He does not call the stranger
who sits next to him 'brother' but he unconsciously embraces him in an
overwhelming outburst of kindly feeling when the favorite player makes
a home run."[136] While socialists may have sneered at working-class leisure
preferences, perhaps Jane Addams grasped something crucial about how
sports shaped a new kind of working-class Fordist masculinity. Sports
produced a new kind of diffuse, extensive solidarity that tied together
workers from different occupations, neighborhoods, and positions on the
production hierarchy into a new kind of collective.

In the United States, of course, racial boundaries fractured these solidarities. Teams, crowds, and even informal chats about the game last night
were all segregated. While the experience of the stadium could create a
diffuse solidarity, spectators were also segmented and segregated. In the
1870s, games were played with little or no permanent infrastructure; wood
grandstands grew in the 1880s, and by the early twentieth century teams
were building massive concrete and steel stadiums. In all four cities, stadiums built in the first decade of the twentieth century remained in use
through the 1960s. In contrast to the unruly crowds of the mid-nineteenth
century, sports spectators now paid for entrance to carefully regulated,
segregated, and hierarchically organized spaces. For the 1891 Championship in Sheffield, the "arrangements for administering the grounds" were
explained in detail to guide spectators through these emerging routines.
Separate entrances were provided for "the five shilling covered stand," for
the "two-shilling stand," and for the "sixpenny" general gate fee.[137] Pittsburgh's Forbes Field and Sheffield's Brammal Lane stadium, pictured in
figure 9.6, exemplified how modern stadiums "classified, segregated, and
ranked" spectators.[138] Forbes Field opened in 1909 with a three-tiered
grandstand that wrapped around home plate, offering the best views and
most comfortable opera chair seating, as well as private boxes; in contrast, far from the main on-field action, in the 25- and 50-cent bleachers, working-class spectators sat on basic wooden planks. Pipe rails and
separate entrances enforced the segregation of different viewing areas.[139]
At around the same time, clubs in Liverpool rebuilt their wooden grandstands into modern steel and concrete structures designed by an expert
architect. By 1910, both Liverpool and Everton had stadiums capable of
accommodating seventy thousand spectators.[140] In the US, price segrega

FIGURES 9.6A AND B Sheffield's Bramall Lane and Pittsburgh's Forbes Field.
New steel and concrete stadiums such as Bramall Lane, built in 1902, and Forbes
Field, built in 1909, provided a physical setting for the organized mass, working-
class Fordist masculinity of the early twentieth century. *Sources*: "Aerial view—
Bramall Lane Football and Cricket Ground, Denby Street Nursery in foreground,
St. Mary's Church and Britannia Brewery, left, Hill Street and Anchor Brewery,
right, Shoreham Street in background," 1920–1939, Picture Sheffield s12356,
Sheffield City Council Archive and Local Studies Library; John K. Gates, "Forbes
Field," 1909–1930, John Gates Photograph Collection, 1890–1910, 9122.156A.GT,
University of Pittsburgh.

tion was supplemented by formal racial segregation, by law in the South, and by organizational choice in the North. In Northern cities like Pittsburgh, African American spectators were confined to the cheapest seats in the bleachers.[141]

Stadiums were clearly important to workers. In Baltimore, the city owned the largest stadium. Baltimore's mayor William Broening opened the Baltimore Municipal Stadium in 1922, "the first to be constructed by a municipality and maintained as a municipal activity."[142] The Baltimore Federation of Labor had endorsed "the building of a stadium" by the city, and they clearly expected to have access to this new municipal structure.[143] In January 1925, a resolution passed declaring that "the Baltimore Federation of Labor favors the opening of the Stadium, under proper supervision, for athletic purposes" to schools and "other organizations of recognized standing in the field of sports," such as the numerous baseball teams organized by local unions in the city.[144] Later that year, the Baltimore Federation of Labor "congratulat[ed] the Park Commissioners . . . for their action" in changing the ticket policy "hitherto prevailing at the Municipal Stadium," since the new policy "would result in cheaper seats for the general masses."[145] A few years later, the Baltimore Federation ordered its business representative to "protest to the proper authorities" the "lack of shelter in the Stadium."[146] During strikes and celebrations, organized labor put stadiums to even more direct use. For instance, during the 1922 railroad strike, union mass meetings were held in baseball stadiums across the country.[147] In one quite literal sense, sports solidarity and union solidarity happened in the same place: the modern stadium.

Perhaps in the whole history of sports, the most dramatic, spectacular form of racial boundary-making is represented by the segregated baseball leagues of the US. This trajectory can be contrasted with Liverpool, where religious divisions shaped but did not define the growth of professional football. In Liverpool, Everton attracted Irish Catholic supporters and Liverpool won support from Protestant fans. However, these associations were never formalized or entrenched the way baseball became segregated in the US. In the late nineteenth century, at least seventy-three African American players were on the rosters of predominantly white professional major league baseball teams in the United States.[148] However, during the late 1880s baseball "hate strikes" by white players drove black players off teams and out of the major leagues. By the end of the decade, most teams had agreed to quotas limiting the number of black players.[149] By the 1890s, professional baseball was whites-only, and segregation remained in place until the 1940s. Baseball, then, like the broader working class, shifted from a degree of fluidity and inclusion in the 1870s and 1880s to strict segregation in the 1890s. Black businesses, athletes, and fans organized the Negro Leagues to provide an alternative. Pittsburgh became a major center for black baseball.[150] The "Blue Ribbon Nine" was one of the first African American teams, organized by black steelworkers at Homestead in 1900. This team eventually became the Homestead Grays, one of the most successful and prominent Negro League teams.[151] The other major black baseball team in the Pittsburgh District also had ties to the steel industry. The Pittsburgh Crawfords were initially organized by Harold "Hooks" Tinker, a black steelworker who migrated from Alabama to work at the Edgar Thomson works in Braddock.[152]

A quite different trajectory characterized football in Liverpool. Religious hostilities between Protestants and Catholics had produced intense conflict over jobs, housing, and the use of public space in the nineteenth century, and predictably these divisions shaped the city's football teams. Everton's managers and owners had close ties with Liberal politics in Liverpool, and thus had close ties with Irish Home Rulers and Irish Nationalists in the city; in contrast, the Liverpool club was closely tied to the Conservative Party and the aggressively Protestant Conservative Workingmen's Association.[153] Everton developed extensive recruiting networks in Ireland, and brought over a significant number of Irish stars, whereas Liverpool recruited from Scotland.[154] Anecdotal evidence has suggested that among fans, Catholics supported Everton and Protestants backed Liverpool up to the 1960s. Despite violent religious riots in Liverpool as late as 1909, football matches never became sites for conflict.[155] In Liverpool, despite the religious and ethnic affiliations of the two clubs, the city's mayor claimed in 1933 that Everton and Liverpool had done more "to cement good fellowship" in the city "than anything said or done in the last 25 years."[156] The disappearing material divisions between Protestants and Catholics in Liverpool allowed sports to become a shared arena of community solidarity.

Conclusion

The rise of organized sports forged a new Fordist masculinity, creating a working-class disposition prepared for membership in expanding bureaucratic unions. The transformation of informal pugilism into regulated boxing, and the transformation of riotous crowds into orderly masses registered a broad transformation of working-class social worlds. Sports also indexed the construction of new racial boundaries that fractured the US working class. In the 1890s, during the same years that the labor movement retreated from early commitments to racial egalitarianism, the color line was drawn in both heavyweight boxing and in baseball. Hate strikes by baseball players directly paralleled the hate strikes of white industrial workers. While the labor market, the production hierarchy, and household wealth provided the crucial material underpinnings of racial inequality, sports made these divisions spectacular and visible within working-class social worlds.

Crowds, Labor Bureaucrats, and the Politics of Redistribution

In 1903, Maryland's Bureau of Statistics noted that "organized labor" had become "stronger numerically than at any time since 1886," and described the recent wave of organizing as the result of a new sense of "fair play between man and master."[1] This reference to the sporting notion of "fair play" was far from isolated. Sports language was often used to narrate the operations of the emerging labor bureaucracy. As British arbitration practices gained traction in the 1870s, the board member given the deciding vote was often called an "umpire," borrowing the "name for the referee in some sports" and suggesting that both unions and employers were expected to negotiate within the sporting "rules of the game."[2] According to the leader of the British Steel Smelters union, "the employers [were] entitled to credit for always having played cricket" in their negotiations.[3] Union leaders were not the only ones who made connections between the rules of the game in sports and collective bargaining. Workers too used sports language to describe union activity. Invoking a baseball metaphor, one steelworker recalled of a prominent organizer: he was "just born with leadership in him" so the "union gave him a job *right off the bat*. They made him a staff man right away."[4] Another Pittsburgh steelworker used football to describe the activities of a union staff organizer: "He just was another guy that was doing things *behind the line of scrimmage* there, trying to sign people" up for the union.[5] In a variety of contexts, the language of bureaucratic sports was used to articulate the operations of the new bureaucratic unions.

In contrast to the artisans and craftsmen of the mid-nineteenth century who informally enforced the customs of their trade, union members in the early twentieth came to occupy a far more passive position in far larger, more bureaucratic unions. During the 1919 steel strike, a researcher investigating the rank and file found that "their conception of trade unionism" was, in his view, "inarticulate."[6] No ordinary worker could "discuss any of the cardinal principles of organized labor," such as the "closed shop," and a "fair number did not know the name of the organization under whose banner they were waging the strike." However, they did know that "the union" aimed to better "the conditions of the workers, and affords them protection against arbitrary, whimsical and discriminatory treatment by superiors." Workers may not have been able to explain the technical details of the emerging labor bureaucracy and collective bargaining, but they usually knew which team they were on in the class struggle. They were on the union team.

The rise of organized labor involved the construction of new, centralized labor bureaucracies that attempted to consolidate, control, and coordinate working-class collective action. This meant a break with the informal street politics of nineteenth-century crowds. As critics have rightly emphasized, union bureaucracies could stifle internal democracy, but a simplistic celebration of the rank and file is as misguided as an unqualified condemnation of labor bureaucrats. Local rank-and-file militancy most often served narrow, privileged interests within the union—most strikingly illustrated in the hate strikes by white workers.[7] Union leaders, whatever their faults, were broadly responsive to the voting power and interests of the median union member, in a broadly inclusive union usually a worker at the mid-point in the production hierarchy between elite craftsmen and common laborers. Organized labor channeled working-class collective action into the bureaucratic machinery of collective bargaining. For some scholars, romantic attachment to the spontaneity of riotous crowds has obscured the limits and declining effectiveness of insurrectionary street politics.[8]

The remaking of working-class social worlds also reoriented working-class collective action toward new political goals. In the nineteenth century, workers had typically demanded autonomy from authorities: autonomy for craftsmen to follow the customs of the trade, autonomy for communities to enjoy informal street leisure free from the meddling of police and moralizing reformers. In the early twentieth century, as we have seen, working-class demands shifted from autonomy to redistribution. The social worlds of the new, working-class suburbs and the experiences of home-based consumption and commercial leisure created workers who sought not autonomy, but more: more money for less time at work, more taxes on the rich, more government transfers to the masses. The new labor history, in exploring the struggle for "workers' control," effectively revealed a rich array of radical demands that went beyond the "bread and butter" business unionism that the old labor history had endorsed. Yet these more radical strands in the labor movement were generally confined to craftsmen whose position in the production hierarchy was threatened by scientific management and the reconstructed Fordist firm.[9] Most workers joined unions not to challenge managerial control, but to keep abusive foremen in check, boost their earnings so they could purchase a new refrigerator, and shorten their workday so they could enjoy more time at home, in the garden, and at the stadium. Such materialistic demands should not be easily dismissed as conservative "business unionism." As E. P. Thompson aimed to "rescue the . . . utopian artisan. . . . from the enormous condescension of posterity," here the aim is to recuperate the aspirations of the typical union member.[10] Almost always a man, and especially in the US, a white man, he wanted more money, shorter hours, and an improved home life for his family.

The demand for more money for less work, especially when the demand is made inclusively, has the potential to challenge the balance of social power and the unequal distribution of income in capitalism. The AFL has often been condemned for its supposedly conservative "pure and simple" demands for more wages, but as Rose Currarino emphasizes, "demands for 'more' constituted efforts to concretize claims to the surplus through higher wages, shorter hours, and greater participation in social and economic life."[11] Many historians, enchanted by nineteenth-century labor republicanism, view the transition from the expansive but nebulous producerism of the Knights of Labor to the concrete, "bread and butter" economism of the AFL with "a pervasive sense of loss," as a "a transition away from a better past to a more problematic and decidedly less virtuous present."[12] Against such nostalgia, one redeeming feature of the AFL was that it offered a clear and compelling case for higher wages, shorter hours, and expanded consumption and leisure for the working class. At the 1897 AFL Convention, Gompers articulated the link between wages, consumption, and economic growth. Organized labor aimed to "give greater leisure and larger opportunities to those who are employed, making of all a greater consumptive power," thus driving the economy forward through working-class consumption.[13]

The New Deal of the 1930s, which undoubtedly marked an unprecedented expansion of the federal government, is often contrasted against the supposedly laissez-faire 1920s. However, World War I was in many ways an even more crucial turning point in both the US and the UK, after which the labor movement increasingly turned to the state for redistributive economic interventions.[14] This is most obvious in the UK, where the Labour Party became the main opposition in the 1920s, and briefly ruled as a minority government. While less visible, a similar process occurred in the US. In the 1920s, redistributive tax policies and cash transfer programs such as pensions became important to working-class politics.

From Riotous Crowds to Centralized Bureaucracies

A momentous shift in working-class collective action, from informal street politics of riotous confrontation to disciplined, planned, authorized, and professionally led strikes occurred between the 1880s and the 1920s.[15] Strikes in the nineteenth century were part of broader repertoires of crowd actions, including bread riots, rescues of prisoners from police, and plebian rituals of popular shaming.[16] The Railroad Uprising of 1877 belonged to the informal world of nineteenth-century street politics; it was not so much a strike as a set of loosely connected community uprisings.[17] The 1880s, with the rise of the first mass, inclusive unions, marked a clear turning point after which spontaneous working-class crowds lost the traditional stamp of legitimacy.[18] Union leaders hoped to gain recognition by promising more orderly solutions to industrial conflicts. As Samuel Gompers testified in 1883, organized labor would eliminate the disorderly street politics of the rioting crowd. Violence erupted "when strikes occur among men who are unorganized, often acting . . . upon passion. . . . [E]ach acts upon his own account without the restraint of organization." Unions would be "conservators of the public peace."[19] In the nineteenth century, local elites genuinely feared the power of riotous crowds, and invested in police forces to tame the tumultuous streets.[20] Suggesting a waning fear of crowds, in 1919, Balfour's Steel in Sheffield decided to no longer carry insurance "against loss arising from damage done through riots." This decision was reversed during the unsettled state of the General Strike in 1926, but in 1927 the decision was once again made to abandon insurance "against damage by riots and civil commotion."[21]

The turn of the century marked the hardening of craft, racial, and nativist boundaries in the US and across the British Empire, and during these same years, labor bureaucracies consolidated, leaving a lasting institutional imprint on organized labor for decades to come.[22] In the mid-nineteenth century, formal organizations barely existed, and formal membership in a union mattered less than the distinction between "good men" who respected the customs of the trade, and the "rats" and "black sheep" who worked under the prevailing wage rate or broke strikes.[23] In the late 1870s British unions began to enforce limited central authority, and it was only in the 1890s that this central authority consolidated.[24] The upsurge of the Knights of Labor in the 1880s highlighted new forms of centralized, bureaucratic bargaining. As noted in the 1886 report of the Bureau of Industrial Statistics of Maryland, the many "trade disputes which were settled by arbitration" directed "the eyes of the entire country . . . to the fact of labor organizations," through which "representatives of tens of thousands of workmen met with the representatives of millions of dollars" of capital and negotiated a settlement "on business principles."[25]

The 1890s marked a pivot toward the consolidation of labor bureaucracies in both countries.[26] From 1890 to 1905, in most of the major US unions, decision-making was elevated "from local bodies to national headquarters."[27] Before 1879, only nine unions in the United States required permission from the national executive to strike; after 1900 that number jumped to fifty.[28] As decision-making centralized, careers emerged for aspiring labor bureaucrats. By the beginning of the twentieth century, US labor leaders "spent much longer moving up the union hierarchy than did their predecessors," and once they reached the peak of the labor bureaucracy, half of union leaders held their offices for fifteen years or more.[29] Pay for union leadership grew from "at best a token fee in the 1870s" to salaries that rivaled those of business executives in the 1920s. Union headquarters that were once "dingy and smelled of stale beer and tobacco" had been transformed by the 1920s into central offices equipped with "the latest in filing cases, and other modern office devices," with a staff of "alert clerks and stenographers."[30]

As union bureaucracies grew, instead of relying on the customs of the trade and local enthusiasm, labor leaders attempted to create new statistical and "scientific" tools to guide their negotiations with employers in order to strategically conserve resources. At the 1890 conference for the Officers of State Labor Bureaus, P. J. McGuire of the United Brotherhood of Carpenters looked forward to unions reaching organization "on a scientific basis," when industrial peace would prevail and a union could devote itself to "acquiring statistics and perfecting them, and of controlling its own forces."[31] McGuire succinctly captured the transformation in how workers engaged in collective action:

The old system of labor organization was the 'hurrah' system. Where there was an improvement in trade, and the men felt that the bosses were making too much money, they would gather together, probably in a hall over some beer saloon or in a beer garden, and pass a resolution, 'Down with the bosses—the capitalists; they are making too much money. . . .' No statistics, no savings, no responsibility, but hit a capitalist's head

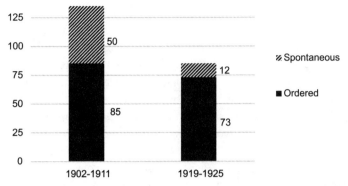

FIGURE 10.1 Spontaneous and ordered strikes in Maryland. *Source*: Collected from the annual reports of the Maryland Bureau of Statistics and Information. Data for 1904 and 1909 are missing in the series from 1902–1911. MSA.

whenever it appeared. The new form of labor organization which has come into existence of later years requires that workmen shall not go into strike without due deliberation, and requires a two-thirds vote instead of the old majority, and a secret ballot at that.

As can be seen in figure 10.1, prior to World War I spontaneous strikes erupting from the rank and file were common in Maryland, but after the war spontaneous strikes had become comparatively rare. In the early twentieth century unions developed calendars and schedules to provide a regular, annually repeated routine for negotiations and formal committee structures to resolve grievances.[32] In return for improved wages and hours, labor bureaucrats promised, and attempted to deliver, more continuous and regular production for employers by avoiding minor disputes and wild-cat strikes. By 1905 the Maryland Bureau of Statistics credited the "more efficient organization of labor" within new bureaucratic unions with largely "preventing strikes" in the state.[33]

The growth of union bureaucracies often had a deadening effect on union democracy. Local union meetings forced workers to come to terms with the power of officials and their regulations. When a Pittsburgh bricklayer contested the 50-cent fine imposed on him by the local president, the District Council "made plain" to him "the duties of a presiding officer . . . and the duty of members to be obedient."[34] While organizers were usually appointed by the executive, locals often attempted to regain democratic control of staff organizers. In 1904, one of the Bricklayers' locals in Pittsburgh moved to have a key staff position, the Walking Delegate, "elected at mass meeting," but the Local Council decided that the position would be "as in the past elected by the Executive Committee."[35] Union staff were routinely deployed to push local union elections in the direction favored by the national leadership.[36] John L. Lewis, the leader of the UMW, was above all a savvy union bureaucrat who knew how to work the coalitional politics of the union's organizational hierarchy.[37] During the 1920s several leading unions retreated from contested, democratic elections to oligarchic control by entrenched leaderships. From 1908 to 1926, the UMW had "hotly contested" elections, but after this Lewis consolidated administration control; in the ILGWU, contests remained lively until 1932, after which David Dubinsky gained uncontested power.[38] Certainly, the power of union bureaucrats was enhanced by the regulatory framework established by the Wagner Act in 1935 and by the elimination of radicals during the Cold War purges of Communists from the labor movement. But the trajectory toward labor bureaucracy was clear by the 1890s and firmly established by the 1920s.

The label "labor bureaucrat" is usually intended as an insult: conservative, careerist, narrowly focused on institutional self-preservation over broader and more transformative goals. While all these critiques carry truth, the construction of durable, permanent institutions that could strategically represent workers' interest was also a remarkable and important achievement, and would not have been possible without centralized, bureaucratic structures. After the mid-nineteenth century, meaningful structural change in the interest of working-class people was unlikely to come solely through spontaneous protest and leaderless movements. Workers needed new ways to contest the power of capital; the labor bureaucracy proved effective in demanding more from both employers and the government. As long as their leaders delivered the goods, rank-and-file workers mostly remained satisfied with these new structures.[39]

Bureaucrats and Crowds: The Baltimore Waterfront Strike of 1912

Sometimes a single event brings larger, long-term historical processes into focus. Such was the 1912 strike by waterfront workers in Baltimore. Already used to introduce racialized strikebreaking in the introduction to this book, as we arrive at its conclusion the strike also illustrates how bureaucratic union officials attempted to discipline and manage the unruly street politics of working-class crowds. The Baltimore strike of 1912 has received only passing attention from historians. Yet the strike was the largest labor conflict in Baltimore prior to World War II. It marked an important, brief experiment at industrial unionism among waterfront workers. As with prior attempts at inclusive organizing in the United States, it was effectively crushed by strikebreakers. The strike erupted informally, without the involvement of union officials. The strike involved "approximately 5,000 men demanding an increase in wages of five cents per hour."[40] Pay in Baltimore was lower than in North Atlantic ports, with wages instead matched the rates in Southern ports such as Newport News and Norfolk.

Reflecting the ongoing importance of nineteenth-century patterns of informal protest, the strike originated as a spontaneous walk-out. However, the newly formed National Transport Workers Federation (NTWF) quickly sent organizers to lead the strike and organize a union. In June 1911, representatives of the US seamen and dockers, with guidance from British trade union leaders, had organized the "Waterfront Federation of New York and Vicinity." After the AFL, ever faithful to craft boundaries, rejected a proposal for an industrial waterfront department, the independent NTWF formed early in 1912. Inspired by, and imported from, Britain, the NTWF was a brief attempt at industrial unionism that would quickly collapse within a year of its founding.[41] The 1912 strike captures the tensions between growing labor bureaucracies and resilient traditions of crowd mobilization in the US. While the new NTWF organizers attempted to channel the demands of workers into formal negotiations, tensions emerged between rank-and-file workers, local leadership, and the central executive in New York. The union officials leading the strike decried violence and attempted to pursue bureaucratic collective bargaining and government arbitration, but street politics and the violence of riotous crowds remained a major factor in 1912.

From its spontaneous start on April 9, the strike remained calm until conflicts between strikers and strikebreakers led to widespread rioting and violence in late April and early May. Despite the extensive recruitment of black strikebreakers, the NTWF managed to mitigate racial hostilities, and hundreds of black workers joined the union. Partial success came for roughly a third of the strikers on May 20, when a group of fourteen stevedore employers as well as the major fruit importing companies agreed to recognize the union and grant the requested wage increase.[42] Further success came a week later when five lumber dealers agreed to the NTWF's demands.[43] However, the most important waterfront employers, the large steamship companies and the railroads, refused to consider union recognition. The strike dragged into early July when it was officially abandoned.[44] Reports claimed that the 1,500 workers who returned to work in early July after three months on strike would not face discrimination as union members. Workers also received half the pay increase demanded. However, no formal bargaining with union representatives would be allowed.[45] Although the strike was largely defeated, and the NTWF quickly collapsed, the International Longshoremen's Association (ILA) picked up the workers organized in 1912. The next summer, in May 1913, a business agent for the ILA who had helped organize the 1912 strike was again in Baltimore to build union locals in the city.[46] Though the NTWF was crushed, a few ILA locals survived. Thus the 1912 strike marks the beginning of durable waterfront unionism in Baltimore.

Baltimore's waterfront had seen occasional, small, and relatively short-lived strikes previously, but there had been little to prepare employers for the scale and intensity of the 1912 mobilization. In 1896 a group of "colored stevedores who handle lumber" successfully went on strike for an increase in wages.[47] In the summer of 1898, Edward McHugh's American Longshoremen's Union claimed to have organized most of the stevedores in Baltimore, but this organization quickly collapsed after a corrupt official absconded with the union's funds.[48] The stevedores handling coffee bags went on strike in 1903, but were defeated when "colored men were employed to take the strikers' places."[49] These prior strikes were short and had little lasting impact. Not so in 1912. Employers were "amazed on learning that the longshoremen heretofore unorganized had been affiliated almost overnight with a union," the NTWF, "that stretches along the Atlantic and Gulf Coasts."[50] A new breed of labor bureaucrat had arrived in Baltimore.

From the start, the NTWF assigned staff organizers and created a formal structure to manage the strike. It drew upon union officials from the constituent unions that had amalgamated to form the NTWF. Charles Sheraton, a national organizer of the International Transport Union, spent the early days of the strike "perfecting plans of organization."[51] He was assisted by Joseph Anderson, a business agent of the Baltimore Atlantic Coast Seamen's Union. Fourteen distinct organizing committees were created to extend the union. Following the general practice of union organizers in the South, black workers were placed in a separate, segregated local. The NTWF planned three locals in Baltimore during the strike: two white locals based on geography for workers at Locust Point and Fells Point, and a third local for all black waterfront workers from across the city. Within a few days, some two thousand members were reportedly enrolled in the union. Signifying membership, workers were issued "a dark blue card . . . identifying its holder as a member of the federation."[52]

From the outset, NTWF leaders expressed a willingness to "submit the proposition to a board of arbitration," since the demand for a raise of 5 cents an hour was "what is just for the stevedores." Union officials hoped that Charles J. Fox, chief of the Maryland Bureau of Statistic and Labor, would step in to mediate "an amicable agreement."[53] Unlike the informal associations of the nineteenth century, labor bureaucracies could centralize and accumulate substantial resources to deploy during strikes. Flexing its financial muscle, the NTWF "organizers promised aid to relieve any member in want as a result of the strike."[54] A month into the strike, these promises were put to the test. A reporter for the *Baltimore Sun*, visiting "where the longshoremen live" in Locust Point, Fells Point, and Canton, found "no suffering among them," since the union had "established a relief station" and distributed "cash in the amount of $4,200" to striking workers, as well as providing for medical care for sick union members.[55] The union treasury could also be used to deal with strikebreakers. Rather than simply intimidating strikebreakers with crowds, unions attempted to use their financial might to dissuade and remove strikebreakers, offering to pay return fares for any strikebreakers imported by employers.[56]

To counter the typical perception of strikers as disorderly rioters, NTWF officials staged carefully choreographed parades in which the union could present the strikers as orderly, respectable representatives of Baltimore's working-class families. For instance, the NTWF organized a children's parade that linked patriotism and the value of families to the cause of the workers on strike:

> With Old Glory waving above their heads, with cheers coming from all sides and with their elders urging them on, children of the striking stevedores paraded through Locust Point last night. . . . Five hundred strong, they formed and began to march, and when they disbanded there were probably 2,000 in line. . . . [T]o the rattle of tin cans and dishpans the children marched, bearing home-made banners inscribed in straggling letters: "My father is a union man." "Sympathize with organized labor" and similar mottos. Quietly gathering together in front of No. 17 Engine House, Fort avenue and Hubert street, the children formed in line. . . . [T]here was surprising order. . . . Mothers dressed in calico and carrying babies in their arms looked on with pride, while many a father, apparently in an effort to hide his feelings, took a fresh grip on his pipe. . . .[57]

Rather than a riotous affair of disorderly immigrants and African Americans, this children's parade emphasized the workers as patriotic, American family men who were supporting their wives and children. Several weeks later, strikers assembled for a mass meeting that was once again carefully choreographed. Instead of the "longshoremen in their garb of blue jeans and the women wearing gingham aprons," for this special demonstration the "men wore suits of tweed and serge and the women were attired in pretty coat suits of white shirtwaists and skirts of dark cloth."[58] Orderly and well-dressed, the strikers were presented as responsible, respectable

American consumers demanding sufficient wages to support their well-dressed families.

These demonstrations achieved their goal: the strike enjoyed broad popular and public support. The German Evangelical Ministerial Union issued a resolution "calling upon the ship owners to meet their employees in a conciliatory manner."[59] The Catholic archbishop of Baltimore and the Maryland governor also urged their service as mediators. The NTWF welcomed these gestures of support, noting that "a great dock workers' strike in England was once settled through the mediation" services of a Catholic cardinal.[60] The conclusions of the "official investigation of the strike situation" by the state of Maryland was seen as a victory for the strikers. The report endorsed both an increase of wages and the recognition of the union.[61]

As strikebreaking escalated tensions between white and black workers on the waterfront, the NTWF labor bureaucrats worked to distance themselves from any kind of violence or riotous street conflict. The *Sun* reported that "business agents and organizers are constantly warning the men against any form of disorder."[62] Even as crowd violence escalated at the end of April, NTWF officials continued to warn the strikers "to refrain from violence."[63] Despite the efforts of NTWF officials to restrain rioting, the visible passage of black strikebreakers through the city unleashed brutal crowd violence by white strikers.

Although the NTWF had attempted to bring inclusive industrial organization to the waterfront, the organization collapsed shortly after the Baltimore strike, and the unions that had amalgamated in the Transport Federation returned to the AFL. By late 1912, former NTWF officials were suing each other "to recover records, books and moneys," a dispute essentially over the material artifacts of a collapsed labor bureaucracy.[64] The craft unions of the AFL gloated at yet another failed attempt at inclusive unionism. The *Coast Seamen's Journal* observed in February 1913 that the NTWF had aimed to "revolutionize. . . . all water-front crafts" and break with the slow and conservative methods of the AFL; yet after "a short and fitful career," the NTWF "tottered and fell." The Boilermakers, kings among the craft labor aristocrats, welcomed the failure of the NTWF and their effort to break with the AFL: "All of the organizations participating in the independent movement will return to the recognized international unions of their craft."[65]

Eric Arnesen, in the only previous scholarly account of the 1912 strike, stressed the widespread violence and the decisive impact of strikebreakers.[66] Arnesen's brief account can be extended in two directions. First, the officials of the NTWF made a concerted and powerful effort to present the strikers as orderly, respectable, American family men. In response to these efforts, Baltimore authorities showed a remarkable degree of support for the strike. In addition, while the strikers failed to win agreements with the large steam shipping companies, and the NTWF soon collapsed, the strike did win pay raises and union recognition for a substantial minority of the dockers, marking the origins of durable unions on Baltimore's waterfront. The ILA took over from the defunct NTWF in 1913, but under the ILA's initial plans for unionization, "only the white workers were to be organized" in Baltimore. The shipping companies objected to bargaining with a racially exclusive union, however, and thus the ILA's organizers were forced to extend their outreach to black workers.[67] Above all, the NTWF and the 1912 strike illustrate how an emerging labor bureaucracy aimed to channel and contain the spontaneous street politics of workers.

From Autonomy to Redistribution: Reorienting Working-Class Politics

The remaking of workers' social worlds in their homes and neighborhoods at the turn of the century underpinned a reorientation of working-class politics from demands for autonomy to materialistic demands for redistribution. The rise of the Labour Party in the United Kingdom provides an obvious marker for this transition, especially in the 1920s when Labour broke with the deep voluntarism of British unions and came to embrace statist forms of redistributive politics.[68] In the United States the shift was more subtle. Most scholars understandably point to the New Deal of the 1930s as the era when workers turned to the state to make redistributive demands.[69] However, a working-class politics of redistribution was already well established in the 1920s. The remaking of working-class life gave new importance to commercial leisure and the conveniences of home life, and these material desires animated a turn toward economistic demands for redistribution. As the Maryland labor bureau put it, an "intensive love of homelife" motivated union organizing in the early twentieth century.[70] Or, as the *Baltimore Afro-American* explained in urging black workers to organize, "trade unionism" could provide "better wages, hours, and conditions of work," and this would allow for "sufficient support of their families" and render "domestic life far more meaningful."[71] Better wages, shorter hours, and a more fulfilling home life were closely bound together in the first decades of the twentieth century. Workers used the new labor bureaucracies to translate their material aspirations into collective bargaining agreements and political policy. The turn toward a labor politics of redistribution in the 1920s can be seen in union activism around income taxes, soldiers' bonuses, and pensions, programs that aimed to capture resources from capital and redistribute cash transfers to working-class families.

The Baltimore Federation of Labor's legislative and lobbying activity during the 1920s suggests a robust politics oriented toward the state and aimed at achieving redistribution in the interests of workers. At the heart of any redistributive politics is the moment of expropriation: income and wealth taxes. Even the conservative craft unionists of Baltimore's AFL unions fought hard to retain the progressive income taxes established during World War I. Once resources were captured by the state, they had to be redistributed, and Baltimore's organized workers provided strong support for direct payments to working-class households in two forms. First, they supported the massively popular Soldiers' Bonuses passed by many states and the federal government after the war. Second, they mobilized for publicly funded old-age pensions. While workers have been ambivalent about the invasive, regulatory dimensions of the welfare state, programs of redistribution that captured resources from the wealthy and reallocated them to working-class households as cash transfers have been among the most popular programs in twentieth-century politics.

Taxation provides the foundation for all redistributive political projects. Organized workers in the 1920s were keenly aware of its importance. In 1922, as the US Chamber and other business interests pushed for a reform of the tax law favorable to the wealthy, the BFL's Political League accused Congress of pursuing a "tax policy" that would "take burdens off the rich and put them on the poor" by repealing the "excess profits tax" and reducing the "surtaxes on incomes," while also making an effort "to enact a general sales tax."[72] Because of the broad popular support for progressive income taxes, organized in part by labor unions, much of the fiscal apparatus created during World War I remained in place.[73] In 1927, the BFL sent a delegation to "appear before a Congressional Committee in behalf of retention of the inheritance tax."[74] While workers were keen to use the state to capture the wealth of the rich, they also wanted to protect their own material possessions, lobbying to shield their homes and automobile fuel from taxation. The BFL endorsed legislation exempting $1,000 from taxation on homes valued at less than $7,000, and in 1927 the Federation's legislative program included "Opposition to a 4 ½ cent gas tax."[75] Support for taxes on the rich, and opposition to taxes on homes, cars, and fuel: this basic configuration of working-class fiscal politics, already apparent in the 1920s, has largely endured.

Although neglected by scholars, among the more pressing and controversial questions of the postwar years was the provision of soldiers' bonuses—lump sums of cash, annuities, or other resources—to the many veterans who served in the war and whose service had deprived them, supporters argued, of the advantages of high wages in the wartime economy. Although promoted primarily through veterans' groups, organized labor also took a prominent role in advocating for soldiers' bonuses after the war. In 1919, the Baltimore Federation endorsed the provision of a soldiers and sailors' bonus in Maryland.[76] Organized capital, on the other hand, was concerned about the precedent of large-scale cash transfers. Through the 1920s, the US Chamber of Commerce reiterated its strong opposition to offering "a general cash bonus" for soldiers, expressing concern over the "burden [it would] place upon the Treasury and the public" in terms of cost as well as the precedent set by the distribution of a "cash bonus given without discrimination."[77] The Chamber warned that "a bonus of any sort for abled-bodied veterans" threatened to undermine the "virtues of democracy." Having "great sums levied by taxes" given to "able-bodied young men" raised the specter of socialist expropriation and majoritarian tyranny in the eyes of the business lobby.[78] Despite the fears of organized capital, soldiers' bonuses proved immensely popular, and substantial programs were passed in many states.[79] Maryland provided for a "Veteran's Relief Fund" in 1924. Governor Albert Ritchie considered it one of his more important accomplishments in the interests of workers, and the state even increased its appropriation in 1929.[80] But soldiers' bonuses were not the only transfer program that gained prominence in these years.

During the 1920s many states created old-age pension programs, with organized labor playing a leading role in lobbying for legislation. These efforts have generally been overshadowed by the New Deal's Social Security program. Yet thirty states had established old age pension laws by the time Social Security was enacted. Too often missed in the misleading perception of the 1920s as a laissez-faire age, statist old-age pensions "were a leading social issue during the 1920s."[81] Already in 1886 when the Knights of Labor swept across the US, old-age pensions were on the minds of some workers. A Baltimore boilermaker interviewed by the newly formed state labor bureau argued that "there should be some provision made for the aged . . . to save them from becoming inmates of almshouses."[82] Despite some deep roots, the BFL was initially uncertain about endorsing the expansion of pensions given the general wariness of craft unions regarding becoming entangled with universal programs administered by the state. In 1920, considerable debate occurred in the BFL when Frank Harper, a representative in the Maryland Legislature and a member of the local Boilermakers Union, asked "the Federation to advise him" on a bill to "provide for a pension for city employees." Initially a motion to oppose pensions

for city employees was made and seconded, but on amendment, the issue was referred to the legislative committee.[83] However, by the middle
of the 1920s any reservations about turning to the state to secure old-age
pensions seems to have evaporated. In 1925, the BFL's Resolution Committee reported favorably on "old age and occupational disease insurance"
and called for a committee to advance these legislative issues.[84] The next
year the BFL wrote to a congressman urging support for a "retirement
bill" providing pensions for employees of the federal government.[85] Once
again in 1927, the BFL's program for the next legislative session included
support for an "Old Age pension law."[86] These sustained efforts bore fruit.
Maryland passed an old-age pension law in 1927. However, its lack of funding and meager provisions meant that the state still lacked a real pension
system. In March of 1928, Abraham Epstein of the National Association for
the Promotion of Old Age Pensions addressed the BFL, and in response,
a joint committee with representatives from several local unions was appointed to work jointly "with other organizations in the city to discuss
ways of making the 'Old Age Pension Bill' now on the statute books of
Maryland effective."[87] In December 1928 the Legislative Program Committee for the BFL recommended "that the Baltimore Labor League be
authorized to call a conference of all parties interested in old age pensions
for the purpose of creating an adequate bill and the lining up of numerous
organizations in its support."[88] The next year the Baltimore Carpenters
appointed three delegates to attend a statewide Old Age Pension Conference aiming to advance legislation, and a "mass meeting" was held in
Baltimore at the Roosevelt Park Recreation Center.[89] A Pennsylvania law
passed in 1923 had been declared unconstitutional, but by the end of the
decade, the Pennsylvania Federation, in conjunction with the Fraternal
Order of Eagles, committed to doing "everything possible. . . . to promote"
the passage of old-age pensions at the next legislative session.[90] Further,
and more consequential, changes would follow during the New Deal, but
labor lobbying on taxes, soldiers' bonuses, and old-age pensions shows
that organized workers had already substantially reoriented toward to
statist redistributive politics in the 1920s.

Conclusion

Workers organized in new ways and toward new goals in the early twentieth century. Nineteenth-century practices of bargaining by riot declined
as labor bureaucrats attempted to coordinate and control working-class
collective action. As the Baltimore waterfront strike of 1912 illustrated,
despite their best efforts, union officials could not always prevent crowd

violence, especially when racialized strikebreaking provoked workers. This was a momentous change in how working people organized to challenge those in power. The pivot of the 1890s when craft, racial, and nativist boundaries all hardened in the United States was also the period during which unions began to build durable, centralized bureaucracies. Even more so, the rise of potentially universal, statist programs of redistribution raised fundamental questions of eligibility, borders, and boundaries, thus extending racial boundary-making into new terrains in the twentieth century.[91] As the welfare state expanded, nativist and racial boundaries were increasingly marked by hostility to ineligible aliens accused of crossing borders as lazy benefit scroungers and unproductive "welfare queens" who abused the benefits system. When the US welfare state expanded in the 1930s, most of its core provisions exempted agricultural and domestic workers, the two most important occupations for black workers. A universal politics of redistribution was clearly on the horizon in the 1920s, but a racially divided working class made a politics of universal redistributive programs extremely difficult.

Conclusion

Sheffield, Liverpool, Baltimore, and Pittsburgh are each wonderful, distinctive cities. Over the course of researching this book, I spent at least a year living and working in each of them. While nearly a century of history sits between where this book ends and the 2010s when I was working in these cities, my time in each offered reminders of the legacies of class, labor mobilization, and racial boundary-making that have endured in some predictable, as well as unexpected, forms. Sheffield and Pittsburgh have both become major research and university centers, exemplary of the "eds and meds" post-industrial reconstruction.[1] As commercial ports and transportation hubs, Liverpool and Baltimore reached their economic peaks somewhat earlier, and their post-Fordist economic redevelopment appears far more uneven and difficult. Today the population in each city is roughly half of its mid-twentieth century peak. A palpable sense of loss, marked in the landscape and registered in conversations with local residents, shapes these communities. But striking differences also stood out. Concentrated poverty and public disinvestment were predictably far more intense and visible in the US cities. Nothing in Liverpool or Sheffield came close to the mass, concentrated, racialized poverty experienced by African Americans. In Baltimore in particular, the carceral arm of the US state was astonishingly omnipresent, with invasive policing and surveillance constantly intervening in working-class neighborhoods. On the other hand, I was surprised by the open, overt racism that was repeatedly expressed by white British residents in casual encounters while living in these cities. In Sheffield in particular, where racialized class formation resonated only faintly during the early twentieth century, the animosity of local white residents toward the city's growing South Asian community was intense, overt, and unapologetic. In contrast, in Liverpool, where class formation was far more fractured by racial boundary-making in the early twentieth century, I was struck to encounter in casual conversations on the streets and in pubs a deep sense of working-class radicalism and international-ism tied to Liverpool's late twentieth-century identity as Britain's most left-wing city.

By ending the narrative in 1929, this analysis closes before the great expansion of inclusive unionism in the US under the CIO in the 1930s. Does this produce a misleading picture? Of course, the rise of the CIO profoundly transformed the labor movement. Industrial unionism spread across the United States, from the Northeast to the Midwest to the West Coast. Yet once again, the shadow of slavery fell on efforts to organize; it proved impossible for CIO unions to organize in the South.[2] Union strength, even during its mid-twentieth-century peak, was always precar-ious if the South beckoned employers with low wages and a non-union workforce.[3] Thus even in 2022, the geography of union strength reflects the geography of slavery. In South Carolina, the heart of the Cotton Kingdom and the state that produced the leaders of proslavery politics, secession, and white supremacy, only 1.7 percent of workers were in unions as of 2022.[4] Less than 5 percent of workers were unionized in Virginia, North Carolina, Georgia, Florida, Louisiana, Arkansas, and Texas.[5] Across the United States, organized labor has been beaten into an appalling retreat, representing a tiny fraction of the broader working class. Offering a glim-mer of hope, a rejuvenated, democratized, and militant United Auto Workers, led by Shawn Fain, has committed real resources to organizing workers across the South.[6]

The rise of the CIO marked a clear break with the racial and craft boundaries forged by the AFL. Black and white workers organized, marched, and campaigned together in unprecedented ways, forging new bonds of solidarity. The longer history explored here suggests the unique and vital role of Communist Party activists in organizing CIO unions. Because they developed a strictly anti-racist internal culture and priori-tized the distinct demands of African Americans, Communist Party ac-tivists and organizers were essential in bridging the racial boundaries that have long proved so insurmountable. Communists were "often both the original, actual builders of [inclusive CIO unions] and the most dedi-cated, talented, and militant activists."[7] Unlike the Knights in the 1880s, the Socialists in the 1910s, and many leftists up to the present, who have argued that universal class interests must be prioritized and that racial grievances only served to divide workers, the Communist Party in the US "was the first largely white US radical group to focus attention" on racism, strictly disciplining white members for discriminatory behavior, and focusing Party organizing and resources on issues of concern to black workers.[8] The Communists' "self-determination" position prioritizing the struggle of African Americans was imposed on the US Party by the 1928 Comintern Congress. While the notion of an autonomous black nation-state carved out of the US South was baffling to many, the approach built on the mass popularity of Garveyism in the 1920s, and more crucially, it rested on the long-standing demand of African Americans for control over the land they had worked as enslaved laborers. Harry Haywood, a leading black Communist, explained the Party's self-determination thesis in terms of the "agrarian and democratic revolution in the South" left unfulfilled in the aftermath of the Civil War: "The revolution had stopped short of a solution to the crucial land question; there was neither confiscation of the big plantations of the former slaveholding class, nor distribution of the land among the Negro freedmen and poor whites," and this failure of land reform "blocked the road to fusion of Blacks and whites into one nation on the basis of equality."[9] In making the distinctive structural position of African Americans central to their understanding of class struggle in the US, the Communist Party gave racial inequality unparalleled importance, and brought thousands of black radicals into the Party.

Yet paradoxically, while the top-down structure of the Comintern initially forced the US Communist Party "to make the fight against racial oppression central to its activities," thus pushing Communist activists to play a powerful and unique role in building the CIO, this undemocratic authoritarianism had fatal costs, and "in the mid-1930s ultimately became an albatross that destroyed the Party."[10] With the shift to the Popular Front after 1936, Communist activists subordinated themselves to more mainstream labor leadership that was uninterested, or hostile, to foregrounding struggles for racial justice, and after 1948, the Taft-Hartley Act required the expulsion of Communist Party members from the US labor movement. Glenda Gilmore shows how this Cold War anti-Communism narrowed the subsequent struggle for civil rights in the 1950s and 1960s to issues of integration and voting rights, foreclosing the longer, more radical struggle for "human rights during the 1930s and 1940s" that had aimed "to eliminate the economic injustices wrought by slavery, debt peonage, and a wage labor system based on degraded black labor."[11]

The inclusive unionism built by the CIO provided substantial wage boosts for all workers, and inclusive bargaining decreased the wage differential across the craft and racial divides.[12] The CIO unquestionably represented a formidable challenge to white supremacy in the US, but ultimately it did very little to mitigate the structural sources of racial boundary-making. There is much to admire and celebrate in what the CIO achieved, but what is ultimately more significant is what was left undone. While union internationals and national labor leaders made verbal commitments to civil rights and racial equality, local unions were far less eager to challenge racial boundaries in the production hierarchy.[13] While rhetorically committed to civil rights from the top down, in the locals, CIO unions followed the well-established path of arguing that "race issues" were not relevant to the labor movement.[14] Echoing Terence Powderly's refusal to see the connections between class and racial domination, one CIO local leader explained: "We tell the blacks to go the NAACP, 'Take it to them.' Or tell the whites if they bring something up, 'You go to the Klan.' That was it. We are here to deal with the working conditions."[15] Several generations on from the height of CIO power, whatever its accomplishments in combating white supremacy, its limits are far more evident in the long run.

Craft divides also proved surprisingly resilient. CIO unions faced the same tensions that made the survival of the Knights of Labor so challenging in the 1880s and 1890s when they attempted to unite common laborers and craft workers together in mixed assemblies. Bryant Etheridge has called attention to the previously overlooked practice of "craft severance" in the 1940s and 1950s. As CIO unions grew, skilled craftsmen would petition the new government agency charged with managing collective bargaining, the National Labor Relations Board (NLRB), to secede from the larger industrial unit and form a separate, exclusive bargaining unit with the AFL.[16] Initially, the NLRB strongly endorsed the industrial unionism of the CIO and rejected petitions for craft severance. Committed to industrial unionism, one NLRB official warned, "The craft organizations ... will build themselves up on the basis of persuading the employees in their respective crafts that if they break away from the industrial union and set themselves up as separate crafts they can get better terms than the industrial unions had so far gotten them."[17] The economic logic for craft severance was hard to deny.

Craft severance was a practice anticipated by the secession of the AFL craft unions from the Knights in 1886. Industrial unions like those in the CIO compressed wages, providing massive improvements for laborers at the bottom of the occupational hierarchy, substantial improvements for the semi-skilled workers who dominated the membership, and only small improvements for the strategically powerful but numerically weak craftsmen. By 1939 AFL leadership was so incensed by the NLRB's rejection of craft severance that it refused to endorse the New Deal at its annual convention.[18] Under pressure from the AFL and conservative politicians, a series of NLRB rulings gradually opened the door to craft severance in the 1940s. Skilled workers flooded the NLRB with petitions to secede from their industrial unions.[19] Once again, craft and racial boundaries were closely intertwined. "Racism was almost certainly a significant motivating factor," since craft severance would allow for the formation of all-white skilled unions.[20] However, what made craft severance so compelling was the ways that craft, racial, and occupational hierarchies continued to reinforce each other. Evidence from specific plants indicate that craft workers were indeed successful in securing higher wages after they seceded from CIO industrial unions and organized separately with the AFL. However, this left the remaining majority of workers in the industrial union in a far weaker bargaining position.[21] While the CIO struggled heroically against the combined boundaries of craft and race that divided the US working class, the CIO's moment of success was brief, and ultimately failed to overcome the racial and craft boundaries that so deeply divided the US working class. It was these structural, material configurations of labor markets and occupational structures that made inclusive unionism of the New Deal era so brief and precarious.

In explaining the "Great Exception" of the New Deal era, Jefferson Cowie's influential account rightly takes note of the "deep divisions in the polity by party, skill, ethnicity, [and] race" as factors undermining working-class solidarity, but his account offers no sense of the material, structural forces producing these divides.[22] Instead, Cowie unconvincingly resurrects Louis Hartz's *The Liberal Tradition in America*, suggesting that the US has been defined by an archaic but enduring political culture of "Jeffersonian individualism" that has prevented even mildly social democratic politics from taking "root in the uniquely challenging ideological soils of the United States."[23] Cowie depicts the United States as somehow a uniquely "complex and conservative place," where individualistic Americans "seem to like to fight each other" instead of confronting elites.[24] Rather than the result of some transcendent individualism, the weakness of the CIO's inclusive unionism, and the limits of the New Deal, were rooted in the structural reality of a racially and regionally divided labor market that reinforced and perpetuated processes of craft, racial, and nativist boundary-making. Not Jeffersonian individualism, but the shadow of slavery, has been the key determinant of the long-term trajectory of labor organizing in the US.[25]

Global inequality remains deeply entrenched in capitalism today. The outlook is not promising. The gap in real wages between the Global North and South continues to grow. The shadow of slavery falls as heavily as ever over the poorer, less powerful, and most populous parts of the world in the early twenty-first century, fueling continually renewed racist boundary-making, closed borders, and mass, populist anti-immigrant nativism across the Global North. Ireland escaped from racialized subordination under unique conditions. Open borders in the nineteenth century meant that Irish emigrants could freely move to favorable high-wage destinations. But borders closed in the early twentieth century, and they have yet to meaningfully reopen, even as many high-wage countries face a demographic crisis of aging populations. Pronatalist, anti-immigrant politics aim to "keep the Global North white" (or to keep Japan Japanese).

While global wage inequality across capitalism combined with uneven development will continue to drive racialized nativism and anti-immigrant politics, internal structures of racialized labor market inequality also remain robust. Labor market discrimination remains rife, and almost wholly unaddressed by public policy. Building on the foundational work of Devah Pager, repeated audit studies have shown that identical white and black job-seekers experience dramatically different outcomes in the labor market. White job-seekers will receive a positive response from employers at twice the rate as identically qualified black job-seekers.[26] Put simply, it is twice as hard to get a job as a black person in the United States. This pervasive labor market discrimination is hardly unique to the US, however. Audit studies across the Global North have found extensive discrimination against non-white job-seekers from the Global South. In fact, comparative research suggests that labor markets in France and Sweden are the most discriminatory against non-white job-seekers, while Germany, the US, and Norway all have comparable levels of racialized labor-market discrimination.[27] Yet in other respects the US also remains distinctive in how racialized inequality continues to shape its broader political economy. Only in the US has punitive policing and mass incarceration emerged as the primary strategy for managing the poverty and social dislocation arising from post-Fordist deindustrialization.[28] Formerly incarcerated black men, a substantial sector of the population in the United States, are effectively locked out of the labor market entirely, further entrenching racialized disparities in wages, income, and housing.

While labor markets remain central sites of inequality and racial boundary-making both globally and locally, during the twentieth century housing replaced land as a key source of security in the Global North. A profound racial wealth gap underpins durable racial inequality in the US, and as seen in figure C.1, the racial gap is by far the most pronounced for those with a high school education or less. After a century of unequal access to the labor market and housing, the racial wealth gap is concentrated in the chasm between the white working class, which enjoys substantial wealth primarily in the form of home ownership, and the black working class, which has been denied access to homeownership. The median wealth of white individuals with a high school education was $78,300,

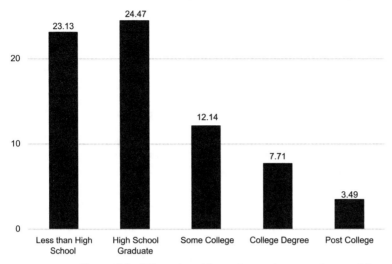

FIGURE C.1 Class and the US racial wealth gap. Ratio of average white wealth to average black wealth at various levels of education. *Source*: Darrick Hamilton et al., "Umbrellas Don't Make It Rain: Why Studying and Working Hard Isn't Enough for Black Americans" (The New School, Duke Center for Social Equality, Insight Center for Community Economic Development, April 2015).

representing a substantial investment in a working-class home. This was nearly twenty-five times the median wealth of black high school graduates, who had a median wealth of only $3,200, little more than a few months' rent. Just as land ownership provided favorable conditions for migrants entering the labor market in the nineteenth century, access to home-ownership offers favorable conditions for participating in the labor market in the twentieth century and into the present. Household wealth has provided white working-class families with insurance against unexpected unemployment, resources for education, and the security and extended time horizons needed for selective employment searches.

As long as black and white workers continue to occupy such different structural positions in the labor market, and as long as vastly unequal rates of homeownership and wealth place black and white families in such profoundly different material circumstances, there is little reason to imagine one, unitary "multi-racial working class" at either a local or global level. White workers, from their structural position of power and material advantage, will not be easily convinced to join inclusive coalitions aiming to elevate the conditions of all. Workers in the Global North will not be inclined to open their labor markets to low-wage migrants. The often reactionary political separatism of white workers across the Global North is not some kind of false consciousness; it articulates the structural reality of a divided working class.

To move from questions of history to the concerns of citizenship and the future, a clear reckoning with material structures driving racial boundary-making must guide future organizing for freedom, democracy, and abundance for all. It is premature to conclude that "there can be no economistic cure for the malady that is 'whiteness.'"[29] No real attempt has ever been made. While material redress is perhaps not the only solution, material redistribution of power and resources must be central to combating racial domination. Material redress would require ongoing reparations globally, paid from the wealth of imperial powers to the dispossessed residents of formerly colonized territories with the aim of equalizing wages and income levels for workers in the Global North and Global South. A return to open borders, as seen with the case of Ireland, would likewise ease the global labor market inequalities that have endured since capitalism's emergence. Material redress would also require reparations for slavery. The Black Reparations Project has targeted the "elimination of the racial wealth gap as the fundamental goal of a plan for reparations for black American descendants of US slavery." As this book also shows, the "promise of forty-acre land grants" stands as the "original source of the debt owed to today's descendants" of slavery and, since "the best economic indicator of America's antiblack history is the racial wealth gap, a reparations plan must provide, *at least*, adequate resources to raise average black wealth on par with average white wealth."[30] Historical injustice and exploitation underpin the moral case of reparations. But it is the future that demands reparations for strategic reasons of class solidarity.[31] Reparations for colonialism and slavery are a structurally necessary precondition for a future with any kind of sustained, deep, and globally inclusive working-class solidarity. "Whiteness" is not some ahistorical constant. Reparations that close the income gap between the Global North and South, as well as reparations for slavery that eliminate the wealth gap between white and black workers, offer a path toward striking down racial boundary-making at its roots. The path from here to there is far from clear, but we must hope for, and work toward, a future beyond the shadow of slavery.

Acknowledgments

The journey that created this book has been unusual. What was initially envisioned as a single chapter grew unexpectedly, and initially against my wishes, into a separate book project. Given this circuitous route, I could not have done it alone. Only a small fraction of those who contributed can be named. My thanks to the many scholars, workers, friends, and family who helped make this possible.

The arguments in this book grew from ideas and approaches I first encountered as an undergraduate at Columbia University. My enduring thanks to Eric Foner, Barbara Fields, Karen Barkey, and Shamus Khan. My gratitude for their early, formative mentorship cannot be adequately expressed. Their words of advice, caution, and encouragement have been a constant guide.

Martin Daunton supervised my efforts to immerse myself in British economic and social history. He generously continued to support me beyond my two years in the United Kingdom. The comparative and global scope of this project could not have been attempted without his support and ongoing guidance.

Sven Beckert's enthusiasm for global history likewise inspired my efforts to develop a comparative approach to political economy. Sven's handwritten comments on countless chapter drafts, continuing for many years after I finished the PhD, provided essential direction and encouragement. A bulky envelope with a dozen stamps affixed arriving from Ghana or Italy or Thailand signaled the arrival of Sven's feedback on yet another piece of writing.

The experience of organizing a union while in graduate school deeply shaped this book. My thanks to Sven for supporting my desire to become fully immersed in the early efforts to organize graduate student workers with the United Auto Workers (UAW), an effort that led to the formation of HGSU-UAW 5118. While admittedly this delayed progress on research at many points, I became a part-time staff organizer for the UAW and attempted to build our union in the Longwood Medical Area. Thousands of walk-throughs of labs, thousands of conversations, and hundreds of cards signed taught me more about the complexities and power of labor organizing than any book could have. My thanks to the UAW, to Josh Gilbert, and most of all to the other organizers who helped build the union in Longwood: Avery, Kate, Sabin, and many others. The first union certification election in 2016 was a harrowing experience, revealing how easily workers could be divided along boundaries of gender, race, and immigration status. This bruising setback, as well as the heroic efforts of a subsequent cohort of organizers to reorganize and win a second election, were foundational experiences that shaped the creation of this book.

Despite the all-consuming effort to organize a union, a dissertation was finally completed. Andrew Gordon prompted an enduring engagement with Japanese labor history, and Elizabeth Hinton pushed me to think more carefully about the intersections of racism, class, and state formation.

This book grew from an incomplete stub of a single chapter that was largely unfinished when the dissertation had to be submitted. I delayed writing the chapter on labor and unions because it felt so close and personal as I myself worked to organize a union. When I eventually got around to writing that chapter in 2021, what I had long envisioned as a single chapter turned into this book. This peculiar path has required additional support, and patience, from the many who have supported me.

My thanks to Lake Forest College, especially my colleagues in the History Department. They provided funds for archival research and for research assistants. My particular thanks to these undergraduate research assistants, whose collaboration has been one of the great joys of working at a small liberal arts college: Kent Beckman, Sarah Coffman, Nicole Ramirez, Aaron Brand, Kieran Artley, and Emilce Baudracco Fabian.

This book was written during the coronavirus pandemic when conferences, workshops, and other venues for feedback were closed. Produced in such isolation, and under such unusual circumstances, I reached out to get feedback and direction and was overwhelmed with the generosity offered. My thanks to Marcel van der Linden, Nelson Lichtenstein, Sam Payne, Brian McCammack, Aundrey Jones, Richard Price, Jonathan Hyslop, Yuting Dong, and Gabe Winant for their comments and feedback on the project. Despite my never having met him, Paul Taillon, a true scholarly comrade, deserves special thanks for providing detailed feedback on the entire manuscript.

My thanks to Peter Cole, Liesl Orenic, Kathyrn Oberdeck, and James

Sparrow for their feedback on a very early draft presented at the Newberry Library Labor History Workshop. Post-pandemic, my thanks to Anthony Chen, Ann Orloff, and the Comparative Historical Social Sciences Workshop at Northwestern. Jonathan Levy and the University of Chicago's Historical Capitalisms and Social Theory Workshop also offered much appreciated guidance and encouragement. Additional thanks to Michael Goldfield for his comments at the Labor and Working-Class History Association conference.

It was library and archive workers whose labor made this research possible. The defunding of libraries, the casualization of library work, and the turn toward short-term contracts in archives threatens the future of historical research. Aside from a few exceptionally wealthy institutions, I saw these pressures in every archive I visited. My conversations with Emily Hikes and David Grinnell, archivists I first met in Pittsburgh, led to a presentation on the shared interests of historical researchers, archivists, and library workers at the 2014 Mid-Atlantic Regional Archives Conference. My thanks also to the library staff at Lake Forest College. Understaffed and undercompensated during the upheavals of the pandemic, they have done miraculous work to support my research.

Tim Mennel, my editor at University of Chicago Press, witnessed firsthand the complicated evolution of this project. Where many editors understandably took flight, Tim remained curious and committed to the ideas. He was unparalleled in his generosity as the project gradually came into focus. During the production process, Andrea Blatz patiently guided me through assembling the final materials and Catherine Osborne provided impressively thoughtful and careful editing, immensely improving the text.

Lastly, and most important, my thanks to my family, who remind me most powerfully that love is what must motivate our struggles for a just world. A special thank you to Rio's grandmas, Corinne and Margarita, who helped us care for our little one. Above all, my partner, Tina Groeger, has shared this journey with me, inspired me, and supported me. I have tested her patience with the winding route to this first book, but she has encouraged and supported me through every step.

Notes

Introduction

1. *Twenty-First Annual Report of the Bureau of Statistics and Information of Maryland 1912* (Baltimore: Mules Printing Co., 1913), 48.

2. No topic has deeper roots in US historiography than the question of "American Exceptionalism," often understood in terms of Sombart's lingering question "Why No Socialism in America?," which highlights the supposedly uniquely narrow, weak, and conservative labor movement in the US. See Larry G. Gerber, "Shifting Perspectives on American Exceptionalism: Recent Literature on American Labor Relations and Labor Politics," *Journal of American Studies* 31, no. 2 (1997): 253–74; Rick Halpern and Jonathan Morris, "The Persistence of Exceptionalism: Class Formation and the Comparative Method," in *American Exceptionalism?*, ed. Rick Halpern and Jonathan Morris (London: Palgrave Macmillan, 1997), 1–13; and George M. Fredrickson, "From Exceptionalism to Variability: Recent Developments in Cross-National Comparative History," *The Journal of American History* 82, no. 2 (1995): 587–604. Among labor historians, political scientists, and comparative historical sociologists, this question has preoccupied generations of scholars. Few scholars today adhere to the old exceptionalist explanations rooted in the frontier, a fundamentally liberal culture, or an absence of class conflict. The new labor history has effectively put these notions to rest. Rather more recent studies generally attribute the narrow labor movement in the US to the exceptional hostility of either employers, the state, or both. See Kim Voss, *The Making of American Exceptionalism: The Knights of Labor and Class Formation in the Nineteenth Century* (Ithaca: Cornell University Press, 1993); Sanford M. Jacoby, *Masters to Managers: Historical and Comparative Perspectives on American Employers* (New York: Columbia University Press, 1991); Robin Archer, *Why Is There No Labor Party in the United States?* (Princeton: Princeton University Press, 2010); Neville Kirk, *Labour and Society in Britain and the USA: Volume Two: Challenge and Accommodation, 1850–1939* (Aldershot, UK: Routledge, 1994); Victoria Charlotte Hattam, *Labor Visions and State Power: The Origins of Business Unionism in the United States* (Princeton: Princeton University Press, 1993); and William E. Forbath, "Courts, Constitutions, and Labor Politics in England and America: A Study of the Constitutive Power of Law," *Law & Social Inquiry* 16, no. 1 (1991): 1–34.

3. "2,500 Men Strike," *BS*, April 12, 1912.

4. "2,500 Men Strike," *BS*, April 12, 1912.

5. "More to Break Strike," *BS*, April 15, 1912.

6. "Armed Women in Strike," *BS*, April 28, 1912.

7. "Armed Women in Strike," *BS*, April 28, 1912.

8. "Armed Women in Strike," *BS*, April 28, 1912.

9. "Strikers Get Allies," *BS*, May 4, 1912.

10. "Strikers Attack," *BS*, April 30, 1912.

11. "Fox Hears Both Sides," *BS*, May 5, 1912.

12. "Fox Favors Increase," *BS*, May 6, 1912.

13. "Armed Women in Strike," *BS*, April 28, 1912.

14. "Armed Women in Strike," *BS*, April 28, 1912.

15. "Strikers Riot," *BS*, April 29, 1912.

16. "Strikers Attack," *BS*, April 30, 1912.

17. "6 Strikers Shot," *BS*, May 1, 1912.

18. "Fox Hears Both Sides," *BS*, May 5, 1912.

19. "Death in Strike," *BS*, May 7, 1912.

20. "Strike Cost Men $50,000," *BS*, July 8, 1912.

21. Comparative history has enormous power to clarify causal mechanisms and social processes, but is sadly a marginal stream of historical research. Recently, a group of South African labor historians have offered compelling critiques of nationally contained labor histories and issued a renewed call for comparative research; see Philip Bonner, Jonathan Hyslop, and Lucien van der Walt, "Rethinking Worlds of Labour: Southern African Labour History in International Context," in *Global Histories of Work*, ed. Andreas Eckert (Berlin: De Gruyter, 2016), 90–122. A comparative approach allows us to "avoid teleological assumptions about the historical trajectory of labour movements," and helps undermine the "sense of national uniqueness that produces a sense of 'exceptionalism'" (92). Additionally, while I adopt the terms of "core" and "periphery" from World Systems Theory, I share Bonner, Hyslop, and van der Walt's reservations about this approach: "Its evident attraction is its very simplicity, as a universal explanation; the same simplicity is its weakness, too, for it posits a closed social analysis, conceived within a functionalist approach, and tends to operate through the static logic of systems theory. It is difficult to see any room for resistance, for the role of ideas, or for ruptures in the structure. . . . By displacing class exploitation within countries by international exploitation between countries, the framework displaces class, and perhaps more importantly, the role of class struggles, from its analysis" (95). Comparison, they argue, productively compels researchers to "question our assumptions" and thereby "expand our conceptual and empirical horizons" (95). Not all scholarship must be rigorously comparative, but the lack of even a passing interest in parallel processes elsewhere in the world in most US scholarship is surely a reflection of an inward-looking intellectual parochialism fostered by nearly a century of global hegemony. On the need for locally grounded comparative studies of racial formation, see Louise Seamster and Victor Ray, "Against Teleology in the Study of Race: Toward the Abolition of the Progress Paradigm," *Sociological Theory* 36, no. 4 (2018): 315–42.

22. James Belich, *Replenishing the Earth: The Settler Revolution and the Rise of the Angloworld* (Oxford: University Press, 2009).

23. Harsha Walia, *Border & Rule: Global Migration, Capitalism, and the Rise of Racist Nationalism* (Chicago: Haymarket Books, 2021); OECD, *IOM Outlook on Migration, Environment and Climate Change* (Paris: Organisation for Economic Co-operation and

Development, 2015), https://www.oecd-ilibrary.org/content/publication/9ba951ac -en; Carmen G. Gonzalez, "Migration as Reparation: Climate Change and the Disruption of Borders Climate Justice Symposium," *Loyola Law Review* 66, no. 2 (2020): 401–44; Nadia Ahmad, "Climate Cages: Connecting Migration, the Carceral State, Extinction Rebellion, and the Coronavirus through Cicero and 21 Savage," *Loyola Law Review* 66, no. 2 (2020): 293–328.

24. For a more detailed exploration of the theoretical and historiographical debates than is possible here, see Rudi Batzell, "Race, Ethnicity, and Global Labor History," in *The Oxford Handbook of Global Labor History*, ed. Sven Beckert and Marcel van der Linden (New York: Oxford, forthcoming).

25. Leo Lucassen, *The Immigrant Threat: The Integration of Old and New Migrants in Western Europe since 1850* (Urbana: University of Illinois Press, 2005).

26. Adam McKeown, "Global Migration, 1846–1940," *Journal of World History* 15, no. 2 (2004): 155–89.

27. This distinction, more sharply defined chronologically here, draws upon to the comparison of racialization by agrarian elites, business interests, and organized labor in Stanley B. Greenberg, *Race and State in Capitalist Development: Studies on South Africa, Alabama, Northern Ireland, and Israel* (New Haven: Yale University Press, 1980).

28. Jean Finot, *The Death-Agony of the "Science" of Race* (London: Stead's Publishing House, 1911), ix–x.

29. While I owe an enormous debt to Barbara Fields's thinking, and share her rejection of "race relations" and fixation on racial identity, the notion that class is real and structural, whereas as race is purely ideological, needs reexamination. Both class formation and racial boundary-making are co-equal, structurally rooted social processes rooted in capitalism's core patterns: inequality, the divide between capital and labor, and the divide between core and periphery. See Karen E. Fields, *Racecraft: The Soul of Inequality in American Life* (London: Verso, 2012); and Paul Heideman, "Racecraft as a Challenge to the Sociology of Race," *Sociology of Race and Ethnicity* 9, no. 1 (January 1, 2023): 119–23, https://doi.org/10.1177/23326492221136164.

30. Onur Ulas Ince, *Colonial Capitalism and the Dilemmas of Liberalism* (Oxford: Oxford University Press, 2018), 4. An excellent essay that brings these global divisions in the organization of labor up to the present is Geoff Eley, "Historicizing the Global, Politicizing Capital: Giving the Present a Name," *History Workshop Journal* 63, no. 1 (2007): 154–88, https://doi.org/10.1093/hwj/dbm010.

31. Cedric J. Robinson, *Black Marxism: The Making of the Black Radical Tradition*, 3rd ed. (Chapel Hill: University of North Carolina Press, 2020). For a lucid discussion of the productive tensions in Robinson's thought, as well as the "racial capitalism" literature more broadly, see Julian Go, "Three Tensions in the Theory of Racial Capitalism," *Sociological Theory* 31, no. 1 (2021): 38–47.

32. On the importance of core-periphery dynamics in the rise of capitalism, especially the sustained flow of raw materials from less free peripheries and the European comparative advantage in fiscal militarism and the use of state power to advance their economic interests, see Kenneth Pomeranz, *The Great Divergence: Europe, China, and the Making of the Modern World Economy* (Princeton: Princeton University Press, 2000); Sven Beckert, *Empire of Cotton: A Global History* (New York: Alfred A. Knopf, 2014); and Charles Tilly, *Coercion, Capital, and European States, AD 990–1992*, rev. ed. (Cambridge, MA: Blackwell, 1992).

33. Neville Kirk, *Comrades and Cousins: Globalization, Workers and Labour Movements in Britain, the USA and Australia from the 1880s to 1914* (London: Merlin, 2003); Jonathan Hyslop, "The Imperial Working Class Makes Itself 'White': White Labourism in Britain, Australia, and South Africa Before the First World War," *Journal of Historical Sociology* 12, no. 4 (1999): 398–421; and George M. Fredrickson, *White Supremacy: A Comparative Study in American and South African History* (New York: Oxford University Press, 1981).

34. Most historians have emphasized the "political construction" of racism and downplayed geographical and economic structures. See Mae Ngai, *The Chinese Question: The Gold Rushes, Chinese Migration, and Global Politics* (New York: Norton, 2021); Alexander Saxton, *The Rise and Fall of the White Republic: Class Politics and Mass Culture in Nineteenth Century America* (London: Verso, 1990). My more materialist position was first partially developed in Rudi Batzell, "Free Labour, Capitalism and the Anti-Slavery Origins of Chinese Exclusion in California in the 1870s," *Past & Present* 225, no. 1 (2014): 143–86.

35. Giovanni Arrighi, "Marxist Century, American Century: The Making and Remaking of the World Labour Movement," *New Left Review*, no. I/179 (1990): 29–63.

36. Eduardo Bonilla-Silva, "Rethinking Racism: Toward a Structural Interpretation," *American Sociological Review* 62, no. 3 (1997): 465–80, https://doi.org/10.2307/2657316; Moon-Kie Jung, *Beneath the Surface of White Supremacy: Denaturalizing US Racisms Past and Present* (Stanford: Stanford University Press, 2015).

37. An older literature on split labor markets is helpful, but far too static in its focus on direct competition in labor markets. See Edna Bonacich, "A Theory of Ethnic Antagonism: The Split Labor Market," *American Sociological Review* 37, no. 5 (1972): 547–59, https://doi.org/10.2307/2093450; and Edna Bonacich, "Advanced Capitalism and Black/White Race Relations in the United States: A Split Labor Market Interpretation," *American Sociological Review* 41, no. 1 (1976): 34–51, https://doi.org/10.2307/2094371. Somewhat recently, an important model of localized, comparative work on racial formation rooted in local labor markets is Evelyn Nakano Glenn, *Unequal Freedom: How Race and Gender Shaped American Citizenship and Labor* (Cambridge: Harvard University Press, 2002).

38. Much can be learned from economic historians, and a rapprochement between the isolated disciplines is long overdue. See Gavin Wright, "Labor History and Labor Economics," in *The Future of Economic History*, ed. Alexander J. Field (Dordrecht: Springer Netherlands, 1987), 313–48, https://doi.org/10.1007/978-94-009-3269-2_7.

39. In emphasizing hierarchies and boundary-making, I follow the work of sociologists including Loïc Wacquant, "Resolving the Trouble with 'Race,'" *New Left Review*, no. 133/134 (2022): 67–88; Andreas Wimmer, *Ethnic Boundary Making: Institutions, Power, Networks* (New York: Oxford University Press, 2013); Jung, *Beneath the Surface of White Supremacy*; Beverly J. Silver, *Forces of Labor: Workers' Movements and Globalization since 1870* (Cambridge: Cambridge: University Press, 2003), 23–27; and Lisa Lowe, *Immigrant Acts: On Asian American Cultural Politics* (Durham: Duke University Press, 1996), ch. 1.

40. There is much to commend in the starting point of this literature; see David R. Roediger, *The Wages of Whiteness: Race and the Making of the American Working Class*, rev. ed. (London: Verso, 2007). An especially useful work in this tradition is Bruce Nelson, *Divided We Stand: American Workers and the Struggle for Black Equal-*

ity (Princeton: Princeton University Press, 2001). The debates around "whiteness studies" have been extensive, polemical, and not entirely productive. For a helpful recent intervention see Cedric Johnson, "The Wages of Roediger: Why Three Decades of Whiteness Studies Has Not Produced the Left We Need," *Nonsite.Org* (blog), September 9, 2019, https://nonsite.org/the-wages-of-roediger-why-three-decades-of -whiteness-studies-has-not-produced-the-left-we-need.

41. W. E. B. Du Bois, *Black Reconstruction in America, 1860–1880* (New York: Free Press, 1998), 216.

42. Du Bois, *Black Reconstruction in America*, 219–22, 122, 274, 337–38, 365–68, 393–95, 601–2, 611.

43. Du Bois, *Black Reconstruction in America*, 217, 596–97.

44. Economists have been far more attentive to strikebreaking than historians; see Warren C. Whatley, "African-American Strikebreaking from the Civil War to the New Deal," *Social Science History* 17, no. 4 (1993): 525–58; Christopher L. Foote, Warren C. Whatley, and Gavin Wright, "Arbitraging a Discriminatory Labor Market: Black Workers at the Ford Motor Company, 1918–1947," *Journal of Labor Economics* 21, no. 3 (July 2003): 493–532, https://doi.org/10.1086/374957; and Joshua L. Rosenbloom, "Strikebreaking and the Labor Market in the United States, 1881–1894," *The Journal of Economic History* 58, no. 1 (March 1998): 183–205.

45. In this Spero and Harris anticipate the influential work of Stephen Castles and Godula Kosack, *Immigrant Workers and Class Structure in Western Europe*, 2nd ed. (Oxford: Oxford University Press, 1985); and Stephen Castles and Godula Kosack, "The Function of Labour Immigration in Western European Capitalism," *New Left Review* 73 (1972): 3–21.

46. Sterling D. Spero and Abram Lincoln Harris, *The Black Worker: The Negro and the Labor Movement* (New York: Columbia University Press, 1931), 33, 244.

47. Stuart Hall, "Race, Articulation, and Domination" in Stuart Hall, *Essential Essays, Volume 1: Foundations of Cultural Studies*, ed. David Morley (Durham: Duke University Press, 2018), 216. Julie Greene's recent essay shares a similar appreciation for Stuart Hall's conception of race. This project aims to answer her call for labor historians to "engage in theoretical reflection" and to "rethink the relationship between workers and settler colonialism, nationalism, and empire." See "Rethinking the Boundaries of Class: Labor History and Theories of Class and Capitalism," *Labor* 18, no. 2 (May 1, 2021): 92, 100–2, https://doi.org/10.1215/15476715-8849628.

48. Hall, "Race, Articulation, and Domination," 175–76.

49. E. P. Thompson, *The Making of the English Working Class* (New York: Vintage Books, 1963); Rudi Batzell et al., "E. P. Thompson, Politics and History: Writing Social History Fifty Years after The Making of the English Working Class," *Journal of Social History* 48, no. 4 (June 1, 2015): 753–58. Katznelson and Zolberg, in their classic formulation of the Thompsonian approach, implicitly assume a given local setting, set aside questions of economic geography, and thus miss racial boundary making as a constitutive dimension of class formation. Katznelson and Zolberg separate the analysis into four levels. Part I of this book corresponds with their first two levels, the "structure of capitalist development" and "work settings and labor markets," while part III explores the more subjective and political dimensions: how "classes are formed into groups, sharing dispositions" and changes in how workers engage in collective action. Part II, on the other hand, foregrounds what is missing

from their influential account of class formation. See Ira Katznelson and Aristide R. Zolberg, *Working-Class Formation: Nineteenth-Century Patterns in Western Europe and the United States* (Princeton: Princeton University Press, 1986), 14–20.

50. Charles Postel, *Equality: An American Dilemma, 1866–1896* (New York: Farrar, Straus and Giroux, 2019), 4.

51. Some of the broader historiographical and theoretical issues raised here, as well as a consideration of antisemitism in this era, are provided in Batzell, "Race, Ethnicity, and Global Labor History."

52. Rudi Batzell, "The Labor of Social Reproduction: Household Work and Gendered Power in the History of Capitalism, 1870–1930," *The Journal of the Gilded Age and Progressive Era* 15, no. 3 (July 2016): 310–30.

53. Initially conceived and researched as a single project on class, race, gender, and empire, for clarity and accessibility the two projects had to be separated as I finalized the manuscripts for publication.

54. My theoretical orientation is rooted in the "reflexive sociology" of Pierre Bourdieu, *Outline of a Theory of Practice*, trans. Richard Nice (New York: Cambridge University Press, 1977); and Pierre Bourdieu, *Distinction: A Social Critique of the Judgement of Taste* (Cambridge, MA: Harvard University Press, 1984).

55. David Neumark, "Experimental Research on Labor Market Discrimination," *Journal of Economic Literature* 56, no. 3 (2018): 799–866.

56. William A. Darity, A. Kirsten Mullen, and Lucas Hubbard, *The Black Reparations Project: A Handbook for Racial Justice* (Oakland: University of California Press, 2023); Ellora Derenoncourt et al., "Wealth of Two Nations: The U.S. Racial Wealth Gap, 1860–2020," Working Paper, National Bureau of Economic Research, June 2022, https://doi.org/10.3386/w30101.

Part 1

1. Du Bois, *Black Reconstruction in America*, 367.

2. Du Bois, *Black Reconstruction in America*, 602.

3. Gavin Wright, *Old South, New South: Revolutions in the Southern Economy since the Civil War* (Baton Rouge: Louisiana State University Press, 1996), 66–70; Roger L. Ransom and Richard Sutch, *One Kind of Freedom: The Economic Consequences of Emancipation*, 2nd ed. (Cambridge: Cambridge University Press, 2001), 195–99.

4. Ray Stannard Baker, *Following the Color Line: An Account of Negro Citizenship in the American Democracy* (New York: Doubleday, Page & Company, 1908), 109.

5. Cindy Hahamovitch and Rick Halpern, "Not a 'Sack of Potatoes': Why Labor Historians Need to Take Agriculture Seriously," *International Labor and Working-Class History*, no. 65 (2004): 3–10.

6. In the most carefully considered comparison, Kirk acknowledges the intensity of employer and state hostility but ultimately makes a sweeping assessment that Britain was "less afflicted" by "anti-union employers" between 1870 and 1914 (*Labour and Society in Britain and the USA*, 5–6, 16–18, 37, 40–44). See Voss, *The Making of American Exceptionalism*; Forbath, "Courts, Constitutions, and Labor Politics in England and America"; Christopher L. Tomlins, *The State and the Unions: Labor Relations, Law, and the Organized Labor Movement in America, 1880–1960* (Cambridge: Cambridge University Press, 1985); Archer, *Why Is There No Labor Party in the United States?* On the question of labor repression and the state, see Robert Justin Goldstein, "Labor

History Symposium: Political Repression of the American Labor Movement during Its Formative Years—A Comparative Perspective," *Labor History* 51, no. 2 (May 2010): 271–93; Chad Pearson, *Reform or Repression: Organizing America's Anti-Union Movement* (Philadelphia: University of Pennsylvania Press, 2016).

Chapter 1

1. Gerard Moran, "James Daly and the Rise and Fall of the Land League in the West of Ireland, 1879–82," *Irish Historical Studies* 29, no. 114 (1994): 197.

2. Kathryn Bernhardt, *Rents, Taxes, and Peasant Resistance: The Lower Yangzi Region, 1840–1950* (Stanford, CA: Stanford University Press, 1992), 55, 82–91, 101–16; Enrico Dal Lago, *Civil War and Agrarian Unrest: The Confederate South and Southern Italy* (Cambridge: Cambridge University Press, 2018).

3. Sir George Campbell, *White and Black: The Outcome of a Visit to the United States* (New York: R. Worthington, 1879), 161.

4. Eric Foner, *Nothing but Freedom: Emancipation and Its Legacy* (Baton Rouge: Louisiana State University Press, 1983), 3. On the debate of how to characterize the freedpeople of the South, see Alex Lichtenstein, "Was the Emancipated Slave a Proletarian?," *Reviews in American History* 26, no. 1 (1998): 124–45. As Barbara Fields argues, in the absence of land reform, African American sharecroppers "became the next thing to wage hands," and thus deprived "of a foundation for economic independence, they could not ultimately hold onto political power." While there were "tremendous obstacles" to widespread land reform in the South, Fields suggests that if it had occurred, "race relations would have been different, and probably better." See Barbara Jeanne Fields, "The Advent of Capitalist Agriculture: The New South in a Bourgeois World," in *Essays on the Postbellum Southern Economy*, ed. Thavolia Glymph and John J. Kushma (College Station: A & M University Press, 1985), 84, 89.

5. Du Bois, *Black Reconstruction in America*, 123.

6. Leon F. Litwack, *Been in the Storm so Long: The Aftermath of Slavery* (New York: Vintage Books, 1980 [1979]), 399.

7. Eric Foner, *Reconstruction: America's Unfinished Revolution, 1863–1877* (New York: Harper Collins, 2002 [1988]), 51.

8. E. Foner, *Reconstruction*, 70–71.

9. E. Foner, *Reconstruction*, 104.

10. Land reform was central in Du Bois's analysis of emancipation's aftermath, and he described the Freedmen's Bureau as "the most extraordinary and far-reaching institution of social uplift that America has ever attempted." See *Black Reconstruction in America 1860–1880*, 219–22, 122, 274, 337–38, 365–68, 393–95, 601–2, 611.

11. E. Foner, *Reconstruction*, 69.

12. E. Foner, *Reconstruction*, 158.

13. Speech in Tennessee on accepting the nomination on June 10, 1864, quoted in Du Bois, *Black Reconstruction in America, 1860–1880*, 245.

14. E. Foner, *Reconstruction*, 159.

15. E. Foner, *Reconstruction*, 161.

16. E. Foner, *Reconstruction*, 163–64.

17. Du Bois, *Black Reconstruction in America*, 395.

18. Roger L. Ransom, "Reconstructing Reconstruction: Options and Limitations

to Federal Policies on Land Distribution in 1866–67," *Civil War History* 51, no. 4 (November 1, 2005): 376.

19. E. Foner, *Reconstruction*, 235.

20. Lawrence Svabek, "To Break the Slave Power: Thaddeus Stevens, Land Confiscation, and the Politics of Reparations," *American Political Thought* 10, no. 4 (September 1, 2021): 537.

21. E. Foner, *Reconstruction*, 304.

22. E. Foner, *Reconstruction*, 375.

23. E. Foner, *Reconstruction*, 302, 374–75.

24. Neil Kinghan, "A Brief Moment in the Sun: Francis Cardozo and Reconstruction in South Carolina" (PhD diss., University College London, 2019), 149.

25. E. Foner, *Reconstruction*, 375; Carol K. Rothrock Bleser, *The Promised Land; the History of the South Carolina Land Commission, 1869–1890* (Columbia: University of South Carolina Press, 1969), 167.

26. Elizabeth Almlie et al., "Prized Pieces of Land: The Impact of Reconstruction on African-American Land Ownership in Lower Richland County, South Carolina," in *Public History Program*, Books and Manuscripts (Columbia: University of South Carolina Press, 2009), 87, https://scholarcommons.sc.edu/pubhist_books/3/.

27. Almlie et al., "Prized Pieces of Land," 87–88.

28. Almlie et al., "Prized Pieces of Land," 88.

29. Campbell, *White and Black*, 155.

30. Campbell, *White and Black*, 155.

31. E. Foner, *Reconstruction*, 376.

32. Richard Edwards, "African Americans and the Southern Homestead Act," *Great Plains Quarterly* 39, no. 2 (2019): 103–29.

33. E. Foner, *Reconstruction*, 451.

34. Rebecca J. Scott, "Defining the Boundaries of Freedom in the World of Cane: Cuba, Brazil, and Louisiana after Emancipation," *The American Historical Review* 99, no. 1 (1994): 81.

35. R. Scott, "Defining the Boundaries of Freedom in the World of Cane," 78.

36. Omar H. Ali, "Standing Guard at the Door of Liberty: Black Populism in South Carolina, 1886–1895," *The South Carolina Historical Magazine* 107, no. 3 (2006): 191, 194–96; Omar H. Ali, *In the Lion's Mouth: Black Populism in the New South, 1886–1900* (Jackson: University Press of Mississippi, 2010).

37. William F. Holmes, "The Demise of the Colored Farmers' Alliance," *The Journal of Southern History* 41, no. 2 (1975): 187–200; Gerald H. Gaither, *Blacks and the Populist Movement: Ballots and Bigotry in the New South*, rev. ed. (Tuscaloosa: University of Alabama Press, 2005).

38. E. Foner, *Reconstruction*, 597.

39. Du Bois, *Black Reconstruction in America*, 601.

40. John W. Dower, *Embracing Defeat: Japan in the Wake of World War II* (New York: W.W. Norton & Co., 1999), 244–51; Yoong-Deok Jeon and Young-Yong Kim, "Land Reform, Income Redistribution, and Agricultural Production in Korea," *Economic Development and Cultural Change* 48, no. 2 (January 2000): 253–68.

41. Du Bois, *Black Reconstruction in America*, 604, 611.

42. Ian D. Ochiltree, "'A Just and Self-Respecting System'?: Black Independence, Sharecropping, and Paternalistic Relations in the American South and South Africa,"

Agricultural History 72, no. 2 (1998): 352–80; Ian Ochiltree, "Mastering the Share-croppers: Land, Labour and the Search for Independence in the US South and South Africa," *Journal of Southern African Studies* 30, no. 1 (March 2004): 41–61; Fredrickson, *White Supremacy*, 213–15.

43. Ransom and Sutch, *One Kind of Freedom*, 177.

44. Fergus Campbell, *Land and Revolution: Nationalist Politics in the West of Ireland, 1891–1921* (Oxford: Oxford University Press, 2005), 13–14.

45. John P. Huttman, "The Impact of Land Reform on Agricultural Production in Ireland," *Agricultural History* 46, no. 3 (1972): 353–54.

46. Timothy W. Guinnane and Ronald I. Miller, "The Limits to Land Reform: The Land Acts in Ireland, 1870–1909," *Economic Development and Cultural Change* 45, no. 3 (April 1997): 593–94.

47. Andrew W. Orridge, "Who Supported the Land War? An Aggregate-Data Analysis of Irish Agrarian Discontent, 1879–1882," *The Economic and Social Review* 12, no. 3 (April 1981): 228.

48. Samuel Clark, *Social Origins of the Irish Land War* (Princeton: Princeton University Press, 2014), 321–23.

49. Samuel Clark, "Strange Bedfellows? The Land League Alliances," in *Land Questions in Modern Ireland, ed. Fergus Campbell and Tony Varley* (Manchester: Manchester University Press, 2013), 93–99. Heather Cox Richardson stresses how class also produced political divides among Southern African Americans, noting that "prominent African-Americans had very different needs and attitudes than the . . . ex-slaves who made up the bulk of the South's population," especially on issues like confiscation and class conflict. See *The Death of Reconstruction Race, Labor, and Politics in the Post-Civil War North, 1865–1901* (Cambridge, MA: Harvard University Press, 2004), 53, 179.

50. Campbell, *Land and Revolution*, 16.

51. Campbell, *Land and Revolution*, 16.

52. Campbell, *Land and Revolution*, 17–18, 22–23.

53. Neil R. McMillen, *Dark Journey: Black Mississippians in the Age of Jim Crow* (Urbana: University of Illinois Press, 1990); Kent Redding and David R. James, "Estimating Levels and Modeling Determinants of Black and White Voter Turnout in the South, 1880 to 1912," *Historical Methods: A Journal of Quantitative and Interdisciplinary History* 34, no. 4 (2001): 141–58.

54. Campbell, *Land and Revolution*, 26.

55. Campbell, *Land and Revolution*, 30–31.

56. Campbell, *Land and Revolution*, ch. 2, 286–89.

57. Guinnane and Miller, "The Limits to Land Reform," 596.

58. Ely M. Janis, *A Greater Ireland: The Land League and Transatlantic Nationalism in Gilded Age America* (Madison: University of Wisconsin Press, 2015), 126, 130–33.

59. Timothy Thomas Fortune, *Black and White: Land, Labor, and Politics in the South* (New York: Washington Square Press, 2007 [1884]), 139, 17–18, 151–53. Fortune became much more conservative after the 1880s, but this first book can be considered a key text in the Black Radical Tradition. See Emma Lou Thornbrough, *T. Thomas Fortune: Militant Journalist* (Chicago: University of Chicago Press, 1972), 43–55, 81, 158.

60. Thomas Alter, "From the Copper-Colored Sons of Montezuma to Comrade Pancho Villa: The Radicalizing Effect of Mexican Revolutionaries on the Texas So-

cialist Party, 1910–1917," *Labor* 12, no. 4 (December 1, 2015): 83–109, https://doi.org /10.1215/15476715-3155161.

61. Harry Haywood, *Black Bolshevik: Autobiography of an Afro-American Communist* (Chicago: Liberator Press, 1978), 205–6.

62. "Farm Labourers' Wages," *Sheffield Independent*, September 3, 1900.

63. McKeown, "Global Migration, 1846–1940," 158.

64. McKeown, "Global Migration, 1846–1940," 166.

65. Baker, *Following the Color Line*, 133.

66. Derek Kramer, "'We Go on Our Own Boats!': Korean Migrants and the Politics of Transportation Infrastructure in the Japanese Empire," *International Review of Social History* (2021): 1–22; Ken C. Kawashima, *The Proletarian Gamble: Korean Workers in Interwar Japan* (Durham: Duke University Press, 2009); Lucassen, *The Immigrant Threat*; Jessica Evans, "The Uneven and Combined Development of Class Forces: Migration as Combined Development," *Cambridge Review of International Affairs* 29, no. 3 (2016): 1061–73; Giovanni Arrighi and Fortunata Piselli, "Capitalist Development in Hostile Environments: Feuds, Class Struggles, and Migrations in a Peripheral Region of Southern Italy," *Review (Fernand Braudel Center)* 10, no. 4 (1987): 649–751; Ewa Morawska, "Labor Migrations of Poles in the Atlantic World Economy, 1880–1914," *Comparative Studies in Society and History* 31, no. 2 (1989): 237–72.

67. Charters Wynn, *Workers, Strikes, and Pogroms: The Donbass-Dnepr Bend in Late Imperial Russia, 1870–1905* (Princeton: Princeton University Press, 2014).

68. Bernhardt, *Rents, Taxes, and Peasant Resistance*, 55, 101.

69. Dal Lago, *Civil War and Agrarian Unrest*, 273–84, 402–4.

70. Jo Guldi, *The Long Land War: The Global Struggle for Occupancy Rights* (New Haven: Yale University Press, 2022).

71. On parallels between Ireland and Mexico see Thomas Murray, "Socio-Economic Rights Versus Social Revolution? Constitution Making in Germany, Mexico and Ireland, 1917–1923," *Social & Legal Studies* 24, no. 4 (2015): 487–508. Mexico likewise illustrates the role of land reform in shaping labor migration. Land reform was unevenly distributed, and some states in Mexico saw no changes to the unequal agrarian order. Most of those who began migrating to the US came from the west-central states that "did not significantly benefit" from the revolutionary land redistribution programs, and by the 1950s, "without further land reform on a large scale, rural people needed to migrate." See Andrew J. Hazelton, *Labor's Outcasts: Migrant Farmworkers and Unions in North America, 1934–1966* (Urbana: University of Illinois Press, 2022), 4, 6.

72. Alan O'Day, "Varieties of Anti-Irish Behaviour in Britain, 1846–1922," in *Racial Violence in Britain, 1840–1950*, ed. P. Panayi (Leicester: Leicester University Press, 1993), 29.

73. Timothy J. Hatton and Jeffrey G. Williamson, "After the Famine: Emigration from Ireland, 1850–1913," *The Journal of Economic History* 53, no. 3 (1993): 579, 596–97.

74. Guinnane and Miller, "The Limits to Land Reform," 600.

75. Hatton and Williamson, "After the Famine," 579, 596–97.

76. Wright, *Old South, New South*, 7–8.

77. Joshua L. Rosenbloom, "The Extent of the Labor Market in the United States, 1870–1914," *Social Science History* 22, no. 3 (1998): 288.

78. Rosenbloom, "The Extent of the Labor Market in the United States," 297.

79. Baker, *Following the Color Line*, 130.

80. Richardson, *The Death of Reconstruction*, 65–65.

81. Philip S. Foner, "A Labor Voice for Black Equality: The *Boston Daily Evening Voice*, 1864–1867," *Science & Society* 38, no. 3 (1974): 304–25.

82. P. Foner, "A Labor Voice for Black Equality," 318–19.

83. Placing Ireland at the root of a century of transformative efforts for land reform, see Guldi, *The Long Land War*, 21–55; Mark R. Rosenzweig, "Rural Wages, Labor Supply, and Land Reform: A Theoretical and Empirical Analysis," *The American Economic Review* 68, no. 5 (1978): 847–61; Klaus Deininger, "Making Negotiated Land Reform Work: Initial Experience from Colombia, Brazil and South Africa," *World Development* 27, no. 4 (April 1999): 651–72; Keijiro Otsuka, "Determinants and Consequences of Land Reform Implementation in the Philippines," *Journal of Development Economics* 35, no. 2 (1991): 339–55; Josef Falkinger and Volker Grossmann, "Oligarchic Land Ownership, Entrepreneurship, and Economic Development," *Journal of Development Economics* 101 (March 2013): 206–15.

84. "A Warning from Blair," *Pittsburgh Dispatch*, March 1, 1891.

85. "The Negro in Iron Mills," *Pittsburgh Dispatch*, July 27, 1889.

86. Untitled, *Pittsburgh Dispatch*, December 16, 1889.

87. C. K., "Largest on Record, A Notable Year in Iron and Steel Production in the Pittsburgh District has Just Been Closed," *Pittsburgh Dispatch*, January 17, 1891.

88. "Cheap Southern Labor," *Pittsburgh Dispatch*, February 26, 1891.

89. Henry W. Hargreaves, Letter to the Editor, *Pittsburgh Dispatch*, February 28, 1891.

90. "Southern Pig Iron," *Pittsburgh Dispatch*, March 28, 1891.

91. "Southern Pig Iron," *Pittsburgh Dispatch*, March 28, 1891.

92. "Forty Cents a Day. The Amazing Cheapness of Southern Mine and Furnace Labor," *Pittsburgh Dispatch*, April 14, 1891.

93. "Forty Cents a Day," *Pittsburgh Dispatch*, April 14, 1891.

94. "The Race Question North and South," *Pittsburgh Daily Post*, December 13, 1904.

95. P. Foner, "A Labor Voice for Black Equality," 309–10.

96. Rosenbloom, "Strikebreaking and the Labor Market in the United States," 201.

97. William J. Collins, "When the Tide Turned: Immigration and the Delay of the Great Black Migration," *The Journal of Economic History* 57, no. 3 (1997): 608.

98. "Classifieds. Wanted," *Pittsburgh Dispatch*, July 27, 1889.

99. "Italian Labor Not Wanted," *Pittsburgh Dispatch*, May 11, 1890.

100. "The Colored Laborers Here," *Pittsburgh Dispatch*, May 15, 1890.

101. "The Colored Laborers Here," *Pittsburgh Dispatch*, May 15, 1890.

102. Carl Kelsey, "Some Causes of Negro Emigration: The Men," Survey, *The Negro in the Cities of the North* (Charity Organization Society, 1905), 16.

103. "Visions of Wealth Dazzle the Eyes of the Colored People of the South When Told of the Wages Paid Here," *Pittsburgh Dispatch*, September 14, 1890.

104. David Killingray and Martin Plaut, "F. Z. S. Peregrino, A Significant but Duplicitous Figure in the Black Atlantic World," *South African Historical Journal* 68, no. 4 (2016): 494.

105. "Visions of Wealth," *Pittsburgh Dispatch*, September 14, 1890.

106. "Visions of Wealth," *Pittsburgh Dispatch*, September 14, 1890.

107. "Classified," *Pittsburgh Dispatch*, August 5, 1891; "Classified," *Pittsburgh Dispatch*, December 10, 12, 1891.

108. Killingray and Plaut, "F. Z. S. Peregrino," 510.

109. Since black workers were channeled into such a narrow set of occupations, new migrants largely competed with, and pushed down the wages of, black workers who were already in the North. See Leah Platt Boustan, *Competition in the Promised Land: Black Migrants in Northern Cities and Labor Markets* (Princeton: Princeton University Press, 2016), 68–71, 88–89.

110. "After Their Rights. Public Meeting of Colored People to Protest Against Discrimination," *Pittsburgh Dispatch*, April 21, 1891.

111. "After Their Rights," *Pittsburgh Dispatch*, April 21, 1891.

112. "Legitimate but Expensive," *Pittsburgh Dispatch*, October 11, 1890.

113. "More than Satisfied. An Exciting Excursion after Some Negro Labor," *Pittsburgh Dispatch*, January 17, 1891.

114. "More than Satisfied," *Pittsburgh Dispatch*, January 17, 1891.

115. Suresh Naidu, "Recruitment Restrictions and Labor Markets: Evidence from the Postbellum U.S. South," *Journal of Labor Economics* 28, no. 2 (2010): 413–14.

116. Naidu, "Recruitment Restrictions and Labor Markets," 417.

117. Amerigo Caruso and Claire Morelon, "The Threat from Within across Empires: Strikes, Labor Migration, and Violence in Central Europe, 1900–1914," *Central European History* 54, no. 1 (2021): 101.

118. Helen Tucker, "The Negroes of Pittsburgh," *Charities and the Commons: A Weekly Journal of Philanthropy and Social Advance* 2 (January 1909): 600.

119. Peter R. Shergold, *Working-Class Life: The "American Standard" in Comparative Perspective, 1899–1913* (Pittsburgh: University of Pittsburgh Press, 1982), 54.

120. Shergold, *Working-Class Life*, 54.

121. John Saville, "Trade Unions and Free Labour: the Background to the Taff Vale Decision," in *Essays in Labour History: In Memory of G. D. H. Cole, 25 September 1889–14 January 1959*, ed. Asa Briggs (New York: Macmillan, 1960), 321.

Chapter 2

1. Karl Marx, *Karl Marx and Frederick Engels on Britain.*, 2nd ed. (Moscow: Foreign Languages Pub. House, 1962).

2. "Head Tax," *PG*, June 20, 1867.

3. "Head Tax," *PG*, June 20, 1867.

4. "Head Tax" *PG*, June 20, 1867.

5. These internal, local tensions will be foregrounded in part II.

6. On the craft exclusiveness of early British unions, see H. A. Clegg et al., *A History of British Trade Unions Since 1889: Vol 1: 1889–1910* (London: Clarendon Press, 1964), 14, 37–38.

7. Spero and Harris, *The Black Worker*, 47.

8. Spero and Harris, *The Black Worker*, 47.

9. "Meeting of the Colored Mechanics," *BS*, January 14, 1870.

10. Voss, *The Making of American Exceptionalism*, 73–75.

11. Among the most important works on the Knights of Labor, which agrees on seeing the 1880s as the key moment of US divergence, but stresses different causes for defeat, especially employer hostility, see Voss, *The Making of American Exceptionalism*. For the remarkable achievements of the Knights in local politics see Leon Fink, *Workingmen's Democracy: The Knights of Labor and American Politics* (Urbana: University of Illinois Press, 1983).

12. Voss, *The Making of American Exceptionalism*, 77–79.

13. Sherry H. Olson, *Baltimore: The Building of an American City* (Baltimore: Johns Hopkins University Press, 1997), 200.

14. Olson, *Baltimore*, 234.

15. Kenneth Kann, "The Knights of Labor and the Southern Black Worker," *Labor History* 18, no. 1 (1977): 50.

16. Kann, "The Knights of Labor and the Southern Black Worker," 54.

17. Melton A. McLaurin, "The Racial Policies of the Knights of Labor and the Organization of Southern Black Workers," *Labor History* 17, no. 4 (Fall 1976): 574–75.

18. McLaurin, "The Racial Policies of the Knights of Labor," 578, 575.

19. Katherine A. Harvey, "The Knights of Labor in the Maryland Coal Fields, 1878–1882," *Labor History* 10, no. 4 (Fall 1969): 558.

20. Harvey, "The Knights of Labor in the Maryland Coal Fields," 570.

21. Harvey, "The Knights of Labor in the Maryland Coal Fields," 570.

22. Kann, "The Knights of Labor and the Southern Black Worker," 56, 52.

23. McLaurin, "Racial Policies of the Knights," 583.

24. Kann, "The Knights of Labor and the Southern Black Worker," 62; Claudia Miner, "The Knights o Labor And 'The Color Line,' Richmond, 1886" (MA thesis, Virginia, College of William and Mary, 1978).

25. Lorenzo Costaguta, *Workers of All Colors Unite: Race and the Origins of American Socialism* (Urbana: University of Illinois Press, 2023), 164.

26. Michael C. Dawson, *Blacks in and out of the Left* (Cambridge, MA: Harvard University Press, 2013), 27–28.

27. Jeffrey B. Perry, *Hubert Harrison: The Voice of Harlem Radicalism, 1883–1918* (New York: Columbia University Press, 2009), 7.

28. McLaurin, "Racial Policies of the Knights," 571.

29. McLaurin, "Racial Policies of the Knights," 585.

30. Thomas C. Weeks, *First Biennial Report of the Bureau of Industrial Statistics and Information of Maryland, 1884–1885* (Baltimore: Guggenheimer, Weil & Co., 1886), footnote, page 12.

31. Weeks, *First Biennial Report*, 13.

32. E. J. Hobsbawm, *Worlds of Labour: Further Studies in the History of Labour* (London: Weidenfeld and Nicolson, 1984), 152.

33. E. J. Hobsbawm, *Labouring Men; Studies in the History of Labour* (New York: Basic Books, 1965), 196.

34. Saville, "Trade Unions and Free Labour," 317.

35. Steven Parfitt, *Knights across the Atlantic: The Knights of Labor in Britain and Ireland* (Liverpool: Liverpool University Press, 2016), 50.

36. Henry Pelling, "The Knights of Labor in Britain, 1880–1901," *The Economic History Review* 9, no. 2 (1956): 321–22.

37. Pelling, "The Knights of Labor in Britain," 322.

38. Pelling, "The Knights of Labor in Britain," 322.

39. Pelling, "The Knights of Labor in Britain," 323.

40. Pelling, "The Knights of Labor in Britain," 329.

41. Clegg, *British Trade Unions, 1889–1910*, 1:56.

42. Clegg, *British Trade Unions, 1889–1910*, 1:71.

43. Hobsbawm, *Worlds of Labour*, 51.

44. Sidney Pollard, *A History of Labour in Sheffield* (Liverpool: Liverpool University Press, 1959), 220.

45. Derek Matthews, "1889 and All That: New Views on the New Unionism," *International Review of Social History* 36, no. 1 (1991): 25–26.

46. Matthews, "1889 and All That," 28–31.

47. Matthews, "1889 and All That," 31.

48. Matthews, "1889 and All That," 32–33.

49. Matthews, "1889 and All That," 36.

50. Clegg, *British Trade Unions*, 1:67–68.

51. E. P. Thompson, "Homage to Tom Maguire," in *Essays in Labour History: In Memory of G. D. H. Cole 25 September 1889–14 January 1959*, ed. Asa Briggs and John Saville (London: Palgrave Macmillan UK, 1960), 300.

52. Clegg, *British Trade Unions*, 1:76.

53. Clegg, *British Trade Unions*, 1:76.

54. Matthews, "1889 and All That," 45–46.

55. Matthews, "1889 and All That," 46, 49, 51.

56. Matthews, "1889 and All That," 56.

57. Arthur J. McIvor, "Employers' Organisation and Strikebreaking in Britain, 1880–1914," *International Review of Social History* 29, no. 1 (1984): 12, Table 1.

58. Hugh Armstrong Clegg, *A History of British Trade Unions Since 1889: Volume II: 1911–1933* (Oxford: Oxford University Press, 1985).

Chapter 3

1. McIvor, "Strikebreaking in Britain," 1.

2. Hobsbawm, *Labouring Men*, 217.

3. Marcel van der Linden, "Proletarian Internationalism: A Long View and Some Speculations," in *Modern World-System in the Longue Duree*, ed. Immanuel Wallerstein (London: Routledge, 2004), 113–16.

4. European labor scholars have been more attentive to the practice; see, for instance, Alessandro Saluppo, "Strikebreaking and Anti-Unionism on the Waterfront: The Shipping Federation, 1890–1914," *European History Quarterly* 49, no. 4 (October 1, 2019): 570–96; Matteo Millan and Alessandro Saluppo, eds., *Corporate Policing, Yellow Unionism, and Strikebreaking, 1890–1930: In Defence of Freedom* (Abingdon, UK: Routledge, 2021). German employers also developed professionalized and centralized strikebreaking services, importing strikebreakers from the lower-wage near-peripheries of Southern Germany, Silesia, Upper Austria, Salzburg, and West Galicia. Galicia was described as an "agents' paradise" for labor recruiters, and in the decade prior to the First World War, Friedrich Hintze in Hamburg and Karl Katzmark in Berlin became recognized as the "most powerful strike breaking agencies in Imperial Germany," with "highly professionalized" cadres of strikebreakers active across German-speaking Central Europe. Hintze claimed in an interview to have six thousand strikebreakers who could be ready to work in only eight days. See Caruso and Morelon, "The Threat from Within across Empires," 88–89, 104–5.

5. One important recent exception that gives sustained attention to rural-industrial labor migration, strikebreaking, the material desires driving workers, and their ambivalence towards emerging union bureaucracies is the wonderful book by Dana M.

Caldemeyer, *Union Renegades: Miners, Capitalism, and Organizing in the Gilded Age* (Urbana: University of Illinois Press, 2021).

6. Rosenbloom, "Strikebreaking and the Labor Market in the United States," 186.

7. Hobsbawm, *Worlds of Labour*, 152.

8. Voss, *The Making of American Exceptionalism*, 79.

9. Richard L. Ehrlich, "Immigrant Strikebreaking Activity: A Sampling of Opinion Expressed in the National Labor Tribune, 1878–1885," *Labor History*, September 1, 1974, 537, https://doi.org/10.1080/00236567408584311.

10. Spero and Harris, *The Black Worker*, 33, 244.

11. Arthur Redford, *Labour Migration in England, 1800–1850*, 2nd ed., ed. and rev. by W. H. Chaloner. (Manchester: Manchester University Press, 1964), 133; Lynn Hollen Lees, *Exiles of Erin: Irish Migrants in Victorian London* (Ithaca, NY: Cornell University Press, 1979), 15–16.

12. Redford, *Labour Migration in England*, 154, 134, 151.

13. Lees, *Exiles of Erin*, 43.

14. Redford, *Labour Migration in England*, 159. It is notable that a mid-twentieth century British scholar would uncritically describe Irish migrants as follows: "The Irish were less provident, and more given to drunkenness; they were slovenly, careless and stupid. On this account they were not usually put in charge of power-driven machinery, and were necessarily given the lower-paid work."

15. Redford, *Labour Migration in England*, 156.

16. Graham Davis, *The Irish in Britain, 1815–1914* (Dublin: Gill and Macmillan, 1991), 86.

17. Redford, *Labour Migration in England*, 162.

18. G. Davis, *The Irish in Britain*, 105.

19. G. Davis, *The Irish in Britain*, 94, 102, 105, 112, 121; Lees, *Exiles of Erin*, 88–94, 98–99.

20. Redford, *Labour Migration in England*, 151.

21. Lees, *Exiles of Erin*, 116.

22. G. Davis, *The Irish in Britain*, 105; Redford, *Labour Migration in England*, 161–63.

23. G. Davis, *The Irish in Britain*, 113.

24. Donald M. MacRaild, *Irish Migrants in Modern Britain, 1750–1922* (London: Macmillan Education UK, 1999), 166.

25. Rachel Vorspant, "The Political Power of Nuisance Law: Labor Picketing and the Courts in Modern England, 1871-Present," *Buffalo Law Review* 46, no. 3 (1998): 618; McIvor, "Strikebreaking in Britain," 13.

26. Karl Marx to S. Meyer and A. Vogt, London, April 9, 1870, in Marx, *Karl Marx and Frederick Engels on Britain*, 552.

27. Marx "could not bring himself to elaborate on the obvious conclusion of his argument when applied to postbellum America: that in the United States, the fracture between Black and white workers represented the key fissure" (Costaguta, *Workers of All Colors Unite*, 43–44).

28. McIvor, "Strikebreaking in Britain," 8.

29. Clegg, *British Trade Unions*, 1:80–81.

30. Saville, "Trade Unions and Free Labour," 330–31.

31. Saville, "Trade Unions and Free Labour," 330.

32. McIvor, "Strikebreaking in Britain," 7–8.

33. R. Bean, "Employers' Associations in the Port of Liverpool, 1890–1914," *International Review of Social History* 21, no. 3 (1976): 364.

34. Bean, 364–65.

35. McIvor, "Strikebreaking in Britain," 9.

36. McIvor, 6–7.

37. Clegg, *British Trade Unions, 1889–1910*, 1:171.

38. Clegg, 1:171–72.

39. Clegg, 1:339.

40. Geoffrey Alderman, "The National Free Labour Association: A Case-Study of Organised Strike-Breaking in the Late Nineteenth and Early Twentieth Centuries," *International Review of Social History* 21, no. 3 (1976): 315.

41. James Holt, "Trade Unionism in the British and US Steel Industries, 1880–1914," *Labor History* 18, no. 1 (1977): 31–32.

42. Kirk, *Labour and Society in Britain and the USA*; Voss, *The Making of American Exceptionalism*.

43. Drafts of Articles by E. N. Simons on the History of Edgar Allen & Co, MD2169-8-6, EASC.

44. Report for Directors Meeting of Jno. Brown & Co Ltd October 30, 1906, 1/2/1/4/1, JB.

45. McIvor, "Strikebreaking in Britain," 9.

46. Bean, "Employers' Associations in the Port of Liverpool," 381.

47. Voss, *The Making of American Exceptionalism*, 245.

48. Jacoby, *Masters to Managers*, 189.

49. Rosemary Feurer and Chad Pearson, "Introduction: Against Labor," in *Against Labor: How US Employers Organized to Defeat Union Activism*, ed. Rosemary Feurer and Chad Pearson (Urbana: University of Illinois Press, 2017), 9.

50. Thomas A. Klug, "Employers' Path to the Open Shop, 1903–1907," in Feurer and Pearson, *Against Labor*, 79.

51. This point is partially acknowledged by Jacoby, but then set aside for an emphasis on state and employer hostitlity: "Ethnic and racial cleavages in the labor force . . . made it easier for American employers to recruit strikebreakers—a tactic that often touched off violence" (*Masters to Managers*, 187).

52. Whatley, "African-American Strikebreaking," 537–38.

53. In the UK, although the overall scale of strikebreaking was much lower in terms of the number of workers, a broadly similar pattern of strikebreaking across industries prevailed. Strikebreakers were used most frequently in transportation strikes (22 percent), and only relatively rarely in coal (3.5 percent). See McIvor, "Strikebreaking in Britain," 14.

54. Stephen H. Norwood, *Strikebreaking & Intimidation: Mercenaries and Masculinity in Twentieth-Century America* (Chapel Hill: University of North Carolina Press, 2002), 78.

55. John H. Keiser, "Black Strikebreakers and Racism in Illinois, 1865–1900," *Journal of the Illinois State Historical Society (1908–1984)* 65, no. 3 (1972): 313–26.

56. R. R. Wright, Jr., "The Negro in Times of Industrial Unrest," in *The Negro in the Cities of the North*, 72.

57. Edward Meeker and James Kau, "Racial Discrimination and Occupational Attainment at the Turn of the Century," *Explorations in Economic History; New York* 14, no. 3 (July 1, 1977): 250–76; Joe T. Darden, "The Effect of World War I On Black

Occupational and Residential Segregation: The Case of Pittsburgh," *Journal of Black Studies* 18, no. 3 (1988): 297–312; Robert A. Margo, "The Competitive Dynamics of Racial Exclusion: Employment Segregation in the South, 1900–1950," Working Paper, Historical Working Paper Series (National Bureau of Economic Research, August 1990), https://doi.org/10.3386/h0014.

58. Wright, "The Negro in Times of Industrial Unrest," 69.

59. Susan D. Olzak, "Causes of Shifts in Occupational Segregation of the Foreign-Born: Evidence from American Cities, 1870–1880," *Social Forces* 68, no. 2 (December 1, 1989): 593–620.

60. John N. Ingham, "A Strike in the Progressive Era: McKees Rocks, 1909," *The Pennsylvania Magazine of History and Biography* 90, no. 3 (1966): 367.

61. Ngai, *The Chinese Question*, 160.

62. Susan Roth Breitzer, "Race, Immigration, and Contested Americanness: Black Nativism and the American Labor Movement, 1880--1930," *Race/Ethnicity: Multidisciplinary Global Contexts* 4, no. 2 (2011): 272.

63. Spero and Harris, *The Black Worker*, 197–98.

64. Spero and Harris, *The Black Worker*, 197–98; Albon P. Man, "Labor Competition and the New York Draft Riots of 1863," *The Journal of Negro History* 36, no. 4 (1951): 375–405; Iver Bernstein, *The New York City Draft Riots: Their Significance for American Society and Politics in the Age of the Civil War* (Oxford: Oxford University Press, 1990).

65. Paul D. Moreno, *Black Americans and Organized Labor: A New History* (Baton Rouge: LSU Press, 2008), 60.

66. Spero and Harris, *The Black Worker*, 249–50; Dennis C. Dickerson, *Out of the Crucible: Black Steel Workers in Western Pennsylvania, 1875–1980* (New York: SUNY Press, 1986), 8.

67. Moreno, *Black Americans and Organized Labor*, 39.

68. Paul Krause, *The Battle for Homestead, 1880–1892: Politics, Culture, and Steel* (Pittsburgh: University of Pittsburgh Press, 1992), 113.

69. "The Labor Troubles," *Pittsburgh Daily Post*, May 22, 1882.

70. Charles Brinton Barnes, *The Longshoremen* (Survey Associates, 1915), 8, 105–6; Spero and Harris, *The Black Worker*, 198.

71. Dickerson, *Out of the Crucible*, 9.

72. Dickerson, *Out of the Crucible*, 9.

73. Raymond A. Hall, "Kings, Knights, and Pawns: Black Coal Miners and Racial Conflict in Washington Territory," *The Pacific Northwest Quarterly* 105, no. 2 (2014): 85–96.

74. Robert Michael Smith, *From Blackjacks to Briefcases: A History of Commercialized Strikebreaking and Unionbusting in the United States* (Athens: Ohio University Press, 2003), 40.

75. R. Smith, *From Blackjacks to Briefcases*.

76. Moreno, *Black Americans and Organized Labor*, 65.

77. "For Homestead Workers They Will Be Given a Limited Time to Return to Work," *Pittsburgh Dispatch*, July 16, 1892.

78. Krause, *The Battle for Homestead*, 346.

79. "Will Not be Discharged," *Pittsburgh Dispatch*, August 3, 1892.

80. "A Matter of Evidence," *Pittsburgh Daily Post*, September 2, 1892.

81. "Colored Laborers at the Elba Works," *Pittsburgh Dispatch*, October 11, 1892.

82. Krause, *The Battle for Homestead*, 346.

83. "Friends of the Colored Race," *BS*, November 15, 1892.

84. "Friends of the Colored Race," *BS*, November 15, 1892.

85. Breitzer, "Race, Immigration, and Contested Americanness," 272–73.

86. Krause, *The Battle for Homestead*, 346.

87. Whatley, "African-American Strikebreaking from the Civil War to the New Deal," 542.

88. Caldemeyer, *Union Renegades*, 103.

89. Eric Arnesen, *Brotherhoods of Color: Black Railroad Workers and the Struggle for Equality* (Cambridge, MA: Harvard University Press, 2001), 29–30.

90. Letter to the Editor from A Coker, "Coke Strike Not Breaking. An Operatives Emphatic Denial of Any Serious Weakness," Scottdale, PA, *Pittsburgh Daily Post*, June 19, 1894.

91. "Colored Labor Imported. Fifty Negroes from Tennessee Quartered on the Southside," *Pittsburgh Daily Post*, May 22, 1895.

92. "A Miners' Strike Brewing," *Pittsburgh Daily Post*, October 9, 1896.

93. Editorial, *Pittsburgh Daily Post*, August 11, 1897.

94. "Negro Labor Imported," *Pittsburgh Daily Post*, July 19, 1899. Although outside the 1890s and outside the Pittsburgh District, another notable instance not covered by Whatley was in the summer of 1902, when the steelworks in Lebanon, Pennsylvania "started up several of its rolling mills with non-union men, all of whom were negroes taken principally from the South." There was "firing of pistols for hours in the vicinity of the iron and steel works" that aimed to terrorize the strikebreakers. See "Troops at Lebanon. Negro Strike-Breakers Terrified by a Big Mob," *BS*, September 24, 1902.

95. Abram Lincoln Harris, Jr., "The New Negro Worker in Pittsburgh" (MA thesis, University of Pittsburgh, 1924), 40. FF467, Box 10, PUL.

96. Interview with F. J. Amormes, 9 Miller Street, Rankin, PA. Pensioned Negro Steel Worker of the American Wire and Steel Company. Interviewed by Alonzo D. Brewer. FF157, Box 3, PUL.

97. Interview with F. J. Amormes, FF157, Box 3, PUL.

98. Spero and Harris, *The Black Worker*, 192.

99. *Twelfth Annual Report of the Bureau of Statistics and Information of Maryland 1903* (Baltimore: The Sun Book and Job Printing, 1904), 44. MSA 2/7/9/17.

100. *Fourteenth Annual Report of the Bureau of Statistics and Information of Maryland for the year 1905* (Baltimore: King Brothers, 1906), 218. MSA 2/7/9/18.

101. Joseph Phillip Goldberg, "American Seamen: A Study in Twentieth Century Collective Action" (PhD diss., Columbia University, 1951), 73.

102. David Brody, *Steelworkers in America: The Nonunion Era* (Urbana: University of Illinois Press, 1998), 67.

103. "Meeting of Mechanics, February 5, 1918," FF149, Box 3, PUL.

104. "Meeting of Mechanics, February 5, 1918," FF149, Box 3, PUL.

105. Dickerson, *Out of the Crucible*, 9.

106. Dickerson, *Out of the Crucible*, 9.

107. *Twelfth Annual Report of the Bureau of Statistics and Information of Maryland 1903* (Baltimore: The Sun Book and Job Printing, 1904), 56. MSA 2/7/9/17.

108. Smith, *From Blackjacks to Briefcases*, 41, 54–55.

109. Chad Pearson, "'Free Shops for Free Men'? The Challenges of Strikebreaking

and Union-Busting in the Progressive Era," in Feurer and Pearson, *Against Labor*, 54, 60–62.

110. Dan McLaughlin, letter to the editor, *UMWJ*, July 23, 1891, quoted in Caldemeyer, *Union Renegades*, 102.

111. Editorial, *Pittsburgh Daily Post*, February 5, 1901.

112. Editorial, *Pittsburgh Daily Post*, February 5, 1901.

113. "Making Big Claims, a West Virginia Coal Operator Tells What He Expects of His State," *Pittsburgh Daily Post*, May 26, 1895.

114. "Along the Wharves. Men Who Handle Freight on River Boats," *Pittsburgh Daily Post*, November 3, 1901.

115. "Curious Race Conflicts," *Pittsburgh Daily Post*, October 29, 1898.

116. Spero and Harris, *The Black Worker*, 224.

117. Whatley, "African-American Strikebreaking from the Civil War to the New Deal," 526.

118. Craig Phelan, *Divided Loyalties: The Public and Private Life of Labor Leader John Mitchell* (Albany: State University of New York Press, 1994), 43.

119. Whatley, "African-American Strikebreaking from the Civil War to the New Deal," 526.

120. "A Colored Exodus from the South," *BS*, September 21, 1916.

121. "Negro Transportation Stopped," *Pittsburgh Daily Post*, June 8, 1917.

122. "Prepaid Orders to Go," *Pittsburgh Daily Post*, June 26, 1917.

123. "A Colored Exodus from the South," *BS*, September 21, 1916.

124. "A Colored Exodus from the South," *BS*, September 21, 1916.

125. "Negro Laborers Move North. Northern Unions and Southern Employers Apprehensive," *BS*, October 12, 1916.

126. "Would Confine Negro to South," *Baltimore Afro American*, November 18, 1916.

127. "Would Confine Negro to South," *Baltimore Afro American*, November 18, 1916.

128. See chapter 7 for a discussion South Africa's parallels with the US experience.

129. Brody, *Steelworkers in America*, 223–24.

130. Dickerson, *Out of the Crucible*, 88.

131. "Minutes of the Welfare Workers' Conference, "September 26, 1919. FF334, Box 7, PUL.

132. Brody, *Steelworkers in America*, 255.

133. McIvor, "Strikebreaking in Britain," Table 1, 12.

134. Dickerson, *Out of the Crucible*, 33.

135. Dickerson, *Out of the Crucible*, 33.

136. Iacobucci, Bert, Oral History, 10, Box 2, Folder 49, BVLHSC.

137. Montini, Ormond, Oral History, Box 2, Folder 55, BVLHSC.

138. Interview with F. J. Amormes, 9 Miller Street, Rankin, PA. Pensioned Negro Steel Worker of the American Wire and Steel Company. Interviewed by Alonzo D. Brewer. FF157, Box 3, PUL.

139. George, Alex Dominic, Oral History, 26, Box 2, Folder 48, BVLHSC.

140. Cliff Brown and Terry Boswell, "Strikebreaking or Solidarity in the Great Steel Strike of 1919: A Split Labor Market, Game-Theoretic, and QCA Analysis," *American Journal of Sociology* 100, no. 6 (1995): 1479–1519.

141. Brown and Boswell, "Strikebreaking or Solidarity," 1496.

142. Brown and Boswell, "Strikebreaking or Solidarity," 1504–5.

143. BFL Meeting Minutes, December 4, 1918, BFL Microfilm, Reel 1.

144. BFL Meeting Minutes, April 10, 1918, BFL Microfilm, Reel 1.

145. *Twenty-Seventh Annual Report of the Maryland State Board of Labor and Statistics 1918* (Baltimore: Meyer & Thalheimer, 1919), 164. MSA 2/7/9/18.

146. "Editorial: A Bad Labor Move," *Baltimore Afro American*, May 16, 1924.

147. Arnesen, *Brotherhoods of Color*, 60–62.

148. "Investigation of Pittsburgh Coal Company Mines at Midland NO. 1 Banning No 2 at Whitsett and banning No 1 at Jacob's Creek," November 2 and 7, 1925, FF109, Box 3, PUL; Interview with F. J. Amormes, 9 Miller Street, Rankin, PA. Pensioned Negro Steel Worker of the American Wire and Steel Company. Interviewed by Alonzo D. Brewer. FF157, Box 3, PUL.

149. Smith, *From Blackjacks to Briefcases*, 73.

150. Wright, *Old South, New South*, 217–19.

151. Nathaniel H. Leff, "Economic Development and Regional Inequality: Origins of the Brazilian Case," *The Quarterly Journal of Economics* 86, no. 2 (1972): 243–62, https://doi.org/10.2307/1880562; Thales Augusto Zamberlan Pereira, "The North-South Divide: Real Wages and Welfare in Brazil during the Early 20th Century," *Revista de Historia Economica—Journal of Iberian and Latin American Economic History* 38, no. 1 (2020): 185–214, https://doi.org/10.1017/S0212610919000132.

152. George Reid Andrews, "Black and White Workers: São Paulo, Brazil, 1888–1928," *Hispanic American Historical Review* 68, no. 3 (August 1, 1988): 501; Maria Helena Pereira Toledo Machado, "From Slave Rebels to Strikebreakers: The Quilombo of Jabaquara and the Problem of Citizenship in Late-Nineteenth-Century Brazil," *Hispanic American Historical Review* 86, no. 2 (2006): 247–74; Sheldon L. Maram, "Labor and the Left in Brazil, 1890–1921: A Movement Aborted," *Hispanic American Historical Review* 57, no. 2 (1977): 254–72.

153. Cliff Brown, "Racial Conflict and Split Labor Markets: The AFL Campaign to Organize Steel Workers, 1918–1919," *Social Science History* 22, no. 3 (October 1, 1998): 334.

Part 2

1. Moreno, *Black Americans and Organized Labor*, 81.

2. Arnesen, *Brotherhoods of Color*, 31.

3. Racism, as Takashi Fujitani writes, is a social logic "common to modernity and hence to modern nation-states, societies, and empires." See *Race for Empire Koreans as Japanese and Japanese as Americans during World War II* (Berkeley: University of California Press, 2011), 31; Wacquant, "Resolving the Trouble with 'Race'"; Loïc Wacquant, "Afropessimism's Radical Abdication," *New Left Review* 144 (December 14, 2023): 97–109.

4. Timothy Yun Hui Tsu, "Japan's 'Yellow Peril': The Chinese in Imperial Japan and Colonial Korea," *Japanese Studies* 30, no. 2 (2010): 165–66, https://doi.org/10.1080/10371397.2010.485553.

5. Kenichi Yasuoka, *Others in Japanese Agriculture: Koreans, Evacuees and Migrants, 1920–1950*, trans. Teresa Castelvetere, ed. Karl Smith (Kyoto: Kyoto University Press, 2018 [2014]), 25.

6. Michael Weiner, *Race and Migration in Imperial Japan* (London: Routledge, 2014), 5.

7. Kawashima, *The Proletarian Gamble*, 4, 11.

8. Kawashima, *The Proletarian Gamble*, 28, 34.

9. Kawashima, *The Proletarian Gamble*, 34.

10. Kawashima, *The Proletarian Gamble*, 61, 73–74.

11. Kawashima, *The Proletarian Gamble*, 98–99.

12. W. Donald Smith, "The 1932 Asō Coal Strike: Korean-Japanese Solidarity and Conflict," *Korean Studies* 20, no. 1 (1996): 112. The National Farmers Union, under influence from Communist Party activists, attempted but failed to bridge divides between Japanese and Korean farmworkers. One pamphlet urged: "Recently the wicked officials have become cunning and are throwing us out of the village and using our Korean brothers and paying them 45 *sen*. It looks like a good deal! However, how can one care for one's elderly parents with such a pittance! . . . Pay Japanese and Koreans equal wages and give us all 30% raises. . . . Japanese and Korean laborers unite!" Yasuoka, *Others in Japanese Agriculture*, 47.

13. Kazuhiro Abe, "Race Relations and the Capitalist State: A Case Study of Koreans in Japan, 1917 through the Mid-1920s," *Korean Studies* 7, no. 1 (1983): 36, https://doi.org/10.1353/ks.1983.0000; Sonia Ryang, "The Great Kanto Earthquake and the Massacre of Koreans in 1923: Notes on Japan's Modern National Sovereignty," *Anthropological Quarterly* 76, no. 4 (2003): 731–48; Hasegawa Kenji, "The Massacre of Koreans in Yokohama in the Aftermath of the Great Kanto Earthquake of 1923," *Monumenta Nipponica* 75, no. 1 (2020): 91–122.

14. Thomas R. Gottschang and Diana Lary, *Swallows and Settlers: The Great Migration from North China to Manchuria* (Ann Arbor: Center for Chinese Studies, The University of Michigan, 2000), 6–10.

15. Victor Seow, *Carbon Technocracy: Energy Regimes in Modern East Asia* (Chicago: The University of Chicago Press, 2021), 57.

16. Gottschang and Lary, *Swallows and Settlers*, 62.

17. Seow, *Carbon Technocracy*, 59.

18. Seow, *Carbon Technocracy*, 97–98.

19. Eiichiro Azuma, *In Search of Our Frontier: Japanese America and Settler Colonialism in the Construction of Japan's Borderless Empire* (Oakland: University of California Press, 2019), 181. Many Japanese settlers in Manchuria had previously suffered from racial hostility in the United States: "Victims of race-based exclusion so easily and willingly turned into enforcers of another kind of racial oppression when they had the power and ideological rationale to do so after moving from North America to Manchuria" (182).

20. Mark Driscoll, *Absolute Erotic, Absolute Grotesque: The Living, Dead, and Undead in Japan's Imperialism, 1895–1945* (Durham, NC: Duke University Press, 2010), 28.

21. Duncan Money and Limin Teh, "Race at Work: A Comparative History of Mining Labor and Empire on the Central African Copperbelt and the Fushun Coalfields, ca. 1907–1945," *International Labor and Working-Class History*, February 2, 2022, 11.

22. Arrighi, "Marxist Century, American Century," 61; Batzell, "Free Labour, Capitalism and the Anti-Slavery Origins of Chinese Exclusion in California in the 1870s." Hobsbawm points to the "White Australia Policy, the Chinese Exclusion Laws in the United States, and anti-black discrimination in South African Industry" as characteristic examples of how fractions of the "favored local working class, afraid of losing its exceptionally advantageous conditions," attempt to impose "strict limitations on entry into the working class" (*Worlds of Labour*, 55).

23. Shergold's study of wages and living standards in Pittsburgh, Birmingham, and Sheffield in the first decade of the twentieth century confirms more specifically that there were far higher wage differentials in the US (*Working-Class Life*, 51–54). Unfortunately, one of the most influential works in the comparative literature, cited in nearly all subsequent work, mistakes the relative craft/common labor wage differential in the US and the UK. Holt suggests that in the UK "wage differentials between skilled and unskilled were greater," leading him to miss a key structural factor explaining the trajectory of the two labor movements. See "Trade Unionism in the British and US Steel Industries, 1880–1914," 18.

24. In the US, Shergold observes that "unions were usually craft-based, and thus far more pressure was exerted upon the wages of the skilled artisans than upon the rates paid to common laborers," whereas in the UK, the New Unionism found "an increasing number of unskilled occupations were organized alongside more skilled ones" (*Working-Class Life*, 53). From the 1890s, it appears that British unions diminished wage inequality, as unionized unskilled workers enjoyed a slightly greater increase in wages compared with non-union workers, while unionized skilled workers enjoyed a somewhat smaller premium over the unorganized. See T. J. Hatton, G. R. Boyer, and R. E. Bailey, "The Union Wage Effect in Late Nineteenth Century Britain," *Economica* 61, no. 244 (1994): 435–56.

25. On the centrality of segmented labor markets in structuring labor organizing see Gary Marks, "Variations in Union Political Activity in the United States, Britain, and Germany from the Nineteenth Century," *Comparative Politics* 22, no. 1 (1989): 83. Antoine Joseph, in his study of skilled workers, identifies four factors in the political economy that push working-class solidarity toward either narrow particularism or broad universalism: (1) internal cleavages based on race, ethnicity and religion, (2) early industrialization and entrenched crafts, (3) economic protectionism, and (4) mass political engagement before inclusive labor organizing. The US exemplifies all four conditions that favor particularism, while the UK has all but one, since free trade prevailed over protectionism until the early twentieth century. In addition, Joseph points to "the centrality of wage differentials in the consolidation of a privileged position of workers in craft unions." See *Skilled Workers' Solidarity: The American Experience in Comparative Perspective* (New York: Garland Pub, 2000), xi–xii, 65, 93. A study of European dockworkers also highlights the importance of a long, early industrialization for creating elaborate skill hierarchies. See Erik Nijhof, John Barzman, and John Lovell, "Dockers' Unions in the Ports of London, Le Havre, Rotterdam and Hamburg, 1850–1914," in *The Emergence of European Trade Unionism*, ed. Jean-Louis Robert, Antoine Prost, and Chris Wrigley (London: Ashgate, 2004), 49.

26. *Eleventh Annual Report of the Bureau of Statistics and Information of Maryland* (Baltimore: The Sun Book and Job Printing, 1903), 1. MSA 2/7/9/17.

Chapter 4

1. Ileen A. DeVault, *United Apart: Gender and the Rise of Craft Unionism* (Ithaca: Cornell University Press, 2004).

2. J. M. Barbalet, "The 'Labor Aristocracy' in Context," *Science & Society* 51, no. 2 (1987): 133–53; Carol Conell and Kim Voss, "Formal Organization and the Fate of Social Movements: Craft Association and Class Alliance in the Knights of Labor,"

American Sociological Review 55, no. 2 (1990): 255; Voss, *The Making of American Exceptionalism*, 178–79.

3. Bernard H. Moss, *The Origins of the French Labor Movement, 1830–1914: The Socialism of Skilled Workers* (Berkeley: University of California Press, 1976); Joan Wallach Scott, *The Glassworkers of Carmaux: French Craftsmen and Political Action in a Nineteenth-Century City* (Cambridge, MA: Harvard University Press, 1974); I. J. Prothero, *Radical Artisans in England and France, 1830–1870* (Cambridge: Cambridge University Press, 1997).

4. Hobsbawm, *Worlds of Labour*, 164, 169.

5. Clegg, *British Trade Unions*, 1:14.

6. Clegg, *British Trade Unions*, 1:37–38.

7. Holt, "Trade Unionism in the British and U.S. Steel Industries," 6.

8. Holt, "Trade Unionism in the British and U.S. Steel Industries," 8.

9. Holt, "Trade Unionism in the British and U.S. Steel Industries," 8.

10. Pollard, *A History of Labour in Sheffield*, 172.

11. Pollard, *A History of Labour in Sheffield*, 235.

12. Clegg, *British Trade Unions*, 1:206.

13. Sam Davies, *Liverpool Labour: Social and Political Influences on the Development of the Labour Party in Liverpool, 1900–1939* (Keele, UK: Keele University Press, 1996), 54–60.

14. Philip J. Waller, *Democracy and Sectarianism: A Political and Social History of Liverpool, 1868–1939* (Liverpool: Liverpool University Press, 1981), 143.

15. Davies, *Liverpool Labour*, 55.

16. Davies, *Liverpool Labour*, 66.

17. Pollard, *A History of Labour in Sheffield*, 170.

18. Pollard, *A History of Labour in Sheffield*, 199.

19. Pollard, *A History of Labour in Sheffield*, 8–9.

20. Gary Marks, *Unions in Politics: Britain, Germany, and the United States in the Nineteenth and Early Twentieth Centuries* (Princeton: Princeton University Press, 1989), 2–4, 210.

21. Paul Michel Taillon, *Good, Reliable, White Men: Railroad Brotherhoods, 1877–1917* (Urbana: University of Illinois Press, 2009), 3–4.

22. Holt, "Trade Unionism in the British and U.S. Steel Industries," 10.

23. Paul Underwood Kellogg, ed., *Wage-Earning Pittsburgh: The Pittsburgh Survey Findings in Six Volumes* (Philadelphia: Wm. F. Fell Co., 1914), 29.

24. H. E. Hoagland, "Trade Unionism in the Iron Industry: A Decadent Organization," *The Quarterly Journal of Economics* 31, no. 4 (1917): 674–89.

25. Michael W. Santos, "Brother against Brother: The Amalgamated and Sons of Vulcan at the A. M. Byers Company, 1907–1913," *The Pennsylvania Magazine of History and Biography* 111, no. 2 (1987): 202–3.

26. Michael W. Santos, "Laboring on the Periphery: Managers and Workers at the A. M. Byers Company, 1900–1956," *Business History Review* 61, no. 1 (1987): 120.

27. Dickerson, *Out of the Crucible*, 15.

28. Lloyd Ulman, *The Rise of the National Trade Union: The Development and Significance of Its Structure, Governing Institutions, and Economic Policies*, 2nd ed. (Cambridge: Harvard University Press, 1966), 323, 333–34.

29. Ulman, *The Rise of the National Trade Union*, 411.

30. Ulman, *The Rise of the National Trade Union*, 414.

31. James Oliver Morris, *Conflict within the AFL: A Study of Craft versus Industrial Unionism, 1901–1938* (Ithaca: Cornell University Press, 1958), 15.

32. David Brian Robertson, *Capital, Labor, and State: The Battle for American Labor Markets from the Civil War to the New Deal* (Lanham, MD: Rowman & Littlefield Publishers, 2000), 69.

33. BFL Meeting Minutes, September 15, 1920, Reel 1.

34. BFL Meeting Minutes, April 4, 18, 25, 1923, Reel 1.

35. Gerald Friedman, "Dividing Labor: Urban Politics and Big-City Construction in Late-Nineteenth-Century America," in *Strategic Factors in Nineteenth Century American Economic History: A Volume to Honor Robert W. Fogel*, ed. Claudia Dale Goldin and Hugh Rockoff (Chicago: University of Chicago Press, 1992), 447–64; and Christopher K. Ansell and Arthur L. Burris, "Bosses of the City Unite! Labor Politics and Political Machine Consolidation, 1870–1910," *Studies in American Political Development* 11, no. 1 (1997): 1–43.

36. The closest approximation of a US-style political machine could be found within the ethnically divided workforce of Liverpool, with its Workingmen's Conservative Association and powerful urban Tory political machine. See Waller, *Democracy and Sectarianism*; Phillip Ingram, "Sectarianism in the North West of England, with Special Reference to Class Relationships in the City of Liverpool 1846–1914" (Preston, Lancashire Polytechnic, 1987); and John Belchem, *Irish, Catholic and Scouse: The History of the Liverpool-Irish, 1800–1939* (Liverpool: Liverpool University Press, 2007).

37. Robertson, *Capital, Labor, and State*, 135; and J. Morris, *Conflict within the AFL*, 10–11.

38. John R. Commons and William M. Leiserson, "Wage-Earners of Pittsburgh," in Kellogg, *Wage-Earning Pittsburgh*, 146.

39. Jno. B. Thomas to Albert C. Ritchie, April 21, 1923; Henry F. Broening to Albert C. Ritchie, March 29, 1923. Folder, "Labor 1919–1930," Labor Box 2//30/2/27, MDGG.

40. Albert C. Ritchie to Henry F. Broening, March 30, 1923; Albert C. Ritchie to Henry F. Broening, May 5, 1923. Folder, "Labor 1919–1930," Labor Box 2//30/2/27, MDGG.

41. Executive Committee Minutes, October 5, 1921. Series I, Box 2, MMA.

42. Clegg, *British Trade Unions*, 1:153–54.

43. Thomas C. Weeks, *First Biennial Report of the Bureau of Industrial Statistics and Information of Maryland, 1884–1885* (Baltimore: Guggenheimer, Weil & Co., 1886), 40.

44. Voss, *The Making of American Exceptionalism*, 198.

45. Hobsbawm, *Labouring Men*, 195.

46. Ulman, *The Rise of the National Trade Union*, 369–75.

47. Conell and Voss, "Formal Organization and the Fate of Social Movements," 266. Similarly, as Oestreicher shows in his study of Detroit in the 1880s and 1890s, the Knights of Labor gave the District Board "great power over the negotiations of local assemblies," and workers in specific crafts repeatedly expressed frustration over the failure of Knights negotiators to prioritize their specific craft demands. See Richard Jules Oestreicher, *Solidarity and Fragmentation: Working People and Class Consciousness in Detroit, 1875–1900* (Urbana: University of Illinois Press, 1986), 192–96.

48. Elizabeth Faue, *Community of Suffering and Struggle: Women, Men, and the Labor Movement in Minneapolis, 1915–1945* (Chapel Hill: University of North Carolina Press, 2016).

49. George Sayers Bain, *Profiles of Union Growth: A Comparative Statistical Portrait of Eight Countries* (Oxford: Blackwell, 1980), 39, 102.

50. Lara Vapnek, *Breadwinners: Working Women and Economic Independence, 1865–1920* (Urbana: University of Illinois Press, 2009), 43, 46.

51. Susan Levine, "Labor's True Woman: Domesticity and Equal Rights in the Knights of Labor," *The Journal of American History* 70, no. 2 (1983): 325.

52. Levine, "Labor's True Woman," 328–29.

53. French Eugene Wolfe, *Admission to American Trade Unions* (Baltimore: Johns Hopkins University Press, 1912), 94.

54. Wolfe, *Admission to American Trade Unions*, 95.

55. DeVault, *United Apart*, 4, 217.

56. Wolfe, *Admission to American Trade Unions*, 85.

57. BFL Meeting Minutes, September 22, 1920. Reel 1.

58. Hobsbawm, *Worlds of Labour*, 159.

59. Susan Trouvé-Finding, "Unionised Women Teachers and Women's Suffrage," in *Suffrage Outside Suffragism: Women's Vote in Britain, 1880–1914*, ed. Myriam Boussahba-Bravard (London: Palgrave Macmillan UK, 2007), 207.

60. Trouvé-Finding, "Unionised Women Teachers," 210.

61. Pat Thane, "Women in the Labour Party and Women's Suffrage," in *Suffrage Outside Suffragism: Women's Vote in Britain, 1880–1914*, ed. Myriam Boussahba-Bravard (London: Palgrave Macmillan UK, 2007), 43.

62. Mathers, "Sheffield Municipal Politics," 200–202.

63. Diana D'Amico, "An Uneasy Union: Women Teachers, Organized Labor, and the Contested Ideology of Profession during the Progressive Era," *Labor: Studies in Working-Class History of the Americas* 14, no. 3 (2017): 35–54.

Chapter 5

1. Moreno, *Black Americans and Organized Labor*, 97.

2. Baker, *Following the Color Line*, 111.

3. C. Vann Woodward, *The Strange Career of Jim Crow* (Oxford: Oxford University Press, 2001 [1955]); George M. Fredrickson, *The Arrogance of Race: Historical Perspectives on Slavery, Racism, and Social Inequality* (Middletown, CT: Wesleyan University Press, 1988), ch. 10. Skeptics of Woodward's thesis of substantial change in the post-bellum Southern racial order include Howard N. Rabinowitz, "From Exclusion to Segregation: Southern Race Relations, 1865–1890," *The Journal of American History* 63, no. 2 (1976): 325–50, https://doi.org/10.2307/1899640; Howard N. Rabinowitz, *Race Relations in the Urban South, 1865–1890* (Athens: University of Georgia Press, 1996); Joel Williamson, *The Crucible of Race: Black-White Relations in the American South since Emancipation* (New York: Oxford University Press, 1984).

4. Glenda Elizabeth Gilmore, *Gender and Jim Crow: Women and the Politics of White Supremacy in North Carolina, 1896–1920*, 2nd ed. (Chapel Hill: The University of North Carolina Press, 2019), 8.

5. Tera W. Hunter, *To 'joy My Freedom: Southern Black Women's Lives and Labors after the Civil War* (Cambridge, MA: Harvard University Press, 1997), 78–81, 98.

6. Hunter, *To 'joy My Freedom*, 116–18.

7. Hunter, *To 'joy My Freedom*, 128. Stressing the pressures of low-wage migration from the Southern countryside, and the desire of white workers to erect a strict occu-

pational color bar, Eric Arnesen's study of the New Orleans waterfront also highlights the importance of the 1890s as period during which racial boundaries hardened. See *Waterfront Workers of New Orleans: Race, Class, and Politics, 1863–1923* (New York: Oxford University Press, 1991), 120–52. See also Glenn, *Unequal Freedom*, 37, 112–20. Henry M. McKiven explores similar labor market and strikebreaking mechanisms, but points to the first two decades of the twentieth century as the key period in Birmingham's steel industry. Semiskilled work unsettled the white/skilled black/ unskilled racial order, leading to intensified efforts at racial boundary-making but also real improvements for black workers in Alabama. See *Iron and Steel: Class, Race, and Community in Birmingham, Alabama, 1875–1920* (Chapel Hill: University of North Carolina Press, 1995), 97–127, 170.

8. Spero and Harris, *The Black Worker*, 9–11.

9. Du Bois, *Black Reconstruction in America*, 18–19, 45–46; Silas Niobeh Tsaba Crowfoot, "Community Development for a White City: Race Making, Improvementism, and the Cincinnati Race Riots and Anti-Abolition Riots of 1829, 1836, and 1841" (PhD diss., Portland State University, 2010).

10. Moreno, *Black Americans and Organized Labor*, 16–18.

11. Moreno, *Black Americans and Organized Labor*, 25.

12. Spero and Harris, *The Black Worker*, 25.

13. Nelson, *Divided We Stand*, 161.

14. Wolfe, *Admission to American Trade Unions*, 115.

15. Du Bois, *Black Reconstruction in America*, 29.

16. Du Bois, *Black Reconstruction in America*, 354–55.

17. Roediger, *The Wages of Whiteness*, 168–70.

18. Spero and Harris, *The Black Worker*, 21.

19. Philip S. Foner, *Organized Labor and the Black Worker, 1619–1973* (New York: International Publishers, 1974), 46, 49.

20. Spero and Harris, *The Black Worker*, 21.

21. Postel, *Equality*, 206, 249.

22. Postel, *Equality*, 253.

23. Moreno, *Black Americans and Organized Labor*, 29.

24. George Bache Du Bois, "The Search for a Better Life: Baltimore's Workers, 1865–1916" (PhD diss., University of Maryland, 1995), 49.

25. P. Foner, *Organized Labor and the Black Worker*, 64.

26. National Urban League, *Negro Membership in American Labor Unions* (New York: The Alexander Press, 1930), 25.

27. P. Foner, *Organized Labor and the Black Worker*, 65.

28. P. Foner, *Organized Labor and the Black Worker*.

29. Spero and Harris, *The Black Worker*, 87–88.

30. Maurice S. Evans, *Black and White in the Southern States; a Study of the Race Problem in the United States from a South African Point of View* (London: Longmans, Green and Co., 1915), 213, http://archive.org/details/blackwhiteinso00evan.

31. P. Foner, *Organized Labor and the Black Worker*, 70.

32. P. Foner, *Organized Labor and the Black Worker*, 71–72. Jeffrey Haydu's insightful comparative study of the Machinists and Engineers in the skilled metal trades in the US and the UK fails to mention the racist policies of the union, indicating the broader lack of attention to white supremacy in most US/Europe comparative work.

See *Between Craft and Class: Skilled Workers and Factory Politics in the United States and Britain, 1890–1922* (Berkeley: University of California Press, 1988).

33. P. Foner, *Organized Labor and the Black Worker*, 71.

34. P. Foner, *Organized Labor and the Black Worker*, 71.

35. P. Foner, *Organized Labor and the Black Worker*, 101.

36. P. Foner, *Organized Labor and the Black Worker*, 74–75.

37. P. Foner, *Organized Labor and the Black Worker*, 76.

38. Gwendolyn Mink, *Old Labor and New Immigrants in American Political Development: Union, Party, and State, 1875–1920* (Ithaca: Cornell University Press, 1986), 97.

39. Whatley, "African-American Strikebreaking from the Civil War to the New Deal," 526.

40. Mink, *Old Labor and New Immigrants*, 97.

41. P. Foner, *Organized Labor and the Black Worker*, 54.

42. P. Foner, *Organized Labor and the Black Worker*, 62–63.

43. Arnesen, *Brotherhoods of Color*, 29.

44. Arnesen, *Brotherhoods of Color*, 29.

45. Arnesen, *Brotherhoods of Color*, 34.

46. Moreno, *Black Americans and Organized Labor*, 121; Taillon, *Good, Reliable, White Men*, 4.

47. Spero and Harris, *The Black Worker*, 250.

48. Dickerson, *Out of the Crucible*, 14.

49. "Local Items," *Pittsburgh Dispatch*, August 17, 1889.

50. Interview with F. J. Amormes, 9 Miller Street, Rankin, PA. Pensioned Negro Steel Worker of the American Wire and Steel Company. Interviewed by Alonzo D. Brewer. FF157, Box 3, PUL.

51. "Race and Wages," *Pittsburgh Daily Post*, July 22, 1893.

52. "Negro Labor Union. National Organization Will Probably Be Inaugurated Here," *Pittsburgh Daily Post*, May 29, 1901.

53. "Will Not Organize. McKeesport Negroes Meet in a Church and Denounce the Amalgamated Association," *Pittsburgh Daily Post*, August 14, 1901.

54. Dickerson, *Out of the Crucible*, 14.

55. Moreno, *Black Americans and Organized Labor*, 107.

56. Moreno, *Black Americans and Organized Labor*, 107.

57. Dickerson, *Out of the Crucible*, 15.

58. R. R. Wright, Jr. "One Hundred Negro Steel Workers," in Kellogg, *Wage-Earning Pittsburgh*, 107.

59. Wright, "One Hundred Negro Steel Workers," 108.

60. Dickerson, *Out of the Crucible*, 11.

61. "Meeting of Mechanics, February 5, 1918," FF149, Box 3, PUL.

62. "Meeting of Mechanics, February 5, 1918," FF149, Box 3, PUL.

63. Abram Lincoln Harris, Jr., "The New Negro Worker in Pittsburgh" (Master's Thesis, University of Pittsburgh, 1924). FF467, Box 10, PUL.

64. "Special Problems of Negro Workers in Pittsburgh," April 6, 1929. FF235, Box 5, PUL.

65. "Special Problems of Negro Workers in Pittsburgh," April 6, 1929. FF235, Box 5, PUL.

66. Spero and Harris, *The Black Worker*, 192.

67. Synopsis of Interview on November 20, 1919 with Mr. K.— Official of the Urban League of Pittsburgh, Pa. HBP.

68. Colin J. Davis, *Power at Odds: The 1922 National Railroad Shopmen's Strike* (Urbana: University of Illinois Press, 1997), 29.

69. Spero and Harris, *The Black Worker*, 201.

70. Quoted in Jacqueline Jones, *American Work: Four Centuries of Black and White Labor* (New York: W.W. Norton, 1998), 314.

71. Rimamo, "White Employees Bar Negroes Says Hill," *Afro American*, August 7, 1926.

72. Baker, *Following the Color Line*, 131–34.

73. W. P. Livingstone, *The Race Conflict: A Study of Conditions in America* (London: Sampson Low, 1911), 16, 118–21, https://catalog.hathitrust.org/Record/000339342.

74. Data Appendix, "Occupations of Black Workers in Pittsburgh, 1870–1900," based on IPUMS microdata from the manuscript census.

75. During World War II, "a wave of hate strikes erupted in Baltimore's heavy industries" despite the anti-racist leadership provided by some CIO unions. Even though African American workers were credited with giving the steelworkers union victory in their 1941 certification election, local representatives "negotiated a series of contracts with Bethlehem that kept discriminatory hiring and promotion practices in place well into the 1960s." For quotation see Christopher Niedt, "The Politics of Prosperity and Crisis in an Industrial Suburb: Dundalk, Maryland, 1920–2005" (PhD thesis, University of California–Berkeley, 2007), 77, 82. See also Eileen Boris, "'You Wouldn't Want One of 'Em Dancing with Your Wife': Racialized Bodies on the Job in World War II," *American Quarterly* 50, no. 1 (1998): 77–108; Bruce Nelson, "Class, Race and Democracy in the CIO: The 'New' Labor History Meets the 'Wages of Whiteness,'" *International Review of Social History* 41, no. 3 (1996): 351; and Allan M. Winkler, "The Philadelphia Transit Strike of 1944," *The Journal of American History* 59, no. 1 (1972): 73–89.

76. Frank Towers, "Job Busting at Baltimore Shipyards: Racial Violence in the Civil War-Era South," *The Journal of Southern History* 66, no. 2 (May 1, 2000): 221–56.

77. Spero and Harris, *The Black Worker*, 18.

78. W. E. B. Du Bois, *The Negro Artisan. Report of a Social Study Made under the Direction of Atlanta University; Together with the Proceedings of the Seventh Conference for the Study of the Negro Problems, Held at Atlanta University, on May 27th, 1902* (Atlanta: Atlanta University Press, 1902), 173.

79. Nelson, *Divided We Stand*, 166.

80. Spero and Harris, *The Black Worker*, 251–52, 254.

81. "Carpenters Confident," BS, March 27, 1903.

82. Norwood, *Strikebreaking & Intimidation*, 102.

83. Boustan, *Competition in the Promised Land*, 73.

84. *Twenty-First Annual Report of the Commissioner of Labor 1906: Strikes and Lockouts* (Washington, DC: Government Printing Office, 1907), 113.

85. BFL Meeting Minutes, March 30, 1921. BFL Microfilm Reel 1.

86. BFL Meeting Minutes, July 15, 1925. Reel 1.

87. "200 Workers at New W. MD. Pier on Strike," BS, April 20, 1929.

88. *Twenty-Seventh Annual Report of the Maryland State Board of Labor and Statistics 1918* (Baltimore: Meyer & Thalheimer, 1919), 174. MSA 2/7/9/18.

89. BFL Meeting Minutes, January 15, 1919. BFL Microfilm Reel 1.

90. Arnesen, *Brotherhoods of Color*, 36–37, 65–70; and Moreno, *Black Americans and Organized Labor*, 99–100.

91. Arnesen, *Brotherhoods of Color*, 80.

92. Joseph Kelly, "Showing Agency on the Margins: African American Railway Workers in the South and Their Unions, 1917–1930," *Labour / Le Travail* 71 (2013): 134, 138.

93. BFL Meeting Minutes, March 16, 1921. BFL Microfilm Reel 1.

94. "Longshoremen Protest," *Afro American*, March 18, 1921.

95. Spero and Harris, *The Black Worker*, 194.

96. Spero and Harris, *The Black Worker*, 194.

97. BFL Meeting Minutes, November 11, 1925. Reel 2.

98. "Should Baltimore Workers Unionize?," *Baltimore Afro American*, March 18, 1921.

99. "Should Servants Organize," *Baltimore Afro American*, May 21, 1919.

100. "Forty Delegates Convene Here," *Baltimore Afro American*, June 13, 1919.

101. "Forty Delegates Convene Here," *Baltimore Afro American*, June 13, 1919.

102. Labor Union Favors Equal Salaries," *Baltimore Afro American*, February 27, 1920.

103. "Labor Meeting Open to All," *Baltimore Afro American*, October 15, 1920.

104. "There is No Race Prejudice in the Industrial Workers of the World According to Benjamin Fletcher Who is One of Them," *Baltimore Afro American*, April 2, 1920.

105. William N. Jones, "Southern Workers Losing Confidence in Unions," *Baltimore Afro American*, June 9, 1928.

106. "Would Confine Negro to South," *Baltimore Afro American*, November 18, 1916.

107. Abram Lincoln Harris, Jr., "The New Negro Worker in Pittsburgh" (Master Thesis, University of Pittsburgh, 1924), 54. FF467, Box 10, PUL.

108. Harris, Jr., "The New Negro Worker in Pittsburgh," 54.

109. Harris, Jr., "The New Negro Worker in Pittsburgh," 55.

110. Peter Cole, *Wobblies on the Waterfront: Interracial Unionism in Progressive-Era Philadelphia* (Urbana: University of Illinois Press, 2007), 148–49.

Chapter 6

1. Gary S. Cross, *Immigrant Workers in Industrial France: The Making of a New Laboring Class* (Philadelphia: Temple University Press, 1983), 30–32; Ulrich Herbert, *A History of Foreign Labor in Germany, 1880–1980: Seasonal Workers, Forced Laborers, Guest Workers* (Ann Arbor: University of Michigan Press, 1990), 75–77; John J. Kulczycki, *The Foreign Worker and the German Labor Movement: Xenophobia and Solidarity in the Coal Fields of the Ruhr, 1871–1914* (Oxford: Berg Publishers, 1994).

2. Ruth Milkman, "Labor's Long Road to Immigrant Inclusion," *Labor* 20, no. 4 (December 1, 2023): 69–75, https://doi.org/10.1215/15476715-10829185.

3. John C. Torpey, *The Invention of the Passport: Surveillance, Citizenship, and the State* (Cambridge, UK: Cambridge University Press, 2000), 105–6. Given the strong, global commitment of organized workers to nativist immigration restriction, it seems necessary to question Marcel van der Linden's characterization of the period from 1894 to 1917 as an "upswing" of proletarian internationalism. Workers were far more likely to try to exclude, than to organize, low-wage migrants anywhere they appeared to potentially have a substantial impact on local labor markets. See "Proletarian In-

ternationalism: A Long View and Some Speculations," in *Modern World-System in the Longue Duree*, ed. *Immanuel Wallerstein* (London: Routledge, 2004), 118–19, 125.

4. Cindy Hahamovitch, *No Man's Land: Jamaican Guestworkers in America and the Global History of Deportable Labor* (Princeton: Princeton University Press, 2011), 14.

5. Batzell, "Free Labour, Capitalism and the Anti-Slavery Origins of Chinese Exclusion in California in the 1870s."

6. Mink, *Old Labor and New Immigrants*, 9, 17, 38.

7. Catherine Collomp, "Unions, Civics, and National Identity," *Labor History* 29, no. 4 (Fall 1988): 468. While Archer initially discounts the importance of nativism in dividing the US working class, he later acknowledges that the American Protective Association "created conflicts within unions" that "led to the collapse of some local organizations, and seriously weakened a number of others," and significantly, the disruptive nativism of the APA was felt most "in just those unions and in those states" where labor was relatively strong, such as among the "steel workers, coal miners, and railroad workers in Pennsylvania, Illinois, and throughout the Midwest." See *Why Is There No Labor Party in the United States?*, 70–71, 205.

8. Robertson, *Capital, Labor, and State*, 84.

9. Seth Rockman, *Scraping By: Wage Labor, Slavery, and Survival in Early Baltimore* (Baltimore: Johns Hopkins University Press, 2009), 9, 42–44. Among the most compelling contributions is Roediger's analysis of how slavery shaped white workers' understanding of unskilled labor in the North (*The Wages of Whiteness*, 145–50, 180).

10. Du Bois, *Black Reconstruction in America*, 700.

11. Alois B. Koukol, "A Slav's a Man For A' That," in Kellogg, *Wage-Earning Pittsburgh*, 73.

12. Michael K. Rosenow, *Death and Dying in the Working Class, 1865–1920* (Urbana: University of Illinois Press, 2015), 30.

13. Brody, *Steelworkers in America*, 119.

14. Brody, *Steelworkers in America*, 119.

15. Gavin Wright, *Slavery and American Economic Development* (Baton Rouge: Louisiana State University Press, 2006), 125.

16. Rosenow, *Death and Dying in the Working Class*, 116.

17. Walter Licht, *Working for the Railroad: The Organization of Work in the Nineteenth Century* (Princeton: Princeton University Press, 1983), 190–91.

18. Marc Linder, "Fatal Subtraction: Statistical MIAs on the Industrial Battlefield," *Journal of Legislation* 20, no. 2 (1994): 103.

19. Linder, "Fatal Subtraction," 104–5.

20. Linder, "Fatal Subtraction," 106.

21. Andrea Salcedo and Derek M. Norman, "A Latino Worker, a Risky Construction Site and a Family in Mourning," *New York Times*, February 17, 2020, https://www.nytimes.com/2020/02/17/nyregion/construction-deaths-latinos-nyc.html.

22. John Mendeloff and Laura Staetsky, "Occupational Fatality Risks in the United States and the United Kingdom," *American Journal of Industrial Medicine* 57, no. 1 (2014): Table 1, 6, https://doi.org/10.1002/ajim.22258.

23. Rick Halpern, "The Peculiarities of Race and Violence in US Labor History," in Melvyn Dubofsky et al., "Labor History Symposium: Responses," *Labor History* 51, no. 2 (May 2010): 302.

24. Eugene E. Leach, "Chaining the Tiger: The Mob Stigma and the Working Class, 1863–1894," *Labor History* 35, no. 2 (1994): 215.

25. *Fifteenth Annual Report of the Bureau of Statistics and Information of Maryland 1906* (Baltimore: Kohn & Pollock, 1907), 118. MSA 2/7/9/18.

26. Terence Finnegan, *A Deed So Accursed: Lynching in Mississippi and South Carolina, 1881–1940* (Charlottesville: University of Virginia Press, 2013); E. M. Beck and Stewart E. Tolnay, "The Killing Fields of the Deep South: The Market for Cotton and the Lynching of Blacks, 1882–1930," *American Sociological Review* 55, no. 4 (1990): 526–39; and Jay Corzine, Lin Huff-Corzine, and James C. Creech, "The Tenant Labor Market and Lynching in the South: A Test of Split Labor Market Theory," *Sociological Inquiry* 58, no. 3 (1988): 261–78. Here again the parallel between the US and Russia is instructive. Both countries experienced exceptionally high rates of violence during strikes, and both also experienced widespread racial terrorism, in the form of the lynching of African Americans in the US South and pogroms against Jews in Russia. See Wynn, *Workers, Strikes, and Pogroms.*

27. Daniel J. Tichenor, *Dividing Lines: The Politics of Immigration Control in America* (Princeton: Princeton University Press, 2002), 117.

28. Janice Fine and Daniel J. Tichenor, "A Movement Wrestling: American Labor's Enduring Struggle with Immigration, 1866–2007," *Studies in American Political Development* 23, no. 1 (2009): 95, https://doi.org/10.1017/S0898588X09000042.

29. John Higham, "Origins of Immigration Restriction, 1882–1897: A Social Analysis," *The Mississippi Valley Historical Review* 39, no. 1 (1952): 81; Tichenor, *Dividing Lines*, 118.

30. "Protect Labor Instead of Monopolies," *Pittsburgh Daily Post*, October 26, 1880.

31. "Campaign Lies Coming Home to Roost," *Pittsburgh Daily Post*, November 20, 1880.

32. "One of Dorsey's Tricks," *Pittsburgh Daily Post*, September 19, 1882.

33. "Promise and Reality," *Pittsburgh Daily Post*, October 1, 1884.

34. "Party Lines Drawn," *Pittsburgh Dispatch*, March 13, 1891.

35. Charles Pearson, Letter to the Editor, "Refutes Mr. Dalzell's Claim That Pittsburgh Workmen are Best Paid," *Pittsburgh Daily Post* April 28, 1911.

36. Higham, "Origins of Immigration Restriction," 87.

37. Donald Louis Kinzer, *An Episode in Anti-Catholicism: The American Protective Association* (Seattle: University of Washington Press, 1964).

38. Kinzer, *An Episode in Anti-Catholicism*, 129.

39. Kinzer, *An Episode in Anti-Catholicism*, 85.

40. K. Gerald Marsden, "Patriotic Societies and American Labor: The American Protective Association in Wisconsin," *The Wisconsin Magazine of History* 41, no. 4 (1958): 293.

41. Kinzer, *An Episode in Anti-Catholicism*, 85, 129–30.

42. Kinzer, *An Episode in Anti-Catholicism*, 293.

43. Kinzer, *An Episode in Anti-Catholicism*, 30.

44. Marsden, "Patriotic Societies and American Labor," 292.

45. Claudia Goldin, "The Political Economy of Immigration Restriction in the United States, 1890 to 1921," in *The Regulated Economy: A Historical Approach to Political Economy*, ed. Claudia Dale Goldin and Gary D. Libecap (Chicago: University of Chicago Press, 1994). A number of unions restricted membership to citizens and those who officially declared their intention to become citizens; see Wolfe, *Admission to American Trade Unions*, 101.

46. UBCDC, Minutes January 16, 1894.

47. UBCDC, Minutes February 6, 1894.

48. UBDC, Minutes March 6, 1894.

49. *First Annual Report of the Commissioner of Labor and Industry 1913* (Harrisburg: Wm. Stanley Bay, 1915), 239. Box 2, PADLI.

50. Caldemeyer, *Union Renegades*, 96.

51. Caldemeyer, *Union Renegades*, 111–12.

52. *First Annual Report of the Commissioner of Labor and Industry 1913* (Harrisburg: Wm. Stanley Bay, 1915), 239. Box 2, PADLI.

53. "May Fight Socialism Workingmen's Political League Will Enter Fall Campaign," *BS*, May 4, 1906; "Girding for the Fray. Workingmen's Political League Elects Officers," *BS*, May 17, 1906.

54. Hunter, *To 'joy My Freedom*, 80–81.

55. "After Their Rights. Public Meeting of Colored People to Protest Against Discrimination," *Pittsburgh Dispatch*, April 21, 1891.

56. Interview with F. J. Amormes, 9 Miller Street, Rankin, PA. Pensioned Negro Steel Worker of the American Wire and Steel Company. Interviewed by Alonzo D. Brewer. FF157, Box 3, PUL.

57. Breitzer, "Race, Immigration, and Contested Americanness," 272.

58. Breitzer, "Race, Immigration, and Contested Americanness," 278; Mark Brilliant, *The Color of America Has Changed: How Racial Diversity Shaped Civil Rights Reform in California, 1941–1978* (New York: Oxford University Press, 2010); Tatishe Nteta, "United We Stand? African Americans, Self-Interest, and Immigration Reform," *American Politics Research* 41, no. 1 (2013): 147–72.

59. Joseph, *Skilled Workers' Solidarity*, 93.

60. D. J. Saposs, "Intellectual Environment of Immigrant Workers in Pittsburgh District," Interchurch World Movement Commission of Inquiry (1919), HBP.

61. Robert Littell, "Under-Cover Men," Interchurch World Movement Commission of Inquiry under supervision of the Bureau of Industrial Research of New York City, HBP.

62. Goldin, "The Political Economy of Immigration Restriction in the United States," in Goldin and Libecap, *The Regulated Economy*, 224.

63. John H. M. Laslett, *Labor and the Left; a Study of Socialist and Radical Influences in the American Labor Movement, 1881–1924* (New York: Basic Books, 1970), 121.

64. Lucas Poy, "The 'World Migration Congress' of 1926 and the Limits of Socialist Internationalism," *Labor* 20, no. 3 (2023): 50, https://doi.org/10.1215/15476715 -10581293.

65. Eric Leif Davin, "Blue Collar Democracy: Ethnic Workers and Class Politics in Pittsburgh's Steel Valley, 1914–1948" (PhD diss., University of Pittsburgh, 1999), 140–42.

66. Goldin, "The Political Economy of Immigration Restriction in the United States," in Goldin and Libecap, *The Regulated Economy*, 226.

67. Goldin, "The Political Economy of Immigration Restriction in the United States," in Goldin and Libecap, *The Regulated Economy*, 239.

68. BFL Meeting Minutes, December 1, 1920. Reel 1.

69. *Thirtieth Annual Report of the Maryland State Board of Labor and Statistics 1921* (Baltimore: Daily Record Company, 1922), 162. MSA 2/7/9/18.

70. "Labor Would Vote 'Reactionaries' Out," *BS*, October 24, 1922.

71. Resolutions Adopted at Fifth Annual Meeting, January 31, February 1 and 2, 1917, Folder "Resolutions 1917–1918," Box 1, USCC.

72. Declarations Adopted at the Eleventh Annual Meeting of the Chamber of Commerce of the United, May 8 to 10, 1923," Folder "Resolutions 1919–1924," Box 1, USCC.

73. Kristofer Allerfeldt, "'And We Got Here First': Albert Johnson, National Origins and Self-Interest in the Immigration Debate of the 1920s," *Journal of Contemporary History* 45, no. 1 (January 1, 2010): 12.

74. Philip Taft, *The A. F. of L. in the Time of Gompers* (New York: Octagon Books, 1957), 308.

75. Allerfeldt, "'And We Got Here First,'" 14.

76. Allerfeldt, "'And We Got Here First,'" 15.

77. Allerfeldt, "'And We Got Here First,'" 18.

78. Allerfeldt, "'And We Got Here First,'" 18.

79. Allerfeldt, "'And We Got Here First,'" 18.

80. PCL, Minutes, January 16, 1930.

81. PCL, Minutes, January 16, 1930.

82. Silver, *Forces of Labor*, 27.

83. Jefferson Cowie, *The Great Exception: The New Deal and the Limits of American Politics* (Princeton: Princeton University Press, 2016), 130–32.

84. Thomas Göbel, "Becoming American: Ethnic Workers and the Rise of the CIO," *Labor History* 29, no. 2 (1988): 174.

85. My deepest thanks to Emilce Baudracco Fabian, my research assistant who helped me to identify and translate the Spanish-language literature used in this section.

86. Nicolás Arceo, Ana L. Fernández, and Mariana L. González, "El mercado de trabajo en el modelo agroexportador en Argentina: el papel de la inmigración," *América Latina en la Historia Económica* 26, no. 3 (2019): e952, https://doi.org/10.18232/alhe.952.

87. Roberto P. Korzeniewicz, "Labor Unrest in Argentina, 1887–1907," *Latin American Research Review* 24, no. 3 (1989): 90–91.

88. Hobsbawm, *Worlds of Labour*, 54.

89. Blanca Sánchez-Alonso, "Making Sense of Immigration Policy: Argentina, 1870–1930," *The Economic History Review* 66, no. 2 (2013): 617; Arceo, Fernández, and González, "El mercado de trabajo en el modelo agroexportador en Argentina," 12–15; and Ruth Mary Thompson, "Organised Labour in Argentina" (PhD diss., University of Oxford, 1979), 12.

90. Thompson, "Organised Labour in Argentina," 19.

91. In the Mendoza region, immigrants occupied the dominant position as landowners and managers, while the native-born population of mixed European and indigenous descent served as agricultural laborers. As Ricardo Salvatore writes, "the arrival of European immigrants accentuated discrimination in favor of immigrants and against Creole workers." See "Control del Trabajo y Discriminación: El Sistema de Contratistas en Mendoza, Argentina, 1880–1920," *Desarrollo Económico* 26, no. 102 (1986): 235, https://doi.org/10.2307/3467032.

92. R. Thompson, "Organised Labour in Argentina," 16.

93. Fernando Devoto, *Historia de la inmigración en la Argentina* (Buenos Aires: Editorial Sudamericana, 2003), 248–49.

94. Blanca Sánchez-Alonso, "La Racionalidad de Las Políticas Migratorias en La

Primera Globalización: El Caso Argentino," *Revista de Instituciones, Ideas y Mercados* 46 (May 2007): 249.

95. Jeremy Adelman, "The Political Economy of Labour in Argentina 1870–1930," in *Essays in Argentine Labour History, 1870–1930*, ed. Jeremy Adelman (London: Palgrave Macmillan UK, 1992), 5.

96. The challenge faced by labor unions and socialist politicians when large sections of the immigrant working class chose to forego naturalization and political participation is explored in Lucas Poy, *El Partido Socialista Argentino* (Santiago: Ariadna Ediciones, 2020), 218.

97. Sánchez-Alonso, "La Racionalidad," 255.

98. Sánchez-Alonso, "La Racionalidad," 236.

99. Eduardo A. Zimmermann, "Racial Ideas and Social Reform: Argentina, 1890–1916," *Hispanic American Historical Review* 72, no. 1 (1992): 37.

100. Colin M. Lewis, "Economic Restructuring and Labour Scarcity: Labour in the 1920s," in *Essays in Argentine Labour History, 1870–1930*, ed. Jeremy Adelman (London: Palgrave Macmillan UK, 1992), 180.

101. National University of Córdoba and National Council for Scientific and Technical Research, "Inmigración, anarquismo y deportación: La criminalización de los extranjeros 'indeseables' en tiempos de las 'grandes migraciones,'" *REMHU: Revista Interdisciplinar Da Mobilidade Humana* 23, no. 45 (2015), https://www.scielo.br/j/remhu/a/Byw45nH6JMGxFmSLfmwCtmn/?lang=es.

102. Sánchez-Alonso, "La Racionalidad," 248, 251.

103. Adelman, "The Political Economy of Labour in Argentina," 21.

104. Fernando J. Devoto, "El Revés de La Trama: Políticas Migratorias y Prácticas Administrativas en La Argentina (1919–1949)," *Desarrollo Económico* 41, no. 162 (2001): 282, https://doi.org/10.2307/3455989.

105. Carolina Biernat, "Las Dos Vías de La Imaginación Poblacionista Argentina: Natalismo e Inmigración Entre 1914 y 1955," *Ciclos En La Historia, La Economia y La Sociedad* 15, no. 30 (2005): 222, http://bibliotecadigital.econ.uba.ar/econ/collection/ciclos/document/ciclos_v15_n30_08.

106. Biernat, "Las Dos Vías," 225.

107. Universidad Museo Social Argentino, *La inmigración después de la guerra* (Buenos Aires: Local social y biblioteca, 1919), vii.

108. Universidad Museo Social Argentino, *La inmigración después de la guerra*, 24.

109. Universidad Museo Social Argentino, *La inmigración después de la guerra*, 25.

110. Universidad Museo Social Argentino, *La inmigración después de la guerra*, 25–26.

111. Universidad Museo Social Argentino, *La inmigración después de la guerra*, 31.

112. Sánchez-Alonso, "La Racionalidad," 254.

113. Sánchez-Alonso, "La Racionalidad," 254.

114. Devoto, "El Revés de La Trama," 283.

115. Devoto, "El Revés de La Trama," 293.

116. Dickerson, *Out of the Crucible*, 79–82.

117. John W. Brown, *World Migration and Labour, Supplemented by Report of World Migration Congress* (Amsterdam: International Federation of Trade Unions, 1926), 17, 19.

118. Walia, *Border & Rule*, 205; Elior Cohen and Jeff Biddle, "Immigration Dis-

ruptions and the Wages of Unskilled Labor in the 1920s," *The Federal Reserve Bank of Kansas City Research Working Papers*, September 27, 2022.

119. Vernon M. Briggs, *Immigration and American Unionism* (Ithaca: Cornell University Press, 2001).

120. Daniel Tichenor, "Nativism and the Bottom Line: Contemporary Legacies of the Immigration Act of 1924," *Labor* 20, no. 4 (2023): 55, https://doi.org/10.1215/15476715-10829157.

Chapter 7

1. "Labour Exiles, South African Leaders in Liverpool," *LDP*, March 16, 1914.

2. Hyslop, "The Imperial Working Class Makes Itself 'White,'" 398–403, quotations from 398–99.

3. This chapter responds to calls for more consideration of political economy and a sense of locality and change over time in interpretations of the British empire; see Richard Price, "One Big Thing: Britain, Its Empire, and Their Imperial Culture," *Journal of British Studies* 45, no. 3 (July 2006): 603–4.

4. Porter has argued, controversially, that empire appeared "only distantly, on the edges of the working classes' perceptions; as someone else's business," and while this reasonably captures the Sheffield experience, issues of empire and racial boundaries resonated much more directly and powerfully in Liverpool. See Bernard Porter, *The Absent-Minded Imperialists: Empire, Society, and Culture in Britain* (Oxford: Oxford University Press, 2004), 225. Class and race were not competing identities or ideologies. Rather, class formation was always implicitly racialized by positions in global capitalism's uneven economic geography. What varied was how relevant, and how explicitly, racial boundary-making appeared for local workers. Thus Neville Kirk's argument that in Britain socialists "asserted the supremacy of class over race and racism" misses the mark by positing class and race as distinct, competing frameworks. See Kirk, *Comrades and Cousins*, 14.

5. Marx, *Karl Marx and Frederick Engels on Britain*, 551.

6. Hobsbawm, *Worlds of Labour*, 51.

7. MacRaild, *Irish Migrants in Modern Britain*, 160–62.

8. Theodore Koditschek, *Liberalism, Imperialism and the Historical Imagination: Nineteenth Century Visions of Greater Britain* (Cambridge: Cambridge University Press, 2011), 327.

9. Lees, *Exiles of Erin*, 54.

10. "Irish Labourers," *SI*, August 13, 1831.

11. "Rotherham—The Railway Men," *SI*, October 20, 1838.

12. "Justice Room, Hemsworth. Disturbance on the North Midland Railway," *SI*, March 7, 1840.

13. "Serious and Alarming Riots on the Chester and Birkenhead Railway," *SI*, October 19, 1839.

14. "Serious and Alarming Riots on the Chester and Birkenhead Railway," *SI*, October 19, 1839.

15. "Riot in South Staffordshire," *SI*, May 15, 1847.

16. "Riot in South Staffordshire," *SI*, May 15, 1847.

17. MacRaild, *Irish Migrants in Modern Britain*, 156.

18. Lees, *Exiles of Erin*, 88, 91–99.

19. MacRaild, *Irish Migrants in Modern Britain*, 49.

20. G. Davis, *The Irish in Britain*, 121.

21. Eric Taplin, "False Dawn of New Unionism? Labour Unrest in Liverpool, 1871–73," in *Popular Politics, Riot and Labour: Essays in Liverpool History, 1790–1940*, ed. John Belcham (Liverpool: Liverpool University Press, 1992), 137.

22. Lees, *Exiles of Erin*, 240–42.

23. O'Day, "Varieties of Anti-Irish Behaviour in Britain," 30.

24. Ingram, "Sectarianism in the North West of England," 281.

25. John Bohstedt, "More Than One Working Class: Protestant-Catholic Riots in Edwardian Liverpool," in Belchem, *Popular Politics, Riot and Labour*, 173–216.

26. Waller, *Democracy and Sectarianism*, 240.

27. Paul Smith, "'A Proud Liverpool Union.' The Liverpool and District Carters' and Motormen's Union, 1889–1946: Ethnicity, Class and Trade-Unionism," *Historical Studies in Industrial Relations*, no. 16 (September 1, 2003): 2.

28. P. Smith, "A Proud Liverpool Union," 5.

29. P. Smith, "A Proud Liverpool Union," 8–9.

30. P. Smith, "A Proud Liverpool Union," 15–16.

31. P. Smith, "A Proud Liverpool Union," 35.

32. P. Smith, "A Proud Liverpool Union," 21.

33. Ingram, "Sectarianism in the North West of England," 281.

34. Ingram, "Sectarianism in the North West of England," 282.

35. Eric Taplin, "The Liverpool General Transport Strike, 1911," *Historical Studies in Industrial Relations*, no. 33 (September 1, 2012): 27.

36. Basil Mogridge, "Militancy and Inter-Union Rivalries in British Shipping, 1911–1929," *International Review of Social History* 6, no. 3 (1961): 382, https://doi.org/10.1017/S0020859000001905.

37. Taplin, "The Liverpool General Transport Strike," 35.

38. Dan Jackson, "'Friends of the Union': Liverpool, Ulster, and Home Rule, 1910–1914," *Transactions of the Historic Society of Lancashire and Cheshire* 152 (2003): 101–29.

39. Waller, *Democracy and Sectarianism*, 207.

40. MacRaild, *Irish Migrants in Modern Britain*, 146.

41. Ingram, "Sectarianism in the North West of England," 145–46.

42. Clegg, *British Trade Unions*, 1:371.

43. Waller, *Democracy and Sectarianism*, 216–17.

44. Waller, *Democracy and Sectarianism*, 233.

45. Laura Tabili, "The Construction of Racial Difference in Twentieth-Century Britain: The Special Restriction (Coloured Alien Seamen) Order, 1925," *Journal of British Studies* 33, no. 1 (1994): 61.

46. Martin J. Daunton, "Jack Ashore: Seamen in Cardiff before 1914," *Welsh History Review* 9, no. 2 (1978): 190.

47. Marika Sherwood, "Race, Nationality and Employment among Lascar Seamen, 1660 to 1945," *Journal of Ethnic and Migration Studies* 17, no. 2 (1991): 231.

48. Sherwood, "Race, Nationality and Employment among Lascar Seamen," 233.

49. Daunton, "Jack Ashore," 191.

50. Tabili, "The Construction of Racial Difference in Twentieth-Century Britain," 63; G. Balachandran, "Workers in the World: Indian Seafarers, c. 1870s–1940s," in *Global Histories of Work*, ed. Andreas Eckert (Berlin: De Gruyter, 2016), 127–31.

51. Daunton, "Jack Ashore," 190, 192.

52. Sherwood, "Race, Nationality and Employment among Lascar Seamen," 234.

53. Diane Frost, *Ethnic Labour and British Imperial Trade: A History of Ethnic Seafarers in the UK* (London: F. Cass, 1995), 26.

54. "Seamen's & Firemen's Conference, The Manning of British Ships," *Liverpool Daily Post*, October 7, 1907.

55. "Seamen's & Firemen's Conference, The Manning of British Ships," *Liverpool Daily Post*, October 7, 1907.

56. For the racialized and national limits of European "internationalism," see Poy, "The 'World Migration Congress' of 1926 and the Limits of Socialist Internationalism," 55.

57. "Colonial Conference. India Opposes Protection, Botha speaks for Freedom," *Liverpool Daily Post*, May 3, 1907; "Asiatics and British Ships," *Liverpool Journal of Commerce*, July 24, 1908.

58. "Shipping Laws. Dominions and Indian Immigration," *Liverpool Echo*, June 20, 1911.

59. "Shipping Laws. Dominions and Indian Immigration," *Liverpool Echo*, June 20, 1911.

60. Hyslop, "The Imperial Working Class Makes Itself 'White,'" 59.

61. "The Yellow Man as Sailor," *Syren and Shipping Illustrated*, March 25, 1908, 390.

62. Kenneth Lunn, "The Seamen's Union and 'Foreign' Workers on British and Colonial Shipping, 1890–1939," *Bulletin—Society for the Study of Labour History* 53, no. 3 (Winter 1988): 5.

63. Lunn, "The Seamen's Union," 5.

64. Hyslop, "The Imperial Working Class Makes Itself 'White,'" 61.

65. Lunn, "The Seamen's Union," 10.

66. Tabili, "The Construction of Racial Difference in Twentieth-Century Britain," 64.

67. Lunn, "The Seamen's Union," 6.

68. Frost, *Ethnic Labour and British Imperial Trade*, 32.

69. J. Jenkinson, "The 1919 Race Riots in Britain: Their Background and Consequences" (PhD diss., University of Edinburgh, 1987), 2–3.

70. Jenkinson, "The 1919 Race Riots in Britain," 164.

71. Roy May and Robin Cohen, "The Interaction Between Race and Colonialism: A Case Study of the Liverpool Race Riots of 1919," *Race and Class* 16, no. 2 (1974): 114.

72. Jenkinson, "The 1919 Race Riots in Britain," 172.

73. May and Cohen, "The Interaction Between Race and Colonialism," 118.

74. Daunton, "Jack Ashore," 195.

75. Sherwood, "Race, Nationality and Employment among Lascar Seamen," 234.

76. Linda May Grant, "Women Workers and the Sexual Division of Labour: Liverpool, 1890–1939" (PhD diss., University of Liverpool, 1987), 266; Eunjae Park, "British Labour Party's Patriotic Politics on Immigration and Race, 1900–1968" (PhD diss., University of York, 2017), 78, 97–98, 104–5, https://etheses.whiterose.ac.uk/20520/.

77. Neville Kirk, "Labour and Empire: Australia and Britain from the Late Nineteenth Century to the Inter-War Years," in *The British Labour Movement and Imperialism*, ed. Billy Frank, Craig Horner, and David Stewart (Newcastle upon Tyne: Cambridge Scholars Publishing, 2010), 41–64; Kirk, *Comrades and Cousins*, 7.

78. The remainder were classed as semi-skilled. See David Pope and Glenn Withers,

"Wage Effects of Immigration in Late-Nineteenth Century Australia," in *Migration and the International Labor Market, 1850–1939*, ed. T. J. Hatton and Jeffrey G. Williamson (New York: Routledge, 1994), 257.

79. Gary Cross, "Labour in Settler-State Democracies: Comparative Perspectives on Australia and the US, 1860–1920," *Labour History*, no. 70 (May 1, 1996): 18, https://doi.org/10.2307/27516407.

80. Cross, "Labour in Settler-State Democracies," 9.

81. Ngai, *The Chinese Question*, 164.

82. Ann Curthoys, "Conflict and Consensus," *Labour History*, no. 35 (November 1978): 48–65.

83. Curthoys, "Conflict and Consensus," 49.

84. Curthoys, "Conflict and Consensus," 58.

85. Curthoys, "Conflict and Consensus," 59.

86. Curthoys, "Conflict and Consensus," 59.

87. Curthoys, "Conflict and Consensus," 60.

88. Curthoys, "Conflict and Consensus," 62.

89. Curthoys, "Conflict and Consensus," 64.

90. Ray Markey, "Explaining Union Mobilisation in the 1880s and Early 1900s," *Labour History*, no. 83 (November 1, 2002): 20–22; and Mark Hearn and Harry Knowles, *One Big Union: A History of the Australian Workers Union, 1886–1994* (Cambridge: Cambridge University Press, 1996), 79.

91. Hearn and Knowles, *One Big Union*, 43.

92. Hearn and Knowles, *One Big Union*, 43.

93. Markey, "Explaining Union Mobilisation in the 1880s and Early 1900s," 27.

94. Arthur McIvor and Christopher Wright, "Managing Labour: UK and Australian Employers in Comparative Perspective, 1900–50," *Labour History*, no. 88 (May 1, 2005): 45–62. Archer stresses employer hostility in the US compared to Australia in determining the survival of New Unionism in *Why Is There No Labor Party in the United States?*

95. Hearn and Knowles, *One Big Union*, 67.

96. Hearn and Knowles, *One Big Union*, 67.

97. Hearn and Knowles, *One Big Union*, 68.

98. Alan Fenna, "Putting the 'Australian Settlement' in Perspective," *Labour History*, no. 102 (May 2012): 99–118.

99. Markey, "Explaining Union Mobilisation in the 1880s and Early 1900s," 27, 30.

100. Bain, *Profiles of Union Growth*, 171.

101. Barry York, "White Australia and the Dictation Test," *Voices: The Quarterly Journal of the National Library of Australia* 6, no. 3 (1996): 27–36.

102. Jeremy Martens, "A Transnational History of Immigration Restriction: Natal and New South Wales, 1896–97," *The Journal of Imperial and Commonwealth History* 34, no. 3 (2006): 324, 333–34.

103. Hearn and Knowles, *One Big Union*, 11.

104. Hearn and Knowles, *One Big Union*, 66.

105. Hearn and Knowles, *One Big Union*, 67.

106. Hearn and Knowles, *One Big Union*, 142.

107. Hearn and Knowles, *One Big Union*, 143.

108. Lenore Layman, "'To Keep up the Australian Standard': Regulating Contract Labour Migration, 1901–50," *Labour History*, no. 70 (1996): 26–35.

109. Carolyn Holbrook, "The Transformation of Labor Party Immigration Policy, 1901–1945," *Journal of Australian Studies* 40, no. 4 (2016): 407.

110. Holbrook, "The Transformation of Labor Party Immigration Policy," 408.

111. Holbrook, "The Transformation of Labor Party Immigration Policy," 409.

112. Michele Langfield, "'White Aliens': The Control of European Immigration to Australia, 1920–30," *Journal of Intercultural Studies* 12, no. 2 (1991): 1–14.

113. Hearn and Knowles, *One Big Union*, 143.

114. Loretta Baldassar, "Italian Migrants in Australia and Their Relationship to Italy: Return Visits, Transnational Caregiving and the Second Generation," *Journal of Mediterranean Studies* 20, no. 2 (2011): 258.

115. Kirk, *Comrades and Cousins*, 77.

116. Peter Alexander, "Race, Class Loyalty and the Structure of Capitalism: Coal Miners in Alabama and the Transvaal, 1918–1922," *Journal of Southern African Studies* 30, no. 1 (2004): 129.

117. Alexander, "Race, Class Loyalty and the Structure of Capitalism," 131–32.

118. Pieter Van Duin, "White Building Workers and Coloured Competition in the South African Labour Market, c. 1890–1940," *International Review of Social History* 37, no. 1 (1992): 59–90.

119. Mats Lundahl and Daniel B. Ndlela, "Land Alienation, Dualism, and Economic Discrimination: South Africa and Rhodesia," *Economy and History* 23, no. 2 (1980): 106–32.

120. Arthur T. Guttery, "An Imperial Scandal," *Sheffield Independent*, July 21, 1914.

121. Alan Jeeves, *Migrant Labour in South Africa's Mining Economy: The Struggle for the Gold Mines' Labour Supply, 1890–1920* (Kingston: McGill-Queen's University Press, 1985), ix.

122. Elaine N. Katz, "Revisiting the Origins of the Industrial Colour Bar in the Witwatersrand Gold Mining Industry, 1891–1899," *Journal of Southern African Studies* 25, no. 1 (1999): 84–85.

123. E. Katz, "Revisiting the Origins of the Industrial Colour Bar," 91; John Higginson, "Privileging the Machines: American Engineers, Indentured Chinese and White Workers in South Africa's Deep-Level Gold Mines, 1902–1907," *International Review of Social History* 52, no. 1 (2007): 15; and Karen Harris, "The 1907 Strike: A Watershed in South African White Miner Trade Unionism," *Kleio* 23, no. 1 (January 1991): 32–51.

124. Colin Bundy, *The Rise and Fall of the South African Peasantry* (Cape Town: David Philip, 1988), 114, https://hdl.handle.net/2027/heb.02568.

125. Bundy, *The Rise and Fall of the South African Peasantry*, 116, 122–25, 135–38.

126. Bundy, *The Rise and Fall of the South African Peasantry*, 207–8.

127. Gary Kynoch, "Controlling the Coolies: Chinese Mineworkers and the Struggle for Labor in South Africa, 1904–1910," *The International Journal of African Historical Studies* 36, no. 2 (2003): 311. Throughout the early twentieth century, "land hunger was an absolutely central feature of black rural consciousness" in South Africa. After interviewing native leaders, one government official reported: "Great question is land, as the Natives have to roam from farm to farm . . . don't understand buying land, consider the country theirs." Quoted in Helen Bradford, *A Taste of Freedom: The ICU in Rural South Africa, 1924–1930* (New Haven: Yale University Press, 1987), 34.

128. Higginson, "Privileging the Machines," 15.

129. Mae M. Ngai, "Trouble on the Rand: The Chinese Question in South Africa

and the Apogee of White Settlerism," *International Labor and Working-Class History* 91 (2017): 59–60.

130. Ngai, "Trouble on the Rand," 60.

131. Jeeves, *Migrant Labour in South Africa's Mining Economy*, 30.

132. Ngai, "Trouble on the Rand."

133. Harris, "The 1907 Strike."

134. Harris, "The 1907 Strike," 44–45.

135. Elaine N. Katz, "The Underground Route to Mining: Afrikaners and the Witwatersrand Gold Mining Industry from 1902 to the 1907 Miners' Strike," *The Journal of African History* 36, no. 3 (1995): 467–89.

136. Jeeves, *Migrant Labour in South Africa's Mining Economy*, 69.

137. Jeeves, *Migrant Labour in South Africa's Mining Economy*, 70–71.

138. Jeeves, *Migrant Labour in South Africa's Mining Economy*, 71.

139. Bundy, *The Rise and Fall of the South African Peasantry*, 136–37, 212.

140. Bundy, *The Rise and Fall of the South African Peasantry*, 213.

141. Bundy, *The Rise and Fall of the South African Peasantry*, 240–43.

142. Jeeves, *Migrant Labour in South Africa's Mining Economy*, 3.

143. Alexander, "Race, Class Loyalty and the Structure of Capitalism," 120.

144. T. Dunbar Moodie, "Maximum Average Violence: Underground Assaults on the South African Gold Mines, 1913–1965," *Journal of Southern African Studies* 31, no. 3 (2005): 547–67. However, with the exception of the 1922 Rand Revolt, mass public violence against black Africans in South Africa was comparatively rare in contrast to the bloody "lynch culture" of the United States. A centralized state in South Africa, unambiguously committed to white supremacy, produced a "bureaucratic tradition" of racial violence, whereas in the US, white supremacy could not be as openly enforced by state authorities, and thus the informal politics of "lynch culture" predominated. See Ivan Evans, *Cultures of Violence: Lynching and Racial Killing in South Africa and the American South* (Manchester: Manchester University Press, 2009).

145. William H. Worger, "Convict Labour, Industrialists and the State in the US South and South Africa, 1870–1930," *Journal of Southern African Studies* 30, no. 1 (2004): 63–86.

146. Frederick A. Johnstone, *Class, Race, and Gold: A Study of Class Relations and Racial Discrimination in South Africa* (London: Routledge & K. Paul, 1976), 169–85.

147. Keith Breckenridge, "'We Must Speak for Ourselves': The Rise and Fall of a Public Sphere on the South African Gold Mines, 1920 to 1931," *Comparative Studies in Society and History* 40, no. 1 (1998): 73.

148. Jonathan Hyslop, "Scottish Labour, Race, and Southern African Empire c. 1880–1922: A Reply to Kenefick," *International Review of Social History* 55, no. 1 (2010): 75, https://doi.org/10.1017/S0020859009990629.

149. Baruch Hirson, "The General Strike of 1922," 3, no. 3 (1993): 69.

150. Breckenridge, "'We Must Speak for Ourselves,'" 76.

151. Breckenridge, "'We Must Speak for Ourselves,'" 84–85.

152. Hirson, "The General Strike of 1922," 72.

153. Bradford, *A Taste of Freedom*, 8–9.

154. Lucien Van Der Walt, "The First Globalisation and Transnational Labour Activism in Southern Africa: White Labourism, the IWW, and the ICU, 1904–1934," *African Studies* 66, no. 2–3 (2007): 238–40.

155. Hirson, "The General Strike of 1922," 74.

156. Keith Breckenridge, "Fighting for a White South Africa: White Working-Class Racism and the 1922 Rand Revolt," *South African Historical Journal* 57, no. 1 (2007): 236, https://doi.org/10.1080/02582470709464719.

157. Breckenridge, "Fighting for a White South Africa," 238.

158. Coleman, "Returning to the Rand Revolt," 89. A recent account of the strike has depicted the racial violence as a "hysteria" that broke with the larger structural conflicts at hand: Jeremy Krikler, "Lost Causes of the Rand Revolt," *South African Historical Journal* 63, no. 2 (2011): 328. However, as a critic has responded, the "major strand of the 1922 strike was a deliberate, violent assault on the political organization of their African working-class peers"; see Breckenridge, "Fighting for a White South Africa," 230.

159. Daniel Coleman, "Returning to the Rand Revolt: Centering Settler Colonialism and Racial Capitalism in Labour History" (MA thesis, University of Cape Town, 2021), 88.

160. Breckenridge, "Fighting for a White South Africa," 242–43.

161. Curiously, Alex Lichtenstein, in a compelling study of the resurgence of black militancy in both countries during the 1940s, seems to have missed this parallel in terms of the exemptions in the coverage of the NLRA when he writes that "the legal barriers to African trade unionism had no counterpart in the United States." See "'The Hope for White and Black'? Race, Labour and the State in South Africa and the United States, 1924–1956," *Journal of Southern African Studies* 30, no. 1 (2004): 136.

162. Duncan Money and Danelle van Zyl-Hermann, "Revisiting White Labourism: New Debates on Working-Class Whiteness in Twentieth-Century Southern Africa," *International Review of Social History* 66, no. 3 (2021): 480, https://doi.org/10.1017/S0020859021000407.

163. Money and van Zyl-Hermann, "Revisiting White Labourism," 480.

164. Yann Béliard, "Imperial Internationalism? Hull Labour's Support for South African Trade-Unionism on the Eve of the Great War," *Labour History Review* 74, no. 3 (2009): 325.

165. Béliard, "Imperial Internationalism?," 327.

166. "Native Labour in South Africa," *LDP*, August 22, 1902.

167. "Chinese Labour Debate," *LDP*, February 18, 1904.

168. "Labour Troubles on the Rand," *LDP*, May 7, 1907; "Popularising Minework among the Natives," *LDP*, May 8, 1907; "House of Commons," *LDP*, May 9, 1907; "The Rand Miners' Strike, Secret Voting," *LDP*, May 11, 1907; "From Our London Correspondent," *LDP*, May 21, 1907; "Rand Mine Strikes," *LDP*, May 23, 1907; "Rand Miners' Strike," *LDP*, May 24, 1907; "White and Black Labour on the Rand," *Liverpool Daily Post*, December 27, 1909; "Future of South Africa," *Liverpool Echo*, September 27, 1909; and "Notes from Greater Britain," *Liverpool Daily Post*, September 19, 1913.

169. "Shall White Labour be Eliminated?," *LDP*, May 27, 1907. The more trade-union friendly *Echo* carried the same article under a different headline: "Labour Sympathy in Cape Colony," *Liverpool Echo*, May 25, 1907.

170. "Shall White Labour be Eliminated?," *LDP*, May 27, 1907.

171. Letter from J. W. Broomhead, Wembury, Gunnersburgy W., "The Future of the Transvaal Goldfields," *LDP*, June 28, 1907.

172. After the strike, J. B. Robinson expressed confidence in expanding the supply of African labor to the mines; see "Briton and Boer. South Africa's Promising Future, Mining Magnates Optimism," *SI*, October 15, 1907.

173. "The Rand Strike," *SI*, May 27, 1907; "The Rand Strike," *SDT*, May 27, 1907; "The Rand's Future. Africa Not a White Man's Country," *Sheffield Daily Telegraph*, March 20, 1908; "Poverty in Gold-Land," *Sheffield Evening Telegraph*, July 13, 1908.

174. "White Labour in South Africa," *Sheffield Daily Telegraph*, August 16, 1907.

175. "South Africa Bill," *LDP*, August 6, 1909.

176. "Rights of Natives. Commons & South African Union," *Sheffield Independent*, August 20, 1909.

177. "Rights of Natives. Commons & South African Union," *Sheffield Independent*, August 20, 1909.

178. "South African Union. Wesleyans and the Colour Bar," *Sheffield Independent*, September 20, 1909.

179. "A Fight For Freedom," *Sheffield Guardian*, August 27, 1909, Sheffield Local Archives.

180. Ambrose Pratt, *The Real South Africa* (London: Holden & Hardingham, 1913).

181. Pratt, *The Real South Africa*, 16–17.

182. Pratt, *The Real South Africa*, 56.

183. Pratt, *The Real South Africa*, 57.

184. Stephen Constantine, "British Emigration to the Empire-Commonwealth since 1880: From Overseas Settlement to Diaspora?," *The Journal of Imperial and Commonwealth History* 31, no. 2 (2003): 16–35. The South African experience, via Lord Milner, would prove crucial for the postwar Oversea Settlement Committee, although the question of whether South Africa was a "fit" destination for white men remained contentious; see Dane Kennedy, "Empire Migration in Post-War Reconstruction: The Role of the Oversea Settlement Committee, 1919–1922," *Albion: A Quarterly Journal Concerned with British Studies* 20, no. 3 (1988): 403–19.

185. "Real South Africa. Vivid Book on the Black Menace," *Sheffield Daily Telegraph*, July 25, 1913.

186. "The Real South Africa," *LDP*, August 22, 1913.

187. "The Life of An Empire," *Liverpool Daily Post*, February 27, 1907.

188. "The Briton Abroad: White and Black in South Africa," *Sheffield Weekly Telegraph*, August 15, 1913.

189. "Labour Party's Difficulty," *LDP*, February 2, 1914; "Future of Deported Leaders," *LDP*, February 26, 1914; "Labour's Welcome to Deportees," *LDP*, February 28, 1914; "The Labour Crisis in South Africa," January 12, 1914; "Labour's Welcome to Deportees," *Liverpool Echo*, February 28, 1914; "Deportees' Visit," *Liverpool Echo*, March 16, 1914; "The Nine Exiles," *Sheffield Independent*, March 2, 1914; "Nine Lions of Labour," *Sheffield Daily Telegraph*, February 23, 1914.

190. "An Object-Lesson," *Sheffield Daily Telegraph*, February 13, 1914. Two weeks prior, the Liberal paper had already anticipated and critiqued this line of argument; see "The Outlook," *Sheffield Independent*, January 30, 1914. In Manchester, a Conservative paper also made the connection in terms of parallel uprisings of irresponsible labor leaders: "It is a far cry from Dublin to the Transvaal, but there is no doubt in the minds of thoughtful people that the distorted ideas of a few extreme Labour leaders are responsible for the disputes in both places"; see "Unrest in South Africa," *Manchester Courier and Lancashire General Advertiser*, January 12, 1914.

191. "South African Deportees in Derby," *Derby Daily Telegraph*, March 28, 1914.

192. Henry J. Phillip, "Labour Victories in the Transvaal," *Sheffield Independent*, April 15, 1914.

193. "Political Power," *Sheffield Independent*, March 2, 1914. The limits of syndicalism as a labor movement strategy were also covered in Liverpool: "Labour Party's Difficulty," *LDP*, February 2, 1914. In the Southwest, the *Western Gazette* argued that the "white worker in South Africa is learning to his cost the blighting influence which Syndicalism brings in its train": "Syndicalism's Curse," *Western Gazette* [Yeovil, England], March 20, 1914.

194. Philip Snowden, MP, "From Labour's Standpoint," *Sheffield Guardian*, March 6, 1914.

195. Searcher, "Life and Labour," *Sheffield Guardian*, January 23, 1914.

196. Searcher, "Life and Labour," *Sheffield Guardian*, January 30, 1914.

197. Searcher, "Life and Labour," *Sheffield Guardian*, January 30, 1914; "Current Events," *Sheffield Guardian*, February 20, 1914; "Current Events," *Sheffield Guardian*, February 27, 1914.

198. "Current Events," *Sheffield Guardian*, February 20, 1914.

199. Philip Snowden, MP, "From Labour's Standpoint," *Sheffield Guardian*, March 6, 1914.

200. "Racialism in South Africa," *Liverpool Echo*, February 21, 1914.

201. "The Deported Leaders," *Liverpool Echo*, March 7, 1914.

202. "Deportees' Visit," *Liverpool Echo*, March 16, 1914.

203. "Labour Exiles, South African Leaders in Liverpool," *LDP*, March 16, 1914.

204. The sharp contrast between maritime Liverpool and industrial Sheffield seems to apply to Britain more broadly, with South African racial hierarchies resonating most clearly in Scottish ports and the southwestern mining districts that supplied a large share of emigrants to South Africa. When the South African tour came to Derby, an interior industrial city comparable to Sheffield, none of the racial context of the South African labor movement came forward. Instead, the South African leaders attempted to elide the differences. "He was asked many times in England what had caused the unrest in South Africa. He might answer that by asking another question, namely, what caused the unrest in England? Was it not because they were trying to have a better time and to share more fully in the pleasures of life. [Conditions in South Africa] were not properly understood by the people of Great Britain" ("South African Deportees in Derby," *Derby Daily Telegraph*, March 28, 1914). In contrast, in the mining districts of Cornwall and the port cities of Scotland, the racial stakes of the South African strike were clearly understood and discussed: "What we fear is that the position of the whites will be worse now than it was before" ("South Africa," *Western Times*, January 17, 1914). See also "Deported Labourist Describes Churchill as Fossilised Brains of Eleventh Century at Demonstration in Dundee," *Dundee Courier*, April 23, 1914; and "South African Deportees at Penzance," *Cornishman*, April 30, 1914. More broadly, "South Africa in A.D. 2010. A Professor's Conclusions. No Room for Whites," *Cornishman* [Penzance], December 22, 1910; "Native Labour in South Africa," *Aberdeen Journal*, January 19, 1911; "White v. Black Labour in South Africa," *Aberdeen Journal*, February 18, 1913; and "The Real South Africa," *Dundee Courier*, October 8, 1913.

205. "Rand Strike," *LDP*, January 6, 1922; "General Smuts and Rand Strike," *LDP*, February 23, 1922; "South Africa's Labour Troubles," *Sheffield Daily Telegraph*, December 30, 1921; and "The Rand Strike," *Sheffield Daily Telegraph*, February 8, 1922.

206. "The Colour Bar, Threatened Trouble on the Rand," *Sheffield Daily Telegraph*, November 7, 1921.

207. "Rand Mining Trouble, The Chamber of Mines the Colour Bar," *Sheffield Daily Telegraph*, January 10, 1922.

208. "The Rand War," *Liverpool Echo*, March 13, 1922.

209. "The Rand Civil War," *LDP*, March 13, 1922.

210. "Cape Mail Train Derailed," *Liverpool Echo*, March 10, 1922.

211. "The Riddle of the Rand: Psychology of the South African Miner by One Who Knows Him," *Sheffield Independent*, March 24, 1922.

212. Arthur T. Guttery, "An Imperial Scandal," *Sheffield Independent*, July 21, 1914.

213. "The Colour Bar," *Sheffield Independent*, December 28, 1918; and "Kaffirs Still Hoping for Relief," *Sheffield Independent*, June 3, 1919.

214. "South Africa's Peril," *Sheffield Daily Telegraph*, October 27, 1920.

215. "Race Problems. Colour Bar Creating a Serious Situation," *Sheffield Independent*, October 8, 1921.

216. "Racial Prejudice. The Labour Colour Bar in South Africa," *Sheffield Daily Telegraph*, October 8, 1921.

217. Basil Matthews, "Solution to the Race Problem," *Sheffield Independent*, November 6, 1926.

218. "Black—and White. Racial Problems Discussed in Sheffield," *Sheffield Independent*, October 1. 1929. A number of other Rotary clubs also hosted discussions of the South African racial and industrial situation in the late 1920s; see "Native Problem in South Africa. Missionary's Address to Dundee Rotarians," *Evening Telegraph* [Dundee] January 27, 1927; and "Colour Problem in South Africa," *Aberdeen Journal*, February 4, 1927.

219. "South African Immigration," *Liverpool Journal of Commerce*, August 12, 1925. See also "Chat on 'Change South African Recovery," *Liverpool Journal of Commerce*, October 22, 1928. Once again, greater understanding and support for white South African workers appears in maritime Scotland and the mining southwest during the 1920s. See "South Africa Note For Whites," *Cornishman* [Penzance], March 7, 1923; "South Africa Menace. General Hertzog and Native Labour," *Aberdeen Journal*, October 19, 1923; and "Black and White," *Aberdeen Journal*, September 30, 1924.

Part 3

1. Alfred Williams, *Life in a Railway Factory* (Library of Alexandria, 1915), 311.

2. McKiven, *Iron and Steel*; David R. Roediger and Elizabeth D. Esch, *The Production of Difference: Race and the Management of Labor in U.S. History* (New York: Oxford University Press, 2012); David Montgomery, *The Fall of the House of Labor: The Workplace, the State, and American Labor Activism, 1865–1925* (Cambridge: Cambridge University Press, 1989).

3. This Du Bois passage explains the "psychological wage of whiteness," which in the original formulation was a collective, socially defined status, not an individualized, intellectualized experience.

4. In the US, see Lizabeth Cohen, *Making a New Deal: Industrial Workers in Chicago, 1919–1939* (Cambridge: Cambridge University Press, 1991); Kathy Lee Peiss, *Cheap Amusements: Working Women and Leisure in Turn-of-the-Century New York* (Philadelphia: Temple University Press, 1986); Nan Enstad, *Ladies of Labor, Girls of Adventure: Working Women, Popular Culture, and Labor Politics at the Turn of the Twentieth Century* (New York: Columbia University Press, 1999). In the UK, see Ross

McKibbin, *The Evolution of the Labour Party, 1910–1924* (Oxford: Oxford University Press, 1974); Ross McKibbin, *The Ideologies of Class: Social Relations in Britain, 1880–1950* (Oxford: Clarendon Press, 1990); Ross McKibbin, *Classes and Cultures: England, 1918–1951* (Oxford: Oxford University Press, 1998).

5. Richard Harris and Robert Lewis, "The Geography of North American Cities and Suburbs, 1900–1950: A New Synthesis," *Journal of Urban History* 27, no. 3 (2001): 272–73.

6. Suggesting a transition from a "politics of property" in the nineteenth century to a "politics of income" in the twentieth century, see Jonathan Levy, *Ages of American Capitalism: A History of the United States* (New York: Random House, 2021); Lawrence B. Glickman, *A Living Wage: American Workers and the Making of Consumer Society* (Ithaca, NY: Cornell University Press, 1997); Richard Price, *Masters, Unions, and Men: Work Control in Building and the Rise of Labour, 1830–1914* (Cambridge: Cambridge University Press, 1980).

7. Cybelle Fox, *Three Worlds of Relief: Race, Immigration, and the American Welfare State from the Progressive Era to the New Deal* (Princeton: Princeton University Press, 2012); Andreas Wimmer, *Nationalist Exclusion and Ethnic Conflict: Shadows of Modernity* (Cambridge: Cambridge University Press, 2002); Torpey, *The Invention of the Passport.*

Chapter 8

1. "Sees Homes as Cure: Banker Declares Owner-Workers Not Inclined to Radicalism," *Baltimore Sun*, September 30, 1919.

2. Rather than consumption redefining the "polity and society" in the 1930s and 1940s, as with Agnew and Cohen, this analysis roots the remaking of the working class in the industrial suburb, and thus suggests that these processes were well under way by the 1880s and fully articulated by the 1920s. Certainly, it was only in the 1950s that aspirations would become reality for most (in the US, white) working-class households. See Jean-Christophe Agnew, "Coming up for Air: Consumer Culture in Historical Perspective," in *Consumption and the World of Goods* (London: Routledge, 1994); Cohen, *Making a New Deal*; Lizabeth Cohen, *A Consumers' Republic: The Politics of Mass Consumption in Postwar America* (New York: Knopf, 2003). My chronology is more in line with that suggested by Livingston, who argues that the 1920s were the "first decade in which consumer demand for new durables—autos, radios, refrigerators, vacuums, washing machines—became the driving force of economic growth," and was "the first decade in which inherited habits of household thrift and saving disappeared and borrowing to buy what you needed became normal." See James Livingston, *Against Thrift: Why Consumer Culture Is Good for the Economy, the Environment, and Your Soul* (New York: Basic Books, 2011), 53. In perhaps the most helpful review of the complicated politics of consumers' role in capitalism, Hilton notes that the left has too often offered an "ascetic, if not downright miserable, retreat from the life of material abundance." See Matthew Hilton, *Consumerism in Twentieth-Century Britain: The Search for a Historical Movement* (Cambridge: Cambridge University Press, 2003), 4–17.

3. Carl H. Nightingale, "The Transnational Contexts of Early Twentieth-Century American Urban Segregation," *Journal of Social History* 39, no. 3 (2006): 668; Carl H. Nightingale, *Segregation: A Global History of Divided Cities* (Chicago: The University of Chicago Press, 2012).

4. Gabriel Winant, *The Next Shift: The Fall of Industry and the Rise of Health Care in Rust Belt America* (Cambridge: Harvard University Press, 2021), 67.

5. This is for households with income between $25,000 and $50,000; see Jung Hyun Choi, "Breaking Down the Black-White Homeownership Gap," The Urban Institute, February 21, 2020, https://www.urban.org/urban-wire/breaking-down-black-white -homeownership-gap.

6. Edward K. Muller and Paul A. Groves, "The Emergence of Industrial Districts in Mid-Nineteenth-Century Baltimore," in Lewis, *Manufacturing Suburbs*, 52.

7. Harris and Lewis, "The Geography of North American Cities and Suburbs," 265, 268.

8. Edward K. Muller, "Industrial Suburbs and the Growth of Metropolitan Pittsburgh, 1870–1920," in Lewis, *Manufacturing Suburbs*.

9. Muller, "Industrial Suburbs," in Lewis, *Manufacturing Suburbs*.

10. Muller, "Industrial Suburbs," in Lewis, *Manufacturing Suburbs*, 130–31.

11. W. Edward Orser, "The Making of a Baltimore Rowhouse Community: The Edmondson Avenue Area, 1915–1945," *Maryland Historical Magazine* 80, no. 3 (1980): 215–18.

12. Personnel Department, "Annual Report B," January 1, 1921, Box 1, USSNDW.

13. June 8, 1890, Director's Minute Book No. 1, MD3169–5, EASC.

14. Report of the President to the Board of Directors of the Jones & Laughlin Steel Company, 1907 partial fiscal year. Folder "Jones & Laughlin Steel Company Annual Stockholders' Meetings 1908 to 1922," JL.

15. William Larimer Jones, Vice President and General Manager, Report to the Stockholders of the Jones and Laughlin Steel Company for the Year 1909, 13. Folder, "Jones & Laughlin Steel Company Annual Stockholders' Meetings 1908 to 1922," JL.

16. "Scunthorpe Housing," Report to the Board, November 22, 1920. 1/2/1/10/1 JB.

17. C. W. D. Townsend, Memorandum. Scunthorpe Works, Works Committee Reports, April 4, 1919. 1/4/1/2/4 JB.

18. "Scunthorpe Housing," Report to the Board, November 22, 1920. 1/2/1/10/1 JB.

19. "Duquesne Light Co. to Build Workers' Homes," *The Pittsburgh Press*, November 14, 1922.

20. "After Their Rights. Public Meeting of Colored People to Protest Against Discrimination" April 21, 1891; "Color Line at Home," *Pittsburgh Daily Post*, April 22, 1891.

21. Jeffrey Snedden, "Histories & Mysteries: Aliquippa emerges from its fiery beginnings to represent the American Dream," *Beaver County Times*, August 11, 2020, https://www.timesonline.com/story/lifestyle/around-town/2020/08/11/histories -mysteries-aliquippa-emerges-from-its-fiery-beginnings-to-represent-american -dream/42201879.

22. Kenneth M. Casebeer, "Aliquippa: The Company Town and Contested Power in the Construction of Law," *Buffalo Law Review* 43 (1995): 643–44.

23. "George Alex Dominic Oral History," 4. Box 2, Folder 48. BVLHSC.

24. "Clark Cobb Oral History," 7–8. Box 2, Folder 42. BVLHSC.

25. "Material For Study for Annual Meeting," undated FF2 Board Correspondence 1923–1925, Box 1, PUL.

26. Peter Scott, *The Making of the Modern British Home: The Suburban Semi and Family Life between the Wars* (Oxford: Oxford University Press, 2013), 6.

27. I Scott, *The Making of the Modern British Home*, 10.

28. Scott, *The Making of the Modern British Home*, 1.

29. Scott, *The Making of the Modern British Home*, 37–38.

30. Scott, *The Making of the Modern British Home*, 41.

31. Scott, *The Making of the Modern British Home*, 43–44.

32. Scott, *The Making of the Modern British Home*, 50, 43.

33. Scott, *The Making of the Modern British Home*, 57.

34. Scott, *The Making of the Modern British Home*, 66.

35. Scott, *The Making of the Modern British Home*, 66.

36. Madeline McKenna, "Municipal Suburbia in Liverpool, 1919–1939," *The Town Planning Review* 60, no. 3 (1989): 304.

37. John Bohstedt, "More than One Working Class: Protestant-Catholic Riots in Edwardian Liverpool," in Belchem, *Popular Politics, Riot and Labour*, 199.

38. Jenkins, "Nationalism and Sectarian Violence in Liverpool and Belfast," 172.

39. David M. P. Freund, *Colored Property: State Policy and White Racial Politics in Suburban America* (Chicago: University of Chicago Press, 2010); and Cohen, *A Consumers' Republic*.

40. Niedt, "The Politics of Prosperity and Crisis in an Industrial Suburb," 15–16.

41. Niedt, "The Politics of Prosperity and Crisis in an Industrial Suburb," 23–24.

42. Niedt, "The Politics of Prosperity and Crisis in an Industrial Suburb," 24.

43. "Sale at Dundalk Soon: 531 Homes to be put on Housing Market," *Baltimore Sun*, November 26, 1919.

44. "Shipyard Needs Homes," *Baltimore Sun*, December 12, 1919.

45. Other cities soon followed Baltimore's example, including Richmond, Norfolk, Roanoke, and Portsmouth, VA, Winston-Salem, NC, Greenville, SC, Birmingham, AL, Atlanta, GA, Louisville, KY, St. Louis, MO, Oklahoma City, OK, New Orleans, LA, Indianapolis, IN, and Dallas, TX. See Antero Pietila, *Not in My Neighborhood: How Bigotry Shaped a Great American City* (Chicago: Ivan R. Dee, 2010), 23–24.

46. Elizabeth A. Herbin-Triant, *Threatening Property: Race, Class, and Campaigns to Legislate Jim Crow Neighborhoods* (New York: Columbia University Press, 2019), 6, 12, 124–25.

47. Garrett Power, "Apartheid Baltimore Style: The Residential Segregation Ordinances of 1910–1913," *Maryland Law Review* 42 (1983): 298–299.

48. Power, "Apartheid Baltimore Style," 289.

49. Paige Glotzer, *How the Suburbs Were Segregated: Developers and the Business of Exclusionary Housing, 1890–1960* (New York: Columbia University Press, 2020), 50–54, 89, 96, 126.

50. Niedt, "The Politics of Prosperity and Crisis in an Industrial Suburb," 59–60.

51. Niedt, "The Politics of Prosperity and Crisis in an Industrial Suburb," 61.

52. Niedt, "The Politics of Prosperity and Crisis in an Industrial Suburb," 26, 50.

53. Andrew J. Cherlin, "'Good, Better, Best': Upward Mobility and Loss of Community in a Black Steelworker Neighborhood," *Du Bois Review* 17, no. 2 (2020): 213, http://dx.doi.org/10.1017/S1742058X20000284.

54. Niedt, "The Politics of Prosperity and Crisis in an Industrial Suburb," 80, 77.

55. S. M. R., "Home Shortage Ally of Radical Unrest," *Baltimore Sun*, November 23, 1919.

56. Referendum 38 on Legislation for Veterans of the World War (Washington, DC: Chamber of Commerce of the United States, 1922). Box 18, Series 1, Sub Series D, USCC.

57. Niedt, "The Politics of Prosperity and Crisis in an Industrial Suburb," 39.

58. Niedt, "The Politics of Prosperity and Crisis in an Industrial Suburb," 39–40.

59. BFL Meeting Minutes, April 26, 1922. Reel 1.

60. BFL Meeting Minutes, June 10, 1925. Reel 1.

61. BFL Meeting Minutes, July 15, 1925. Reel 1.

62. BFL Meeting Minutes, October 8, 1924. Reel 1.

63. BFL Meeting Minutes, January 14, 1925. Reel 1.

64. BFL Meeting Minutes, March 12, 1924. Reel 1.

65. Clarence S. Stein, "Community Planning of Homes," *American Federationist* 33, no. 3 (1926): 340.

66. Albert J. Kennedy, *Social Conditions in the Twenty-Seventh Ward of Pittsburgh: A Report to the Buhl Foundation upon a Study Made Between November 1929 and November 1930* (Pittsburgh: 1930), 6. Box 13, NCA.

67. John E. Bodnar, Roger D. Simon, and Michael P. Weber, *Lives of Their Own: Blacks, Italians, and Poles in Pittsburgh, 1900–1960* (Urbana: University of Illinois Press, 1982), table 30, p. 211.

68. David J. Saposs, "How the Rank and File of the Workers View the Strike," Inter Church World Movement Commission of Inquiry (New York Bureau of Industrial Research, 1919). HBP.

69. Albert J. Kennedy, *Social Conditions in the Twenty-Seventh Ward of Pittsburgh: A Report to the Buhl Foundation upon a Study Made Between November 1929 and November 1930* (Pittsburgh: 1930), 71. Box 13, NCA, 70–71.

70. "League Program for 1925," FF2, Box 1, PUL.

71. *Negro Survey of Pennsylvania* (Harrisburg: Commonwealth of Pennsylvania Department of Welfare, 1926). FF303, Box 7, PUL. Citations in this paragraph are from p. 31, 33, 40, and 26.

72. Margaret Black, "Woman's Column, Letter from Dean Russell of Teachers College," *Baltimore Afro-American*, May 13, 1916.

73. "Prof. Fudge Says," *Baltimore Afro-American*, December 14, 1923.

74. Louis R. Lauter, "Development of C. M. A. Stores to be Nation-Wide," *Afro American*, August 30, 1930.

75. Scott, *The Making of the Modern British Home*, 16–17.

76. Vyta Baselice, Dante Burrichter, and Peter N. Stearns, "Debating the Birthday: Innovation and Resistance in Celebrating Children," *The Journal of the History of Childhood and Youth* 12, no. 2 (2019): 276–79.

77. Leigh Eric Schmidt, "The Commercialization of the Calendar: American Holidays and the Culture of Consumption, 1870–1930," *The Journal of American History* 78, no. 3 (1991): 887–916.

78. Herbin-Triant, *Threatening Property*, 120.

79. Rose C. Feld, "Now That They Have It: Intimate Talks with the Steel-Workers about the Eight-Hour Day," *Century Magazine* (October 1924): 756.

80. Johnstone, *Class, Race, and Gold*, 189.

81. Livingston, *Against Thrift*, 79–80.

82. George Bailey Wilson, *Alcohol and the Nation: A Contribution to the Study of the Liquor Problem in the United Kingdom from 1800 to 1935)* (London: Nicholson and Watson, 1940); James Nicholls, *Politics of Alcohol: A History of the Drink Question in England* (Manchester: Manchester University Press, 2009); Perry Duis, *The Saloon: Public Drinking in Chicago and Boston, 1880–1920* (Urbana: University of Illinois Press,

1983); Lisa McGirr, *The War on Alcohol: Prohibition and the Rise of the American State* (New York: W.W. Norton & Company, 2016).

83. A. E. Dingle, "Drink and Working-Class Living Standards in Britain, 1870–1914," *The Economic History Review* 25, no. 4 (1972): 611.

84. Arthur Pugh, *Men of Steel* (London: Iron and Steel Trades Confederation, 1951), 22.

85. David Hey, *A History of Sheffield* (Lancaster: Carnegie Pub., 1998), 199.

86. J. M. Golby, *The Civilisation of the Crowd: Popular Culture in England, 1750–1900* (New York: Schocken Books, 1985), 125; and Pollard, *A History of Labour in Sheffield.*, 196.

87. "Miss Barnum's Statement of Conditions at Fall River," *Charities: A Weekly Review of Local and General Philanthropy* 13 (February 4, 1905): 415.

88. Whiting Williams, *What's on the Worker's Mind, By One Who Put on Overalls to Find Out* (New York: Charles Scribner's Sons, 1920), 199.

89. A. Williams, *Life in a Railway Factory*, 262–63.

90. "Horticultural Show," *The Edgar Allen Imperial Works and Sports Magazine* (July 1921).

91. "In Your Garden," *Sheffield Daily Telegraph*, January 3, 1925; "Today in the Garden," *Liverpool Echo*, June 6, 1925.

92. Feld, "Now That They Have It," 751.

93. Scott, *The Making of the Modern British Home*, 176.

94. Scott, *The Making of the Modern British Home*, 179.

95. Scott, *The Making of the Modern British Home*, 180.

96. Steven M. Gelber, *Hobbies: Leisure and the Culture of Work in America* (New York: Columbia University Press, 1999), 30.

97. Feld, "Now That They Have It," 756.

98. "Hobbies Competition," *Liverpool Echo*, February 7, 1925.

99. *Eleventh Annual Report of the Bureau of Statistics and Information of Maryland* (Baltimore: The Sun Book and Job Printing, 1903), 20. MSA 2/7/9/17.

100. Christopher Thomas Potter, "An Exploration of Social and Cultural Aspects of Motorcycling During the Interwar Period" (PhD diss., University of Northumbria at Newcastle, 2007), 190–91; Eric Hopkins, "Working Class Life in Birmingham Between the Wars, 1918–1939," *Midland History* 15, no. 1 (January 1, 1990): 129–50.

101. Miss Marian D. Savage, "Family Budgets and Living Conditions," 22–23, Interchurch World Movement Commission of Inquiry, HBP.

102. BFL Meeting Minutes, April 14, 1926. Reel 2.

103. Feld, "Now That They Have It," 753.

104. McKibbin, *Classes and Cultures*, 165, 193, 197, 519.

105. D. J. Saposs, "Intellectual Environment of Immigrant Workers in Pittsburgh District," 3. Interchurch World Movement Commission of Inquiry (1919). HBP.

106. Feld, "Now That They Have It," 749.

107. Steven M. Gelber, "Do-It-Yourself: Constructing, Repairing and Maintaining Domestic Masculinity," *American Quarterly* 49, no. 1 (1997): 67.

108. Feld, "Now That They Have It," 751.

109. Feld, "Now That They Have It," 755.

110. Feld, "Now That They Have It,"; and Scott, *The Making of the Modern British Home*, 191.

111. Sam Mitrani, *The Rise of the Chicago Police Department: Class and Conflict, 1850–1894* (Urbana: University of Illinois Press, 2013).

112. Martin J. Daunton, *House and Home in the Victorian City: Working Class Housing, 1850–1914* (London: E. Arnold, 1983), 13–14.

113. Daunton, *House and Home,* 15.

114. Douglas A. Reid, "Playing and Praying," in *Cambridge Urban History of Britain,* ed. Martin J. Daunton (Cambridge: Cambridge University Press, 2008), 777.

115. Hey, *A History of Sheffield,* 195.

116. Joseph C. Rosalski, "In Perspective: Ferdinand C. Latrobe's Mayoral Terms and Progressive Influences on the City of Baltimore, 1875–1895" (MA thesis, University of Maryland, Baltimore County, 2010), 63, 68.

117. Stephen G. Jones, "State Intervention in Sport and Leisure in Britain between the Wars," *Journal of Contemporary History* 22, no. 1 (1987): 167.

118. James H. Preston, *Mayor's General Message to the City Council* (Baltimore: King Brothers, 1918), 63.

119. Preston, *Mayor's General Message to the City Council,* 64.

120. "'Jazz' Tabooed In Park Concerts; To Begin Sunday," *Pittsburgh Post,* July 7, 1921. Box 2, FF15. Civic Club of Allegheny County. AIS 70:2. University of Pittsburgh.

121. Citizens Committee on City Plan of Pittsburgh, *Pittsburgh Playgrounds: A Part of the Pittsburgh Plan* (June 1920), 3, 5. Box 14, NCA.

122. Rob Ruck, *Sandlot Seasons: Sport in Black Pittsburgh* (Urbana: University of Illinois Press, 1987), 17.

123. James Roland Coates, "Recreation and Sport in the African-American Community of Baltimore, 1890–1920" (PhD diss., University of Maryland, College Park, 1991), 153.

124. Coates, "Recreation and Sport," 153–165.

125. Angelique D. Jessup, "Backyard Battles: Local Struggles for African American Political Advancement in Baltimore, 1920–1944" (PhD diss., University of Michigan–Ann Arbor, 2010), 79–82.

126. Ruck, *Sandlot Seasons,* 17.

127. *Negro Survey of Pennsylvania* (Harrisburg: Commonwealth of Pennsylvania Department of Welfare, 1926), 53. FF303, Box 7, PUL.

128. John T. Clark, Executive Secretary of Urban League of Pittsburgh to George Gerwig, Secretary, Board of Education, June 18, 1925. FF47, Box 2, PUL.

129. Reid, "Playing and Praying."

130. Elizabeth Roberts, *A Woman's Place: An Oral History of Working-Class Women, 1890–1940* (New York: Blackwell, 1984), 123; and Reid, "Playing and Praying," 776.

131. Michael Aronson, *Nickelodeon City: Pittsburgh at the Movies, 1905–1929* (Pittsburgh: University of Pittsburgh Press, 2008).

132. Samuel E. Eliot, "Report and recommendations of the Director of the Woods Run Industrial Settlement Read at the Annual Meting of the Association, December 11, 1911," Box 2, NCA.

133. David Nasaw, *Going Out: The Rise and Fall of Public Amusements* (Cambridge, MA: Harvard University Press, 1999); and Peiss, *Cheap Amusements.*

134. Robert C. Allen, "Manhattan Myopia; Or, Oh! Iowa! Robert C. Allen on Ben Singer's 'Manhattan Nickelodeons: New Data on Audiences and Exhibitors," *Cinema Journal* 35, no. 3 (1996): 96, https://doi.org/10.2307/1225767.

135. BFL Meeting Minutes, February 10, 1926. Reel 2.

136. Andor D. Skotnes, "The Black Freedom Movement and the Workers' Movement in Baltimore, 1930–39" (PhD diss., Rutgers University, 1991), 50.

137. John T. Clark, Annual Report of the Work of the Urban League of Pittsburgh for 1924. FF246, Box 6, PUL; *Negro Survey of Pennsylvania* (Harrisburg: Commonwealth of Pennsylvania Department of Welfare, 1926), 55. FF303, Box 7, PUL.

138. Williams, *Life in a Railway Factory*, 314.

Chapter 9

1. Jane Addams, "Public Recreation and Social Morality," *Charities: A Weekly Review of Local and General Philanthropy* 18 (August 3, 1907): 491; see also, on similar lines, William Chauncy Langdon, "The Juvenile City League," *Charities: A Weekly Review of Local and General Philanthropy* 10 (September 10, 1904): 924; Joseph Lee, "Play as School of the Citizen," *Charities: A Weekly Review of Local and General Philanthropy* 18 (August 3, 1907): 489.

2. Sidney S. Pexotta, "The Aims of a Boys' Club: The Necessity for System and Order in Developing Boys' Club Work," *Charities: A Weekly Review of Local and General Philanthropy* 19 (October 19, 1907): 906.

3. Sidney S. Peixotta, "The Aims of a Boys' Club: Gangs and Original Initiative and Dues," *Charities: A Weekly Review of Local and General Philanthropy* 19 (November 2, 1907): 980–81.

4. "Baseball as Organized Play," *Charities: A Weekly Review of Local and General Philanthropy* 21 (December 19, 1908): 440–41.

5. Percy Strickney Grant, "Children's Street Games," *The Survey* (November 13, 1909): 235–36.

6. Personnel Department, "Report A" 1920" Box 1, USSNDW.

7. As a leading example, Lizabeth Cohen's account of changes in working-class culture in the early twentieth century, *Making a New Deal*, offers a single paragraph on employer-sponsored sports. On sports history's still marginal place in the US historiography, see Susan K. Cahn, "Turn, Turn, Turn: There Is a Reason (for Sports History)," *The Journal of American History* 101, no. 1 (2014): 181–83. On the productive dialog between sports and labor history in UK historiography, see Matthew Taylor, "Parallel Fields: Labour History and Sports History," *International Journal of the History of Sport* 32, no. 15 (2015): 1769–74. A number of recent projects have drawn connections, including Daryl Leeworthy, "Partisan Players: Sport, Working-Class Culture, and the Labour Movement in South Wales, 1920-1939," *Labor History* 55, no. 5 (2014): 580–93; Ryan S. Pettengill, "'Fair Play in Bowling': Sport, Civil Rights, and the UAW Culture of Inclusion, 1936–1950," *Journal of Social History* 51, no. 4 (2018): 953–79; and Fiona Skillen, "Preventing 'Robotised Women Workers': Women, Sport and the Workplace in Scotland, 1919-1939," *Labor History* 55, no. 5 (2014): 594–606.

8. McKibbin, *Classes and Cultures*, 340.

9. McKibbin, *Classes and Cultures*, 340.

10. For the importance of not simply seeing sports as a straightforward instrument of elite control, see Alan Ingham and Stephen Hardy, "Sport: Structuration, Subjugation and Hegemony," *Theory, Culture & Society* 2, no. 2 (1984): 85–103.

11. Ralph Miliband, *Marxism and Politics*, Marxist Introductions (Oxford: University Press, 1977), 52; John Hargreaves, *Sport, Power and Culture: A Social and Historical Analysis of Popular Sports in Britain* (Cambridge, UK: Polity Press, 1986); and Stephen

G. Jones, *Workers at Play: A Social and Economic History of Leisure, 1918–1939* (London: Routledge & Kegan Paul, 1986).

12. R. J. Holt, "Football and the Urban Way of Life in Nineteenth-Century Britain," in *Pleasure, Profit, Proselytism*, ed. J. A. Mangan (New York: Routledge, 1988), 68.

13. Caroline Oldcorn Reid, "Middle Class Values and Working Class Culture in Nineteenth Century Sheffield" (1976), 291; and Christopher Philip Stevens, "A Study of Urban Conservatism, with Reference to Sheffield, 1885–1906" (University of Teesside, 1997), 393.

14. Wright, *Old South, New South*, 75; Bodnar, Simon, and Weber, *Lives of Their Own*, 57.

15. Hobsbawm, *Worlds of Labour*, 212.

16. Bradford, *A Taste of Freedom*, 11.

17. Faue, *Community of Suffering and Struggle*, 15.

18. J. S. Hurt, *Elementary Schooling and the Working Classes, 1860–1918* (London: Routledge, 1979); and Malcolm Mercer, *Schooling the Poorer Child: Elementary Education in Sheffield, 1560–1902* (Sheffield: Sheffield Academic, 1996).

19. J. H. Bingham, *The Period of the Sheffield School Board, 1870–1903* (Sheffield: Northend, 1949), 87; *Twelfth Annual Report of the Condition of the Public Schools of Pittsburgh for the School Year Ending August 31st, 1880* (Pittsburgh: James McMiller, 1881); Carole Shammas, "Did Democracy Give the United States an Edge in Primary Schooling?," *Social Science History* 39, no. 3 (2015): 315–38.

20. The Board of Public Education School District of Pittsburgh, *Second Annual Report for the Year Ending December 31, 1913* (1914), 29.

21. "Police Court. School Board Prosecutions," *SI*, June 5, 1897.

22. Philip Gooderson, "'Noisy and Dangerous Boys': The Slogging Gang Phenomenon in Late Nineteenth-Century Birmingham," *Midland History* 38, no. 1 (2013): 58–79.

23. "Our Office Boys' Biographies: No. 4. S Bates," *The Edgar Allen Imperial Works and Sports Magazine* (June 1921).

24. Michael James Childs, *Labour's Apprentices: Working-Class Lads in Late Victorian and Edwardian England* (Montreal: McGill-Queen's University Press, 1992), 49.

25. Scott, *The Making of the Modern British Home*, 55; McKenna, "Municipal Suburbia in Liverpool," 303–4.

26. Fidel Makoto Campet, "Housing in Black Pittsburgh: Community Struggles and the State, 1916–1973" (PhD diss., Carnegie Mellon University, 2011); Jessup, "Backyard Battles"; Power, "Apartheid Baltimore Style."

27. Jessup, "Backyard Battles," 125–36.

28. Abram Lincoln Harris, Jr., "The New Negro Worker in Pittsburgh" (Master Thesis, University of Pittsburgh, 1924), 59. FF467, Box 10, PUL.

29. "Go to High School—Go to College Campaign," FF47, Box 2, PUL. The League also funded a research fellow at the University of Pittsburgh to study educational provision for African American children; see Report of the President, E. C. May, at the 9th Annual Meeting, January 17, 1927. FF36, Box 1, PUL.

30. Cristina Viviana Groeger, *The Education Trap: Schools and the Remaking of Inequality in Boston* (Cambridge, MA: Harvard University Press, 2021).

31. Williams, *Life in a Railway Factory*, 64, 82.

32. "Athletics in Elementary Schools," *Edinburgh Evening*, November 30, 1892.

33. "Saturday's Schoolboy Match," *SDT*, February 4, 1904; "Athletics. Sheffield

Elementary School Sports," *SDT*, June 16, 1896; "Facts and Fancies," *SI*, April 27, 1897; "Sheffield Schools Football Association," *SDT*, February 1, 1896; "Sheffield Schools Football Association," *SDT*, December 11, 1895; "Clegg Challenge Shield. Final Tie Sharrow Lane v. Lowfield," *SI*, May 3, 1892; "Sheffield Boys v. London Boys," *SDT*, May 16, 1891.

34. See Data Appendix, "Social Background of Sheffield Youth Football," 1890–1904. Two youths were residents of an orphan home; they were classed as "laborers" for family context given their precarious position and lack of kinship ties.

35. "Poly is Champion: Great Public School Game Goes Against City College," *BS*, November 21, 1908; "To Test Football Fans. City and Poly Will Play Many Games Here In Future if Policy Pays," *BS*, September 24, 1916.

36. Woods Run Settlement, *Annual Statement for the Fiscal Year 1926–1927* (Pittsburgh, 1927). Box 2, NCA.

37. Bold in original; Woods Run Settlement, *Annual Statement for the Fiscal Year 1926–1927* (Pittsburgh, 1927). Box 2, NCA; and Jane Thomas, "November 1, 1912," *The Stenographer Writes: Annual Report of the Woods Run Settlement Association, 1912–1913* (Pittsburgh, 1913). Box 2, NCA.

38. Jane Thomas, December 1, 1912, *The Stenographer Writes: Annual Report of the Woods Run Settlement Association, 1912–1913* (Pittsburgh, 1913), 8. Box 2, NCA.

39. Daniel Katz, *All Together Different: Yiddish Socialists, Garment Workers, and the Labor Roots of Multiculturalism* (New York: NYU Press, 2011), 78–79.

40. "Recreational Activities of Labor Organizations," *Monthly Labor Review* 26, no. 5 (1928): 16.

41. BFL Meeting Minutes, March 23, 1927. Reel 2.

42. BFL Meeting Minutes, March 30, April 6, Mary 11, June 1, June 8, 1927. Reel 2.

43. BFL Meeting Minutes, June 29, 1927. Reel 2.

44. BFL Meeting Minutes, November 9, 1927. Reel 2. 1920s.

45. The camp appears to have continued to flourish in the late 1920s. BFL Meeting Minutes, June 6, July 11, July 25, 1928, June 5, 1929. Reel 2.

46. John Thomas Preston, "The Origins and Development of Association Football in the Liverpool District, c. 1879 until c. 1915" (PhD diss., University of Central Lancashire, 2007), 193.

47. Preston, "The Origins and Development of Association Football," 193.

48. "Schools' FA Chief Dies," *Liverpool Echo*, April 15, 1985.

49. Preston, "The Origins and Development of Association Football," 174.

50. Preston, "The Origins and Development of Association Football," 175.

51. "Football Notes," *SDT*, December 30, 1884.

52. "Outdoor Sports," *LM*, April 8, 1899.

53. "Liverpool Shield Competition," *LM*, March 4, 1895.

54. "Steamship League," *Liverpool Echo*, February 7, 1925.

55. "Sheffield Works League," *The Edgar Allen Imperial Works and Sports Magazine*, January 1922.

56. "Sports Notes," *The Edgar Allen Imperial Works and Sports Magazine*, March 1922.

57. Works Committee Report, January 15, 1919. 1/4/1/2/4 JB.

58. Works Committee Report, January 15, 1919. 1/4/1/2/4 JB. In 1921, Firths and John Brown worked to purchase a cricket ground at Pitsmoor; see Report to Board of Directors, October 24, 1921. Board Papers 1921, 1/2/3/2/204-216, FSC. Balfour's and

Edgar Allen steel were also concerned with providing adequate recreational space for their employees; see Directors Meeting, November 22, 1923, BDR 79; October 4, 1918, Directors Minute Book No. 2, MD2169-5, EASC.

59. Directors Meeting, October 14, 1929, BDR 79; Directors Meeting, January 15, 1930, BDR 79.

60. "B. and O., 1; Sparrows Point, 0." BS, August 6, 1905; "Railroad Men Lost. B. and O. Defeated By Sparrows Point 6 to 4," BS, August 27, 1905.

61. David M. Vrooman, *Daniel Willard and Progressive Management on the Baltimore & Ohio Railroad* (Columbus: Ohio State University Press, 1991), 23.

62. Vrooman, *Daniel Willard*, 20.

63. *Second Annual Report of the Commissioner of Labor and Industry of the Commonwealth of Pennsylvania 1914* (Harrisburg: Wm. Stanley Ray, 1915), 17.

64. Personnel Department, "Report A" 1920. Box 1, USSNDW.

65. Leeworthy, "Partisan Players."

66. "Recreational Activities of Labor Organizations," 5.

67. PCL, Minutes January 16, 1930; PCL Minutes, July 17, 1930.

68. BFL Meeting Minutes, May 22, June 5, June 26, August 21, August 38, October 30, 1929. Reel 2.

69. BFL Meeting Minutes, June 26, 1929. Reel 2.

70. Ruck, *Sandlot Seasons*, 20–29.

71. Industrial Welfare Workers Minutes, May 18, 1918. FF334, Box 7, PUL; Industrial Welfare Workers Minutes, January 8, 1921. FF335, Box 7, PUL; Industrial Welfare Workers Minutes, February 5, 1921. FF335, Box 7, PUL.

72. Industrial Welfare Workers Minutes, May 25, 1921. FF335, Box 7, PUL.

73. Industrial Welfare Workers Informal Meeting, June 1, 1921. FF335, Box 7, PUL.

74. Industrial Welfare Workers Minutes, May 25, 1921. FF335, Box 7, PUL.

75. Alan Metcalfe, *Leisure and Recreation in a Victorian Mining Community: The Social Economy of Leisure in North-East England, 1820–1914* (Psychology Press, 2006), 111–14.

76. "'Mill' on Fifth Street" *PG*, June 10, 1867; for a similar fight, a week later, see an untitled item in *PG*, June 18, 1867.

77. G. Halliwell, "Fifty Years On," *NWC* 19 January 1895, cited in Metcalfe, *Leisure and Recreation*, 112. For examples of informal fights see "Birkenhead Police Court," *LDP*, January 22, 1867; "Brutal Assault on a Police Officer," *LDP*, June 4, 1867; "A Youthful Prizefighter," *SI*, January 2, 1868; "Alleged Fighting at Clown," *SI*, June 2, 1868.

78. "Birmingham Stabbing Case," *PG*, June 12, 1867. Occupations for named participants in fights were identified through the manuscript census on Ancestry.com. The US Census manuscript reports Munn as a "glass blower" although the newspaper report states that he was a teamster at a glass works. His son worked as a moulder, according to the United States Census of 1870; Census Place: South Pittsburgh, Allegheny, Pennsylvania; Roll: M593_1296; Page: 44B; Image: 92; Family History Library Film: 552795.

79. No title, *SI*, January 29, 1867. For occupations, see Census of England in 1871. Class: RG10; Piece: 4687; Folio: 112; Page: 28; GSU roll: 847233; Census of England in 1871. Class: RG10; Piece: 4702; Folio: 78; Page: 14; GSU roll: 847241; Census of England in 1871. Class: RG10; Piece: 4669; Folio: 17; Page: 27; GSU roll: 847224.

80. "The Prize Ring," *PG*, January 11, 1868. United States Census 1870; Census

Place: Pittsburgh Ward 5, Allegheny, Pennsylvania; Roll: M593_1295; Page: 564A; Image: 433; Family History Library Film: 552794.

81. "Pugilistic," *PG*, June 15, 1867.

82. "Prize Fighters and Their Admirers in Trouble," *SI*, January 12, 1867.

83. "Brutal Assault on a Police Officer," *LDP*, June 4, 1867.

84. This change came in the UK with the Coney decision of 1882; see Jack Anderson, "Pugilistic Prosecutions: Prize Fighting and the Courts in Nineteenth Century Britain," *Sports Historian* 21, no. 2 (2001): 50. In the US, states regulated this, and in Pennsylvania the decision was given in 1883 that "sparring exhibitions" could go ahead if they had the sanction of the local mayor that they would not cause a breach of the peace. See Thomas M. Croak, "The Professionalization of Prizefighting: Pittsburgh at the Turn of the Century," *Western Pennsylvania History: 1918–2016* 62, no. 4 (1979): 336.

85. Kenneth G. Sheard, "Aspects of Boxing in the Western 'Civilizing Process,'" *International Review for the Sociology of Sport* 32, no. 1 (1997): 35–38.

86. Sheard, "Aspects of Boxing," 37.

87. Matt Horgan, "Blood Sport in Pittsburgh: An Analysis of Prize Fighting and Cock Fighting in an American Industrial City," *The Sloping Halls Review* (2013): 26.

88. Horgan, "Blood Sport in Pittsburgh," 25.

89. Croak, "The Professionalization of Prizefighting," 337, 340.

90. Horgan, "Blood Sport in Pittsburgh," 27.

91. "Big Crowd Sees Mills," *BS*, August 2, 1910; "In the Boxing Ring," *Liverpool Echo*, February 7, 1925.

92. Croak, "The Professionalization of Prizefighting," 335–36.

93. "Report of the State Athletic Commission of Maryland, 1923," in Folder "State Athletic Commission," Box Loose Reports MdHR 2/3/6/12.

94. "Report of the State Athletic Commission of Maryland, 1926," in Folder "State Athletic Commission," Box Loose Reports MdHR 2/3/6/12.

95. Jones, "State Intervention in Sport and Leisure in Britain between the Wars," 168–69.

96. *Negro Survey of Pennsylvania* (Harrisburg: Commonwealth of Pennsylvania Department of Welfare, 1926). FF303, Box 7, PUL.

97. Dan Streible, "A History of the Boxing Film, 1894–1915: Social Control and Social Reform in the Progressive Era," *Film History* 3, no. 3 (1989): 235–57.

98. Streible, "A History of the Boxing Film."

99. Streible, "A History of the Boxing Film," 242.

100. Streible, "A History of the Boxing Film," 243.

101. Streible, "A History of the Boxing Film," 245.

102. Ruck, *Sandlot Seasons*, 14.

103. Streible, "A History of the Boxing Film, 1894–1915," 247.

104. Burt Solomon, *Where They Ain't: The Fabled Life and Untimely Death of the Original Baltimore Orioles, the Team That Gave Birth to Modern Baseball* (New York: Free Press, 1999); Steven A. Riess, *Touching Base: Professional Baseball and American Culture in the Progressive Era* (Westport, CT: Greenwood Press, 1980); William E. Benswanger, ed., "Professional Baseball in Pittsburgh," *Western Pennsylvania History*, 1947; Peter Morris et al., *Base Ball Pioneers, 1850–1870: The Clubs and Players Who Spread the Sport Nationwide* (McFarland, 2012); G. Kitching, "The Origins of Football: History, Ideology and the Making of 'The People's Game,'" *History Workshop*

Journal 79, no. 1 (2015): 127–53; Matthew Taylor, *The Association Game: A History of British Football* (Harlow: Pearson Longman, 2008); David Kennedy, "And Then There Were Two: Everton and Liverpool Football Clubs, 1892–1902," *Soccer & Society* 12, no. 4 (2011): 523–37; Tony Mason, *Association Football and English Society, 1863–1915* (Brighton: Harvester Press, 1981); and N. L. Tranter, *Sport, Economy, and Society in Britain, 1750–1914* (Cambridge: Cambridge University Press, 1998).

105. "Football. Sheffield v. London," *SDT*, March 4, 1872.

106. Kitching, "The Origins of Football," 149–50.

107. Stephen G. Jones, *Sport, Politics, and the Working Class: Organised Labour and Sport in Inter-War Britain* Manchester: Manchester University Press, 1988), 57–62.

108. "Baseball," *BS*, June 1, 1883.

109. "Modern Professional Football," *SDT*, October 17, 1892.

110. "Afternoon Contests. Baltimore Defeats Washington Again, This Time at Oriole Park," *BS*, July 5, 1890.

111. "Football. Sheffield Wednesday v. Sheffield United," *SDT*, December 27, 1895; "Everton v. Liverpool," *LM*, April 20, 1897; "'The Rivals': At Brammall Lane," *SDT*, December 28, 1896.

112. "Football Notes," *LM*, December 27, 1897.

113. Preston, "Association Football in Liverpool," 236–39; Riess, *Touching Base*, 13–15.

114. "Football and Health," *SDT*, December 22, 1904.

115. "Some News and Old Birds in Action at Oriole Park," *BS*, March 19, 1911.

116. Riess, *Touching Base*, 15.

117. Matt Simm, in the *Northern Democrat* (1908), quoted in Chris Waters, *British Socialists and the Politics of Popular Culture, 1884–1914* (Manchester: Manchester University Press, 1990), 35.

118. Waters, *British Socialists and the Politics of Popular Culture*, 41, 167, 181–82; David Vessey, "'People Want Newspapers Far More than Weekly Collections of Articles': The Sheffield Guardian, the Labour Party and the Left-Wing Press," *Labour History Review* 80, no. 3 (2015): 249–73, https://doi.org/10.3828/lhr.2015.11.

119. Williams, *Life in a Railway Factory*, 303.

120. Reid, "Playing and Praying," 775–76.

121. "Baseball on for Good," *BS*, April 27, 1907.

122. "Play Ball!," *BS*, April 23, 1909.

123. Riess, *Touching Base*, 44.

124. "Football. English Association Cup," *SI*, February 28, 1891.

125. "Football. National Cup Competition," *SDT*, March 4, 1890.

126. "Scene at a Football Match," *SDT*, December 27, 1890; "Brutal Attack on the Flint Goalkeeper," *SET*, November 1, 1894.

127. "Football," *SDT*, February 5, 1892.

128. "Football. The Stoning of the Wednesday Players," *SDT*, April 9, 1903.

129. "Scene on the Football Field at Doncaster," *SI*, March 21, 1893; "Alleged Football Riot at Owlerton," *SDT*, January 14, 1901.

130. "Rowdyism at a Football Match," *SDT*, April 21, 1896.

131. "Crowd at Oriole Park Vents Its Displeasure on Mr. Gifford," *BS*, July 1, 1904; "Riot at Oriole Park," *BS*, June 7, 1908.

132. "Football. The Home Coming of the English Cup," *SDT*, April 21, 1896.

133. "With the Crowd in the Street," *LM*, April 2, 1894.

134. Rollin Lynde Hartt, *The People at Play* (New York: Houghton Mifflin, 1909), 303–7.

135. "Football. Wednesday v. United at Olive Grove," *SDT*, October 18, 1892.

136. Quoted in Riess, *Touching Base*, 28.

137. "Football. English Association Cup," *SI*, February 28, 1891.

138. P. J. Carlino, "Bleacher Bugs and Fifty-Centers: The Social Stratification of Baseball Fans through Stadium Design, 1880–1920," *Buildings & Landscapes: Journal of the Vernacular Architecture Forum* 28, no. 1 (2021): 7, 18.

139. Carlino, "Bleacher Bugs and Fifty-Centers," 16–17.

140. Preston, "Association Football in Liverpool," 228–32.

141. Riess, *Touching Base*, 49; Carlino, "Bleacher Bugs and Fifty-Centers," 12.

142. William F. Broening, *Mayor's Message and General Summary to the City Council, 1919–1923* (Baltimore: King Brothers, 1923), 12; William F. Broening, *Mayor's Message to the Members of the City Council, May 26, 1930* (Baltimore: King Brothers, 1930), 31.

143. BFL Meeting Minutes, February 15, 1922. Reel 1.

144. BFL Meeting Minutes, January 21, 1925. Reel 1; BFL Meeting Meetings, January 28, 1925. Reel 1.

145. BFL Meeting Minutes, December 2, 1925. Reel 2.

146. BFL Meeting Minutes, September 18, 1929. Reel 2.

147. Davis, *Power at Odds*, 85.

148. Riess, *Touching Base*, 194.

149. Riess, *Touching Base*, 194–95.

150. Ruck, *Sandlot Seasons*; Shawn Morris, "The Negro Leagues and Regional Historiography," *Black Ball* 7 (2014): 44–53.

151. Pamela Annette Smoot, "Black Self Help and Institution Building in Pittsburgh, Pennsylvania, 1830–1945" (PhD diss., Michigan State University, 1999), 427.

152. Smoot, "Black Self Help and Institution Building in Pittsburgh," 438.

153. David Kennedy, "Red and Blue and Orange and Green?," *Soccer & Society* 12, no. 4 (2011): 556.

154. Kennedy, "Red and Blue and Orange and Green?," 558–60.

155. Preston, "Association Football in Liverpool," 21–22, 254, 257.

156. Quoted in Kennedy, "Red and Blue and Orange and Green?," 561.

Chapter 10

1. *Twelfth Annual Report of the Bureau of Statistics and Information of Maryland 1903* (Baltimore: The Sun Book and Job Printing, 1904), 60. MSA 2/7/9/17.

2. Howell Harris, "Between Convergence and Exceptionalism: Americans and the British Model of Labor Relations, c. 1867–1920," *Labor History* 48, no. 2 (2007): 145, https://doi.org/10.1080/00236560701224726.

3. Holt, "Trade Unionism in the British and U.S. Steel Industries," 30.

4. Emphasis mine. Montini, Ormond Oral History, Box 2, Folder 55. BVLHSC.

5. Emphasis mine. George Alex Dominic Oral History, Box 2, Folder 48. BVLHSC.

6. David J. Saposs, "How the Rank and File of the Workers View the Strike," Inter Church World Movement Commission of Inquiry (New York Bureau of Industrial Research, 1919), 9. HBP.

7. Nelson, "Class, Race and Democracy in the CIO," 364–68.

8. Joshua Clover, *Riot. Strike. Riot: The New Era of Uprisings* (London: Verso, 2016).

9. Montgomery, *The Fall of the House of Labor.*

10. Thompson, *The Making of the English Working Class.*

11. Rosanne Currarino, *The Labor Question in America: Economic Democracy in the Gilded Age* (Urbana: University of Illinois Press, 2011), 5.

12. Currarino, *The Labor Question in America,* 7.

13. Currarino, *The Labor Question in America,* 91.

14. Julie Greene has put to rest the widespread, but deeply misguided, notion that the AFL was somehow "apolitical," but it is unfortunate that her account of the AFL breaks off during World War I, and misses the expansion of labor's political agenda in the 1920s. See *Pure and Simple Politics: The American Federation of Labor and Political Activism, 1881-1917* (New York: Cambridge University Press, 1998).

15. Dick Geary, *European Labour Protest, 1848-1939* (London: Methuen, 1981), 27-28, 31-34; David Montgomery, "Strikes in Nineteenth-Century America," *Social Science History* 4, no. 1 (1980): 81-104; and James Cronin, "Strikes and Power in Britain, 1870-1920," *International Review of Social History* 32, no. 2 (1987): 153.

16. David Grimsted, "Ante-Bellum Labor: Violence, Strike, and Communal Arbitration," *Journal of Social History* 19, no. 1 (1985): 5-28. See also Montgomery, "Strikes in Nineteenth-Century America."

17. David O. Stowell offers an effective critique of the dominant interpretation, in which there was "community support" for a national railroad strike. Rather, the protests should be understood as locally distinct "community uprisings" focused on the use and control of public space in these cities. See *Streets, Railroads, and the Great Strike of 1877* (Chicago: University of Chicago Press, 1999), 7-11.

18. Leach, "Chaining the Tiger," 209.

19. Leach, "Chaining the Tiger," 207-8.

20. Mitrani, *The Rise of the Chicago Police Department.*

21. Directors Weekly Conference, August 26, 1919, BDR 80; Directors Meeting, January 4, 1927, BDR 79.

22. Price, *Masters, Unions, and Men,* 55-56; and George W. Alcock, *Fifty Years of Railway Trade Unionism,* (London [etc.]: Co-operative printing society limited, 1922), 31.

23. Price, *Masters, Unions, and Men,* 65.

24. Price, *Masters, Unions, and Men,* 69.

25. Thomas C. Weeks, *First Biennial Report of the Bureau of Industrial Statistics and Information of Maryland, 1884-1885* (Baltimore: Guggenheimer, Weil & Co., 1886), footnote, page 12.

26. Price, *Masters, Unions, and Men,* 225.

27. Warren R. Van Tine, *The Making of the Labor Bureaucrat: Union Leadership in the United States, 1870-1920* (Amherst: University of Massachusetts Press, 1973), 53.

28. Van Tine, *The Making of the Labor Bureaucrat,* 68.

29. Van Tine, *The Making of the Labor Bureaucrat,* 30.

30. Van Tine, *The Making of the Labor Bureaucrat,* 31.

31. *Proceedings of the Eighth National Convention of Officers of Bureaus of Labor Statistics in the United States* (Philadelphia; n.p., 1891), 116. MSA Box 2/7/9/17.

32. *Twelfth Annual Report of the Bureau of Statistics and Information of Maryland 1903* (Baltimore: The Sun Book and Job Printing, 1904), 58. MSA 2/7/9/17; Taplin, "The Liverpool General Transport Strike, 1911," 28.

33. *Fourteenth Annual Report of the Bureau of Statistics and Information of Maryland for the year 1905* (Baltimore: King Brothers, 1906), 214. MSA 2/7/9/18.

34. IUBAC Minutes, March 21, 1912. See also another instance in which a member and local president nearly came to blows, and the District Council and the International became involved, in IUBAC Minutes, May 21, 1912.

35. IUBAC Minutes of Locals 3, 33, and 82 of BM&PIU, January 26, 1904.

36. Van Tine, *The Making of the Labor Bureaucrat*, 153–54.

37. Melvyn Dubofsky, *John L. Lewis: A Biography*, abridged ed. (Urbana: University of Illinois Press, 1986).

38. American Civil Liberties Union Committee on Democracy in Trade Unions, *Democracy in Trade Unions, a Survey, with a Program of Action* (New York: American Civil Liberties Union, 1943), 51.

39. Caldemeyer, *Union Renegades*, 133–56.

40. *Twenty-First Annual Report of the Bureau of Statistics and Information of Maryland 1912* (Baltimore: Mules Printing Co., 1913), 48.

41. Goldberg, "American Seamen," 72–75; Johnathan Thayer, "Merchant Seamen, Sailortowns, and the Shaping of U.S. Citizenship, 1843–1945" (PhD diss., The Graduate Center, City University of New York, 2018), 120–47.

42. "Stevedore Firms Yield," *BS*, May 21, 1912.

43. "Strikers Confer Today," *BS*, May 27, 1912.

44. "Strike Cost Men $50,000," *BS*, July 8, 1912.

45. "Strike Cost Men $50,000," *BS*, July 8, 1912.

46. "Stevedores' Strike is Expected to Spread," *BS*, May 20, 1913.

47. *Fifth Annual Report of the Bureau of Industrial Statistics of Maryland* (Baltimore: King Brothers, 1897), 157. MSA 2/7/9/17.

48. "Meeting of Longshoremen," *BS*, June 2, 1898.

49. *Twelfth Annual Report of the Bureau of Statistics and Information of Maryland 1903* (Baltimore: The Sun Book and Job Printing, 1904), 44. MSA 2/7/9/17.

50. "2,500 Men Strike," *BS*, April 12, 1912.

51. "2,500 Men Strike," *BS*, April 12, 1912.

52. "Will Fight to the End," *BS*, April 14, 1912.

53. "More to Break Strike," *BS*, April 15, 1912.

54. "2,500 Men Strike," *BS*, April 12, 1912.

55. "Strikers Look to Peace," *BS*, May 13, 1912.

56. Barnes, *The Longshoremen*, 120.

57. "Strike Children March," *BS*, May 3, 1912.

58. "Women Want to March," *BS*, May 20, 1912.

59. "Death in Strike," *BS*, May 7, 1912.

60. "Cardinal is Willing," *BS*, May 11, 1912.

61. "Fox Favors Increase," *BS*, May 6, 1912.

62. "Says Strikers Will Hold Out," *BS*, April 21, 1912.

63. "Strikers Attack," *BS*, April 30, 1912.

64. "Sue for Union's Records," *Boston Evening Transcript*, January 29, 1912.

65. "Transport Workers Disintegrate," *The Journal of the International Brotherhood of Boilermakers, Iron Ship Builders and Helpers of America* 24, no. 7 (July 1, 1912).

66. Eric Arnesen, "'It Aint Like They Do In New Orleans': Race Relations, Labor Markets, and Waterfront Labor Movements in the American South, 1880–1923," in *Racism and the Labour Market: Historical Studies*, ed. Dik van Arkel and Marcel van

der Linden (Bern: P. Lang, 1995), 83–85. The strike is also discussed in Thomas L. Hollowak, *A History of Polish Longshoremen and Their Role in the Establishment of a Union at the Port of Baltimore* (Baltimore: History Press, 1996).

67. National Urban League, *Negro Membership in American Labor Unions*, 50.

68. Martin James Daunton, "Payment and Participation: Welfare and State-Formation in Britain 1900–1951," *Past & Present*, no. 150 (1996): 169–216.

69. Cohen, *Making a New Deal*.

70. *Twelfth Annual Report of the Bureau of Statistics and Information of Maryland 1903* (Baltimore: The Sun Book and Job Printing, 1904), 60. MSA 2/7/9/17.

71. "Should Baltimore Workers Unionize?," *Baltimore Afro American*, March 18, 1921.

72. "Labor Would Vote 'Reactionaries' Out," *BS*, October 24, 1922.

73. Ajay K. Mehrotra, *Making the Modern American Fiscal State: Law, Politics, and the Rise of Progressive Taxation, 1877–1929* (New York: Cambridge University Press, 2013).

74. BFL Meeting Minutes, November 16, 1927. Reel 2.

75. BFL Meeting Minutes, January 12, 1927. Reel 2.

76. BFL Meeting Minutes, November 5, 1919.

77. "Declarations Adopted at the Eighth Annual Meeting of the Chamber of Commerce of the United States, April 27 to 29, 1920," Folder "Resolutions 1919–1924," Box 1, USCC; Referendum 38 on Legislation for Veterans of the World War (Washington, DC: Chamber of Commerce of the United States, 1922). Box 18, Series I, Sub Series D, USCC.

78. "Declarations Adopted at the Twelfth Annual Meeting of the Chamber of Commerce of the United States May 6 to 8, 1924," Folder "Resolutions 1919–1924," Box 1, USCC.

79. Charles Kettleborough, "Soldiers' Bonus," *The American Political Science Review* 16, no. 3 (1922): 455–60; Charles Kettleborough, "Soldiers' Bonus," *The American Political Science Review* 18, no. 3 (1924): 559–65.

80. Herbert Levy to Albert C. Ritchie, August 8, 1930. Folder, "Labor 1919–1930," Labor Box 2//30/2/27, MDGG.

81. Christopher Anglim and Brian Gratton, "Organized Labor and Old Age Pensions," *The International Journal of Aging and Human Development* 25, no. 2 (1987): 91–107; Gabriel Winant, "The Natural Profits of Their Years of Labor," *Radical History Review* (2021): 75–102.

82. Thomas C. Weeks, *First Biennial Report of the Bureau of Industrial Statistics and Information of Maryland, 1884–1885* (Baltimore: Guggenheimer, Weil & Co., 1886), 216.

83. BFL Meeting Minutes, February 18, 1920. Reel 1.

84. BFL Meeting Minutes, May 27, 1925. Reel 1.

85. BFL Meeting Minutes, April 14, 1926. Reel 2.

86. BFL Meeting Minutes, January 12, 1927. Reel 2.

87. BFL Meeting Minutes, March 7, 1928. Reel 2.

88. BFL Meeting Minutes, December 12, 1928. Reel 2.

89. BFL Minutes, January 9, 30, 1929. Reel 2.

90. PCL Minutes, June 5, 19, 1930.

91. Fox, *Three Worlds of Relief*; Torpey, *The Invention of the Passport*; Wimmer, *Nationalist Exclusion and Ethnic Conflict*.

Conclusion

1. Winant, *The Next Shift*.

2. Michael K. Honey, *Southern Labor and Black Civil Rights: Organizing Memphis Workers* (Urbana: University of Illinois Press, 1993).

3. Michael Goldfield, *The Southern Key: Class, Race, and Radicalism in the 1930s and 1940s* (New York: Oxford University Press, 2020).

4. Manisha Sinha, *The Counterrevolution of Slavery: Politics and Ideology in Antebellum South Carolina* (Chapel Hill: University of North Carolina Press, 2000).

5. "Union Members—2022," USDL-23-0071. For Release on Thursday, January 19, 2023. https://www.bls.gov/news.release/pdf/union2.pdf.

6. Alex Press, "The UAW has Set Its Sights on the Anti-Union South," *Jacobin*, March 6, 2024. https://jacobin.com/2024/03/uaw-organizing-mercedes-benz-alabama.

7. Goldfield, *The Southern Key*, 332.

8. Goldfield, *The Southern Key* 346; Robin D. G. Kelley, *Hammer and Hoe: Alabama Communists during the Great Depression* (Chapel Hill: University of North Carolina Press, 1990); Glenda Gilmore, *Defying Dixie: The Radical Roots of Civil Rights, 1919–1950* (New York: W.W. Norton & Co., 2008); Hosea Hudson and Nell Irvin Painter, *The Narrative of Hosea Hudson: The Life and Times of a Black Radical* (New York: Norton, 1994); and Dawson, *Blacks in and out of the Left*.

9. Haywood, *Black Bolshevik*, 222, 231.

10. Goldfield, *The Southern Key*, 332. Goldfield provides a clear-eyed assessment of both the achievements and importance of Communist organizers in fighting for civil rights and building inclusive, democratic unions, while also stressing their "sectarian stupidity," authoritarian, undemocratic internal party structures, rigid adherence to political lines dictated from Moscow, and defense of "the most horrific policies of the terror and gulags," 250, 360–62.

11. Gilmore, *Defying Dixie*, 8.

12. Cherrie Bucknor, "Black Workers, Unions, and Inequality" (Center for Economic and Policy Research, August 2016), https://cepr.net/images/stories/reports/black-workers-unions-2016-08.pdf.

13. Nelson, "Class, Race and Democracy in the CIO"; Nelson, *Divided We Stand*; Greenberg, *Race and State in Capitalist Development*, 351–54.

14. Andor Skotnes, *A New Deal for All?: Race and Class Struggles in Depression-Era Baltimore* (Durham: Duke University Press, 2012).

15. Greenberg, *Race and State in Capitalist Development*, 354.

16. Bryant Etheridge, "Contesting the Great Compression: The National Labor Relations Board and Skilled Workers' Struggle to Control Wage Differentials, 1935–1955," *Journal of Policy History* 32, no. 2 (2020): 183–213.

17. Edwin W. Smith, quoted in Etheridge, "Contesting the Great Compression," 191.

18. Etheridge, "Contesting the Great Compression," 192.

19. Etheridge, "Contesting the Great Compression," 195–97.

20. Etheridge, "Contesting the Great Compression," 201.

21. Etheridge, "Contesting the Great Compression," 202.

22. Cowie, *The Great Exception*, 17.

23. Cowie, *The Great Exception*, 26, 149, 186; Louis Hartz, *The Liberal Tradition in*

America: An Interpretation of American Political Thought since the Revolution (New York: Harcourt, Brace & World, 1963).

24. Cowie, *The Great Exception*, 31–32.

25. Remarkably, the material structures of racism, labor markets, and wage differentials are largely absent from many discussions of the New Deal's demise, while intellectuals, right-wing political activity, and political culture loom large. See for instance, Romain Huret, Nelson Lichtenstein, and Jean-Christian Vinel, *Capitalism Contested: The New Deal and Its Legacies* (Philadelphia: University of Pennsylvania Press, 2020).

26. Devah Pager, "The Mark of a Criminal Record," *American Journal of Sociology* 108, no. 5 (2003): 937–75; Devah Pager, Bart Bonikowski, and Bruce Western, "Discrimination in a Low-Wage Labor Market: A Field Experiment," *American Sociological Review* 74, no. 5 (2009): 777–99.

27. Lincoln Quillian et al., "Do Some Countries Discriminate More than Others? Evidence from 97 Field Experiments of Racial Discrimination in Hiring," *Sociological Science* 6 (2019): 467–96, https://doi.org/10.15195/v6.a18.

28. Bruce Western and Katherine Beckett, "How Unregulated Is the U.S. Labor Market? The Penal System as a Labor Market Institution," *American Journal of Sociology* 104, no. 4 (1999): 1030–60, https://doi.org/10.1086/210135; Elizabeth Hinton, *From the War on Poverty to the War on Crime* (Cambridge: Harvard University Press, 2016); Ruth Wilson Gilmore, *Golden Gulag: Prisons, Surplus, Crisis, and Opposition in Globalizing California* (Berkeley: University of California Press, 2007); and Cedric Johnson, *After Black Lives Matter: Policing and Anti-Capitalist Struggle* (London: Verso, 2023).

29. Nelson, *Divided We Stand*, 293.

30. Darity, Mullen, and Hubbard, *The Black Reparations Project*, 3, 18.

31. Symbolic reparations, or "apologies" for past harm, do little to address the entrenched structural inequalities driving racial boundary-making, and often distract attention from issues of class, as noted in Cedric Johnson's important critique of some reparations proposals, "An Open Letter to Ta-Nehisi Coates and the Liberals Who Love Him," *Jacobin*, February 3, 2016, https://jacobin.com/2016/02/ta-nehisi-coates-case-for-reparations-bernie-sanders-racism/.

Bibliography

Archival Collections Identified by Abbreviations

APTI: Association of Principals of Technical Institutions, A/PTI London Metropolitan Archives

BAC: Baltimore Association of Commerce Records, R0006-BAC, Baltimore Regional Studies Archives, University of Baltimore

BDR: Balfour Steel Co. Directors Records, Sheffield Archives

BFL: Baltimore Federation of Labor, Microfilm of Executive and General Meeting Minutes, 2 Reels, University of Maryland Special Collections and Archives, College Park, Maryland

BVLHSC: Beaver Valley Labor History Society Collection, Archives of Industrial Society 81:8, University of Pittsburgh

EASC: Edgar Allen Steel Company, MD, Sheffield Archives

FSC: Firth Steel Company, X306, Sheffield Archives

HBP: Heber Blankhorn Papers, Archives of Industrial Society 66:15, University of Pittsburgh

IUBAC: International Union of Bricklayers and Allied Craft Workers Local 33, Archives of Industrial Society: 2000:10, University of Pittsburgh

JB: John Brown & Company, X308 Sheffield Archives

JBKI: John Brown & Company, Kelham Island Industrial Museum, Sheffield

JHM: James H. Mathews & Co., Pittsburgh Business Records, 1875–1939, Archives of Industrial Society, 65:17, University of Pittsburgh

JL: Jones & Laughlin, Archives of Industrial Society 78:9 Box 1, University of Pittsburgh

JLMisc: Jones and Laughlin Corporation Historical Miscellanea, 1871–1953, Archives of Industrial Society 73:7, University of Pittsburgh

LSOA: Liverpool Steamship Owners Association, Mersey Maritime Museum, Liverpool

MDBW: Board of Welfare (Minutes), S250, 1923–1939, Maryland State Archives, Annapolis

MDGG: Governor (General File), 1920–1935 Public Schools, MSA S1041, Maryland State Archives, Annapolis

MMA: Merchants and Manufacturers Association, R0074-MMA, Baltimore Regional Studies Archives, University of Baltimore

NCA: Neighborhood Center Association Woodlawn Settlement House, Archives of Industrial Society 64:28, University of Pittsburgh

OISC: Oliver Iron and Steel Company Papers, Archives of Industrial Society 64:6, University of Pittsburgh

PADLI: Pennsylvania Department of Labor and Industry, RG 16, Pennsylvania State Archives, Harrisburg

PCL: Pittsburgh Central Labor Union, UE/Lab 96:4 Box 1, University of Pittsburgh

PUL: Pittsburgh Urban League, Archives of Industrial Society, 81:11, University of Pittsburgh

UBCDC: United Brotherhood of Carpenters District Council of Western Pennsylvania, UE/LAB 96:12 Microfilm, University of Pittsburgh

USCC: United States Chamber of Commerce, AC 1960, Hagley Museum and Archive, Wilmington, Delaware

USSNDW: United States Steel National-Duquesne Works, UE/Lab 91:6, University of Pittsburgh

WJG: William J. Gaughan Collection, Archives of Industrial Society 94:3, University of Pittsburgh

Newspapers Identified by Abbreviations

BS   Baltimore Sun
LDP   Liverpool Daily Post
PG   Pittsburgh Gazette
SDT   Sheffield Daily Telegraph
SI   Sheffield Independent

Books and Articles

Abe, Kazuhiro. "Race Relations and the Capitalist State: A Case Study of Koreans in Japan, 1917 through the Mid-1920s." *Korean Studies* 7, no. 1 (1983): 35–60. https://doi.org/10.1353/ks.1983.0000.

Adelman, Jeremy. "The Political Economy of Labour in Argentina, 1870–1930." In *Essays in Argentine Labour History, 1870–1930*, edited by Jeremy Adelman, 1–34. London: Palgrave Macmillan UK, 1992.

Agnew, Jean-Christophe. "Coming up for Air: Consumer Culture in Historical Perspective." In *Consumption and the World of Goods*, edited by John Brewer and Roy Porter, 19–39. London: Routledge, 1994.

Ahmad, Nadia. "Climate Cages: Connecting Migration, the Carceral State, Extinction Rebellion, and the Coronavirus through Cicero and 21 Savage." *Loyola Law Review* 66, no. 2 (2020): 293–328.

Alcock, George W. *Fifty Years of Railway Trade Unionism*. London [etc.]: Co-operative Printing Society Limited, 1922.

Alderman, Geoffrey. "The National Free Labour Association: A Case-Study of Organised Strike-Breaking in the Late Nineteenth and Early Twentieth Centuries." *International Review of Social History* 21, no. 3 (December 1976): 309–36.

Alexander, Peter. "Race, Class Loyalty and the Structure of Capitalism: Coal Miners in Alabama and the Transvaal, 1918–1922." *Journal of Southern African Studies* 30, no. 1 (2004): 115–32.

Ali, Omar H. *In the Lion's Mouth: Black Populism in the New South, 1886–1900.* Jackson: University Press of Mississippi, 2010.

———. "Standing Guard at the Door of Liberty: Black Populism in South Carolina, 1886–1895." *The South Carolina Historical Magazine* 107, no. 3 (2006): 190–203.

Allen, Robert C. "Manhattan Myopia; Or, Oh! Iowa! Robert C. Allen on Ben Singer's 'Manhattan Nickelodeons: New Data on Audiences and Exhibitors,' 'Cinema Journal' 34, No. 3 (Spring 1995)." *Cinema Journal* 35, no. 3 (1996): 75–103. https://doi.org/10.2307/1225767.

Allerfeldt, Kristofer. "'And We Got Here First': Albert Johnson, National Origins and Self-Interest in the Immigration Debate of the 1920s." *Journal of Contemporary History* 45, no. 1 (2010): 7–26.

Almlie, Elizabeth, Angi Fuller Wildt, Ashley Bouknight, Amanda Bowman, Lee Durbetaki, Keri Fay, Haley Grant, et al. "Prized Pieces of Land: The Impact of Reconstruction on African-American Land Ownership in Lower Richland County, South Carolina." In *Public History Program*, 123. Books and Manuscripts. Columbia: University of South Carolina Press, 2009. https://scholar commons.sc.edu/pubhist_books/3/.

Alter, Thomas. "From the Copper-Colored Sons of Montezuma to Comrade Pancho Villa: The Radicalizing Effect of Mexican Revolutionaries on the Texas Socialist Party, 1910–1917." *Labor* 12, no. 4 (2015): 83–109. https://doi.org/10.1215/1547 6715-3155161.

American Civil Liberties Union Committee on Democracy in Trade Unions. *Democracy in Trade Unions, a Survey, with a Program of Action.* New York: American Civil Liberties Union, 1943.

Anderson, Jack. "Pugilistic Prosecutions: Prize Fighting and the Courts in Nineteenth Century Britain." *Sports Historian* 21, no. 2 (2001): 35–53.

Andrews, George Reid. "Black and White Workers: São Paulo, Brazil, 1888–1928." *Hispanic American Historical Review* 68, no. 3 (August 1, 1988): 491–524.

Anglim, Christopher, and Brian Gratton. "Organized Labor and Old Age Pensions." *The International Journal of Aging and Human Development* 25, no. 2 (1987): 91–107.

Ansell, Christopher K., and Arthur L. Burris. "Bosses of the City Unite! Labor Politics and Political Machine Consolidation, 1870–1910." *Studies in American Political Development* 11, no. 1 (1997): 1–43.

Arceo, Nicolás, Ana L. Fernández, and Mariana L. González. "El mercado de trabajo en el modelo agroexportador en Argentina: el papel de la inmigración." *América Latina en la Historia Económica* 26, no. 3 (2019): e952. https://doi.org /10.18232/alhe.952.

Archer, Robin. *Why Is There No Labor Party in the United States?* Princeton: Princeton University Press, 2010.

Arkel, Dik van, and Marcel van der Linden. *Racism and the Labour Market: Historical Studies.* Bern: P. Lang, 1995.

Arnesen, Eric. *Brotherhoods of Color: Black Railroad Workers and the Struggle for Equality.* Cambridge, MA: Harvard University Press, 2001.

———. "'It Aint Like They Do In New Orleans': Race Relations, Labor Markets, and Waterfront Labor Movements in the American South, 1880–1923." In *Racism and the Labour Market: Historical Studies*, edited by Dik van Arkel and Marcel van der Linden, 57–100. Bern: P. Lang, 1995.

————. *Waterfront Workers of New Orleans: Race, Class, and Politics, 1863–1923.* New York: Oxford University Press, 1991.

Aronson, Michael. *Nickelodeon City: Pittsburgh at the Movies, 1905–1929.* Pittsburgh: University of Pittsburgh Press, 2008.

Arrighi, Giovanni. "Marxist Century, American Century: The Making and Remaking of the World Labour Movement." *New Left Review*, no. I/179 (1990): 29–63.

Arrighi, Giovanni, and Fortunata Piselli. "Capitalist Development in Hostile Environments: Feuds, Class Struggles, and Migrations in a Peripheral Region of Southern Italy." *Review (Fernand Braudel Center)* 10, no. 4 (1987): 649–751.

Azuma, Eiichiro. *In Search of Our Frontier: Japanese America and Settler Colonialism in the Construction of Japan's Borderless Empire.* Oakland: University of California Press, 2019.

Bain, George Sayers. *Profiles of Union Growth: A Comparative Statistical Portrait of Eight Countries.* Oxford: Blackwell, 1980.

Baker, Ray Stannard. *Following the Color Line: An Account of Negro Citizenship in the American Democracy.* New York: Doubleday, Page & Company, 1908.

Balachandran, G. "Workers in the World: Indian Seafarers, c. 1870s–1940s." In *Global Histories of Work*, edited by Andreas Eckert, 125–45. Berlin: De Gruyter, 2016.

Baldassar, Loretta. "Italian Migrants in Australia and Their Relationship to Italy: Return Visits, Transnational Caregiving and the Second Generation." *Journal of Mediterranean Studies* 20, no. 2 (2011): 255–82.

Barbalet, J. M. "The 'Labor Aristocracy' in Context." *Science & Society* 51, no. 2 (1987): 133–53.

Barnes, Charles Brinton. *The Longshoremen.* New York: Survey Associates, 1915.

Baselice, Vyta, Dante Burrichter, and Peter N. Stearns. "Debating the Birthday: Innovation and Resistance in Celebrating Children." *The Journal of the History of Childhood and Youth* 12, no. 2 (2019): 262–84.

Batzell, Rudi. "Free Labour, Capitalism and the Anti-Slavery Origins of Chinese Exclusion in California in the 1870s." *Past & Present* 225, no. 1 (2014): 143–86.

————. "The Labor of Social Reproduction: Household Work and Gendered Power in the History of Capitalism, 1870–1930." *The Journal of the Gilded Age and Progressive Era* 15, no. 3 (2016): 310–30.

————. "Race, Ethnicity, and Global Labor History." In *The Oxford Handbook of Global Labor History*, edited by Sven Beckert and Marcel van der Linden. New York: Oxford, forthcoming.

Batzell, Rudi, Sven Beckert, Andrew Gordon, and Gabriel Winant. "E. P. Thompson, Politics and History: Writing Social History Fifty Years after *The Making of the English Working Class*." *Journal of Social History* 48, no. 4 (2015): 753–58. https://doi.org/10.1093/jsh/shv036.

Bean, R. "Employers' Associations in the Port of Liverpool, 1890–1914." *International Review of Social History* 21, no. 3 (1976): 358–82.

Beck, E. M., and Stewart E. Tolnay. "The Killing Fields of the Deep South: The Market for Cotton and the Lynching of Blacks, 1882–1930." *American Sociological Review* 55, no. 4 (1990): 526–39.

Beckert, Sven. *Empire of Cotton: A Global History.* New York: Alfred A. Knopf, 2014.

Belchem, John. *Irish, Catholic and Scouse: The History of the Liverpool-Irish, 1800–1939*. Liverpool: Liverpool University Press, 2007.

———, ed. *Popular Politics, Riot and Labour: Essays in Liverpool History, 1790–1940*. Liverpool: Liverpool University Press, 1992.

Béliard, Yann. "Imperial Internationalism? Hull Labour's Support for South African Trade-Unionism on the Eve of the Great War." *Labour History Review* 74, no. 3 (2009): 319–29.

Belich, James. *Replenishing the Earth: The Settler Revolution and the Rise of the Angloworld*. Oxford: Oxford University Press, 2009.

Benswanger, William E. "Professional Baseball in Pittsburgh." *Western Pennsylvania History* 30, no. 1-2 (1947): 9–14.

Bernhardt, Kathryn. *Rents, Taxes, and Peasant Resistance: The Lower Yangzi Region, 1840–1950*. Stanford, CA: Stanford University Press, 1992.

Bernstein, Iver. *The New York City Draft Riots: Their Significance for American Society and Politics in the Age of the Civil War*. Oxford: Oxford University Press, 1990.

Biernat, Carolina. "Las Dos Vías de La Imaginación Poblacionista Argentina: Natalismo e Inmigración Entre 1914 y 1955." *Ciclos En La Historia, La Economia y La Sociedad* 15, no. 30 (2005). http://bibliotecadigital.econ.uba.ar/econ/collection/ciclos/document/ciclos_v15_n30_08.

Bingham, J. H. *The Period of the Sheffield School Board, 1870–1903*. Sheffield: Northend, 1949.

Bleser, Carol K. Rothrock. *The Promised Land: The History of the South Carolina Land Commission, 1869–1890*. Columbia: University of South Carolina Press, 1969.

Bodnar, John E., Roger D. Simon, and Michael P. Weber. *Lives of Their Own: Blacks, Italians, and Poles in Pittsburgh, 1900–1960*. Urbana: University of Illinois Press, 1982.

Bonacich, Edna. "A Theory of Ethnic Antagonism: The Split Labor Market." *American Sociological Review* 37, no. 5 (1972): 547–59. https://doi.org/10.2307/2093450.

———. "Advanced Capitalism and Black/ White Race Relations in the United States: A Split Labor Market Interpretation." *American Sociological Review* 41, no. 1 (1976): 34–51. https://doi.org/10.2307/2094371.

Bonilla-Silva, Eduardo. "Rethinking Racism: Toward a Structural Interpretation." *American Sociological Review* 62, no. 3 (1997): 465–80. https://doi.org/10.2307/2657316.

Bonner, Philip, Jonathan Hyslop, and Lucien van der Walt. "Rethinking Worlds of Labour: Southern African Labour History in International Context." In *Global Histories of Work*, edited by Andreas Eckert, 90–122. Berlin: De Gruyter, 2016.

Boris, Eileen. "'You Wouldn't Want One of 'Em Dancing with Your Wife': Racialized Bodies on the Job in World War II." *American Quarterly* 50, no. 1 (1998): 77–108.

Bourdieu, Pierre. *Distinction: A Social Critique of the Judgement of Taste*. Cambridge, MA: Harvard University Press, 1984.

———. *Outline of a Theory of Practice*. Translated by Richard Nice. New York: Cambridge University Press, 1977.

Boustan, Leah Platt. *Competition in the Promised Land: Black Migrants in Northern Cities and Labor Markets*. Princeton: Princeton University Press, 2016.

Bradford, Helen. *A Taste of Freedom: The ICU in Rural South Africa, 1924–1930*. New Haven: Yale University Press, 1987.

Breckenridge, Keith. "Fighting for a White South Africa: White Working-Class Racism and the 1922 Rand Revolt." *South African Historical Journal* 57, no. 1 (January 2007): 228–43. https://doi.org/10.1080/02582470709464719.

———. "'We Must Speak for Ourselves': The Rise and Fall of a Public Sphere on the South African Gold Mines, 1920 to 1931." *Comparative Studies in Society and History* 40, no. 1 (January 1998): 71–108.

Breitzer, Susan Roth. "Race, Immigration, and Contested Americanness: Black Nativism and the American Labor Movement, 1880–1930." *Race/Ethnicity: Multidisciplinary Global Contexts* 4, no. 2 (2011): 269–83.

Briggs, Asa, and John Saville, ed. *Essays in Labour History: In Memory of G. D. H. Cole, 25 September 1889–14 January 1959*. London: Macmillan, 1960.

Briggs, Vernon M. *Immigration and American Unionism*. Ithaca: Cornell University Press, 2001.

Brilliant, Mark. *The Color of America Has Changed: How Racial Diversity Shaped Civil Rights Reform in California, 1941–1978*. New York: Oxford University Press, 2010.

Brody, David. *Steelworkers in America: The Nonunion Era*. Urbana: University of Illinois Press, 1998.

Brown, Cliff. "Racial Conflict and Split Labor Markets: The AFL Campaign to Organize Steel Workers, 1918–1919." *Social Science History* 22, no. 3 (October 1, 1998): 319–47.

Brown, Cliff, and Terry Boswell. "Strikebreaking or Solidarity in the Great Steel Strike of 1919: A Split Labor Market, Game-Theoretic, and QCA Analysis." *American Journal of Sociology* 100, no. 6 (1995): 1479–1519.

Brown, John W. *World Migration and Labour, Supplemented by Report of World Migration Congress*. Amsterdam: International Federation of Trade Unions, 1926.

Bucknor, Cherrie. "Black Workers, Unions, and Inequality." Center for Economic and Policy Research, August 2016. https://cepr.net/images/stories/reports /black-workers-unions-2016-08.pdf.

Bundy, Colin. *The Rise and Fall of the South African Peasantry*. Cape Town: David Philip, 1988.

Cahn, Susan K. "Turn, Turn, Turn: There Is a Reason (for Sports History)." *The Journal of American History* 101, no. 1 (2014): 181–83.

Caldemeyer, Dana M. *Union Renegades: Miners, Capitalism, and Organizing in the Gilded Age*. Urbana: University of Illinois Press, 2021.

Campbell, Fergus. *Land and Revolution: Nationalist Politics in the West of Ireland, 1891–1921*. Oxford: Oxford University Press, 2005.

Campbell, Sir George. *White and Black: The Outcome of a Visit to the United States*. New York: R. Worthington, 1879.

Campet, Fidel Makoto. "Housing in Black Pittsburgh: Community Struggles and the State, 1916–1973." PhD diss., Carnegie Mellon University, 2011.

Carlino, P. J. "Bleacher Bugs and Fifty-Centers: The Social Stratification of Baseball Fans through Stadium Design, 1880–1920." *Buildings & Landscapes: Journal of the Vernacular Architecture Forum* 28, no. 1 (2021): 5–29.

Caruso, Amerigo, and Claire Morelon. "The Threat from Within across Empires: Strikes, Labor Migration, and Violence in Central Europe, 1900–1914." *Central European History* 54, no. 1 (2021): 86–111.

Casebeer, Kenneth M. "Aliquippa: The Company Town and Contested Power in the Construction of Law." *Buffalo Law Review* 43 (1995): 617–87.

Castles, Stephen, and Godula Kosack. *Immigrant Workers and Class Structure in Western Europe.* 2nd ed. Oxford: Oxford University Press, 1985.

———. "The Function of Labour Immigration in Western European Capitalism." *New Left Review* 73 (1972): 3–21.

Cherlin, Andrew J. "'Good, Better, Best': Upward Mobility and Loss of Community in a Black Steelworker Neighborhood." *Du Bois Review* 17, no. 2 (Fall 2020): 211–31. http://dx.doi.org/10.1017/S1742058X20000284.

Childs, Michael James. *Labour's Apprentices: Working-Class Lads in Late Victorian and Edwardian England.* Montreal: McGill-Queen's University Press, 1992.

Clark, Samuel. *Social Origins of the Irish Land War.* Princeton: Princeton University Press, 2014.

———. "Strange Bedfellows? The Land League Alliances." In *Land Questions in Modern Ireland,* edited by Fergus Campbell and Tony Varley, 87–116. Manchester: Manchester University Press, 2013.

Clegg, H. A., et al. *A History of British Trade Unions Since 1889: Volume 1: 1889–1910.* London: Clarendon Press, 1964.

Clegg, Hugh Armstrong. *A History of British Trade Unions Since 1889: Volume II: 1911–1933.* Oxford: Oxford University Press, 1985.

Clover, Joshua. *Riot. Strike. Riot: The New Era of Uprisings.* London: Verso, 2016.

Coates, James Roland. "Recreation and Sport in the African-American Community of Baltimore, 1890–1920." PhD diss., University of Maryland, College Park, 1991.

Cohen, Elior, and Jeff Biddle. "Immigration Disruptions and the Wages of Unskilled Labor in the 1920s." *The Federal Reserve Bank of Kansas City Research Working Papers,* September 27, 2022.

Cohen, Lizabeth. *A Consumers' Republic: The Politics of Mass Consumption in Post-war America.* New York: Knopf, 2003.

———. *Making a New Deal: Industrial Workers in Chicago, 1919–1939.* Cambridge: Cambridge University Press, 1991.

Cole, Peter. *Wobblies on the Waterfront: Interracial Unionism in Progressive-Era Philadelphia.* Urbana: University of Illinois Press, 2007.

Coleman, Daniel. "Returning to the Rand Revolt: Centering Settler Colonialism and Racial Capitalism in Labour History." MA thesis, University of Cape Town, 2021.

Collins, William J. "When the Tide Turned: Immigration and the Delay of the Great Black Migration." *The Journal of Economic History* 57, no. 3 (1997): 607–32.

Collomp, Catherine. "Unions, Civics, and National Identity." *Labor History* 29, no. 4 (Fall 1988): 450–74.

Conell, Carol, and Kim Voss. "Formal Organization and the Fate of Social Movements: Craft Association and Class Alliance in the Knights of Labor." *American Sociological Review* 55, no. 2 (1990): 255.

Constantine, Stephen. "British Emigration to the Empire-Commonwealth since 1880: From Overseas Settlement to Diaspora?" *The Journal of Imperial and Commonwealth History* 31, no. 2 (2003): 16–35.

Corzine, Jay, Lin Huff-Corzine, and James C. Creech. "The Tenant Labor Market and Lynching in the South: A Test of Split Labor Market Theory." *Sociological Inquiry* 58, no. 3 (1988): 261–78.

Costaguta, Lorenzo. *Workers of All Colors Unite: Race and the Origins of American Socialism*. Urbana: University of Illinois Press, 2023.

Cowie, Jefferson. *The Great Exception: The New Deal and the Limits of American Politics*. Princeton: Princeton University Press, 2016.

Croak, Thomas M. "The Professionalization of Prizefighting: Pittsburgh at the Turn of the Century." *Western Pennsylvania History: 1918–2016* 62, no. 4 (1979): 333–44.

Cronin, James. "Strikes and Power in Britain, 1870–1920." *International Review of Social History* 32, no. 2 (1987): 144–67.

Cross, Gary. "Labour in Settler-State Democracies: Comparative Perspectives on Australia and the US, 1860–1920." *Labour History* 70 (May 1996): 1–24. https://doi.org/10.2307/27516407.

———. *Immigrant Workers in Industrial France: The Making of a New Laboring Class*. Philadelphia: Temple University Press, 1983.

Crowfoot, Silas Niobeh Tsaba. "Community Development for a White City: Race Making, Improvementism, and the Cincinnati Race Riots and Anti-Abolition Riots of 1829, 1836, and 1841." PhD diss., Portland State University, 2010.

Currarino, Rosanne. *The Labor Question in America: Economic Democracy in the Gilded Age*. Urbana: University of Illinois Press, 2011.

Curthoys, Ann. "Conflict and Consensus." *Labour History*, no. 35 (November 1978): 48–65.

Dal Lago, Enrico. *Civil War and Agrarian Unrest: The Confederate South and Southern Italy*. Cambridge: Cambridge University Press, 2018.

D'Amico, Diana. "An Uneasy Union: Women Teachers, Organized Labor, and the Contested Ideology of Profession during the Progressive Era." *Labor: Studies in Working-Class History of the Americas* 14, no. 3 (2017): 35–54.

Darden, Joe T. "The Effect of World War I on Black Occupational and Residential Segregation: The Case of Pittsburgh." *Journal of Black Studies* 18, no. 3 (March 1, 1988): 297–312.

Darity, William A., A. Kirsten Mullen, and Lucas Hubbard. *The Black Reparations Project: A Handbook for Racial Justice*. Oakland: University of California Press, 2023.

Daunton, Martin J. *House and Home in the Victorian City: Working Class Housing, 1850–1914*. London: E. Arnold, 1983.

———. "Jack Ashore: Seamen in Cardiff before 1914." *Welsh History Review* 9, no. 2 (1978): 176–203.

———. "Payment and Participation: Welfare and State-Formation in Britain, 1900–1951." *Past & Present* 150 (1996): 169–216.

Davies, Sam. *Liverpool Labour: Social and Political Influences on the Development of the Labour Party in Liverpool, 1900–1939*. Keele, UK: Keele University Press, 1996.

Davin, Eric Leif. "Blue Collar Democracy: Ethnic Workers and Class Politics in Pittsburgh's Steel Valley, 1914–1948." PhD diss., University of Pittsburgh, 1999.

Davis, Colin J. *Power at Odds: The 1922 National Railroad Shopmen's Strike*. Urbana: University of Illinois Press, 1997.

Davis, Graham. *The Irish in Britain, 1815–1914*. Dublin: Gill and Macmillan, 1991.

Dawson, Michael C. *Blacks in and out of the Left*. The W.E.B. Du Bois Lectures. Cambridge, MA: Harvard University Press, 2013.

Deininger, Klaus. "Making Negotiated Land Reform Work: Initial Experience from Colombia, Brazil and South Africa." *World Development* 27, no. 4 (April 1999): 651–72.

Derenoncourt, Ellora, Chi Hyun Kim, Moritz Kuhn, and Moritz Schularick. "Wealth of Two Nations: The U.S. Racial Wealth Gap, 1860–2020." Working Paper. National Bureau of Economic Research, June 2022. https://doi.org/10.3386/w30101.

DeVault, Ileen A. *United Apart: Gender and the Rise of Craft Unionism*. Ithaca: Cornell University Press, 2004.

Devoto, Fernando. *Historia de la inmigración en la Argentina*. Buenos Aires: Editorial Sudamericana, 2003.

———. "El Revés de La Trama: Políticas Migratorias y Prácticas Administrativas En La Argentina (1919–1949)." *Desarrollo Económico* 41, no. 162 (2001): 281–304. https://doi.org/10.2307/3455989.

Dickerson, Dennis C. *Out of the Crucible: Black Steel Workers in Western Pennsylvania, 1875–1980*. New York: SUNY Press, 1986.

Dingle, A. E. "Drink and Working-Class Living Standards in Britain, 1870–1914." *The Economic History Review* 25, no. 4 (1972): 608–22.

Dower, John W. *Embracing Defeat: Japan in the Wake of World War II*. New York: W.W. Norton & Co., 1999.

Driscoll, Mark. *Absolute Erotic, Absolute Grotesque: The Living, Dead, and Undead in Japan's Imperialism, 1895–1945*. Durham, NC: Duke University Press, 2010.

Du Bois, George Bache. "The Search for a Better Life: Baltimore's Workers, 1865–1916." PhD diss., University of Maryland, 1995.

Du Bois, W. E. B. *Black Reconstruction in America, 1860–1880*. New York: Free Press, 1998 [1935].

———. *The Negro Artisan. Report of a Social Study Made under the Direction of Atlanta University; Together with the Proceedings of the Seventh Conference for the Study of the Negro Problems, Held at Atlanta University, on May 27th, 1902*. Atlanta: Atlanta University Press, 1902.

Dubofsky, Melvyn. *John L. Lewis: A Biography*. Abridged ed. Urbana: University of Illinois Press, 1986.

Dubofsky, Melvyn, Rick Halpern, Gary Marks, and Robert Justin Goldstein. "Labor History Symposium: Responses." *Labor History* 51, no. 2 (May 2010): 295–318.

Duin, Pieter Van. "White Building Workers and Coloured Competition in the South African Labour Market, c. 1890–1940." *International Review of Social History* 37, no. 1 (1992): 59–90.

Duis, Perry. *The Saloon: Public Drinking in Chicago and Boston, 1880–1920*. Urbana: University of Illinois Press, 1983.

Edwards, Richard. "African Americans and the Southern Homestead Act." *Great Plains Quarterly* 39, no. 2 (2019): 103–29.

Ehrlich, Richard L. "Immigrant Strikebreaking Activity: A Sampling of Opinion Expressed in the National Labor Tribune, 1878–1885." *Labor History*, September 1, 1974. https://doi.org/10.1080/00236567408584311.

Eley, Geoff. "Historicizing the Global, Politicizing Capital: Giving the Present a Name." *History Workshop Journal* 63, no. 1 (2007): 154–88. https://doi.org/10.1093/hwj/dbm010.

Enstad, Nan. *Ladies of Labor, Girls of Adventure: Working Women, Popular Culture, and Labor Politics at the Turn of the Twentieth Century.* New York: Columbia University Press, 1999.

Etheridge, Bryant. "Contesting the Great Compression: The National Labor Relations Board and Skilled Workers' Struggle to Control Wage Differentials, 1935–1955." *Journal of Policy History* 32, no. 2 (April 2020): 183–213.

Evans, Ivan. *Cultures of Violence: Lynching and Racial Killing in South Africa and the American South.* Manchester: Manchester University Press, 2009.

Evans, Jessica. "The Uneven and Combined Development of Class Forces: Migration as Combined Development." *Cambridge Review of International Affairs* 29, no. 3 (2016): 1061–73.

Evans, Maurice S. *Black and White in the Southern States; a Study of the Race Problem in the United States from a South African Point of View.* London: Longmans, Green and Co., 1915. http://archive.org/details/blackwhiteinso00evan.

Falkinger, Josef, and Volker Grossmann. "Oligarchic Land Ownership, Entrepreneurship, and Economic Development." *Journal of Development Economics* 101 (March 2013): 206–15.

Faue, Elizabeth. *Community of Suffering and Struggle: Women, Men, and the Labor Movement in Minneapolis, 1915–1945.* Chapel Hill: University of North Carolina Press, 2016.

Fenna, Alan. "Putting the 'Australian Settlement' in Perspective." *Labour History*, no. 102 (May 2012): 99–118.

Feurer, Rosemary, and Chad Pearson, eds. *Against Labor: How US Employers Organized to Defeat Union Activism.* Urbana: University of Illinois Press, 2017.

Fields, Barbara Jeanne. "The Advent of Capitalist Agriculture: The New South in a Bourgeois World." In *Essays on the Postbellum Southern Economy*, edited by Thavolia Glymph and John J. Kushma, 73–94. College Station: A&M University Press, 1985.

Fields, Karen E. *Racecraft: The Soul of Inequality in American Life.* London: Verso, 2012.

Fine, Janice, and Daniel J. Tichenor. "A Movement Wrestling: American Labor's Enduring Struggle with Immigration, 1866–2007." *Studies in American Political Development* 23, no. 1 (2009): 84–113. https://doi.org/10.1017/S0898588X090 00042.

Fink, Leon. *Workingmen's Democracy: The Knights of Labor and American Politics.* Urbana: University of Illinois Press, 1983.

Finnegan, Terence. *A Deed So Accursed: Lynching in Mississippi and South Carolina, 1881–1940.* Charlottesville: University of Virginia Press, 2013.

Finot, Jean. *The Death-Agony of the "Science" of Race.* London: Stead's Publishing House, 1911.

Foner, Eric. *Nothing but Freedom: Emancipation and Its Legacy.* Baton Rouge: Louisiana State University Press, 1983.

———. *Reconstruction: America's Unfinished Revolution, 1863–1877.* New York: Harper Collins, 2002 [1988].

Foner, Philip S. "A Labor Voice for Black Equality: The *Boston Daily Evening Voice*, 1864–1867." *Science & Society* 38, no. 3 (1974): 304–25.

———. *Organized Labor and the Black Worker, 1619–1973.* New York: International Publishers, 1974.

Foote, Christopher L., Warren C. Whatley, and Gavin Wright. "Arbitraging a Discriminatory Labor Market: Black Workers at the Ford Motor Company, 1918–1947." *Journal of Labor Economics* 21, no. 3 (July 2003): 493–532. https://doi.org/10.1086/374957.

Forbath, William E. "Courts, Constitutions, and Labor Politics in England and America: A Study of the Constitutive Power of Law." *Law & Social Inquiry* 16, no. 1 (1991): 1–34.

Fortune, Timothy Thomas. *Black and White: Land, Labor, and Politics in the South.* New York: Washington Square Press, 2007 [1884].

Fox, Cybelle. *Three Worlds of Relief: Race, Immigration, and the American Welfare State from the Progressive Era to the New Deal.* Princeton: Princeton University Press, 2012.

Fredrickson, George M. "From Exceptionalism to Variability: Recent Developments in Cross-National Comparative History." *The Journal of American History* 82, no. 2 (1995): 587–604.

———. *The Arrogance of Race: Historical Perspectives on Slavery, Racism, and Social Inequality.* Middletown, CT: Wesleyan University Press, 1988.

———. *White Supremacy: A Comparative Study in American and South African History.* New York: Oxford University Press, 1981.

Freund, David M. P. *Colored Property: State Policy and White Racial Politics in Suburban America.* Chicago: University of Chicago Press, 2010.

Friedman, Gerald. "Dividing Labor: Urban Politics and Big-City Construction in Late-Nineteenth-Century America." In *Strategic Factors in Nineteenth Century American Economic History: A Volume to Honor Robert W. Fogel,* edited by Claudia Dale Goldin and Hugh Rockoff, 447–64. Chicago: University of Chicago Press, 1992.

Frost, Diane. *Ethnic Labour and British Imperial Trade: A History of Ethnic Seafarers in the UK.* London: F. Cass, 1995.

Fujitani, Takashi. *Race for Empire: Koreans as Japanese and Japanese as Americans during World War II.* Berkeley: University of California Press, 2011.

Gaither, Gerald H. *Blacks and the Populist Movement: Ballots and Bigotry in the New South.* Rev. ed. Tuscaloosa: University of Alabama Press, 2005.

Geary, Dick. *European Labour Protest, 1848–1939.* London: Methuen, 1981.

Gelber, Steven M. "Do-It-Yourself: Constructing, Repairing and Maintaining Domestic Masculinity." *American Quarterly* 49, no. 1 (1997): 66–112.

———. *Hobbies: Leisure and the Culture of Work in America.* New York: Columbia University Press, 1999.

Gerber, Larry G. "Shifting Perspectives on American Exceptionalism: Recent Literature on American Labor Relations and Labor Politics." *Journal of American Studies* 31, no. 2 (1997): 253–74.

Gilmore, Glenda. *Defying Dixie: The Radical Roots of Civil Rights, 1919–1950.* New York: W.W. Norton & Co., 2008.

———. *Gender and Jim Crow: Women and the Politics of White Supremacy in North Carolina, 1896–1920.* 2nd ed. Chapel Hill: University of North Carolina Press, 2019.

Gilmore, Ruth Wilson. *Golden Gulag: Prisons, Surplus, Crisis, and Opposition in Globalizing California.* Berkeley: University of California Press, 2007.

Glenn, Evelyn Nakano. *Unequal Freedom: How Race and Gender Shaped American Citizenship and Labor.* Cambridge, MA: Harvard University Press, 2002.

Glickman, Lawrence B. *A Living Wage: American Workers and the Making of Consumer Society*. Ithaca, NY: Cornell University Press, 1997.

Glotzer, Paige. *How the Suburbs Were Segregated: Developers and the Business of Exclusionary Housing, 1890–1960*. New York: Columbia University Press, 2020.

Go, Julian. "Three Tensions in the Theory of Racial Capitalism." *Sociological Theory* 31, no. 1 (2021): 38–47.

Göbel, Thomas. "Becoming American: Ethnic Workers and the Rise of the CIO." *Labor History* 29, no. 2 (March 1988): 173–98.

Golby, J. M., and A. W. Purdue. *The Civilisation of the Crowd: Popular Culture in England, 1750–1900*. New York: Schocken Books, 1985 [1984].

Goldberg, Joseph Phillip. "American Seamen: A Study in Twentieth Century Collective Action." PhD diss., Columbia University, 1951.

Goldfield, Michael. *The Southern Key: Class, Race, and Radicalism in the 1930s and 1940s*. New York: Oxford University Press, 2020.

Goldin, Claudia Dale, and Gary D. Libecap, eds. *The Regulated Economy: A Historical Approach to Political Economy*. Chicago: University of Chicago Press, 1994.

Goldstein, Robert Justin. "Labor History Symposium: Political Repression of the American Labor Movement during Its Formative Years—A Comparative Perspective." *Labor History* 51, no. 2 (2010): 271–93.

Gonzalez, Carmen G. "Migration as Reparation: Climate Change and the Disruption of Borders Climate Justice Symposium." *Loyola Law Review* 66, no. 2 (2020): 401–44.

Gooderson, Philip. "'Noisy and Dangerous Boys': The Slogging Gang Phenomenon in Late Nineteenth-Century Birmingham." *Midland History* 38, no. 1 (2013): 58–79.

Gottschang, Thomas R., and Diana Lary. *Swallows and Settlers: The Great Migration from North China to Manchuria*. Ann Arbor: Center for Chinese Studies, The University of Michigan, 2000.

Grant, Linda May. "Women Workers and the Sexual Division of Labour: Liverpool, 1890–1939." PhD diss., University of Liverpool, 1987.

Greenberg, Stanley B. *Race and State in Capitalist Development: Studies on South Africa, Alabama, Northern Ireland and Israel*. New Haven: Yale University Press, 1980.

Greene, Julie. *Pure and Simple Politics: The American Federation of Labor and Political Activism, 1881–1917*. New York: Cambridge University Press, 1998.

———. "Rethinking the Boundaries of Class: Labor History and Theories of Class and Capitalism." *Labor* 18, no. 2 (2021): 92–112. https://doi.org/10.1215/15476715-8849628.

Grimsted, David. "Ante-Bellum Labor: Violence, Strike, and Communal Arbitration." *Journal of Social History* 19, no. 1 (1985): 5–28.

Groeger, Cristina Viviana. *The Education Trap: Schools and the Remaking of Inequality in Boston*. Cambridge, MA: Harvard University Press, 2021.

Guinnane, Timothy W., and Ronald I. Miller. "The Limits to Land Reform: The Land Acts in Ireland, 1870–1909." *Economic Development and Cultural Change* 45, no. 3 (1997): 591–612.

Guldi, Jo. *The Long Land War: The Global Struggle for Occupancy Rights*. New Haven: Yale University Press, 2022.

Hahamovitch, Cindy. *No Man's Land: Jamaican Guestworkers in America and the Global History of Deportable Labor*. Princeton: Princeton University Press, 2011.

Hahamovitch, Cindy, and Rick Halpern. "Not a 'Sack of Potatoes': Why Labor Historians Need to Take Agriculture Seriously." *International Labor and Working-Class History*, no. 65 (2004): 3–10.

Hall, Raymond A. "Kings, Knights, and Pawns: Black Coal Miners and Racial Conflict in Washington Territory." *The Pacific Northwest Quarterly* 105, no. 2 (2014): 85–96.

Hall, Stuart. *Essential Essays, Volume 1: Foundations of Cultural Studies*. Edited by David Morley. Durham: Duke University Press, 2018.

Halpern, Rick, and Jonathan Morris. "The Persistence of Exceptionalism: Class Formation and the Comparative Method." In *American Exceptionalism? US Working-Class Formation in an International Context*, edited by Rick Halpern and Jonathan Morris, 1–13. London: Palgrave Macmillan, 1997.

Hargreaves, John. *Sport, Power and Culture: A Social and Historical Analysis of Popular Sports in Britain*. Cambridge, UK: Polity Press, 1986.

Harris, Howell. "Between Convergence and Exceptionalism: Americans and the British Model of Labor Relations, c. 1867–1920." *Labor History* 48, no. 2 (May 1, 2007): 141–73. https://doi.org/10.1080/00236560701224726.

Harris, Karen. "The 1907 Strike: A Watershed in South African White Miner Trade Unionism." *Kleio* 23, no. 1 (January 1991): 32–51.

Harris, Richard, and Robert Lewis. "The Geography of North American Cities and Suburbs, 1900–1950: A New Synthesis." *Journal of Urban History* 27, no. 3 (2001): 262–92.

Hartt, Rollin Lynde. *The People at Play*. New York: Houghton Mifflin, 1909.

Hartz, Louis. *The Liberal Tradition in America: An Interpretation of American Political Thought since the Revolution*. New York: Harcourt, Brace & World, 1963.

Harvey, Katherine A. "The Knights of Labor in the Maryland Coal Fields, 1878–1882." *Labor History* 10, no. 4 (1969): 555.

Hattam, Victoria Charlotte. *Labor Visions and State Power: The Origins of Business Unionism in the United States*. Princeton: Princeton University Press, 1993.

Hatton, T. J., G. R. Boyer, and R. E. Bailey. "The Union Wage Effect in Late Nineteenth Century Britain." *Economica* 61, no. 244 (1994): 435–56.

Hatton, Timothy J., and Jeffrey G. Williamson. "After the Famine: Emigration from Ireland, 1850–1913." *The Journal of Economic History* 53, no. 3 (1993): 575–600.

Haydu, Jeffrey. *Between Craft and Class: Skilled Workers and Factory Politics in the United States and Britain, 1890–1922*. Berkeley: University of California Press, 1988.

Haywood, Harry. *Black Bolshevik: Autobiography of an Afro-American Communist*. Chicago: Liberator Press, 1978.

Hazelton, Andrew J. *Labor's Outcasts: Migrant Farmworkers and Unions in North America, 1934–1966*. Urbana: University of Illinois Press, 2022.

Hearn, Mark, and Harry Knowles. *One Big Union: A History of the Australian Workers Union, 1886–1994*. Cambridge: Cambridge University Press, 1996.

Heideman, Paul. "Racecraft as a Challenge to the Sociology of Race." *Sociology of Race and Ethnicity* 9, no. 1 (2023): 119–23. https://doi.org/10.1177/233264922 21136164.

Herbert, Ulrich. *A History of Foreign Labor in Germany, 1880–1980: Seasonal Workers, Forced Laborers, Guest Workers.* Ann Arbor: University of Michigan Press, 1990.

Herbin-Triant, Elizabeth A. *Threatening Property: Race, Class, and Campaigns to Legislate Jim Crow Neighborhoods.* New York: Columbia University Press, 2019.

Hey, David. *A History of Sheffield.* Lancaster: Carnegie Pub., 1998.

Higginson, John. "Privileging the Machines: American Engineers, Indentured Chinese and White Workers in South Africa's Deep-Level Gold Mines, 1902–1907." *International Review of Social History* 52, no. 1 (2007): 1–34.

Higham, John. "Origins of Immigration Restriction, 1882–1897: A Social Analysis." *The Mississippi Valley Historical Review* 39, no. 1 (1952): 77–88.

Hilton, Matthew. *Consumerism in Twentieth-Century Britain: The Search for a Historical Movement.* Cambridge: Cambridge University Press, 2003.

Hinton, Elizabeth. *From the War on Poverty to the War on Crime.* Cambridge, MA: Harvard University Press, 2016.

Hirson, Baruch. "The General Strike of 1922." *Searchlight South Africa* 3, no. 3 (1993): 63-94.

Hoagland, H. E. "Trade Unionism in the Iron Industry: A Decadent Organization." *The Quarterly Journal of Economics* 31, no. 4 (1917): 674–89.

Hobsbawm, E. J. *Labouring Men: Studies in the History of Labour.* New York: Basic Books, 1965.

———. *Worlds of Labour: Further Studies in the History of Labour.* London: Weidenfeld and Nicolson, 1984.

Holbrook, Carolyn. "The Transformation of Labor Party Immigration Policy, 1901–1945." *Journal of Australian Studies* 40, no. 4 (2016): 403–17.

Hollowak, Thomas L. *A History of Polish Longshoremen and Their Role in the Establishment of a Union at the Port of Baltimore.* Baltimore: History Press, 1996.

Holmes, William F. "The Demise of the Colored Farmers' Alliance." *The Journal of Southern History* 41, no. 2 (1975): 187–200.

Holt, James. "Trade Unionism in the British and US Steel Industries, 1880–1914." *Labor History* 18, no. 1 (1977): 5.

Holt, R. J. "Football and the Urban Way of Life in Nineteenth-Century Britain." In *Pleasure, Profit, Proselytism,* edited by J. A. Mangan, 67–85. New York: Routledge, 1988.

Honey, Michael K. *Southern Labor and Black Civil Rights: Organizing Memphis Workers.* Urbana: University of Illinois Press, 1993.

Hopkins, Eric. "Working Class Life in Birmingham Between the Wars, 1918–1939." *Midland History* 15, no. 1 (January 1, 1990): 129–50.

Horgan, Matt. "Blood Sport in Pittsburgh: An Analysis of Prize Fighting and Cock Fighting in an American Industrial City." *The Sloping Halls Review* (2013): 21–29.

Hudson, Hosea, and Nell Irvin Painter. *The Narrative of Hosea Hudson: The Life and Times of a Black Radical.* New York: Norton, 1994.

Hunter, Tera W. *To 'joy My Freedom: Southern Black Women's Lives and Labors after the Civil War.* Cambridge, MA: Harvard University Press, 1997.

Huret, Romain, Nelson Lichtenstein, and Jean-Christian Vinel. *Capitalism Contested: The New Deal and Its Legacies.* Philadelphia: University of Pennsylvania Press, 2020.

Hurt, J. S. *Elementary Schooling and the Working Classes, 1860–1918.* London: Routledge & Keegan Paul, 1979.

Huttman, John P. "The Impact of Land Reform on Agricultural Production in Ireland." *Agricultural History* 46, no. 3 (1972): 353–68.

Hyslop, Jonathan. "Scottish Labour, Race, and Southern African Empire c. 1880–1922: A Reply to Kenefick." *International Review of Social History* 55, no. 1 (April 2010): 63–81. https://doi.org/10.1017/S0020859009990629.

———. "The Imperial Working Class Makes Itself 'White': White Labourism in Britain, Australia, and South Africa Before the First World War." *Journal of Historical Sociology* 12, no. 4 (1999): 398–421.

Ince, Onur Ulas. *Colonial Capitalism and the Dilemmas of Liberalism.* Oxford: Oxford University Press, 2018.

Ingham, Alan, and Stephen Hardy. "Sport: Structuration, Subjugation and Hegemony." *Theory, Culture & Society* 2, no. 2 (1984): 85–103.

Ingham, John N. "A Strike in the Progressive Era: McKees Rocks, 1909." *The Pennsylvania Magazine of History and Biography* 90, no. 3 (1966): 353–77.

Ingram, Phillip. "Sectarianism in the North West of England, with Special Reference to Class Relationships in the City of Liverpool, 1846–1914." PhD diss., Lancashire Polytechnic, 1987.

Jackson, Dan. "'Friends of the Union': Liverpool, Ulster, and Home Rule, 1910–1914." *Transactions of the Historic Society of Lancashire and Cheshire* 152 (2003): 101–29.

Jacoby, Sanford M. *Masters to Managers: Historical and Comparative Perspectives on American Employers.* New York: Columbia University Press, 1991.

Janis, Ely M. *A Greater Ireland: The Land League and Transatlantic Nationalism in Gilded Age America.* Madison: The University of Wisconsin Press, 2015.

Jeeves, Alan. *Migrant Labour in South Africa's Mining Economy: The Struggle for the Gold Mines' Labour Supply, 1890–1920.* Kingston: McGill-Queen's University Press, 1985.

Jenkinson, J. "The 1919 Race Riots in Britain: Their Background and Consequences." PhD diss., University of Edinburgh, 1987.

Jeon, Yoong-Deok, and Young-Yong Kim. "Land Reform, Income Redistribution, and Agricultural Production in Korea." *Economic Development and Cultural Change* 48, no. 2 (2000): 253–68.

Jessup, Angelique D. "Backyard Battles: Local Struggles for African American Political Advancement in Baltimore, 1920–1944." PhD diss., University of Michigan–Ann Arbor, 2010.

Johnson, Cedric. *After Black Lives Matter: Policing and Anti-Capitalist Struggle.* London: Verso, 2023.

———. "An Open Letter to Ta-Nehisi Coates and the Liberals Who Love Him." *Jacobin*, February 3, 2016. https://jacobin.com/2016/02/ta-nehisi-coates-case-for-reparations-bernie-sanders-racism.

———. "The Wages of Roediger: Why Three Decades of Whiteness Studies Has Not Produced the Left We Need." *Nonsite.Org* (blog), September 9, 2019. https://nonsite.org/the-wages-of-roediger-why-three-decades-of-whiteness-studies-has-not-produced-the-left-we-need.

Johnstone, Frederick A. *Class, Race, and Gold: A Study of Class Relations and Racial Discrimination in South Africa.* London: Routledge & K. Paul, 1976.

Jones, Jacqueline. *American Work: Four Centuries of Black and White Labor.* New York: W.W. Norton, 1998.

Jones, Stephen G. *Sport, Politics, and the Working Class: Organised Labour and Sport in Inter-War Britain.* Manchester: Manchester University Press, 1988.

———. "State Intervention in Sport and Leisure in Britain between the Wars." *Journal of Contemporary History* 22, no. 1 (1987): 163–82.

———. *Workers at Play: A Social and Economic History of Leisure, 1918–1939.* London: Routledge & Kegan Paul, 1986.

Joseph, Antoine. *Skilled Workers' Solidarity: The American Experience in Comparative Perspective.* New York: Garland, 2000.

Jung, Moon-Kie. *Beneath the Surface of White Supremacy: Denaturalizing US Racisms Past and Present.* Stanford: Stanford University Press, 2015.

Kann, Kenneth. "The Knights of Labor and the Southern Black Worker." *Labor History* 18, no. 1 (Winter 1977): 49.

Katz, Daniel. *All Together Different: Yiddish Socialists, Garment Workers, and the Labor Roots of Multiculturalism.* New York: NYU Press, 2011.

Katz, Elaine N. "Revisiting the Origins of the Industrial Colour Bar in the Witwatersrand Gold Mining Industry, 1891–1899." *Journal of Southern African Studies* 25, no. 1 (1999): 73–97.

———. "The Underground Route to Mining: Afrikaners and the Witwatersrand Gold Mining Industry from 1902 to the 1907 Miners' Strike." *The Journal of African History* 36, no. 3 (1995): 467–89.

Katznelson, Ira, and Aristide R. Zolberg. *Working-Class Formation: Nineteenth-Century Patterns in Western Europe and the United States.* Princeton: Princeton University Press, 1986.

Kawashima, Ken C. *The Proletarian Gamble: Korean Workers in Interwar Japan.* Durham: Duke University Press, 2009.

Keiser, John H. "Black Strikebreakers and Racism in Illinois, 1865–1900." *Journal of the Illinois State Historical Society (1908–1984)* 65, no. 3 (1972): 313–26.

Kelley, Robin D. G. *Hammer and Hoe: Alabama Communists during the Great Depression.* Chapel Hill: University of North Carolina Press, 1990.

Kellogg, Paul Underwood, ed. *Wage-Earning Pittsburgh: The Pittsburgh Survey Findings in Six Volumes.* Philadelphia: Wm. F. Fell Co., 1914.

Kelly, Joseph. "Showing Agency on the Margins: African American Railway Workers in the South and Their Unions, 1917–1930." *Labour / Le Travail* 71 (2013): 123–48.

Kelsey, Carl. "Some Causes of Negro Emigration: The Men," *The Negro in the Cities of the North* (Charity Organization Society, New York, 1905): 15–17.

Kenji, Hasegawa. "The Massacre of Koreans in Yokohama in the Aftermath of the Great Kanto Earthquake of 1923." *Monumenta Nipponica* 75, no. 1 (2020): 91–122.

Kennedy, Dane. "Empire Migration in Post-War Reconstruction: The Role of the Oversea Settlement Committee, 1919–1922." *Albion: A Quarterly Journal Concerned with British Studies* 20, no. 3 (1988): 403–19.

Kennedy, David. "And Then There Were Two: Everton and Liverpool Football Clubs, 1892–1902." *Soccer & Society* 12, no. 4 (July 2011): 523–37.

———. "Red and Blue and Orange and Green?" *Soccer & Society* 12, no. 4 (July 2011): 552–64.

Kettleborough, Charles. "Soldiers' Bonus." *The American Political Science Review* 16, no. 3 (1922): 455–60.

———. "Soldiers' Bonus." *The American Political Science Review* 18, no. 3 (1924): 559–65.

Killingray, David, and Martin Plaut. "F. Z. S. Peregrino, a Significant but Duplicitous Figure in the Black Atlantic World." *South African Historical Journal* 68, no. 4 (October 1, 2016): 493–516.

Kinghan, Neil. "A Brief Moment in the Sun: Francis Cardozo and Reconstruction in South Carolina." PhD diss., University College London, 2019.

Kinzer, Donald Louis. *An Episode in Anti-Catholicism: The American Protective Association.* Seattle: University of Washington Press, 1964.

Kirk, Neville. *Comrades and Cousins: Globalization, Workers and Labour Movements in Britain, the USA and Australia from the 1880s to 1914.* London: Merlin, 2003.

———. "Labour and Empire: Australia and Britain from the Late Nineteenth Century to the Inter-War Years." In *The British Labour Movement and Imperialism*, edited by Billy Frank, Craig Horner, and David Stewart, 41–64. Newcastle upon Tyne: Cambridge Scholars Publishing, 2010.

———. *Labour and Society in Britain and the USA: Volume Two: Challenge and Accommodation, 1850–1939.* Aldershot, UK: Routledge, 1994.

Kitching, G. "The Origins of Football: History, Ideology and the Making of 'The People's Game.'" *History Workshop Journal* 79, no. 1 (April 1, 2015): 127–53.

Koditschek, Theodore. *Liberalism, Imperialism and the Historical Imagination: Nineteenth Century Visions of Greater Britain.* Cambridge: Cambridge University Press, 2011.

Korzeniewicz, Roberto P. "Labor Unrest in Argentina, 1887–1907." *Latin American Research Review* 24, no. 3 (1989): 71–98.

Kramer, Derek. "'We Go on Our Own Boats!': Korean Migrants and the Politics of Transportation Infrastructure in the Japanese Empire." *International Review of Social History* 67, no. 2 (2021): 1–22.

Krause, Paul. *The Battle for Homestead, 1880–1892: Politics, Culture, and Steel.* Pittsburgh: University of Pittsburgh Press, 1992.

Krikler, Jeremy. "Lost Causes of the Rand Revolt." *South African Historical Journal* 63, no. 2 (2011): 318–38.

Kulczycki, John J. *The Foreign Worker and the German Labor Movement: Xenophobia and Solidarity in the Coal Fields of the Ruhr, 1871–1914.* Oxford: Berg Publishers, 1994.

Kynoch, Gary. "Controlling the Coolies: Chinese Mineworkers and the Struggle for Labor in South Africa, 1904–1910." *The International Journal of African Historical Studies* 36, no. 2 (2003): 309–29.

Langfield, Michele. "'White Aliens': The Control of European Immigration to Australia, 1920–30." *Journal of Intercultural Studies* 12, no. 2 (1991): 1–14.

Laslett, John H. M. *Labor and the Left; a Study of Socialist and Radical Influences in the American Labor Movement, 1881–1924.* New York: Basic Books, 1970.

Layman, Lenore. "'To Keep up the Australian Standard': Regulating Contract Labour Migration 1901–50." *Labour History*, no. 70 (1996): 25–52.

Leach, Eugene E. "Chaining the Tiger: The Mob Stigma and the Working Class, 1863–1894." *Labor History* 35, no. 2 (1994): 187–215.

Lees, Lynn Hollen. *Exiles of Erin: Irish Migrants in Victorian London*. Ithaca, NY: Cornell University Press, 1979.

Leeworthy, Daryl. "Partisan Players: Sport, Working-Class Culture, and the Labour Movement in South Wales, 1920–1939." *Labor History* 55, no. 5 (2014): 580–93.

Leff, Nathaniel H. "Economic Development and Regional Inequality: Origins of the Brazilian Case." *The Quarterly Journal of Economics* 86, no. 2 (1972): 243–62. https://doi.org/10.2307/1880562.

Levine, Susan. "Labor's True Woman: Domesticity and Equal Rights in the Knights of Labor." *The Journal of American History* 70, no. 2 (1983): 323–39.

Levy, Jonathan. *Ages of American Capitalism: A History of the United States*. New York: Random House, 2021.

Lewis, Colin M. "Economic Restructuring and Labour Scarcity: Labour in the 1920s." In *Essays in Argentine Labour History, 1870–1930*, edited by Jeremy Adelman, 177–98. London: Palgrave Macmillan UK, 1992.

Lewis, Robert D., ed. *Manufacturing Suburbs: Building Work and Home on the Metropolitan Fringe*. Philadelphia: Temple University, 2004.

Licht, Walter. *Working for the Railroad: The Organization of Work in the Nineteenth Century*. Princeton: Princeton University Press, 1983.

Lichtenstein, Alex. "'The Hope for White and Black'? Race, Labour and the State in South Africa and the United States, 1924–1956." *Journal of Southern African Studies* 30, no. 1 (2004): 133–53.

———. "Was the Emancipated Slave a Proletarian?" *Reviews in American History* 26, no. 1 (1998): 124–45.

Linden, Marcel van der. "Proletarian Internationalism: A Long View and Some Speculations." In *Modern World-System in the Longue Duree*, edited by Immanuel Wallerstein, 107–31. London: Routledge, 2004.

Linder, Marc. "Fatal Subtraction: Statistical MIAs on the Industrial Battlefield." *Journal of Legislation* 20, no. 2 (1994): 99–145.

Litwack, Leon F. *Been in the Storm so Long: The Aftermath of Slavery*. New York: Vintage Books, 1980 [1979].

Livingston, James. *Against Thrift: Why Consumer Culture Is Good for the Economy, the Environment, and Your Soul*. New York: Basic Books, 2011.

Livingstone, W. P. *The Race Conflict: A Study of Conditions in America*. London: Sampson Low, 1911. https://catalog.hathitrust.org/Record/000339342.

Lowe, Lisa. *Immigrant Acts: On Asian American Cultural Politics*. Durham: Duke University Press, 1996.

Lucassen, Leo. *The Immigrant Threat: The Integration of Old and New Migrants in Western Europe since 1850*. Urbana: University of Illinois Press, 2005.

Lundahl, Mats, and Daniel B. Ndlela. "Land Alienation, Dualism, and Economic Discrimination: South Africa and Rhodesia." *Economy and History* 23, no. 2 (1980): 106–32.

Lunn, Kenneth. "The Seamen's Union and 'Foreign' Workers on British and Colonial Shipping, 1890–1939." *Bulletin—Society for the Study of Labour History* 53, no. 3 (1988): 5–13.

Machado, Maria Helena Pereira Toledo. "From Slave Rebels to Strikebreakers: The Quilombo of Jabaquara and the Problem of Citizenship in Late-Nineteenth-Century Brazil." *Hispanic American Historical Review* 86, no. 2 (2006): 247–74.

MacRaild, Donald M. *Irish Migrants in Modern Britain, 1750–1922.* London: Macmillan Education UK, 1999.

Man, Albon P. "Labor Competition and the New York Draft Riots of 1863." *The Journal of Negro History* 36, no. 4 (1951): 375–405.

Maram, Sheldon L. "Labor and the Left in Brazil, 1890–1921: A Movement Aborted." *Hispanic American Historical Review* 57, no. 2 (1977): 254–72.

Margo, Robert A. "The Competitive Dynamics of Racial Exclusion: Employment Segregation in the South, 1900–1950." National Bureau of Economic Research, August 1990. https://doi.org/10.3386/h0014.

Markey, Ray. "Explaining Union Mobilisation in the 1880s and Early 1900s." *Labour History* 83 (November 2002): 19–42.

Marks, Gary. "Variations in Union Political Activity in the United States, Britain, and Germany from the Nineteenth Century." *Comparative Politics* 22, no. 1 (October 1, 1989): 83–104.

———. *Unions in Politics: Britain, Germany, and the United States in the Nineteenth and Early Twentieth Centuries.* Princeton: Princeton University Press, 1989.

Marsden, K. Gerald. "Patriotic Societies and American Labor: The American Protective Association in Wisconsin." *The Wisconsin Magazine of History* 41, no. 4 (1958): 287–94.

Martens, Jeremy. "A Transnational History of Immigration Restriction: Natal and New South Wales, 1896–97." *The Journal of Imperial and Commonwealth History* 34, no. 3 (September 2006): 323–44.

Marx, Karl. *Karl Marx and Frederick Engels on Britain.* 2nd ed. Moscow: Foreign Languages Pub. House, 1962.

Mason, Tony. *Association Football and English Society, 1863–1915.* Brighton: Harvester Press, 1981.

Mathers, Helen Elisa. "Sheffield Municipal Politics, 1893–1926. Parties, Personalities and the Rise of Labour." PhD Diss., University of Sheffield, 1979.

Matthews, Derek. "1889 and All That: New Views on the New Unionism." *International Review of Social History* 36, no. 1 (1991): 24–58.

May, Roy, and Robin Cohen. "The Interaction Between Race and Colonialism: A Case Study of the Liverpool Race Riots of 1919." *Race and Class* 16, no. 2 (1974).

McGirr, Lisa. *The War on Alcohol: Prohibition and the Rise of the American State.* New York: W.W. Norton & Company, 2016.

McIvor, Arthur J. "Employers' Organisation and Strikebreaking in Britain, 1880–1914." *International Review of Social History* 29, no. 1 (April 1984): 1–33.

McIvor, Arthur, and Christopher Wright. "Managing Labour: UK and Australian Employers in Comparative Perspective, 1900–50." *Labour History*, no. 88 (May 1, 2005): 45–62.

McKenna, Madeline. "Municipal Suburbia in Liverpool, 1919–1939." *The Town Planning Review* 60, no. 3 (1989): 287–318.

McKeown, Adam. "Global Migration, 1846–1940." *Journal of World History* 15, no. 2 (2004): 155–89.

McKibbin, Ross. *Classes and Cultures: England, 1918–1951.* Oxford: Oxford University Press, 1998.

———. *The Evolution of the Labour Party, 1910–1924.* Oxford: Oxford University Press, 1974.

—— . *The Ideologies of Class: Social Relations in Britain, 1880–1950*. Oxford: Clarendon, 1990.

McKiven, Henry M. *Iron and Steel: Class, Race, and Community in Birmingham, Alabama, 1875–1920*. Chapel Hill: University of North Carolina Press, 1995.

McLaurin, Melton A. "The Racial Policies of the Knights of Labor and the Organization of Southern Black Workers." *Labor History* 17, no. 4 (1976): 568.

McMillen, Neil R. *Dark Journey: Black Mississippians in the Age of Jim Crow*. Urbana: University of Illinois Press, 1990.

Meeker, Edward, and James Kau. "Racial Discrimination and Occupational Attainment at the Turn of the Century." *Explorations in Economic History: New York* 14, no. 3 (1977): 250–76.

Mehrotra, Ajay K. *Making the Modern American Fiscal State: Law, Politics, and the Rise of Progressive Taxation, 1877–1929*. New York: Cambridge University Press, 2013.

Mendeloff, John, and Laura Staetsky. "Occupational Fatality Risks in the United States and the United Kingdom." *American Journal of Industrial Medicine* 57, no. 1 (2014): 4–14. https://doi.org/10.1002/ajim.22258.

Mercer, Malcolm. *Schooling the Poorer Child: Elementary Education in Sheffield, 1560–1902*. Sheffield: Sheffield Academic, 1996.

Metcalfe, Alan. *Leisure and Recreation in a Victorian Mining Community: The Social Economy of Leisure in North-East England, 1820–1914*. New York: Routledge, 2006.

Miliband, Ralph. *Marxism and Politics*. Oxford: Oxford University Press, 1977.

Milkman, Ruth. "Labor's Long Road to Immigrant Inclusion." *Labor* 20, no. 4 (2023): 69–75. https://doi.org/10.1215/15476715-10829185.

Millan, Matteo, and Alessandro Saluppo, eds. *Corporate Policing, Yellow Unionism, and Strikebreaking, 1890–1930: In Defence of Freedom*. Abingdon, UK: Routledge, 2021.

Miner, Claudia. "The Knights of Labor and 'The Color Line,' Richmond, 1886." MA thesis, College of William and Mary, 1978.

Mink, Gwendolyn. *Old Labor and New Immigrants in American Political Development: Union, Party, and State, 1875–1920*. Ithaca, NY: Cornell University Press, 1986.

Mitrani, Sam. *The Rise of the Chicago Police Department: Class and Conflict, 1850–1894*. Urbana: University of Illinois Press, 2013.

Mogridge, Basil. "Militancy and Inter-Union Rivalries in British Shipping, 1911–1929." *International Review of Social History* 6, no. 3 (1961): 375–412. https://doi.org/10.1017/S0020859000001905.

Money, Duncan, and Limin Teh. "Race at Work: A Comparative History of Mining Labor and Empire on the Central African Copperbelt and the Fushun Coalfields, ca. 1907–1945." *International Labor and Working-Class History* 101 (Spring 2022): 100–117.

Money, Duncan, and Danelle van Zyl-Hermann. "Revisiting White Labourism: New Debates on Working-Class Whiteness in Twentieth-Century Southern Africa." *International Review of Social History* 66, no. 3 (2021): 469–91. https://doi.org/10.1017/S0020859021000407.

Montgomery, David. "Strikes in Nineteenth-Century America." *Social Science History* 4, no. 1 (1980): 81–104.

————. *The Fall of the House of Labor: The Workplace, the State, and American Labor Activism, 1865–1925.* Cambridge: Cambridge University Press, 1989.

Moodie, T. Dunbar. "Maximum Average Violence: Underground Assaults on the South African Gold Mines, 1913–1965." *Journal of Southern African Studies* 31, no. 3 (2005): 547–67.

Moran, Gerard. "James Daly and the Rise and Fall of the Land League in the West of Ireland, 1879–82." *Irish Historical Studies* 29, no. 114 (1994): 189–207.

Morawska, Ewa. "Labor Migrations of Poles in the Atlantic World Economy, 1880–1914." *Comparative Studies in Society and History* 31, no. 2 (1989): 237–72.

Moreno, Paul D. *Black Americans and Organized Labor: A New History.* Baton Rouge: LSU Press, 2008.

Morris, James Oliver. *Conflict within the AFL: A Study of Craft versus Industrial Unionism, 1901–1938.* Ithaca: Cornell University Press, 1958.

Morris, Peter, William J. Ryczek, Jan Finkel, and Leonard Levin. *Base Ball Pioneers, 1850–1870: The Clubs and Players Who Spread the Sport Nationwide.* Jefferson, NC: McFarland, 2012.

Morris, Shawn. "The Negro Leagues and Regional Historiography." *Black Ball* 7 (2014): 44–53.

Moss, Bernard H. *The Origins of the French Labor Movement, 1830–1914: The Socialism of Skilled Workers.* Berkeley: University of California Press, 1976.

Murray, Thomas. "Socio-Economic Rights Versus Social Revolution? Constitution Making in Germany, Mexico and Ireland, 1917–1923." *Social & Legal Studies* 24, no. 4 (2015): 487–508.

Naidu, Suresh. "Recruitment Restrictions and Labor Markets: Evidence from the Postbellum US South." *Journal of Labor Economics* 28, no. 2 (2010): 413–45.

Nasaw, David. *Going Out: The Rise and Fall of Public Amusements.* Cambridge, MA: Harvard University Press, 1999.

National University of Córdoba and National Council for Scientific and Technical Research. "Inmigración, anarquismo y deportación: La criminalización de los extranjeros 'indeseables' en tiempos de las 'grandes migraciones.'" *REMHU: Revista Interdisciplinar da Mobilidade Humana* 23, no. 45 (2015). https://www.scielo.br/j/remhu/a/Byw45nH6JMGxFmSLfmwCtmn/?lang=es.

National Urban League. *Negro Membership in American Labor Unions.* New York: The Alexander Press, 1930.

Nelson, Bruce. "Class, Race and Democracy in the CIO: The 'New' Labor History Meets the 'Wages of Whiteness.'" *International Review of Social History* 41, no. 3 (1996): 351.

————. *Divided We Stand: American Workers and the Struggle for Black Equality.* Princeton: Princeton University Press, 2001.

Neumark, David. "Experimental Research on Labor Market Discrimination." *Journal of Economic Literature* 56, no. 3 (2018): 799–866.

Ngai, Mae. *The Chinese Question: The Gold Rushes, Chinese Migration, and Global Politics.* New York: Norton, 2021.

————. "Trouble on the Rand: The Chinese Question in South Africa and the Apogee of White Settlerism." *International Labor and Working-Class History* 91 (2017): 59–78.

Nicholls, James. *Politics of Alcohol: A History of the Drink Question in England.* Manchester: Manchester University Press.

Nijhof, Erik, John Barzman, and John Lovell. "Dockers' Unions in the Ports of London, Le Havre, Rotterdam and Hamburg, 1850–1914." In *The Emergence of European Trade Unionism*, edited by Jean-Louis Robert, Antoine Prost, and Chris Wrigley, 33–53. London: Ashgate, 2004.

Niedt, Christopher. "The Politics of Prosperity and Crisis in an Industrial Suburb: Dundalk, Maryland, 1920–2005." PhD diss., University of California, 2007.

Nightingale, Carl H. "The Transnational Contexts of Early Twentieth-Century American Urban Segregation." *Journal of Social History* 39, no. 3 (2006): 667–702.

———. *Segregation: A Global History of Divided Cities*. Chicago: University of Chicago Press, 2012.

Norwood, Stephen H. *Strikebreaking & Intimidation: Mercenaries and Masculinity in Twentieth-Century America*. Chapel Hill: University of North Carolina Press, 2002.

Nteta, Tatishe. "United We Stand? African Americans, Self-Interest, and Immigration Reform." *American Politics Research* 41, no. 1 (2013): 147–72.

Ochiltree, Ian. "Mastering the Sharecroppers: Land, Labour and the Search for Independence in the US South and South Africa." *Journal of Southern African Studies* 30, no. 1 (2004): 41–61.

———. "'A Just and Self-Respecting System'? Black Independence, Sharecropping, and Paternalistic Relations in the American South and South Africa." *Agricultural History* 72, no. 2 (1998): 352–80.

O'Day, Alan. "Varieties of Anti-Irish Behaviour in Britain, 1846–1922." In *Racial Violence in Britain, 1840–1950*, edited by P. Panayi, 26–43. Leicester: Leicester University Press, 1993.

OECD. *IOM Outlook on Migration, Environment and Climate Change*. Paris: Organisation for Economic Co-operation and Development, 2015. https://www.oecd-ilibrary.org/content/publication/9ba951ac-en.

Oestreicher, Richard Jules. *Solidarity and Fragmentation: Working People and Class Consciousness in Detroit, 1875–1900*. Urbana: University of Illinois Press, 1986.

Olson, Sherry H. *Baltimore: The Building of an American City*. Baltimore: Johns Hopkins University Press, 1997.

Olzak, Susan D. "Causes of Shifts in Occupational Segregation of the Foreign-Born: Evidence from American Cities, 1870–1880." *Social Forces* 68, no. 2 (1989): 593–620.

Orridge, Andrew W. "Who Supported the Land War? An Aggregate-Data Analysis of Irish Agrarian Discontent, 1879–1882." *The Economic and Social Review* 12, no. 3 (1981): 203–33.

Orser, W. Edward. "The Making of a Baltimore Rowhouse Community: The Edmondson Avenue Area, 1915–1945." *Maryland Historical Magazine* 80, no. 3 (1980): 203–27.

Otsuka, Keijiro. "Determinants and Consequences of Land Reform Implementation in the Philippines." *Journal of Development Economics* 35, no. 2 (1991): 339–55.

Pager, Devah. "The Mark of a Criminal Record." *American Journal of Sociology* 108, no. 5 (2003): 937–75.

Pager, Devah, Bart Bonikowski, and Bruce Western. "Discrimination in a Low-Wage Labor Market: A Field Experiment." *American Sociological Review* 74, no. 5 (2009): 777–99.

Parfitt, Steven. *Knights across the Atlantic: The Knights of Labor in Britain and Ireland.* Liverpool: Liverpool University Press, 2016.

Park, Eunjae. "British Labour Party's Patriotic Politics on Immigration and Race, 1900–1968." PhD diss., University of York, 2017.

Pearson, Chad. *Reform or Repression: Organizing America's Anti-Union Movement.* Philadelphia: University of Pennsylvania Press, 2016.

Peiss, Kathy Lee. *Cheap Amusements: Working Women and Leisure in Turn-of-the-Century New York.* Philadelphia: Temple University Press, 1986.

Pelling, Henry. "The Knights of Labor in Britain, 1880–1901." *The Economic History Review* 9, no. 2 (1956): 313–31.

Pereira, Thales Augusto Zamberlan. "The North-South Divide: Real Wages and Welfare in Brazil during the Early 20th Century." *Revista de Historia Economica—Journal of Iberian and Latin American Economic History* 38, no. 1 (2020): 185–214. https://doi.org/10.1017/S0212610919000132.

Perry, Jeffrey B. *Hubert Harrison: The Voice of Harlem Radicalism, 1883-1918.* New York: Columbia University Press, 2009.

Pettengill, Ryan S. "'Fair Play in Bowling': Sport, Civil Rights, and the UAW Culture of Inclusion, 1936–1950." *Journal of Social History* 51, no. 4 (2018): 953–79.

Phelan, Craig. *Divided Loyalties: The Public and Private Life of Labor Leader John Mitchell.* Albany: State University of New York Press, 1994.

Pietila, Antero. *Not in My Neighborhood: How Bigotry Shaped a Great American City.* Chicago: Ivan R. Dee, 2010.

Pollard, Sidney. *A History of Labour in Sheffield.* Liverpool: Liverpool University Press, 1959.

Pomeranz, Kenneth. *The Great Divergence: Europe, China, and the Making of the Modern World Economy.* Princeton: Princeton University Press, 2000.

Pope, David, and Glenn Withers. "Wage Effects of Immigration in Late-Nineteenth-Century Australia." In *Migration and the International Labor Market, 1850–1939,* edited by T. J. Hatton and Jeffrey G. Williamson, 240–82. New York: Routledge, 1994.

Porter, Bernard. *The Absent-Minded Imperialists: Empire, Society, and Culture in Britain.* Oxford: Oxford University Press, 2004.

Postel, Charles. *Equality: An American Dilemma, 1866–1896.* New York: Farrar, Straus and Giroux, 2019.

Potter, Christopher Thomas. "An Exploration of Social and Cultural Aspects of Motorcycling During the Interwar Period." PhD diss., University of Northumbria at Newcastle, 2007.

Power, Garrett. "Apartheid Baltimore Style: The Residential Segregation Ordinances of 1910–1913." *Maryland Law Review* 42 (1983): 289–328.

Poy, Lucas. *El Partido Socialista Argentino.* Santiago: Ariadna Ediciones, 2020.

———. "The 'World Migration Congress' of 1926 and the Limits of Socialist Internationalism." *Labor* 20, no. 3 (2023): 33–59. https://doi.org/10.1215/15476715-10581293.

Pratt, Ambrose. *The Real South Africa.* London: Holden & Hardingham, 1913.

Preston, John Thomas. "The Origins and Development of Association Football in the Liverpool District, c. 1879 until c. 1915." PhD diss., University of Central Lancashire, 2007.

Price, Richard. *Masters, Unions, and Men: Work Control in Building and the Rise of Labour, 1830–1914*. Cambridge, UK: Cambridge University Press, 1980.

———. "One Big Thing: Britain, Its Empire, and Their Imperial Culture." *Journal of British Studies* 45, no. 3 (July 2006): 602–27.

Prothero, I. J. *Radical Artisans in England and France, 1830–1870*. Cambridge: Cambridge University Press, 1997.

Pugh, Arthur. *Men of Steel*. London: Iron and Steel Trades Confederation, 1951.

Quillian, Lincoln, Anthony Heath, Devah Pager, Arnfinn Midtbøen, Fenella Fleischmann, and Ole Hexel. "Do Some Countries Discriminate More than Others? Evidence from 97 Field Experiments of Racial Discrimination in Hiring." *Sociological Science* 6 (2019): 467–96. https://doi.org/10.15195/v6.a18.

Rabinowitz, Howard N. "From Exclusion to Segregation: Southern Race Relations, 1865–1890." *The Journal of American History* 63, no. 2 (1976): 325–50. https://doi.org/10.2307/1899640.

———. *Race Relations in the Urban South, 1865–1890*. Athens: University of Georgia Press, 1996.

Ransom, Roger L. "Reconstructing Reconstruction: Options and Limitations to Federal Policies on Land Distribution in 1866–67." *Civil War History* 51, no. 4 (2005): 364–77.

Ransom, Roger L., and Richard Sutch. *One Kind of Freedom: The Economic Consequences of Emancipation*. 2nd ed. Cambridge: Cambridge University Press, 2001.

"Recreational Activities of Labor Organizations." *Monthly Labor Review* 26, no. 5 (1928): 5–20.

Redding, Kent, and David R. James. "Estimating Levels and Modeling Determinants of Black and White Voter Turnout in the South, 1880 to 1912." *Historical Methods: A Journal of Quantitative and Interdisciplinary History* 34, no. 4 (2001): 141–58.

Redford, Arthur. *Labour Migration in England, 1800–1850*. 2nd ed., edited and revised by W. H. Chaloner. Manchester: Manchester University Press, 1964.

Reid, Caroline Oldcorn. "Middle-Class Values and Working-Class Culture in Nineteenth Century Sheffield." PhD diss., University of Sheffield, 1976.

Reid, Douglas A. "Playing and Praying." In *Cambridge Urban History of Britain*, edited by Martin J. Daunton, 745–807. Cambridge: Cambridge University Press, 2008.

Richardson, Heather Cox. *The Death of Reconstruction: Race, Labor, and Politics in the Post-Civil War North, 1865–1901*. Cambridge, MA: Harvard University Press, 2004.

Riess, Steven A. *Touching Base: Professional Baseball and American Culture in the Progressive Era*. Westport, CT: Greenwood Press, 1980.

Robert, Jean-Louis, Antoine Prost, and Chris Wrigley, eds. *The Emergence of European Trade Unionism*. London: Ashgate, 2004.

Roberts, Elizabeth. *A Woman's Place: An Oral History of Working-Class Women, 1890–1940*. New York: Blackwell, 1984.

Robertson, David Brian. *Capital, Labor, and State: The Battle for American Labor Markets from the Civil War to the New Deal*. Lanham, MD: Rowman & Littlefield Publishers, 2000.

Robinson, Cedric J. *Black Marxism: The Making of the Black Radical Tradition*. 3rd ed. Chapel Hill: University of North Carolina Press, 2020.

Rockman, Seth. *Scraping By: Wage Labor, Slavery, and Survival in Early Baltimore.* Baltimore: Johns Hopkins University Press, 2009.

Roediger, David R. *The Wages of Whiteness: Race and the Making of the American Working Class.* Rev. ed. London: Verso, 2007.

Roediger, David R., and Elizabeth D. Esch. *The Production of Difference: Race and the Management of Labor in US History.* New York: Oxford University Press, 2012.

Rosalski, Joseph C. "In Perspective: Ferdinand C. Latrobe's Mayoral Terms and Progressive Influences on the City of Baltimore, 1875–1895." MA thesis, University of Maryland, Baltimore County, 2010.

Rosenbloom, Joshua L. "Strikebreaking and the Labor Market in the United States, 1881–1894." *The Journal of Economic History* 58, no. 1 (1998): 183–205.

———. "The Extent of the Labor Market in the United States, 1870–1914." *Social Science History* 22, no. 3 (1998): 287–318.

Rosenow, Michael K. *Death and Dying in the Working Class, 1865–1920.* Urbana: University of Illinois Press, 2015.

Rosenzweig, Mark R. "Rural Wages, Labor Supply, and Land Reform: A Theoretical and Empirical Analysis." *The American Economic Review* 68, no. 5 (1978): 847–61.

Ruck, Rob. *Sandlot Seasons: Sport in Black Pittsburgh.* Urbana: University of Illinois Press, 1987.

Ryang, Sonia. "The Great Kanto Earthquake and the Massacre of Koreans in 1923: Notes on Japan's Modern National Sovereignty." *Anthropological Quarterly* 76, no. 4 (2003): 731–48.

Salcedo, Andrea, and Derek M. Norman. "A Latino Worker, a Risky Construction Site and a Family in Mourning." *New York Times*, February 17, 2020. https:// www.nytimes.com/2020/02/17/nyregion/construction-deaths-latinos-nyc .html.

Saluppo, Alessandro. "Strikebreaking and Anti-Unionism on the Waterfront: The Shipping Federation, 1890–1914." *European History Quarterly* 49, no. 4 (2019): 570–96.

Salvatore, Ricardo D. "Control del Trabajo y Discriminación: El Sistema de Contratistas en Mendoza, Argentina, 1880–1920." *Desarrollo Económico* 26, no. 102 (1986): 229–53. https://doi.org/10.2307/3467032.

Sánchez-Alonso, Blanca. "Making Sense of Immigration Policy: Argentina, 1870–1930." *The Economic History Review* 66, no. 2 (2013): 601–27.

———. "La Racionalidad de Las Políticas Migratorias en La Primera Globalización: El Caso Argentino." *Revista de Instituciones, Ideas y Mercados* 46 (May 2007): 233–64.

Santos, Michael W. "Brother against Brother: The Amalgamated and Sons of Vulcan at the A. M. Byers Company, 1907–1913." *The Pennsylvania Magazine of History and Biography* 111, no. 2 (1987): 195–212.

———. "Laboring on the Periphery: Managers and Workers at the A. M. Byers Company, 1900–1956." *Business History Review* 61, no. 1 (1987): 113–33.

Saville, John. "Trade Unions and Free Labour: The Background to the Taff Vale Decision." In Briggs and Saville, *Essays in Labour History: In Memory of G. D. H. Cole*, ed. Asa Briggs and John Saville. London: Macmillan, 1960, 317–350.

Saxton, Alexander. *The Rise and Fall of the White Republic: Class Politics and Mass Culture in Nineteenth Century America.* London: Verso, 1990.

Schmidt, Leigh Eric. "The Commercialization of the Calendar: American Holidays and the Culture of Consumption, 1870–1930." *The Journal of American History* 78, no. 3 (1991): 887–916.

Scott, Joan Wallach. *The Glassworkers of Carmaux: French Craftsmen and Political Action in a Nineteenth-Century City.* Cambridge, MA: Harvard University Press, 1974.

Scott, Peter. *The Making of the Modern British Home: The Suburban Semi and Family Life between the Wars.* Oxford: Oxford University Press, 2013.

Scott, Rebecca J. "Defining the Boundaries of Freedom in the World of Cane: Cuba, Brazil, and Louisiana after Emancipation." *The American Historical Review* 99, no. 1 (1994): 70–102.

Seamster, Louise, and Victor Ray. "Against Teleology in the Study of Race: Toward the Abolition of the Progress Paradigm." *Sociological Theory* 36, no. 4 (2018): 315–42.

Seow, Victor. *Carbon Technocracy: Energy Regimes in Modern East Asia.* Chicago: The University of Chicago Press, 2021.

Shammas, Carole. "Did Democracy Give the United States an Edge in Primary Schooling?" *Social Science History* 39, no. 3 (2015): 315–38.

Sheard, Kenneth G. "Aspects of Boxing in the Western 'Civilizing Process.'" *International Review for the Sociology of Sport* 32, no. 1 (1997): 38–57.

Shergold, Peter R. *Working-Class Life: The "American Standard" in Comparative Perspective, 1899–1913.* Pittsburgh: University of Pittsburgh Press, 1982.

Sherwood, Marika. "Race, Nationality and Employment among Lascar Seamen, 1660 to 1945." *Journal of Ethnic and Migration Studies* 17, no. 2 (1991): 229–44.

Silver, Beverly J. *Forces of Labor: Workers' Movements and Globalization since 1870.* Cambridge, UK: Cambridge University Press, 2003.

Sinha, Manisha. *The Counterrevolution of Slavery: Politics and Ideology in Antebellum South Carolina.* Chapel Hill: University of North Carolina Press, 2000.

Skillen, Fiona. "Preventing 'Robotised Women Workers': Women, Sport and the Workplace in Scotland, 1919–1939." *Labor History* 55, no. 5 (2014): 594–606.

Skotnes, Andor. *A New Deal for All? Race and Class Struggles in Depression-Era Baltimore.* Durham: Duke University Press, 2012.

———. "The Black Freedom Movement and the Workers' Movement in Baltimore, 1930–39." PhD diss., Rutgers University, 1991.

Smith, Paul. "'A Proud Liverpool Union.' The Liverpool and District Carters' and Motormen's Union, 1889–1946: Ethnicity, Class and Trade-Unionism." *Historical Studies in Industrial Relations* 16 (September 2003): 1–38.

Smith, Robert Michael. *From Blackjacks to Briefcases: A History of Commercialized Strikebreaking and Unionbusting in the United States.* Athens: Ohio University Press, 2003.

Smith, W. Donald. "The 1932 Asō Coal Strike: Korean-Japanese Solidarity and Conflict." *Korean Studies* 20, no. 1 (1996): 94–122.

Smoot, Pamela Annette. "Black Self Help and Institution Building in Pittsburgh, Pennsylvania, 1830–1945." PhD diss., Michigan State University, 1999.

Solomon, Burt. *Where They Ain't: The Fabled Life and Untimely Death of the Original Baltimore Orioles, the Team That Gave Birth to Modern Baseball.* New York: Free Press, 1999.

Spero, Sterling D., and Abram Lincoln Harris. *The Black Worker: The Negro and the Labor Movement*. New York: Columbia University Press, 1931.

Stevens, Christopher Philip. "A Study of Urban Conservatism, with Reference to Sheffield, 1885–1906." PhD diss., University of Teesside, 1997.

Stowell, David O. *Streets, Railroads, and the Great Strike of 1877*. Chicago: University of Chicago Press, 1999.

Streible, Dan. "A History of the Boxing Film, 1894–1915: Social Control and Social Reform in the Progressive Era." *Film History* 3, no. 3 (1989): 235–57.

Svabek, Lawrence. "To Break the Slave Power: Thaddeus Stevens, Land Confiscation, and the Politics of Reparations." *American Political Thought* 10, no. 4 (2021): 523–51.

Tabili, Laura. "The Construction of Racial Difference in Twentieth-Century Britain: The Special Restriction (Coloured Alien Seamen) Order, 1925." *Journal of British Studies* 33, no. 1 (1994): 54–98.

Taft, Philip. *The A. F. of L. in the Time of Gompers*. New York: Octagon Books, 1957.

Taillon, Paul Michel. *Good, Reliable, White Men: Railroad Brotherhoods, 1877–1917*. Urbana: University of Illinois Press, 2009.

Taplin, Eric. "The Liverpool General Transport Strike, 1911." *Historical Studies in Industrial Relations* 33 (2012): 25–38.

Taylor, Matthew. "Parallel Fields: Labour History and Sports History." *International Journal of the History of Sport* 32, no. 15 (2015): 1769–74.

———. *The Association Game: A History of British Football*. Harlow: Pearson Longman, 2008.

Thane, Pat. "Women in the Labour Party and Women's Suffrage." In *Suffrage Outside Suffragism: Women's Vote in Britain, 1880–1914*, edited by Myriam Boussahba-Bravard, 35–51. London: Palgrave Macmillan UK, 2007.

Thayer, Johnathan. "Merchant Seamen, Sailortowns, and the Shaping of US Citizenship, 1843–1945." PhD diss., The Graduate Center, City University of New York, 2018.

Thompson, E. P. "Homage to Tom Maguire." In Briggs and Saville, *Essays in Labour History*, 276–316.

———. *The Making of the English Working Class*. New York: Vintage Books, 1963.

Thompson, Ruth Mary. "Organised Labour in Argentina." PhD diss., University of Oxford, 1979.

Thornbrough, Emma Lou. *T. Thomas Fortune: Militant Journalist*. Chicago: University of Chicago Press, 1972.

Tichenor, Daniel. "Nativism and the Bottom Line: Contemporary Legacies of the Immigration Act of 1924." *Labor* 20, no. 4 (2023): 52–59. https://doi.org/10.1215/15476715-10829157.

———. *Dividing Lines: The Politics of Immigration Control in America*. Princeton: Princeton University Press, 2002.

Tilly, Charles. *Coercion, Capital, and European States, AD 990–1992*. Rev. ed. Cambridge, MA: Blackwell, 1992.

Tomlins, Christopher L. *The State and the Unions: Labor Relations, Law, and the Organized Labor Movement in America, 1880–1960*. Cambridge: Cambridge University Press, 1985.

Torpey, John C. *The Invention of the Passport: Surveillance, Citizenship, and the State*. Cambridge: Cambridge University Press, 2000.

Towers, Frank. "Job Busting at Baltimore Shipyards: Racial Violence in the Civil War–Era South." *The Journal of Southern History* 66, no. 2 (2000): 221–56.

Tranter, N. L. *Sport, Economy, and Society in Britain, 1750–1914*. Cambridge: Cambridge University Press, 1998.

Trouvé-Finding, Susan. "Unionised Women Teachers and Women's Suffrage." In *Suffrage Outside Suffragism: Women's Vote in Britain, 1880–1914*, edited by Myriam Boussahba-Bravard, 205–30. London: Palgrave Macmillan UK, 2007.

Tsu, Timothy Yun Hui. "Japan's 'Yellow Peril': The Chinese in Imperial Japan and Colonial Korea." *Japanese Studies* 30, no. 2 (2010): 161–83. https://doi.org/10.1080/10371397.2010.485553.

Tucker, Helen. "The Negroes of Pittsburgh." *Charities and the Commons: A Weekly Journal of Philanthropy and Social Advance* 2 (January 1909): 599–608.

Ulman, Lloyd. *The Rise of the National Trade Union: The Development and Significance of Its Structure, Governing Institutions, and Economic Policies*. 2nd ed. Cambridge, MA: Harvard University Press, 1966.

Universidad Museo Social Argentino. *La inmigración después de la guerra*. Buenos Aires: Local social y biblioteca, 1919.

Van Der Walt, Lucien. "The First Globalisation and Transnational Labour Activism in Southern Africa: White Labourism, the IWW, and the ICU, 1904–1934." *African Studies* 66, no. 2–3 (2007): 223–51.

Van Tine, Warren R. *The Making of the Labor Bureaucrat: Union Leadership in the United States, 1870–1920*. Amherst: University of Massachusetts Press, 1973.

Vapnek, Lara. *Breadwinners: Working Women and Economic Independence, 1865–1920*. Urbana: University of Illinois Press, 2009.

Vessey, David. "'People Want Newspapers Far More than Weekly Collections of Articles': The Sheffield Guardian, the Labour Party and the Left-Wing Press." *Labour History Review* 80, no. 3 (2015): 249–73. https://doi.org/10.3828/lhr.2015.11.

Vorspant, Rachel. "The Political Power of Nuisance Law: Labor Picketing and the Courts in Modern England, 1871–Present." *Buffalo Law Review* 46, no. 3 (1998): 113.

Voss, Kim. *The Making of American Exceptionalism: The Knights of Labor and Class Formation in the Nineteenth Century*. Ithaca, NY: Cornell University Press, 1993.

Vrooman, David M. *Daniel Willard and Progressive Management on the Baltimore & Ohio Railroad*. Columbus: Ohio State University Press, 1991.

Wacquant, Loïc. "Afropessimism's Radical Abdication." *New Left Review* 144 (December 14, 2023): 97–109.

———. "Resolving the Trouble with 'Race.'" *New Left Review* 133/134 (April 13, 2022): 67–88.

Walia, Harsha. *Border & Rule: Global Migration, Capitalism, and the Rise of Racist Nationalism*. Chicago: Haymarket Books, 2021.

Waller, Philip J. *Democracy and Sectarianism: A Political and Social History of Liverpool, 1868–1939*. Liverpool: Liverpool University Press, 1981.

Waters, Chris. *British Socialists and the Politics of Popular Culture, 1884–1914*. Manchester: Manchester University Press, 1990.

Weiner, Michael. *Race and Migration in Imperial Japan*. London: Routledge, 2014.

Western, Bruce, and Katherine Beckett. "How Unregulated Is the U.S. Labor

Market? The Penal System as a Labor Market Institution." *American Journal of Sociology* 104, no. 4 (1999): 1030–60. https://doi.org/10.1086/210135.

Whatley, Warren C. "African-American Strikebreaking from the Civil War to the New Deal." *Social Science History* 17, no. 4 (1993): 525–58.

Williams, Alfred. *Life in a Railway Factory.* CreateSpace Independent Publishing Platform, 2017 [1915].

Williams, Whiting. *What's on the Worker's Mind, by One Who Put on Overalls to Find Out.* New York: Charles Scribner's Sons, 1920.

Williamson, Joel. *The Crucible of Race: Black-White Relations in the American South since Emancipation.* New York: Oxford University Press, 1984.

Wilson, George Bailey. *Alcohol and the Nation: A Contribution to the Study of the Liquor Problem in the United Kingdom from 1800 to 1935.* London: Nicholson and Watson, 1940.

Wimmer, Andreas. *Ethnic Boundary Making: Institutions, Power, Networks.* New York: Oxford University Press, 2013.

———. *Nationalist Exclusion and Ethnic Conflict: Shadows of Modernity.* Cambridge: Cambridge University Press, 2002.

Winant, Gabriel. "The Natural Profits of Their Years of Labor." *Radical History Review* 139 (January 1, 2021): 75–102.

———. *The Next Shift: The Fall of Industry and the Rise of Health Care in Rust Belt America.* Cambridge, MA: Harvard University Press, 2021.

Winkler, Allan M. "The Philadelphia Transit Strike of 1944." *The Journal of American History* 59, no. 1 (1972): 73–89.

Wolfe, French Eugene. *Admission to American Trade Unions.* Baltimore: Johns Hopkins University Press, 1912.

Woodward, C. Vann. *The Strange Career of Jim Crow.* Oxford: Oxford University Press, 2001 [1955].

Worger, William H. "Convict Labour, Industrialists and the State in the US South and South Africa, 1870–1930." *Journal of Southern African Studies* 30, no. 1 (2004): 63–86.

Wright, Gavin. "Labor History and Labor Economics." In *The Future of Economic History*, edited by Alexander J. Field, 313–48. Dordrecht: Springer Netherlands, 1987.

———. *Old South, New South: Revolutions in the Southern Economy since the Civil War.* Baton Rouge: Louisiana State University Press, 1996.

———. *Slavery and American Economic Development.* Baton Rouge: Louisiana State University Press, 2006.

Wynn, Charters. *Workers, Strikes, and Pogroms: The Donbass-Dnepr Bend in Late Imperial Russia, 1870–1905.* Princeton: Princeton University Press, 2014.

Yasuoka, Kenichi. *Others in Japanese Agriculture: Koreans, Evacuees and Migrants, 1920–1950.* Translated by Teresa Castelvetere. Edited by Karl Smith. Kyoto: Kyoto University Press, 2018 [2014].

York, Barry. "White Australia and the Dictation Test." *Voices: The Quarterly Journal of the National Library of Australia* 6, no. 3 (1996): 27–36.

Zimmermann, Eduardo A. "Racial Ideas and Social Reform: Argentina, 1890–1916." *Hispanic American Historical Review* 72, no. 1 (1992): 23–46.

Index